D1342717

ELECTIONS BEFORE DEMOCRACY: THE HISTORY OF ELECTIONS IN EUROPE AND LATIN AMERICA

INSTITUTE OF LATIN AMERICAN STUDIES SERIES

General Editor: Victor Bulmer-Thomas, Professor of Economics and Director, Institute of Latin American Studies, University of London

The Institute of Latin American Studies, a member of the School of Advanced Study of the University of London, was founded in 1965. The Institute is dedicated to research on Latin America in the social sciences and humanities. The purpose of this series is to disseminate to a wide audience the new work based on the research programmes and projects organised by academic staff and Associate Fellows of the Institute of Latin American Studies.

Victor Bulmer-Thomas (*editor*)
THE NEW ECONOMIC MODEL IN LATIN AMERICA AND ITS
IMPACT ON INCOME DISTRIBUTION AND POVERTY

Victor Bulmer-Thomas, Nikki Craske and Mónica Serrano (*editors*)
MEXICO AND THE NORTH AMERICAN FREE TRADE
AGREEMENT: WHO WILL BENEFIT?

Walter Little and Eduardo Posada-Carbó (*editors*)
POLITICAL CORRUPTION IN EUROPE AND LATIN AMERICA

Eduardo Posada-Carbó (*editor*)
ELECTIONS BEFORE DEMOCRACY: THE HISTORY OF
ELECTIONS IN EUROPE AND LATIN AMERICA

Rachel Sieder (*editor*)
CENTRAL AMERICA: FRAGILE TRANSITION

John Weeks (*editor*)
STRUCTURAL ADJUSTMENT AND THE AGRICULTURAL
SECTOR IN LATIN AMERICA AND THE CARIBBEAN

Elections before Democracy: The History of Elections in Europe and Latin America

Edited by

Eduardo Posada-Carbó
Lecturer in History
Institute of Latin American Studies
University of London

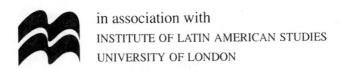

in association with
INSTITUTE OF LATIN AMERICAN STUDIES
UNIVERSITY OF LONDON

First published in Great Britain 1996 by
MACMILLAN PRESS LTD
Houndmills, Basingstoke, Hampshire RG21 6XS
and London
Companies and representatives
throughout the world

A catalogue record for this book is available
from the British Library.

ISBN 0–333–65841–8

First published in the United States of America 1996 by
ST. MARTIN'S PRESS, INC.,
Scholarly and Reference Division,
175 Fifth Avenue,
New York, N.Y. 10010

ISBN 0–312–15885–8

Library of Congress Cataloging-in-Publication Data applied for

---

10   9   8   7   6   5   4   3   2   1
05   04   03   02   01   00   99   98   97   96

Printed and bound in Great Britain by
Antony Rowe Ltd, Chippenham, Wiltshire

CONTENTS

ACKNOWLEDGEMENTS

This book is the result of a workshop held at the Institute of Latin American Studies (ILAS) in the University of London. I wish to express my gratitude to Victor Bulmer-Thomas, Director of the Institute, who supported the organisation of the event and encouraged me to publish this volume.

My initial interest in the history of Latin-American elections, particularly those of Colombia, originated in my conversations with Malcolm Deas, who, in various essays, has for a long time remarked on the subject's neglect. I owe to Malcolm the intellectual stimulus for embarking on this project. All the contributors to this book are leading scholars in the field. I want to thank them all for their participation and for their patience in seeing this volume through what became a long editorial process.

Thanks to a grant from the Isobel Thornley Bequest, we were able to translate into English two of the chapters of the book. Penny Simmons was very helpful in editing the manuscript.

This book would not have been possible without the support of Tony Bell, Administrative Secretary of ILAS. Tony helped with translations, general editing and computer problems, speeding up production of the book. Obviously, responsibility for any errors is mine alone.

Eduardo Posada-Carbó
Institute of Latin American Studies, London.

NOTES ON CONTRIBUTORS

Margaret Lavinia Anderson is Associate Professor of History at the University of California, Berkeley. She is the author of *Windhorst. A Political Biography* (Oxford, 1981). She has published extensively on German political and electoral history, including articles in the *American Historical Review, Central European History, Historical Journal* and *Journal of Modern History.*

Paula Alonso is a Research Fellow at the Department of Politics and International Studies, University of Warwick, and a visiting professor at the Universidad di Tella in Argentina. She completed her D.Phil. at Oxford University with the thesis, 'The origins of the Argentina Radical Party, 1889-1898'. She has published on Argentine electoral history in the *Journal of Latin American Studies.*

Antonio Annino is Professor of History at the University of Florence. He is the co-editor of *El liberalismo en Mexico* (Hamburg, 1992), and *De los imperios a la nación* (Madrid, 1994). He is a contributor on Mexican electoral history to *Quaderni Storici.*

Carlos Dardé is Professor of History at the Universidad de Cantabria, Spain. He has published widely on Spanish electoral history in various Spanish journals. He is a contributor to Javier Tusell (ed.), *El Sufragio Universal* (Madrid, 1991); N. Townson (ed.), *El republicanismo en España, 1830-1975* (Madrid, 1994), and G. Corázar (ed.), *Nación y estado en la España liberal* (Madrid, 1994).

Malcolm Deas is Faculty Fellow and University Lecturer at St Antony's College, Oxford. He has worked extensively on Colombian history. He is a contributor to the *Cambridge History of Latin America.* His publications include: *Del Poder y la Gramática* (Bogotá, 1994); (with F. Gaitán) *Dos ensayos especulativos sobre la violencia en Colombia* (Bogotá, 1995), and (co-editor with Carlos Ossa), *El gobierno Barco* (Bogotá, 1994). He is one of the editors of *Historia Andina*, currently under preparation.

Marie-Danielle Demélas-Bohy is Professor of History at the Centre de Recherches d'Histoire de l'Amérique Latine et du Monde Ibérique,

Université de Paris. She is the author of *L'invention politique. Bolivie, Equateur, Pérou au XIXe siècle* (Paris, 1992).

François-Xavier Guerra is Professor of History at the Centre de Recherches d'Histoire de l'Amérique Latine et du Monde Ibérique. He is the author of *México: del antiguo régimen a la revolución* (Mexico, 1988) and *Modernidad e independencias* (Madrid, 1992). He has published on Latin American electoral history in the *Journal of Latin American Studies* and *Caravelle*.

K. Theodore Hoppen is Reader in History at the University of Hull. He is the author of *Elections, Politics and Society in Ireland* (Oxford, 1984), and *Ireland since 1800: Conflict and Conformity* (London, 1989). He has published extensively on Irish electoral history, including articles in *English Historical Review, History* and *Quaderni Storici*.

Juan Maiguashca is Professor of History at the University of York in Toronto, Canada. He is the editor of *Historia y Región en el Ecuador, 1830-1930* (Quito, 1994). He is also one of the general editors of *Historia Andina*, currently under preparation.

Frank O' Gorman is Professor of History at the University of Manchester. He is the author of several books, including *Voters, Patrons and Parties: The Unreformed Electorate of Hanoverian England* (Oxford, 1989). He has published extensively on English electoral history, including articles in *Past and Present, Journal of Modern History*, and *Social History*.

Eduardo Posada-Carbó is Lecturer in History at the Institute of Latin American Studies, University of London. He is the author of *The Colombian Caribbean: A Regional History, 1870-1930*, (Oxford, 1996), and with Walter Little he is co-editor of *Political Corruption in Europe and Latin America* (Basingstoke, 1996). He has published on Colombian electoral history in the *Journal of Latin American Studies*.

J. Samuel Valenzuela is Professor of Sociology at the University of Notre Dame. He is the author of *Democratización vía reforma: la expansión del sufragio en Chile* (Buenos Aires, 1985).

LIST OF TABLES

LIST OF FIGURES

INTRODUCTION

ELECTIONS BEFORE DEMOCRACY: SOME CONSIDERATIONS ON ELECTORAL HISTORY FROM A COMPARATIVE APPROACH

Eduardo Posada-Carbó

'With the acquisition of universal suffrage in Great Britain and the passing of the Old Prussian system', Charles Seymour and Donald Paige Frary wrote in 1918, 'a definite milestone on the road of political evolution has been reached'. Indeed Seymour and Frary's optimism about the developments of a popular electoral franchise apparently knew few boundaries: '...if a League of Nations is to become a reality, removing trade barriers between countries, diminishing the likelihood of war, and promoting a common intercourse of things material and intellectual, there can be no reason for delimiting elections upon lines of dead frontiers'. Thus they concluded: 'an international franchise, limited, no doubt, to elections of general interests, is a possiblity of the future'.[1]

Their optimism was soon to be disappointed. Yet at the time they published their two-volume work, *How the World Votes*, Seymour and Frary's optimism was not that unfounded. In 1918 all British adult males who had hitherto not qualified for the vote were enfranchised, as were then women ratepayers of 30 years old. Elsewhere in the continent male universal suffrage had been gaining ground: it was introduced, for example, in Spain in 1890, in Italy in 1912, in Belgium in 1919.[2] The process of expansion of the electorate was by no means a gradual one, nor did it follow the same pattern in all countries. France, where universal suffrage was adopted first in 1792 and then in 1848, experienced a 'deuxième naissance du suffrage universel' in 1870-77 following the frustrations of the Second Republic.[3] While in Spain the expansion of the franchise was not the result of any pressure from below, the granting of universal suffrage in Belgium was preceded by popular mobilisation in favour of electoral reforms, most notably the mass demonstration of 10 August 1890 and the general strike of 14 April 1913.[4]

Beyond the European frontiers the Americas also experienced a wave of electoral reforms at the turn of the century. In the United States, with a relatively wide franchise since the early nineteenth-century, the issue was not so much the expansion of the electorate as electoral corruption. There was much more than elections at stake in the reform movements that swept across the United States from the 1890s to 1917, but the 'progressives' certainly targeted the electoral bosses and their party machines.[5] Elsewhere in the hemisphere there was no shortage of electoral politics, though their development varied from country to country. In Chile, where the electorate had significantly expanded after the 1874 reforms, the debate was centred on the need to free the electoral process from the influences of the executive. After the parliamentary reaction against President José M. Balmaceda in 1891, Chileans entered a new period of political history. Similarly in Colombia, pressures for reform were focused on the rules to guarantee a fair electoral process. Likewise in Argentina, where male universal suffrage had been adopted since 1853, the showpiece of electoral legislation – the Sáenz Peña Law of 1912 – was geared towards guaranteeing free elections.[6]

These were crucial developments, both in Europe and in the Americas, whose importance today is often undervalued or simply dismissed. As Peter Steinbach has observed, 'social scientists have lost a sense of the fundamental significance of the democratic franchise for the emergence of a modern political system..., they neglect the historical preconditions of a political culture that, after all, represents the outcome of a process rather than the sum of attitudes and values'.[7] Moreover elections in what are considered 'pre-modern', 'pre-democratic' societies have not received much scholarly attention. Whenever they are studied, with a few notable exceptions, they tend to be identified exclusively with the practices of patronage and clientelism, or merely with fraud and coercion. At a more sophisticated level, elections in these societies are perceived as mechanisms of social control or as conferring legitimacy to the oligarchies and their political systems.

Indeed, as the franchise expanded, the diffusion of voting practices faced several obstacles, and any study of the history of elections cannot fail to take into account all those factors that tended to distort the electoral process: the power of landlords, the clergy and government officials over voters; the manipulation of the electoral register; the use of fraud, intimidation or direct bribery. The apparent predominance of these 'glaring anomalies' in England during the eighteenth century led many to neglect the significance of elections before the Reform Act of 1832: 'The whole business was pure, or perhaps more accurately impure, theatre'.[8] For similar reasons, in 1918, the electoral process in the Iberian peninsula and Latin America was characterised as 'denatured', or simply as 'a pure sham'. Set against the progress of democracy in the English electoral system throughout the nineteenth-century, elections in Spain and Latin America were regarded as 'peculiar' or, as C. E. Chapman put it, a 'curious phenomenon'.[9]

This view of electoral history has recently been subject to close scrutiny. In particular, the work of Frank O'Gorman has provided a new perspective on elections in pre-reformed England, a stimulating approach that could be useful in studying pre-reformed elections elsewhere. O'Gorman's point of departure is to dispute some of the traditional assumptions about the eighteenth-century English elections: that 'very few of the voters were free to vote as they wished', that elections were an exclusive rather than a participatory process, that the vast majority of electors were politically unaware and, therefore, elections were only a conflict of material and personal pressures rather than a conflict of values and ideas.[10] O'Gorman moves away from the hitherto dominant interpretation which tends to concentrate on exposing the anomalies of the electoral system. Instead he sets himself the task of answering, among others, the following questions: 'Was the electorate growing in size, and if so, at what rate? If it was growing in size, was it becoming harder to influence and control? ... How was the electorate organized and with what degree of efficiency? ... Could the (electoral) campaign influence the outcome of an electoral contest?'[11]

The result is a detailed study of electoral behaviour that goes beyond the traditional explanation of a client-patron relationship. Local politics are at the centre of O'Gorman's analysis, although he does not neglect the impact of national issues in local life. Local families were obviously in control of the electoral system, but their influence was conditioned by 'habits of widespread political involvement'. The way patronage mechanisms worked varied according to the different types of constituencies, but in most cases patronage alone could not secure a seat. Of particular interest is O'Gorman's emphasis on the significance of electioneering and canvassing, since political support did not automatically follow any status, but had to be worked for. In addition, electoral canvassing provided 'great community occasions': far from being exclusive, electoral politics became an increasingly active and participatory experience. Furthermore, given their involvement in elections, the ruling class became committed to Parliament and thus to 'representative forms of government and processes'. All in all, the value of O'Gorman's approach lies in providing us with an explanatory framework of an electoral order where pressures for reform are undermining patronage structures. Alongside patron-client relationships, he identifies a rich electoral life that requires an explanation of its own. It was the strength of the electoral continuities, and the electoral culture that was therefore being created, upon which, according to O'Gorman, the representative democracy of the Victorian era was to be erected.[12]

In the first chapter of this book, Frank O'Gorman thus elaborates further on the concept of 'electoral culture', and examines how this culture developed in England between the late seventeenth century and the First World War. He calls our attention to the significance of electoral campaigns and processes in encouraging the emergence of a popular electoral culture. This culture, greatly influenced by the printed word, experienced its fullest development between the 1780s and 1832. Among some of the assumptions underlying electoral culture, O'Gorman points out that elections were a departure from the rhythm of normal life, that electors had a mind of their own, and that elections were ritualistic events with wider social and political implications. His chapter also offers some suggestions for comparative research, although he is cautious to warn of the difficulties involved in extending the English experience elsewhere. Nevertheless his suggestions are worthy of consideration, and not necessarily just in looking for replicas of English electoral culture. As John H. Elliot has observed, 'the value of comparative history lies not so much in discovering the similarities as in identifying the differences'.[13]

One major feature in the history of elections in the Hispanic world, contrasting sharply with the English tradition, is the revolutionary origins of the electoral process. In England, as Charles Seymour pointed out, there was a constant though slow 'advance towards democracy in elections.'[14] In both Spain and Spanish America the system of elective representation came about abruptly, following the Napoleonic invasion of the peninsula and the abdication of Ferdinand VII. To fill the sudden vacuum of power, the Hispanic world was forced to enter a period of electoral agitation hitherto unknown.

The first general elections took place in 1809 when the Americans were asked to send their representatives to the *Junta Central* in Sevilla. These elections, and the ones which followed in the next four years, including those to select deputies to the Cortes, were major formative events for the emerging independent nations in Spanish America. As François-Xavier Guerra and Marie-Danielle Demélas-Bohy show in chapter 2 of this book, from the spring of 1809 to the winter of 1810 the electoral experience in Spanish America, from Sonora to Chile, was particularly meaningful. They encouraged political mobilisation throughout the continent in an unprecedented fashion. More than one hundred cities were involved in this electoral process. In places such as Valladolid (Morelos in Mexico today) and Córdoba in the River Plate, elections be-

came occasions where local disputes were bitterly aired through anonymous leaflets which kept these cities in a state of confrontation. Indeed
political language itself changed. The press played a significant role in
spreading new values. Above all elections were participatory events, in-
volving all social sectors in the cities where they took place.[15]
    The electoral process might initially have been felt more intensely in
Spain than in Spanish America. In both the metropolis and the colonies it
received a setback with the restoration of the Monarchy in 1814. But in
1820 elections were again at the forefront of politics in the Hispanic
world, mobilising public opinion through the publication of newspapers,
leaflets, and sermons from the pulpit. Even plays highlighted the significance of elections.[16] In the colonies, where the question of 'equal
representation' became so central to the debate, the electoral process
served to widen the distance with the metropolis and encouraged independence. As Guerra and Demélas-Bohy observe, the elections *were* the
revolution.
    The adoption of elections did not mean that liberal institutions pre-
vailed overnight. Indeed Guerra and Demélas-Bohy suggest that there
coexisted in contradiction a modern political discourse and electoral
practices in societies that remained traditional overall. This proposition is
examined systematically by Antonio Annino regarding the experience of
New Spain (Mexico today) between 1812 and 1820 (chapter 3). By 1820,
more than 600 elective councils existed in New Spain, providing evidence of widespread representative institutions. Annino shows how
indigenous communities adapted to and even reshaped the newly adopted
franchise: voting practices enjoyed consensus by the communities, but
the new concept of 'sovereignty' was not accepted. This had unpredict-
able outcomes. Annino argues that elections unleashed a process of
decentralisation with long lasting consequences for the later life of republican Mexico.
    This reappraisal of the electoral process during the first two decades
of the nineteenth-century serves to highlight at least two significant
points: the early existence of a relatively wide suffrage in the Hispanic
World, and the way in which electoral politics mobilised large sections of
society in that period. The acceptance of an extended franchise varied
from region to region. As David Bushnell has suggested, a comparative
analysis of electoral legislation is of immense value to a better understanding of the Spanish American emerging nations.[17] In Venezuela, the
military were given privileged voting rights unparalleled in Colombia.
But by the mid-nineteenth century Venezuela enjoyed 'one of the most
democratic electoral systems (for that period) in the world'.[18] Similarly

some provinces in Argentina adopted a wide franchise shortly after independence, although they sometimes discriminated against blacks (a
paradox, since blacks were few in Argentina). Colombia, in contrast,
adopted a more restricted franchise than in some of Argentina's provinces
but there were no special clauses discriminating against the relatively
large black population.[19] Both Colombia and Argentina accepted male
universal suffrage in 1853, though a restricted franchise was reintroduced
in some Colombian states following the federal constitution of 1863, and
further restrictive legislation was adopted in 1886. No general pattern
therefore emerged. However, it seems that, with a few exceptions, in most
Latin American countries the idea of an extended suffrage gained ground
during the first half of the nineteenth century to an extent which has few
parallels in the Western world. This in itself is of interest to the intellectual history of the region. But the precociousness of the Latin American
electorate had wider political and social consequences.

Most significantly the emergence of new political nations with voting
rights was a major source of instability. As J. H. Plumb has observed,
until the English electorate that came into being during the seventeeth
century was 'reduced, subjected, or prevented from voting, there was no
hope whatsoever that England would achieve political stability'.[20] Plumb
shows how the struggle to control the electorate, with its new methods of
propaganda and electioneering and subtler forms of corruption and manipulation, 'involved far more than Parliament and Court: it touched the
entire political nation; on its resolution depended the pattern of power in
the counties, cities and boroughs'.[21] Since nineteenth-century politics in
Latin America have been largely neglected, very little attention has been
given to the electoral dimensions of the recurrent civil conflicts in the region. Even Chile, considered as an exceptionally stable country, did not
escape these struggles: the four major civil wars of the nineteenth century
(1829-30, 1851, 1859, and 1891) coincided with an electoral campaign.
The 1880 presidential contest in Argentina was the source of one of the
bitterest conflicts of the century, but other elections also ended up in
war.[22] Likewise in Colombia the civil wars of 1859-60, 1875, 1885 and
even the *Guerra de los Mil Días* (1889-1902) were linked to the electoral
struggle in one way or another.[23]

By its very nature, the electoral process involved an element of pre-
cariousness with regard to public order. Since, at least in theory, elections
opened up the possibility of a transfer of power, those in government saw
their authority weakened during any elections whose results were uncertain. That is why wherever elections developed, with a few exceptions,
they were accompanied by violence.[24] In Spanish America, this problem

was exacerbated by the unresolved complex question of 'legitimacy', brought about by the wars of independence. A weak state was often a passive witness of partisan struggles. In some countries, as Malcolm Deas shows in chapter 7 on Colombia, the Army became, although reluctantly, the arbiter of electoral conflicts.[25]

Perhaps inevitably, some of these conflicts revolved around the rules of the game, the fairness of elections, the process that after all was to determine the final allocation of power. But as Pierre Rosanvallon has observed regarding elections in mid-nineteenth-century France, the theme of electoral reform was wide-embracing. It 'played the role of universal political remedy, which should provide answers to the great problems of the moment: the supression of corruption, installation of affordable government, respect for the general good, guarantee of social peace'.[26] Juan Maiguascha in chapter 4 illustrates how the 1861 electoral reforms in Ecuador not only involved demands for social inclusion, but also crucial political claims. His is also a contribution to the neglected field of constitutional history.

The emergence of these political nations with voting rights in Latin America has often been overlooked by historians. Very few dispute that the acceptance of a wide franchise meant the early inclusion of popular sectors in the electorate.[27] But easy assumptions are made about how this electorate was controlled or manipulated from above, undervaluing its significance. As noted, Guerra has readdressed the meaning of elections during the first decades of the nineteenth-century, and how they encouraged political mobility with widespread social consequences. He nevertheless suggests that political participation decreased as the century wore on, leading to the consolidation of regimes characterised as 'fictitious democracies'.[28]

This appears to be the case for Mexico during the *Porfiriato* (1876-1910). But before the rise of Porfirio Díaz, Mexican politics remained volatile and turbulent – a turbulence which involved much electioneering.[29] Elsewhere the picture varied significantly over time and place. Chile certainly saw the steady expansion of an electorate – with a brief interlude in the 1880s – that became less amenable to control. Party organisation followed, as was also the experience of Argentina, where the system of conventions to select candidates – with the United States as the model – was adopted. But even in the case of Brazil, where nineteenth-century elections were apparently controlled by the landed elites, Richard Graham admits that voters in the cities were hard to manipulate and that in the countryside *agregados* – who were not tied to the land – required constant attention from the patron, who could not rely on their deference or loyalty.[30] As the century wore on the situation certainly became more complex. Mauricio Font shows how in São Paulo elections were most significant political events during the first three decades of this century.[31]

Whatever degree of control was exercised by those in positions of power over the voters, it was not always unconditional. In an interesting document, quoted at length in Malcolm Deas's chapter, the Colombian Liberal ideologue Manuel Murillo Toro acknowledged in 1855 that the influence of priests and landlords over the electorate was often limited. The electorate in Hanoverian England was not free of control by the local etites either, but as O'Gorman demonstrates, it was a control exercised 'at great cost, with great care, with great difficulty, with much effort, and sometimes for no very great return'.[32] To what extent these conditions applied in Latin America or elsewhere in Europe and how they developed over time is still in most cases an open question. We need further detailed studies on government participation in elections as well as on other agents and institutions involved in electoral politics.[33]

One such institution was the Church. Three chapters in this book look at the role of the Catholic Church in elections in Ireland, Germany and Colombia. As a 'distinctly Catholic electoral bloc' emerged in Ireland after the 1820s, the clergy became involved in electioneering. The expansion of the franchise, as happened in Germany during the 1870s, encouraged the participation of a beleaguered Catholic Church in the electoral process. The resurrection of the Centrum Party went hand in hand with the mobilisation of Catholics and the rise of a partisan clergy. In Colombia the clergy was involved in electoral politics from the very foundation of the republic, and its role became crucial in the Liberal-Conservative divide that clearly demarcated the political nation by the mid-nineteenth century.

In all three countries, the participation of the clergy in elections was therefore significant. There was of course a major difference between the nature of the disputes that led to the involvement of the Catholic Church in the politics of Ireland and Germany and its involvement in Colombia. In the former, Catholic politics were a means to oppose a dominant Protestant majority, conferring on the conflict a deeply religious and even ethnic dimension. In the latter, the debate over Church issues was mostly a debate within a community which was by and large Catholic, although the commitment to Catholicism varied a great deal from region to region.

In all cases, however, clerical involvement in elections raises similarly interesting questions, addressed in this book by K. Theodore Hoppen (chapter 5), Margaret Lavinia Anderson (chapter 6) and Malcolm Deas (chapter 7): how effective was the clergy's participation in electioneering; under which circumstances could priests exercise power over their parishioners; who guided the electoral process; what were the consequences of clerical electioneering for the politics of these countries? For some contemporaries 'clerical influence became the sin against the free election'.[34] The Liberals' defeat in Colombia in 1856, after the first presidential election under male universal suffrage, encouraged the view among fellow partisans that the rural poor were easily manipulated by the Church in favour of the Conservatives. Likewise in Germany, the successful mobilisation of Catholic voters by the Centrum Party in the 1871 elections raised fears among Protestants and Liberals. Yet the extent to which the clergy controlled the votes of their flock needs to be closely reexamined. As J. H. Whyte put the question regarding the Irish experience: 'how far the clergy actually altered the voting: in other words, how far they induced electors to vote for candidates whom they would otherwise have opposed?'.[35]

K. Theodore Hoppen argues that in Irish politics priests 'were never more than one powerful group among many'. Locally their power was often impressive. But when it came to national politics their effectiveness was questionable. At all events, as Hoppen shows, their monopoly over spiritual and theological matters was not always 'accompanied by a similar deference in the field of politics'. Their involvement in politics was sometimes encouraged by laymen: it was Daniel O'Connell 'who had approached the clergy in the 1820s, not the other way about'.[36] Furthermore the leadership of Catholic politics, when most effective, remained in lay hands. And priests, as in Colombia and Germany, had to be cautious: they were most effective in mobilising the Catholic electorate when their views coincided with their flock.

In the words of Margaret Lavinia Anderson regarding the case of Germany, 'the power of the priest lay in his ability to define community, or at least to articulate the community's own view of itself'. And in Catholic Germany the influence of the clergy in electioneering seems to have no parallel either in Europe or in America: priests distributed ballots, organised campaign rallies, spoke at the hustings, but they were also elected as deputies in large numbers, although their real leverage remained outside parliament. In Colombia too, as described by Malcolm Deas, the clergy was heavily involved in electioneering: priests voted *en masse*, and organised village mobs against Liberal speakers. Yet Anderson suggests that 'nowhere else...did clerical influence on elections become so widespread, so continuous, or so effective as in Catholic Germany. Nowhere else was it institutionalised in a powerful party'. The Catholic laity looked towards the leadership of the party for direction, and in some cases, particularly at the local level, that leadership was clerical.

At all events, wherever one looks at clerical electioneering – in Ireland, in Colombia or in Germany – it is useful to bear in mind Hoppen's conclusion: '"clerical influence" over elections must, as a conceptre-main imprecise both as to nature and degree'. Hoppen also underlines how easy it is 'to mistake energy for effectiveness'. In addition, contemporary anti-clerical literature can be misleading. Malcolm Deas notes 'how intensely political all post-election polemic is', and 'how necessary anticlericalism was to the Liberal cause': it increased 'Liberal enthusiasm'.

If 'clerical influences', as a concept, should remain imprecise, what about other influences? In the 1828 elections in Chile, for example, the traditional power of landords was said to have been displaced 'by the audacity of electoral agents'.[37] After 1830 the President gained the upper hand over the electoral process – the 'venia del ejecutivo' (literally permission from the executive) usually was a guarantee to be elected. This power, however, was not unlimited. In a convincingly revisionist approach, J. Samuel Valenzuela in chapter 10 shows that the opposition was 'an ever present ingredient' in Chilean nineteenth-century politics. In the face of opposition the government had to be cautious in interpreting the public mood. The process of selection of candidates could not neglect local feelings.[38] President Manuel Montt, for example, could not impose his successor in 1861. Furthermore, the reading of electoral results must be taken with a pinch of salt. As Valenzuela suggests, electoral contests were judged on the basis of those districts where the opposition presented a challenge. An overall victory, as occured in 1849 when the opposition won in Valparaíso, could turn into moral defeat: in this case, the government was forced to change the cabinet.[39] At all events, the executive's influence over elections was increasingly challenged; as the opposition gained space the pressure to reform the system mounted.

Contested elections in nineteenth-century Chile were far from being exceptional. Electoral competition often encouraged electoral organisation, particularly in the opposition ranks for, as D. E. Ginter has observed regarding the English general election of 1790, without organisation there was no way that the opposition groups could defeat the government.[40] The Chilean experience also serves to illustrate how electoral organisation developed in an intense electoral agenda. In the 1840s there were conscious efforts to organise popular sectors for electoral purposes. Political clubs were established, canvassing was intensified, while new means for the selection of candidates were adopted. In 1859, for example, a *Club de la*

Oposición was set up in Valparaíso. Their members met at the evenings in Teatro de la Victoria, where popular orators attracted large gatherings. In the 1860s, the Radicals organised electoral assemblies, considered by Julio Heise as a novelty in the political struggle.[41] Electoral conventions became the norm after 1874, when Liberal delegates from all over the country selected Aníbal Pinto as their presidential candidate. Likewise in Argentina, particularly in Buenos Aires where elections were heavily contested, electoral competition brought about changes in electoral organisation. Paula Alonso in chapter 8 pays attention to these changes in the political life of Buenos Aires from the 1860s to the turn of the century. Prominent among them was the new organisation of the emergent parties, with their permanent committees whose activities differed from the old electoral clubs.

Electoral organisation was also crucial in the struggles against electoral corruption. As the Colombian Liberal Enrique Santos observed in 1915, fraud became more difficult in the face of an organised opposition party.[42] Manifestations of electoral corruption, however, were varied in nature and from country to country. Carlos Dardé in chapter 9 deals with a specific aspect of electoral fraud, namely the falsification of electoral results in Spain. In his view, there is a historiographical consensus about the extent of fraud in Spain during the Restoration period (1875-1925), which seems to characterise Spanish elections at the time. Dardé reviews the different mechanisms used to rig electoral results and turns his attention to the passivity of the Spanish electorate as a possible explanation for the persistence of fraud. He does acknowledge that in large cities, such as Madrid, Barcelona, Valencia and Bilbao, electoral results often reflected the will of the electorate.

The subject of electoral fraud and corruption is indeed rich and complex. To start with, the evidence is elusive: the English investigation committees of the nineteenth century 'found as great difficulty as do historians in determining the exact truth of each specific allegation...'.[43] Denunciation of fraud, or of other forms of electoral corruption, was often a political weapon used by all parties in dispute. Wherever electoral contests developed, fraud might have been one of many factors determining the outcome of what was, after all, a competitive struggle. In addition, the historian ought to be able to distinguish electoral fraud pure and simple – that is, the physical adulteration of votes – from other forms of electoral corruption, including the venality of electors and intimidation.

Fraud and corruption were ever-present characteristics in the history of elections in Europe and Latin America. The universality of electoral

corruption indicates the need for a comparative approach to appreciate
its nature in the countries where elections developed. Indeed, in putting
together different essays on various aspects of elections, the purpose of
this book is to suggest that electoral practices and behaviour ought to be
properly considered in the context of comparative history. There are obvious limitations. The paucity of research, particularly in Latin
America, impedes systematic comparative analysis. That is why, while
offering interesting material for further comparisons, most of these chapters concentrate on national histories. Comparative history, as John H.
Elliot has pointed out, faces some other challenges: 'should we confine
our comparisons to societies in much the same geographical or temporal
frame... or can we profitably extend the comparison across the centuries
to look at very different societies at moments when they might be regarded as having reached broadly similar stages of development?'⁴⁴ As
Latin America has long moulded its political traditions in a Western
framework, comparisons with Europe are not only valid but appropriate.
Moreover, in the case of electoral history, it seems useful to extend the
comparative analysis to the United States.

As the title of this book suggests, its various chapters deal with aspects of elections in what political scientists and sociologists may
consider to be pre-democratic societies. There is, however, another angle
to *Elections Before Democracy* that this book is intended to highlight: the
historical significance of elections to democratic developments. This is
what Samuel J. Valenzuela refers to as 'building aspects of democracy
before democracy'. Or, in the words of Frank O'Gorman: 'the widespread diffusion of traditions and practices of electoral culture may be
taken to be one of the most indispensable pre-requisites for representative
government'.

Notes

1. Charles Seymour and Donald Paige Frary, *How the World Votes. The Story
    of Democratic Developments in Elections* (Springfield, Mass., 1918), vol. 1,
    p. v, and vol. 2, pp. 310–11.
2. See Eric J. Evans, *The Great Reform Act of 1832* (London and New York,
    1994), p. 2; Javier Tusell (ed.), *El sufragio universal* (Madrid, 1991), pp.
    17 and 118; C. Dardé, 'El sufragio universal en España: causas y efectos',
    Historia Contemporánea. Anales de la Universidad de Alicante, No. 7
    (1989-90), pp. 85-101; J. Stengers, 'Histoire de la législation électorale en
    Belgique', in S. Noiret (ed.), *Political Strategies and Electoral Reforms:
    Origins of Voting Systems in Europe in the 19th and 20th Centuries* (Baden

Baden, 1990), p. 77.
3. Raymond Huard, *Le suffrage universel en France, 1848-1946* (Aubier, 1991), pp. 9 and 101.
4. Tusell, *El sufragio universal*, p. 17, and Janet L. Polasky, 'A Revolution for Socialist Reforms: the Belgian General Strike for Universal Suffrage', *Journal of Contemporary History*, vol. 27 (1992), pp. 449–66.
5. R. McCormick, *The Party Period and Public Policy. American Politics from the Age of Jackson to the Progressive Era* (New York and Oxford, 1986), p. 277. In fact, 'many new laws redefined the eligible electorate by excluding certain people from voting and including others', *idem.* See *ibid.*, note 25 for further reading suggestions. See also R. F. Wesser, *A Response to Progressivism: The Democratic Party and New York Politics, 1902-1918* (New York and London, 1986). For a contemporary description of US electoral politics, see James Bryce, *The American Commonwealth* (London and New York, 1895), vol. II.
6. See R. Donoso, *Las ideas políticas en Chile* (México, 1946), pp. 381-439; N. R. Botana, *El orden conservador. La política argentina entre 1880 y 1916* (Buenos Aires, 1977), pp. 217-346; D. Cullen, 'Electoral Practices in Argentina, 1898-1904', unpublished D. Phil. thesis, University of Oxford, 1994; F. Barón, *La reforma electoral* (Bogotá, 1915).
7. P. Steinbach, 'Reichstag Elections in the Kaiserreich: The Prospects for Electoral Research in the Interdisciplinary Context', in L. E. Jones *et al.* (eds.), *Elections, Mass Politics and Social Change in Modern Germany* (Cambridge, 1992), p. 120.
8. Evans, *The Great Reform Act*, p. 10. Nevertheless, Evans acknowledges recent advances in the literature, providing a rather different picture of elections before 1832, of which more later in this introduction; see *idem*, pp. 11-4.
9. C. E. Chapman, 'The Age of the Caudillos: A Chapter in Hispanic American History', *Hispanic American Historical Review*, vol. XII (1932), p. 292; see also Seymour and Frary, *How the World Votes*, vol. 1, p. v, and vol. 2, p. 267.
10. F. O'Gorman, *Voters, Patrons and Parties: the Unreformed Electorate of Hanoverian England, 1734-1832* (Oxford, 1989), pp. 2-4.
11. *Ibid.*, p. 4.
12. *Ibid.*, pp. 384-93.
13. J. H. Elliot, *National and Comparative History. An Inaugural Lecture Delivered Before the University of Oxford* (Oxford, 1991), p. 24.
14. Charles Seymour, *Electoral Reform in England and Wales. The Development and Operation of the Parliamentary Franchise, 1832-1885* (1915) (Hamden, 1970), pp. vii-viii.
15. These points also receive systematic attention in F.-X. Guerra, *Modernidad e independencias. Ensayo sobre las revoluciones hispánicas* (Madrid, 1992); see in particular pp. 140, 144, 177-226, and 275-318. See also V. Peralta, 'Elecciones, constitucionalismo y revolución: el Cusco entre 1809-

1815', unpublished paper presented at the Instituto Ortega y Gasset, February 1994.

16. 'El buen cura y sus feligreses. Diálogo patriótico, acomodado a la inteligencia del pueblo para fijar su opinión estraviada sobre constitución, y dirigir su conducta en el delicado e importantísimo asunto de elecciones' (1820), in B. E. Buldaín Jaca (ed.), *Las elecciones de 1820. La época y su publicística* (Madrid, 1993), pp. 119-48.

17. David Bushnell, 'El sufragio en la Argentina y en Colombia hasta 1853', *Revista del Instituto de Historia del Derecho*, no. 19 (Buenos Aires, 1968), pp. 11-29, and 'La evolución del derecho del sufragio en Venezuela', *Boletín Histórico*, vol. 29, Caracas (May 1972), pp. 189-206.

18. Bushnell, 'La evolución del derecho de sufragio en Venezuela', p. 202. Two recent books shed light on the elections of Venezuela during the first half of the nineteenth century: A. Navas Blanco, *Las elecciones presidenciales en Venezuela del siglo XIX, 1830-1854* (Caracas, 1993), and E. Gabaldón, *Las elecciones presidenciales de 1835* (Caracas, 1986).

19. Bushnell, 'El sufragio en la Argentina y en Colombia', p. 20.

20. J. H. Plumb, *The Growth of Political Stability in England, 1675-1725* (London, 1967), p. 41.

21. Plumb, *The Growth of Political Stability*, pp. 41, 45, 46.

22. Maurice Zeitlin, *The Civil Wars in Chile* (Princeton, 1984); and Lia E. M. Sanucci, *La renovación presidencial de 1880* (La Plata, 1955).

23. See my 'Elections and civil wars in nineteenth-century Colombia: The 1875 presidential campaign', *Journal of Latin American Studies*, vol. 26, pt. 3 (Oct. 1994), pp. 621-50.

24. For electoral violence, see, for example, O'Gorman, *Voters, Patrons and Parties*, pp. 255-9; I. Gilmour, *Riot, Rising and Revolution. Governance and Violence in 18th century England* (London, 1992), pp. 207-23; K.T. Hoppen, *Elections, Politics and Society in Ireland, 1832 - 1885* (Oxford, 1984), pp. 388-408; R. M. Brown, *No Duty to Retreat. Violence and Values in American History and Society* (Oxford, 1991), p. 10; R. Graham, *Patronage and Politics in Nineteenth-century Brazil* (Stanford, 1990), p. 141; S. Wilson, *Feuding, Conflict and Banditry in Nineteenth-century Corsica* (Cambridge, 1988), pp. 324-34.

25. See also P. Pinzón de Lewin, *El ejército y las elecciones* (Bogotá, 1994).

26. P. Rosanvallon, 'The republic of universal suffrage', in B. Fontana (ed.), *The Invention of the Modern Republic* (Cambridge, 1994).

27. For examples of how 'men of certain social position... do not attend the polls' in Argentina, see H. Sábato, 'Citizenship, Political Participation and the Formation of the Public Sphere in Buenos Aires, 1850-1880', *Past and Present*, vol. 136 (1992), pp. 142-8. A more systematic analysis of who voted in Buenos Aires is in P. Alonso, 'Politics and Elections in Buenos Aires, 1890-1898', *Journal of Latin American Studies*, vol. 25 (1993), pp. 465-87. For the case of Chile, see J. Samuel Valenzuela, *Democratización vía reforma. La expansión del sufragio en Chile* (Buenos Aires, 1985).

Introduction 15

David Sowell demonstrates how artisans were heavily involved in the electoral politics of Bogotá, Colombia, since the early years of the republic; see his *The Early Colombian Labor Movement* (Philadephia, 1992).

28. See his 'The Spanish-American Tradition of Representation and its European Roots', *Journal of Latin American Studies*, vol. 26, pt.1 (Feb.1994), pp. 1-36.

29. For a study of how Santa Anna, the archetype Mexican caudillo, was unable to control the electoral process, and how contested Mexican elections were during the first half of the nineteenth century, see M. P. Costeloe, 'Generals versus Politicians: Santa Anna and the 1842 Congressional Elections in Mexico', *Bulletin of Latin American Research*, vol. 8, no. 2 (1989), pp. 257-74. An exceptional defence of the significance of elections in Mexico between 1857 and 1876 is in Daniel Cosío Villegas, *La constitución de 1857 y sus críticos* (Mexico and Buenos Aires, 1957), pp. 122-50.

30. Graham, *Patronage and politics in nineteenth-century Brazil*, pp. 34 and 86.

31. See his *Coffee, Contention and Change. The Making of Modern Brazil* (Cambridge, Mass., and Oxford, 1990).

32. O'Gorman, *Voters, Patrons and Parties*, pp. 384-5.

33. See, for example, M. L. Anderson, 'Voter, Junker, Landrat, Priest: The Old Authorities and the New Franchise in Imperial Germany', *American Historical Review*, vol. 98, no. 5 (December 1993), pp. 1448-74.

34. See chapter 6 in this book.

35. J. H. Whyte, 'The Influence of the Catholic Clergy on Elections in Nineteenth-Century Ireland', *English Historical Review*, no. 75 (1960), p. 245.

36. See Hoppen's chapter in this book (chap. 5). See also his *Elections, Politics, and Society in Ireland*, p. 232.

37. Donoso, *Las ideas políticas en Chile*, p. 389.

38. See also Valenzuela, *Democratización vía reforma*, pp. 55, 70, 72.

39. See also Donoso, *Las ideas políticas en Chile*, pp. 403-4; A. Edwards, *El gobierno de don Manuel Montt, 1851-1861* (Santiago, 1932), p. 16; and I. Errázuriz, *Historia de la administración Errázuriz* (Santiago, 1935), pp. 312-3.

40. D. E. Ginter (ed.), *Whig Organization in the General Election of 1790* (Berkeley and Los Angeles, 1967), p. xlvii. For a suggestive approach to electoral organisation see also: H. J. Hanham, *Elections and Party Management* (Sussex, 1978), and J. H. Silbey, *The American Political Nation, 1838-1893* (Stanford, 1991).

41. See P. P. Figueroa, *Historia de la revolución constituyente (1858-1859) escrita sobre documentos completamente inéditos* (Santiago, 1889), pp. 479-85; and J. Heise González, *El período parlamentario, 1861-1925* (Santiago, 1982), vol. II, pp. 36-7.

42. E. Santos (Calibán), 'Las causas de las derrotas', *La Linterna*, 12 Feb. 1915, in his *La Danza de las Horas y otros escritos* (Bogotá, 1969), p. 59

43. Seymour, *Electoral Reform in England and Wales*, p. 401.

44. Elliot, *National and Comparative History*, p. 22.

CHAPTER 1

THE CULTURE OF ELECTIONS IN ENGLAND: FROM THE GLORIOUS REVOLUTION TO THE FIRST WORLD WAR, 1688-1914

Frank O'Gorman

The culture of elections and election campaigns acquired a continuous existence in England when elections became a regular and necessary part of the political system. In the sixteenth and seventeenth centuries parliament was dissolved and elections held at the personal whim and political convenience of the monarch. The management of parliament was essential to effective royal government. To avoid opposition in parliament monarchs would simply try to govern without it for as long as they could rather than risk an appeal to the political nation. Consequently, for example, there were no elections in England between 1629 and 1640, but then there were two in 1640 and 1641. To take another example, elections were not held between 1661 and 1679, but between 1679 and 1681 there were three. In these circumstances it was difficult for electoral traditions to develop. Elections were exceptional appeals to the country to resolve deadlocks within the parliamentary classes. They were not yet regular and integral elements of the political and social process.

They began to be so with the passing of the Triennial Act of 1694. This Act was part of the Revolution Settlement in England in which the hitherto arbitrary powers of the monarchy were brought under parliamentary control. Parliament was now to become independent of the monarchy and more subject to regular elections than to the royal manipulation and control to which it had been earlier subjected. The Triennial Act stated that the period between elections could not exceed three years (in practice it was more like two). Given the regularity of elections under the Triennial Act, election campaigns became more closely contested, more exciting and more elaborate. Indeed, the electorate could not be controlled and government majorities were frequently uncertain.[1]

And as elections became more regular so the process by which landlords, corporations and other groups had been able to secure compliant acceptance of their candidates became more complicated. In the sixteenth and seventeenth centuries election procedures had made local contests between candidates more difficult. They were designed to frustrate opposition. 'Logistical difficulties, long delays and the longer deliberations of candidates and officials all worked to prevent divisive elections'.[2] As we shall see, however, such electoral processes were able to act as the agencies for the emergence of a vibrant and, to some extent, popular, electoral culture. From 1694 Britain entered a period of sharpening political conflict and increasing party commitment that lasted until the Septennial Act of 1716.[3]

The Act of 1694 was replaced by the Septennial Act in 1716 which defined the period between elections as not more than seven years (in practice it was more like six). The Act of 1694 had been too successful in giving full play to political disagreements at both the local and national levels. The Septennial Act reduced the frequency of their expression, but it did not remove them. Most of all, it did not seriously affect the emergence of a specific form of electoral culture.

Definition of Electoral Culture

I have elsewhere described the forms and rituals of this electoral culture: the formal entries of candidates into their constituencies amidst scenes of popular acclaim together with the processions of local people, organised into hierarchies of occupation and status; the formal etiquette of the canvas of electors; the municipal ceremony of the nomination of the candidates; the rituals of treating, dining and toasting; the nightly speeches and paradings at the close of the poll each day and, not least, the formal healing of wounds signified in the chairing of the victorious candidates around the constituency.[4]

This electoral culture may initially be treated as reciprocating between the 'official', formal, political culture of the patronal classes, on the one hand, and the (to some extent) subversive traditions of popular culture, on the other. To understand this electoral culture, it is not enough to provide a literal description of what happened during election campaigns. Historians have for two centuries chosen to distort the meanings of these events and to denounce the morality of these rituals because they are so different from the electoral culture of the twentieth century. Yet they can only be reconstructed if the assumptions underlying them are clearly understood.

Indeed, there can be no mistaking the existence of common assumptions among *both the electors and the non-electors* that election campaigns signified a departure from the rhythms of normal life. Parades and processions, music and song, entertainments and treatings were all laid on for the benefit of the latter. Normal life was suspended as carnival came to town. Furthermore, the deluge of propaganda which accompanied every contested election hammered home the same values: that the electors were the privileged orders now; that their social superiors must contend for their support and for their approval. Electors were not passive recipients of 'social control', but independent agents with minds and consciences of their own. Voters were, and were supposed to be, prickly and sensitive, alive to the interests of the constituency. Voters weighed the issues of the election with due seriousness. However predictable their votes, they did, at least, wish to be seen to be responsible and conscientious. At the same time, electors and non-electors alike were entitled to demand favours for themselves and for their families as well as for the constituency.

There was an agreed intellectual foundation for this set of assumptions. English constitutional liberties depended upon preserving the balance of the constitution, of which the independence of the House of Commons was an indispensable element. The independence of the House of Commons was constantly being threatened by royal and/or aristocratic interference. It could only be protected by the steadfast independence of the electors. Indeed, a Standing Order of the House of Commons of 1701 sought to inhibit the intervention of peers in elections. Although the Order was ignored in practice, it was constantly cited in the constituencies.

Although it is possible to identify the intellectual origins of the social asumptions underpinning electoral culture, it remains true that festive behaviour had a curiously ambiguous quality. To a patrician observer a particular pattern of behaviour may appear dutiful, orderly and even deferential. To the plebeians involved, however, it may have had a totally different and essentially subversive meaning. The Chairing of the victorious candidates at the conclusion of the Poll might have appeared to the patricians as a pleasing and even memorable occurence – and even endorsement – of the official procedure of the election. To the crowd, however, the Chairing might simply have been the somewhat tiresome preliminary to the real event of the day: the 'Mock Chairing' of mock candidates. In these 'Mock Chairings' small boys, fat ladies, chimney sweeps, labourers, lunatics or even animals might be 'chaired' around the constituency, just as the candidates had been, in a calculated act of defiance and ridicule of the official election and the official candidates.[5] In this sense, then, electoral culture could permit, and even encourage, the expression of a conflict between groups who wished to impart different messages and meanings to traditional festive behaviour.

Obviously, electoral culture is embodied in repetitive, essentially ritualistic, events. The election campaign creates both the climate and the context of these events, these festivities and rituals. It endows them with meanings that are immediately political, but which have unmistakably social implications. These latter convey the popular toleration of a hierarchy of superiors while stressing the obligations which social superiors owe to the community.[6]

At the heart of electoral culture in England in this period, then, is a conflict between two forces: first, the need felt by members of the political nation to appeal to a popular audience not only for votes, but for a much more popular endorsement of candidates and their policies and, indeed, of the electoral process in general; second, the need to preserve order and discipline while doing so. Electoral culture, then, is a reciprocity of mutually tolerating, if harshly contrasting, social and political forces. It does not represent a polite and obedient acceptance by the electors of the social and political values of their superiors. Nor does it represent a noisy and riotous repudiation of those values. It represents the clash and the intermingling of these two traditions.

An alternative approach to defining electoral culture in these centuries is to stress the organic drama of the election campaign, to regard the election campaign as a narrative, or even as a text.[7] The election has a cast of characters (the candidates and their managers), a stage on which the drama is set (the streets of the town and the surrounding area), a script or a story which can be both drama and farce, epic and nonsense as the reader chooses (the events of the campaign as served to the observer through the eyes of commentators). This approach is illuminating and instructive, but it contains a number of deficiencies. First, it is not an approach which is endorsed to any significant degree in contemporary sources, which stress the pastness and timelessness of electoral ritual. Second, it tends to exagerate the extent of local variation in electoral culture. It is undeniable that electoral traditions are locally generated and refer to local men and matters. Nevertheless, it is the surprising uniformity in these patterns of electoral ritual which require emphasis, not their endless variations.

Dynamics of Electoral Culture

These patterns of electoral culture developed and achieved maturity during the eighteenth century. There is considerable evidence that they became more elaborate and more complex as the century advanced, feeding off themselves and the traditions and the nostalgia to which they gave rise. The period of their fullest development may be taken to be the half century from the closing years of the American War of Independence in the early 1780s to the First Reform Act of 1832. The War of Independence aroused enormous political concern in England and the issues to which it gave rise yielded massive popular involvement in the General Election of 1784.[8] Their slow decline after 1832 will be traced later.

Patterns of electoral ritual must not be detached from their cultural context. During the eighteenth century the older patterns of seasonal civic ritual were in decline.[9] To some extent these were overtaken by political rituals with a national as much as a local context: the celebration of naval and military victories, the idolisation of individual politicians (Chatham, Wilkes, Pitt and Fox, for example) and, of course, the growing currency in enfranchised towns of electoral ritual.

Central to this argument is the point that ritual is an enormously flexible social and, indeed, political instrument. An electoral ritual, such as the ceremonial entry of the candidates into a town may be interpreted as nothing more than a social occasion: an opportunity to mobilise the hierarchies of a community in an attempt to obtain popular acceptance, recognition and acclaim – and thus renewal – of those patterns of status. Such a ritual, however, could easily become politicised if one or other of the candidates chose to make political capital out of such an occasion.[10] For example, one of the best opportunities for the politicisation of electoral ritual was the speech at the nomination of the candidates. Although such speeches were traditionally unexceptionable and platitudinous, by the end of the eighteenth century, they had largely become political occasions.[11] A further example of the politicisation of electoral culture was the emergence of the political canvass. By the early nineteenth century the canvass had become the canvass of political opinions rather than the straightforward introduction of candidates to electors.[12] Similarly, speeches, dinners, toasts, cartoons, satires and handbills could quite easily be converted from social comment to political propaganda.

Politicisation does not take place in a void and one of the most effective agencies of politicisation in this period was the local political party.[13] Competitive ritual meant that one side had to do – and outdo – what the other side did. The politicisation of ritual was a competitive phenomenon. Party issues found their way into election speeches. Government was supported or denounced. The parliamentary record of sitting members was carefully scrutinised and discussed.[14] The successful incorporation of political, indeed, party political, propaganda into electoral ritual was one of the most powerful reasons for its intricate and elaborate development and, indeed, its long survival.

The politicisation of electoral ritual was accompanied by a development of equal significance: the recording of election campaigns by the printed word. Although few towns had newspapers before the end of the eighteenth century, the use of pamphlets, resolutions, addresses, squibs, cartoons and handbills ensured that a constituency was deluged in print for the duration of the election campaign. In this way the non-electors as well as the electors were drawn into the campaign as actors in the local drama. The election campaign was an open event, a public spectacle, inclusive and popular. This quite simple fact is itself of immense significance. However powerful the elements of persuasion, control and even intimidation may have been in the electoral system in the eighteenth century, the campaign itself was built upon the assumption that electoral choices were there to be made, that propaganda might serve to persuade, that ideas were not fixed and that political support might legitimately be sought in any part of the community.[15]

The Decline of Old Electoral Culture

Quite soon after the passing of the 1832 Reform Act the sources start to register the passing of the old electoral rituals with which we have been concerned. This was not a rapid development. Indeed, in many places the old culture seemed to be thriving just when, in others, there were signs of its slow demise. The first sign was the abandonment of Chairing, which was in many ways one of the most tumultuous and most popular of them all.[16] Thereafter, other aspects of the old electoral culture began to disappear. There were three sets of reasons for this stifling of the old festive electoral culture: legal changes, developments in political organisation and a gradual transformation in political morality.

Oddly, the Reform Act of 1832 almost certainly inaugurated the process leading to the disappearance of traditional and festive electoral culture. The Registration clauses of the Act served to define the electorate much more closely, and thus give official recognition to those who were, and to those who were not, entitled to participate in electoral affairs. Hitherto, the franchise had been vague and uncertain. Consequently, the distinction between electors and non-electors became more discernible after 1832. Furthermore, the limitation of the poll to two days restricted the length of the carnival campaign. As Dr Vernon has pointed out, this carried with it the possibility of a swift mid-week election, from which the mass of the people might be excluded.[17] Finally, the clause of the Act requiring returning officers to make polling places available per 600 electors at different geographical points around the constituency may have facilitated the act of voting for the electors. However, it served seriously to fragment electoral proceedings and to render it difficult for the non-electors to participate in the central and vociferous manner that they had hitherto. Such legal restrictions upon the rights of non-electors were fatal to old electoral practices. The Ballot Act of 1872 took them to their logical conclusion. Not only was the act of voting now to be secret and private. Non-voters were now to be entirely excluded from the place of nomination and polling.[18]

Nevertheless, the demise of the old electoral culture was much more than the consequence of legal restrictions. Quite simply, many of the functions that electoral culture had served could now be performed through other, more controllable agencies. The partisanship and the competitiveness could be furthered by more modern styles of political organisation. More particularly, the development of centrally organised, mass-based, national political parties ultimately rendered redundant the old festive culture. As I have remarked elsewhere, 'political feeling and political identity became better defined and, as time went on, more satisfyingly expressed through the political and religious agencies of the Conservative and Liberal parties: the local party branches, the local and national party press, the churches, the chapels and the pressure groups incorporated the local committees which had traditionally organised the old election activities'.[19] Although party identities and party loyalties had been important at the national level, and to some extent at the local level, too, before 1832 they had been thoroughly entangled in a locally-based and traditionally defined political universe within the constituency. For example, in most places party labels were less compelling than traditional party colours. At Ipswich and at Coventry, for example, the Blues fought the Yellows. And while MPs, once elected, would engage in the party conflict at Westminster between Whigs and Tories, those national lines of distinction would only rarely correspond to local party labels. After 1832 they began to correspond much more closely. Local idiosyncracies began to give way to national distinctions between Liberals and Conservatives. The great national parties began to establish their own local associations everywhere after the Reform Act and, ultimately, they came to absorb and to displace the old informal clubs and committees which had organised and officered the old electoral system. It was to be a slow process, however, and the coexistence of the two organisational structures must be deemed one of the abiding and most fascinating features of the electoral system after 1832.[20]

Finally, and gradually, the old electoral values became redundant and unacceptable in the Victorian era. The old ways had offered drama, excitement and amusement. Such needs came to be satisfied in the second half of the nineteenth century by mass entertainment, organised sports and growing leisure facilities. At another level, the vociferous, aggressive, noisy and sometimes violent aspects of the old electoral culture were none too appealing to the new, and often highly respectable, electors of Victorian England. Ever since the 1770s radical critics had been remarking unfavourably upon the corruption, drunkenness and violence which too often accompanied the old politics. Now, these cries were taken up by Liberals. It was indeed, frequently Liberal candidates, responding to a very definite set of moral canons, not least those of temperance and sabbatarianism, who abandoned the old rituals and embarrasing customs. (How the Conservatives responded to being left holding this particular baby we shall leave to another ocassion!)

To some extent the decline of old corruption was a question of numbers. In the new constituencies with their thousands of electors after 1832, and their tens of thousands after 1867, the personal tie between candidates and voters could not possibly endure. In the heaving towns of nineteenth-century England, unbridled processing and parading might be deemed a luxury that could not be risked. The street politics of the eighteenth century could not continue indefinitely into the nineteenth century without considerable refinement and control. Nor, at the financial level, could they be afforded. It was, perhaps, practical considerations, as much as moral imperatives, which weakened the old culture.

The Future of Research into Electoral Culture

This chapter has been proceeding upon the assumption that we should look not merely to the forms of an electoral system – the legalities of the franchise, the formal, manifesto issues of the election and to the official outcomes of the electoral process – but to the cultural patterns which underpin it. Both dimensions deserve recognition. Their interactions require future study. As I have been strongly hinting, the official or elite stage of the election may well provide an arena for a very different sort of political, and, of course, theatrical, production. One of the most promising arenas for further investigations into and understanding of electoral culture must be into its comparative manifestations. This chapter now proceeds to advance a suggested agenda for comparative research into electoral culture in pre-modern, pre-democratic political systems.

1) We should first notice the relevance of social role-playing to these patterns of cultural behaviour. Here are some suggestions. Candi-

dates need to conform to a fairly sophisticated and very well understood set of norms defining the roles expected of them. These are very frequently articulated, and thus recycled and renewed, whenever election competition takes place. In my study of the English electoral system, for example, I noticed a complex set of requirements relating to a) age, b) family, c) place of residence, d) type, value and amount of property holding, e) type of occupational background, f) quality of local service, g) what may be termed manners and approachability, h) standing, in what may be termed the ranks of honour and i) last, but perhaps not least, political opinions.[21] I should remark here that a really enduring comparative perspective will be achieved less by producing the kind of menu – immensely detailed and thus rather unmanageable – which I have just produced, useful though that may be to start with, but by adopting a much more rigorous theoretical perspective. Here, I mention Erving Goffman who in his book *The Presentation of Self in Everyday Life* as far back as 1958 related the entire issue of role and role playing to concepts like 'performance', 'face', and 'personal space'.

2) We need offer no apology for drawing attention to the relevance of family and kinship to electoral culture, as, indeed, to so many other historical issues. Here, I would like to draw attention to just two areas of possible significance. The first of these is the propensity of voters linked in family groupings to vote in similar or, at least, a non-contradictory manner. Although the methodology can be very complex, there can be little doubt that membership of a family group provides a most potent predictor of voting behaviour. Sons vote the same way as their fathers, brothers votes the same way as brother. The second is thus the hereditary nature of electoral behaviour. Because family groups at the electoral level tend to behave homogeneously, the electorate may to some extent be viewed not as a number of atomistic individuals but as clusters of hereditary dynasties both as voters and, frequently, as electoral activists – canvassers, committee men and so on – and, of course, as candidates.

3) It would be difficult to avoid raising the issue of 'community' in any comparative study of electoral systems and of electoral culture. My study of the English electoral system in the pre-democratic era encountered an extremely complex set of variables. I was not seriously tempted, for example, to try to relate electoral behaviour to any kind of settlement pattern, to any kind of environmental context or to issues of size or even dominant industry. More useful, I believe, might be to approach the problem of community through regular instances of community behaviour. Inevitably, and, I think, indisputably, this must entail some concentration upon ritual. We should not focus our attention upon elec-

toral ritual alone. We should not lose sight of *the context* of ritual within which electoral ritual is produced. We should, therefore, examine calendrical and annual patterns of civic ritual both ecclesiastical and secular, in order to re-establish what Professor Cohen termed *The Symbolic Construction of Community* in his book of that name in 1985.[22] In such an enquiry we should be concerned to examine the extent to which electoral conflicts thus ritualised correspond with other conflicts within the community. In this we would wish to discern the elements of division within the community as well as the elements of disunity.

4) It would hardly be possible to conduct worthwhile comparative examinations of electoral culture without estimating the *functions* which electoral culture fulfils. I have already drawn attention to one extremely important function which I believe electoral ritual in England fulfilled in the pre-democratic era: what I have termed 'a willing, yet conditional, acceptance of the leadership of the local community by its traditional elites and institutions'.[23] This socially conservative reading of electoral culture may, or may not, be confirmed by research into the history of other societies. At the same time, electoral culture invites and intensifies participation in the electoral process by voters and non-voters alike. The popular elements in electoral culture are played up, even exaggerated. Even at its most docile, electoral culture is needed to convey at least the impression of popular endorsement *not only for the candidates, but for the electoral process and the social system which it underpins*. It may or may not be the same point, but there seems little doubt that electoral culture exists to raise criticism and to bring vexed issues to the notice of the local elite. The plain speaking that election campaigns encouraged permitted a form of public debate upon the performance by that elite of its paternalistic obligations.

5) This logically raises the question of ideological consensus and the extent to which electoral culture epitomised profound ideological and even moral community norms. It may be the case, for example, that election campaigns were vehicles for the articulation of agreed values about the conditions within which the local elite ruled and which were recognised as legitimate by those they governed. This endorsement of the local political and social order – or the lack of it – may have been an essential component of political adaptability and even of political stability.

This certainly does not mean, and is not meant to imply, that there was no opposition within the English electoral system. There was a very great deal of opposition, dissidence and sensitivity. The point is that such opposition could be channelled in traditional ways. Particular issues and particular individuals could provoke intense indignation, but it was rare for electoral culture itself to be challenged. Electoral practices which were a violation of its norms or its spirit were very vigorously challenged indeed, but the legitimacy of the old electoral culture was not seriously doubted. Furthermore, such opposition and such challenges necessarily recognised limits and boundaries to that challenge. Elite groups had to exercise restraint in pursuing their political vendettas. For if they could not control their own political differences, then how could they expect their social inferiors to exercise restraint in pursuing theirs?

6) And on the issue of social inferiors, the question of popular participation has flitted in and out of this chapter since the outset. Let us now state the issue as clearly as possible: the mass of the people appear to have been as vitally concerned in the process and in the outcome of election campaigns as the voters and as the local elite.[24] In view of the importance of the issue of popular participation, we ought now to place it on the agenda for comparative research. Popular electoral culture in England was characterised by its propensity to draw the mass of the people, the non-voters as well as the voters, the plebeians as well as the patrons, into the theatrical and ritualistic performances which characterised the days and weeks of the election campaign. Even when these trembled on the verge of violence and anarchy, an unfortunate candidate had to accept any degradations to which the mass of the people might wish to subject him, and then to thank them for their attentions.[25] Committee men found themselves in the ludicrous position of having to satisfy the popular desire to make a mockery of the entire proceedings that they were conducting.[26] Now, it is not for this historian to pontificate on the popular character of electoral culture elsewhere, to characterise it and to account for it. Local specialists may be left to work this particular vein and to extract the valuable, if sometimes elusive, ore of popular participation in such pre-democratic electoral campaigns.

Was England Exceptional?

Understandably, we must confront the issue of how 'typical' England was in the type of electoral culture with which we have been dealing. In spite of her national propaganda, we should not leap to the conclusion that England was totally out of line with the rest of the continent of Europe. After all, the culture of elections owes very much indeed to the culture of carnival. Although England had no direct experience of carnival, many of the characteristics of old election culture may be traced back to traditions of European carnival: the social inversion, the suspension of the normal social codes and hierarchies, the sense of burlesque and mockery, the satire, the street processions, the popular involvement by the crowd.

Interestingly, we know that many of these cultural traditions crossed the Atlantic to be used against the British during the years of the American Revolution. The popular radical, John Wilkes, for example, was just as much of a popular hero in the United States as in England. Stylised rituals of obeisance to Wilkes 'insolently imitated the rituals of royalty, especially the king's birthday'.[27] Such mockery of the monarchy was continued with the later revolutionary leaders playing the part earlier played by Wilkes.[28] In the present state of knowledge we could not assert with confidence that the whole panoply of electoral culture crossed the Atlantic to North America, but it is quite certain that the more general traditions of popular culture made the crossing. In the New World they survived, assumed their own local variants and were then mobilised effectively against the mother country.

We should not exaggerate this process. English festive forms were not always typical of those in Europe. Reading the pages of Nona Ozouf's *Festivals and the French Revolution*, we notice the significant differences between France and England in the 1790s. In England, for example, it would be impossible to argue that the festival 'was a dynamic image of the gathering, rather than a description of an assembled community', misleading to claim that 'the people joined in only as gatecrashers'.[29]

After all, electoral culture is characterised by its powerful local references and local variants, on the one hand, and by its overwhelmingly backward-looking, and hence highly specific, orientation, on the other. It does make sense – indeed, it can only make sense – to subsume these variants within a specifically English framework of historical narrative and an intellectual structure with an overwhelmingly English, and thus anti-French and anti-Catholic political meaning. These simply cannot be casually generalised into other cultural situations. The intellectual structures and the belief systems of different civilisations are frequently expressed in their ritual more explicitly than in other cultural patterns. Electoral ritual should not be given undue prominence over other forms of ritual but it will, nevertheless, provide an indispensable window into the nature of past societies in Europe and in the Americas.

Conclusions

This does not exhaust the number of vital issues with which research into the field of electoral culture ought to concern itself. In particular, I am very conscious indeed that I have not had the opportunity to comment on at least two other matters of first importance: the character and the role of violence and/or implied violence in electoral culture. Further, I have said nothing about the role of women in electoral culture. Nevertheless, we need to bring together a number of issues with which we *have* been concerned even if only in a rhetorical manner. These are little more than provocative comments that arise in the mind of one historian who has immersed himself almost entirely within one electoral system and inside one electoral culture. But is it not the case that a viable electoral culture is necessarily linked into conceptions of the national interest and the national welfare, which in turn relate to sentiments of national pride and patriotism? Is it an accident that the rise of such a viable electoral culture in England coincides with the emergence of patriotism? It also coincides with the emergence – a very slow and intermittent emergence, it must be conceded – of a newspaper press in England during the eighteenth century. News, information, exhortation, rumour, counter-rumour and appeals to action are obviously the very stuff of electoral campaigning. It would have been much harder to mobilise the numbers that were mobilised without broadside, cartoon, paragraph and newspaper. However traditionally minded the electoral culture of the eighteenth and nineteenth centuries may have been, it depended for its survival and its proliferation upon the technology of the printing press.

It is, furthermore, so obvious that it seeems hardly worth stating: the necessary vehicle for the 'performance' of electoral culture is a party system operating at local level. By this we mean a system of legal competition for political power between local groups, organised around different political (and perhaps religious) principles and with different versions of the recent, and not-so-recent, history of the local town or region. In the English context, these local parties ultimately looked to parliament and to nationally competing political groups and political traditions (Whigs and Tories) as the external objective of their local conflict.

Finally, it may be ventured that more fundamental to the emergence of a mature representative system than a given level of economic development or a particular pattern of historical development is the widespread recognition that there are boundaries – legal and moral – to political life and political power. This means that different aspects of life have their own domain, their own autonomy. Whether this is interpreted as the habit of 'civic culture'[30] or whether this is taken to be the more positive assertion of one or other aspect of individual freedom, such as religious toleration, is not immediately at issue. In the last analysis, electoral culture is about the restraint of political power and the conditionality of the influence of the elite. Insofar as this may be the case, we must conclude that the widespread diffusion of traditions and practices of electoral culture may be taken to be one of the most indispensable pre-requisites for representative government.

Notes

1. For the Triennial Act see E.N. Williams, *The Eighteenth Century Constitution* (Cambridge, 1970), pp. 49-50. In fact, a Triennial Act had been passed in 1664 but Charles II had simply ignored it. The intention of the Act of 1694 was clearly to restrict the king's ability to summon and dissolve parliament. After the passing of the Act 'the country remained almost continually in the grip of election fever'. See J. Miller, *The Glorious Revolution* (London, 1983), p. 71.
2. M. Kishlansky, *Parliamentary Selection: Social and Political Choice in Early Modern England* (Cambridge, 1986), p. 64.
3. J. Carter, 'The Revolution and the Constitution', in G. Holmes (ed.), *Britain after the Glorious Revolution* (Basingstoke, 1969), p. 45.
4. These rituals and ceremonies, together with some attempt to interpret them, are the subject of my 'Campaign Rituals and Ceremonies: the Social Meaning of Elections in England, 1780-1860', *Past and Present*, no. 135 (May 1992), pp. 79-115.
5. Mock chairings are discussed in *ibid.*, pp. 111-12.
6. This 'conservative' interpretation of electoral culture is given at some length in *ibid.*, pp. 108-11.
7. See, for example, J. Vernon, *Politics and the People: A Study in English Political Culture, c.1815-1867* (Cambridge, 1993), pp. 99-104.
8. This point was first raised in the extended introduction to D. E. Ginter, *Whig Organization at the General Election of 1790* (Berkeley, 1967).
9. The argument is treated authoritatively in P. Borsay, 'All the Town's a Stage: Urban Ritual and Ceremony, 1600-1800', in P. Clark (ed.), *The Transformation of English Provincial Towns* (London, 1974), pp. 246-8.
10. Examples of both types of entry may be found. At Lancaster and at Somerset, the entry was entirely symbolic and lacked any political significance; *An Impartial Statement... of the Late Election* (London, 1818), pp. 164, 281. At sedate North Derbyshire in 1837, however, the entry was marked with flags and banners making political statements. J. Roberts (ed.), *Poll Book for the Northern Division* (Chesterfield, 1837).
11. There are some interesting examples of politicised nomination speeches at the (largely uncontroversial) general election of 1802. See, for example, the speech of John Scudamore at Hereford which dealt with Habeas Corpus, Parliamentary Reform, the politics of Ireland, etc. At Norfolk, too, nomination speeches concentrated on the past records of the sitting members. At Hull they were full of political references. *The Picture of Parliament or a History of the General*

Election of 1802 (London, 1802), pp. 33, 91, 156-7. Indeed, at the Kent nomination in 1818 there was much questioning of the candidates. One persistent questioner 'conceived that the candidates came there for the purpose of being catechized'. And at Middlesex in the same year the crowd began to catechise one of the candidates on his support for the Corn Laws and Habeas Corpus Suspension. See *An Impartial Statement*, pp. 160-224.

12. See my 'Campaign Rituals and Ceremonies', pp. 112-3.
13. See my *Voters, Patrons and Parties: The Unreformed Electorate of Hanoverian England, 1734-1832* (Oxford, 1989), chapter six.
14. 'Campaign Rituals and Ceremonies', pp. 112-13.
15. *Ibid.*, p. 98.
16. For the gradual abandonment of Chairing, see *ibid.*, p. 124. See also Vernon, *Politics and the People*, pp. 231-32.
17. For these effects on the 1832 Reform Act, see Vernon, *Politics and the People*, pp. 99-102.
18. Charles Seymour, *Electoral Reform in England and Wales* (New Haven, 1915), pp. 430-1.
19. See my 'Campaign Rituals and Ceremonies', p. 115.
20. This is noticed in Vernon, *Politics and the People*, but for a more detailed treatment see the unpublished Ph.D. dissertation by H. B. Raymond, 'English Political Parties and Electoral Organization, 1832-67', University of Harvard, 1952.
21. See my *Voters, Patrons and Parties*, pp. 117-26.
22. A. P. Cohen, *The Symbolic Construction of Community* (Chichester, 1985).
23. 'Campaign Rituals and Ceremonies', p. 107.
24. There seems nothing surprising in this fact. As Professor David Underwood has shown, the common people in the seventeenth century were capable of exhibiting enormous interest in contemporary political matters. See his *Revel, Riot and Rebellion* (Oxford, 1985), pp. 3-6.
25. At the Westminster election of 1818 an unpopular candidate, Sir Murray Maxwell, was the subject of stone-throwing. One stone hit him painfully in the eye. He did not flinch, preferring to bow, as if in gratitude. At the end of the poll he gave a speech which included the following words: 'The so nearly fatal consequences to myself I most sincerely forgive, and consider it an honour of inestimable value to have received these indignities'... *An Impartial Statement*, pp. 366, 375.
26. There is a good example in Liverpool in 1790 when committee men penned rhymes ridiculing the entire election campaign of which they were the most essential exponents. See the rhyme 'Lord Penrhyn's the Man for Me', in T. Johnson (ed.), *The Poll for the Election* (Liverpool, 1790), p. 63.
27. P. Shaw, *American Patriots and the Rituals of Revolution* (Cambridge, Mass., 1981), p. 67.
28. *Ibid.*, p. 188.
29. N. Ozouf, *Festivals and the French Revolution* (Cambridge, Mass., 1988).
30. G. A. Almond and S. Verba, *The Civic Culture: Political Attitudes and Democracy in Five Nations* (Princeton, 1963).

CHAPTER 2

THE HISPANIC REVOLUTIONS:
THE ADOPTION OF MODERN FORMS OF
REPRESENTATION IN SPAIN AND AMERICA (1808-1810)

M.-D. Demélas-Bohy and F.-X. Guerra

Twenty years after the French Revolution, and following its example, Spain and its Empire entered a revolutionary cycle which was to culminate in the disappearance of Spain as a great power, in the birth of multiple independent states in Spanish America and in the emergence of modern political forms in all the Spanish domains. In the long run this was one of the most important consequences of the French Revolution.

Despite its importance, the development of this process is not well known: it has not been considered from a global perspective and there has sometimes been a tendency to view it through the eyes of 19th century historians, either Spanish American or Spanish, some of whom aimed to recount, through the Independence revolutions, the emancipation of the American 'nations', whereas for others the *Spanish revolution* – that of the Cortes of Cádiz, the source of Spanish liberalism[1] – was sufficient in itself. In addition, over recent decades the predominance of socio-economic analysis in the social sciences has produced a similar divergence since, from this point of view, Spanish America is completely diverse. At any event the most striking features of these revolutionary movements – their simultaneity and their similarity – have been forgotten.

National histories are, however, under re-examination, and the re-emergence of the political factor helps to elucidate what the sources have always shown: the constant overlapping of events in Spain with those in America. As with the collapse of the Soviet Empire in our day, the independence of the Spanish American countries cannot be understood without reference to the crisis in political unity from which it originated. If revolutionary phenomena emerged in similar ways on both sides of the Atlantic, it was because all the provinces of the Spanish monarchy, despite their differences, possessed institutions in common, an identical political culture, a single authority; if they came about at the same time it was because they derived from the same political crisis. In fact everything bears witness to a

single revolution which ended in the disintegration of an Empire.
It was, nevertheless, a paradoxical revolution, which first declared
its loyalty to the King, but soon proclaimed the sovereignty of the nation;
the work of patriots who were fighting against France, but at the same
time took their inspiration from the French model in the wish to destroy
the old regime; a movement which in its early days gathered together
Spaniards and Spanish Americans in the same patriotic fervour, only to
lead then to the independence of Spanish America.

The problem of political representation and electoral practice occupied a central place in this process because it went to the heart of
revolutionary action: a new legitimacy born of the 'nation' whose sovereignty was declared at the first session of the Cortes at Cádiz, on 24
September 1810.

Yet even before this outcome, from May 1808 on, the question of
representation lay at the centre of all political debate, in Spain as much as
in Spanish America. In order to resist Napoleon and to constitute a provisional government, it was necessary to appeal to the rights of the
nation, the kingdom, the people.... Since legitimacy could only derive
from society, the representation of society was becoming an urgent necessity. There then began a period of intense political activity in which the
constitution of provisional powers, political debate and elections were in-
cessantly intermingled on both continents. It was in this key period that
the foundations of modern politics in the Hispanic world were laid and
political practices emerged that promised a good future.

Through the debate on representation, the Hispanic elites turned towards a new frame of reference. For to debate representation was to
tackle two key themes which opened the door to revolution as well as to
American independence: what is the nation and what respective places do
Spain and America occupy in it? The second term of the debate posed,
through the question of the parity of representation of the two continents,
the problem of the political status of America, the principal cause of its
independence. The first question, which was at the heart of the French
Revolution, led to the opposition of two concepts of society. Was the nation formed of old political communities, with their orders and privileged
bodies, or of equal individuals? Was the nation the product of history or
the result of free association? Was it already constituted or did it remain
to be formed? Was sovereignty vested in the nation, and what was its nature?

Being simultaneously a manifestation and a pledge of this demand for
legitimacy, the elections which marked out this period were, from a certain point of view, the revolution itself. Between 1809 and 1814 there

were no less than five sorts of elections. In 1809, the patriciates of the American provinces elected representatives to the Central Spanish Junta; between 1810 and 1812, Spain and loyalist America designated deputies and substitutes[2] to the extraordinary Cortes; from 1812 on, by virtue of the constitution of Cádiz, it was necessary to proceed to the selection of deputies for the ordinary Cortes and to draw up municipal councils and provincial deputations. The rapid succession of these elections which were carried out under different electoral rules (in 1809 under the old system of representation; in 1810 under a mixed system in which the old type of representation and suffrage of family heads were intermingled; from 1812 on, finally, under almost universal suffrage) allows us to follow step by step the spread of modern political forms. We will limit ourselves to the first three elections, prior to the Cádiz constitution – the most important ones for the development of the revolution.[3]

The End of Absolutism and the Renaissance of Representation

At the end of May 1808, in the cities where the *Gazeta de Madrid* had arrived, giving an account of the abdications of Charles IV and Ferdinand VII in Bayonne, popular uprisings at once installed defence Juntas. These insurrectionary bodies, product of a wounded patriotism, could only derive their legitimacy from the action of the people since the constituted authorities seemed to accept the *fait accompli*.

In the proclamations that were published by the Juntas to justify their refusal to accept the abdications, and in the burgeoning political literature of the period, the words 'vassals', 'fidelity', 'loyalty' were repeated in obsessive exaltation of Ferdinand VII, 'the beloved King' to whom the nation had sworn allegiance. Transcending his physical personage, these terms referred to a pact between King and nation which belonged to classical Spanish political thought, but broke with the eighteenth century theory and practice of absolutism.

Even if the foundations of this pact were varied, based on traditional as well as modern concepts, *vacatio regis* caused the collapse, not only practical but also theoretical, of absolutism, which offered no base for the resistance movement. Conceivable from an absolutist perspective, the abdication of the King was impossible according to the conceptions of a mutual pact. Since the bilateral relationship between the King and the community could not be broken off unilaterally, the rejection of the usurper and the reversion of sovereignty to the political community followed naturally.

An improvised representation: the Spanish Juntas
Under various formulations all the insurrectionary Juntas based themselves
on these principles. If the process of their formation is still not well known,
their composition gives a fairly certain clue as to how the patriots conceived the Kingdom in those early revolutionary times.[4]

Everywhere there are signs of the care taken to represent the variety
of institutions, orders and bodies befitting a society of the old regime.
Once more we find members of the Juntas of the royal authorities: cap-
tains-general, governors, *intendentes, corregidores;* members of the
audiencias, cabildos (town councils) and ecclesiastical chapters; representatives of various corporations – the order of lawyers, university,
merchants, craftsmen; members of privileged orders – bishops and
priests of the main parishes, the superiors of religious orders, titled no-
blemen, knights – soldiers, representatives of minor towns etc. This
diversity showed the unanimity of the uprising: it represented a society
that had become sovereign again as the actors viewed it – as an assembly
of groups.

Once the urgency of the first days of the uprising had passed, when
the resistance needed uncontested powers,[5] just as the machinery of monarchy needed central government, each region turned first towards the old
representative institutions of medieval origin. Some, such as the assembly of the Principality of the Asturias, were still active; others were no
longer in existence, such as the Cortes of the Kingdoms, which had constituted the Crown of Spain[6] and which were brought back to life in quite
new circumstances. The Cortes of Aragón assembled in June 1808;
Galicia, Old Castile and León all prepared to summon Cortes. In order to
meet a situation without precedent, the Juntas turned instinctively towards the past, a far off and partially mythic past. So it is of little
importance what novel things the return to tradition comprised: it was
necessary to give to the *de facto* powers the legitimacy which sprang
from historical representation.

The same concern was paramount in the formation of a central
power capable of ensuring the conduct of the war, negotiating with
England, and maintaining links with America. While the abundant free
press, roused by the patriotism of the moment, demanded the meeting
of the Cortes Generales, the representatives of the provincial Juntas
managed to constitute, on 25 September 1808 at Aranjuez, a Supreme
Central Junta for the Government of the Kingdom, made up of two delegates for each Junta of the Kingdom.[7] This new institution still
reflected an old concept of the Crown of Spain – pre-Bourbon, one
might say, for it reflected the pluralist structure of the Habsburg mon-

archy – founded on an idea of representation that was likewise old. Within the Central Junta it was the kingdoms that were represented, not their populations.

The bases of the Central Junta's authority offered the same mixture of tradition and modernism. It governed in the name and in the place of Ferdinand VII, in the role of 'repository of sovereign authority' until the King's return – a clear and yet ambiguous formula, for the King had not formulated an explicit delegation and it was in fact the representatives of the Kingdoms who had formed the Junta. That is why it was gradually considered as the organ of national representation, of an almost modern kind. Those of its members who had received imperative mandates had to be given, then, the most extensive powers.

Freed of their imperative mandate and enjoying immunity, the members of the Central Junta were already sketching out the statute of the future deputies of the present day Cortes. Nevertheless they still belonged, through their origins, to the elites of the society of the old regime and one cannot consider them as representatives of a Third Estate originating in the new social classes. Most were members of the privileged orders, clergy (15%) and nobility (51%) forming an overwhelming majority.[8]

Being a mere outline of a national representative body, the Central Junta governed for a little more than a year, until January 1810. During this difficult period it attempted with varying success to organise the country and direct the war. But as the military defeats lessened its prestige and a modern public opinion began to develop, it had to concern itself with improving national representation and bringing about reforms.

The political status of America

To improve national representation meant first of all to summon the Cortes Generales, the *'grande affaire'*,[9] from the month of May 1809 (we will return to this). But before this date, a first attempt inaugurated the electoral period of this revolutionary epoch: the Central Junta asked the American provinces to elect representatives. This was a major decision which brought about the first elections of the Hispanic Empire regulated by a general law and which opened the debate about equality between Spain and America, the principal cause of American independence. How had this resolution become inevitable?

American loyalty had been universally solid since the beginning of the Spanish crisis. Not only had Spanish America unanimously refused to recognise the change of dynasty but through its subsidiaries it had supported, in a decisive way, resistance in the peninsula. That does not mean, however, that it was a mere passive follower of events. The disappearance of the King posed Spanish America the same problem of substituting power and, as in Spain, as soon as the abdications were known, the first reaction was also one of mutual pacts: the American provinces wanted to form their own Juntas. The difficulties they encountered came from the authorities there who, unlike those of the peninsula, had not suffered the discredit of an oath sworn to the usurper King and carried on in their posts. Absolutism still found supporters in America, for whom certain initiatives which necessity demanded in the metropolis were not accepted in the overseas provinces which had to accept whatever government was constituted in Spain. In fact only the almost simultaneous arrival of the news of the abdication and the emissaries of a provincial Junta, that of Seville, which, in order to lay a false trail, had called itself the Supreme Junta of Spain and the Indies, prevented the formation of American Juntas in 1808.

Rightly so in certain cases. The *cabildo* of Caracas was preparing to set up 'a State Junta with power to represent the sovereign authority'. Mexico had gone further along this road. Following arguments derived from the medieval *Partidas,* the *cabildo* of Mexico had declared the abdications null and void, since they had been decided without the consent of the nation, and they demanded the convocation of the Council of the Kingdom of New Spain. The preparatory Juntas, in which the representatives of the different orders and bodies participated, took place during the summer of 1808 and their deliberations were only interrupted by a *coup d'état* carried out in September by a group of *peninsulares* who were determined to put an end to any desire for autonomy.

The other American capitals recognised the Seville Junta, either because they believed they were dealing with the Spanish resistance government, or in order not to complicate things by expressing misgivings. Then, in the course of 1809, one after another, they accepted the authority of the Central Junta. At the same time the arrival of a vast amount of correspondence and printed material from Spain alerted the Americans to the uncertainties of the political and military situation. They thus learnt of the lost battles, the quarrels between the different metropolitan Juntas, the doubts expressed publicly on the legitimacy of the Central Junta.

So, even though it was accepted by the overseas provinces, the Central Junta understood the need to associate them in government. A month after its installation, on 27 October 1808, it considered an unprecedented proposal on American representation, and on 22 January 1809, an edict was published setting out its rationale and its forms. It began with a declaration taken up countless times by the Americans:

>...the Supreme Central Junta of the government of the Kingdom, bearing in mind that the vast and precious domains that Spain possesses in the Indies are not strictly colonies or trading posts, as are those of other nations, but rather an integral part of the Spanish monarchy, and desiring to strengthen indissolubly the sacred bonds between both domains, as well as responding to the heroic loyalty and patriotism which they have recently demonstrated towards Spain... has decided that they must henceforth be represented nationally to his Royal Highness and be part of the Central Junta of the Kingdom's government through their representatives...[10]

The apparent generosity of the statement concealed serious deficiencies. The edict seemed inspired by the equality of rights between the two factions of the monarchy but the fact of arguing in terms of colonies[11] or, even worse, trading posts contradicted what the Indies had always represented in law and in the imagination of the Americans: kingdoms of the same status as the other kingdoms of the Spanish Crown. 'Spain' designated the whole and not just one of the parts. (That is why people often said 'Spain of the two hemispheres' or 'The Spains'). It was an even more serious error than to try to present participation in national representation as a reward earned by American loyalty; this was to deny equality while proclaiming it.

The same inequality was revealed in the number of representatives. The four vice-royalties (New Spain, Peru, New Granada and the River Plate) and the five captaincy-generals (Cuba, Puerto Rico, Guatemala, Chile, Venezuela and the Philippines)[12] were only permitted to designate one deputy each: why not two like the Spanish Juntas? And why reduce representation to these territories alone, which was tantamount to having America represented by nine members as against twenty-six on the peninsula, whereas the population of the Indies was greater? One might advance the theory that, as far as representation of the kingdoms was concerned, proportionality was of no importance, but it appears that in this case, as later in the membership of the Cortes, this measure above all reflected the Spanish fear of being in the minority.

The first American general elections
The Americans were torn between the satisfaction of taking part in national representation and the disappointment when confronted with its unfairness.[13] Despite this, these elections, which represented an extraordinary innovation, in Spain as well as in Spanish America, did take

place, and they occupied the administrative apparatus and the political life of the cities for months. From the Spring of 1809 to the Winter of 1810, from Sonora to Chile, all Spanish America lived according to the rhythm of this first experience of general elections.

The electoral system that the Central Junta had chosen was of an old type, with multiple filters and a trust in chance to impede the action of the parties; old too was the concept of representation by kingdom. As a first stage representatives had to be elected by the municipal councils of the district (*partido*); the aldermen selected three individuals (a *terna*) from whom the city's choice was then determined by the drawing of lots; it was said that man selected and God decided. Then, in the capital of the viceroyalty or of the captaincy-general the Viceroy or the Captain General and the *audiencia* together selected a *terna* from among those elected by the cities and in a final drawing of lots the deputy to the Central Junta was designated.

There is nothing more traditional than this intermixing of electoral procedures. It was not individuals who were represented but rather the kingdoms, conceived in their turn as a totality of cities dominating a territory and its subordinate towns.[14] These capitals were considered, and perceived themselves, as naturally representing the section of the body politic which they administered. Besides, the right to representation was looked on as a privilege bound up with the prestige of the city, as the protests of the cities that were left out reveal. Inside the city the municipal bodies – in fact, the urban patriciates – were the citizens. The edict which defined the qualities of the elected as 'a good citizen and a zealous patrician' encouraged this interpretation. Patrician, instead of denoting 'native of the area', served most often to describe the members of the creole oligarchies.

It was also very much part and parcel of an old world mental outlook that care should be taken to avoid 'the factionalism which can be seen to prevail [at election time]'.[15] The ideal of the representation of corporate bodies was a unanimist representation; it was a question of choosing not the supporters of a programme but rather individuals 'of known probity, talent and learning, free from any stain which might blemish their reputation'; all of which excluded candidacies and electoral campaigns. The archaic drawing of lots was considered simultaneously as a way of avoiding factionalism and as an intervention of providence, the ultimate guarantor of the natural order.[16]

By means of these measures the edict of January 1809 remained faithful to the representative system of the old Cortes, in which the body politic of the realm was made up of 'good towns' represented by a patriciate who held purchasable offices. The great innovation, prelude to upheavals to come, lay in extending representation to the Spanish American kingdoms and in the number of towns consulted – more than a hundred – which contrasted with the 37 cities of Spain which alone had the right to vote to the Cortes in the eighteenth century.

On examining the men elected by the *cabildos* to be subsequently selected by the drawing of lots, great differences between the regions can be detected.[17] In New Spain each province designated its own elites. In contrast, in Chile, with its very limited and homogeneous population, the elites of Santiago imposed their own candidates throughout. In Peru, dominated by Lima, the elected who were of provincial origin were excluded from the final vote, to the advantage of those from Lima itself. Universally the choice was made from the holders of the highest offices, civil, clerical or military, of the society of the old regime, the ordering of the three names faithfully reproducing the hierarchy of prestige and honour.

Close study of electoral objections proves decisively that practice rarely corresponded with the ideal of a unanimous election. Most of the cities were divided by party in-fighting, large groupings linked by blood ties, friendship, *compadrazgo*, clientelism, revolving around the big families. These rival 'parties' used all the means at their disposal – even fraud – to attain their ends and they succeeded in certain places such as Valladolid de Michoacán[18] in Mexico, or Córdoba[19] in Río de la Plata in blocking the electoral process almost totally.

The predominantly traditional nature of the society is revealed in the powers and instructions that each city entrusted to its deputy. Elected by the whole kingdom, he was to receive as many powers and instructions as there were cities taking part in his election. Hence he remained to all intents and purposes a representative of the old kind, representing the pyramid of the communities which had designated him: cities, provinces, kingdom and the entire nation. We will confine ourselves to the study of the powers and instructions of New Spain, which comprise the most complete corpus.[20]

These powers, although 'endowing [the deputy] with the power to represent and to have authority together with all the supplementary privileges which he might need', in fact demarcated the limits of his power to act; and the instructions constituted a form of imperative mandate. Some of these limits were of a general nature, and appear in all the documents: loyalty to King Ferdinand VII, the indissoluble tie between Spain and Spanish America, the defence of the Catholic religion. As far as realising these objectives, they reveal an America of a more traditional character than the peninsula. In these documents there is no mention of the wish for, nor even the very word, constitution, as was by then so prevalent in Spain. Mexico spoke of the 'wise and holy laws which govern us' and committed itself only to the 'observance of the laws, the reform of some of them and the addition of others which might be more useful than the old ones'. Puebla alluded to the 'laws, usages and customs [of the monarchy]', as well as to 'basic laws' of the kingdom, a keyword of the historical constitutional movement, attached to the restoration of medieval freedoms. San Luis Potosí risked a vague allusion 'to the reforms that the present day constitution of this America requires', but all its extrapolations bore on the specific interests of the region.

Only the *cabildo* of the powerful mining town of Zacatecas, which had members of the great mining nobility, often *peninsulares* of Basque origin, seemed inspired by a reformism comparable to that of Spain. It demanded the restoration of the nation's rights through the renaissance of the Cortes, the struggle against the arbitrary power of ministers and the separation of powers. Above all it demanded parity of representation between Spain and America in new representative institutions, an essential demand for New Spain, as much within the framework of political representation as in access to public employment.[21] Were the elites of Zacatecas more advanced than those of other cities? Did they enjoy a greater liberty because of their peninsular origin and the financial help which they had never stopped proffering to the Crown?

It is certain that the crucial political demand of New Spain which appears with more or less fervour in the documents of this period was equality between the two Spains. As for other matters, powers and instructions were devoted to questions of local interest. The prospect of being represented in the central government of the Empire gave these distant provinces the hope of being heard at last at the highest level, without an intermediary, and speedily to receive satisfaction.

Even if none of the American deputies arrived in Spain in time to take their seats in the Central Junta, it was nevertheless the case that for the first time – and even before Spain – Spanish America had elected representatives to the central government of the monarchy. Its participation was achieved and it was on the topics of parity of representation and modes of election that the rest of the debate would revolve.

The Summoning of the Cortes

While America was electing representatives to the Central Junta, the

Spanish situation was changing swiftly. The meeting of the Cortes was at the centre of a vigorous political debate in which were sketched out the contours of political groupings. Conservatives, moderates or liberals, all those who desired the meeting of the Cortes, could remember only the model of the medieval assemblies, as if since the times of Charles V there had been no other sort. However, in contradiction to France, the custom of summoning the Cortes had not changed in Spain. Still powerful in the seventeenth century in the various kingdoms, the unitary Cortes of the monarchy had been summoned five times in the eighteenth century, the last session in 1789 being cut short through fear of an aimless drifting similar to that of the Estates General in France.

Yet for the men of 1808 their assemblies had lost their value and legitimacy because of their restricted powers and poor level of representativeness. In fact, these Cortes, in effect the successors to those of Castile, by excluding from their deliberations the nobility and the clergy made up only a 'third estate' which did not correspond to the plebeian Third Estate but rather to the privileged towns, governed by hereditary aldermen or, very often, by the nobility. So when it was necessary to create a means of representation for resistance Spain, nobody considered the assemblies of the previous century and reference was made to the medieval Cortes and freedoms.

Despite the appeals to the past, there was a need to innovate. The more moderate were inspired by the English example. The more radical were thinking of a national assembly along the lines of the French model, but did not expressly say so. All knew what was at stake in this debate and they also knew that the convocation of a new assembly could lead to a revolution.

Two years were required to come to an understanding on the way to form the assembly and on its powers.[22] On 22 May 1809, the Central Junta announced its intention to assemble the Cortes and to create a commission with the task of studying the method of its convocation.[23] There was discussion as to whether it would be administered according to a modified tradition in three Estates or whether only the third Estate would assemble; would it meet separately or together, would voting be in social blocks or individually? Would the presidency revert, according to tradition, to the representatives of the King or to the assembly itself? There was also a need to decide what its powers would be; would they be limited to the conduct of the war, would they be extended to carry out certain reforms or even go so far as to elaborate a constitution?

In accordance with the replies given to these questions, the Cortes would either result in the restoration of old institutions, with representation of the three Estates, or they would constitute a unique assembly of representatives of the nation. The debate which was conducted in France on the convocation of the Estates General, from their first sessions until the proclamation of the National Assembly, was repeated in the Hispanic world between 1808 and 1810.[24]

This debate was of exceptional length. Its central arguments took place in Spain and were continued in America.[25] It opposed the 'historical constitutionalists', grouped around Jovellanos, against the revolutionaries – the future liberals – whose leader was then undoubtedly the poet Manuel José Quintana.

In order to aid the commission in its task, the Central Junta requested the constituted bodies and the enlightened individuals of the realm to pass on to it their thoughts and their plans.[26] This consultation was used by the innovators in order to make the weight of 'public opinion' felt: the start of a new legitimacy, a recent product of press freedom established *de facto* since the uprisings and the swift development of modern forms of sociability. In the struggle which would bring them into opposition first of all with the rear guard of absolutism, and later with the moderates, the revolutionaries were able to rely on the support of a network of societies which became more and more substantial – *tertulias*[27] for the most part – and a political press in full flood.

Among the host of memoranda that the commission received, some dealt with the topic of the convocation, but most, favourable to the principle of a representative monarchy, presented global reforms and constitutions. This did not fail to comfort the supporters of a constituent assembly: these represented for them the majority opinion. In January 1810, when the Central Junta, which was in disarray before the French offensive, had to give way in Cádiz to a Regency, it set out in a final document that the Cortes would retain their division into three Estates which would meet separately and that executive power would be exercised by the Regency.

The moderates seemed to carry the day, but progress towards a modern representative system was already largely under way. A majority of deputies elected by the 'commons' without distinction of rank would take their seats alongside the privileged orders, in a number proportionate to the population of the provinces. Even if the system was mixed – for it was also anticipated that some deputies would be elected by the towns which had seats in the old Cortes and by the insurrectionary Juntas of the provinces – the basis of representation rested already on individuals and no longer on corporate bodies.

The problem of American representation
If the debate on representation was provisionally closed in Spain, it was just beginning in America, whose representation had become inevitable after the election of deputies to the Central Junta. But the *peninsulares,* whether they were moderates or revolutionaries, were far from understanding the aspirations of the Americans.

When on 23 October 1809 a decree of the Central Junta established the date of the meeting of the Cortes, it seemed that the shortness of notice would prevent America from being represented.[28] The protests of the Americans were not long in coming. What they had tolerated in 1808, at the time of the Junta's constitution, was no longer acceptable;[29] the complaints which had built up about the inequality of representation in the Junta grew as the Cortes approached – the Americans risked being absent at the moment when the future assembly seemed certain to reform the monarchy.

Partly aware of this problem, the Central Junta then invented an unusual system to overcome the problem of the American absence: the designation in Spain of substitutes empowered to represent America. This was a solution that could be justified under the constraints of war, but which posed more problems than it solved.

In fact representation by substitutes was barely defensible, whatever might be the context. All representation, even if it is always in part a myth, requires the manifestation, though it may be merely symbolic, of the will of the person who is represented. The use of substitutes was repugnant to a society accustomed to representation of the old type, which imposed an imperative mandate on the *procuradores* of the towns.

Added to the problem posed by the doubtful legitimacy of the system of substitutes was that of inequality. American representation would be considerably less numerous than that of the metropolis, where one deputy would be designated per 50,000 inhabitants. The Central Junta assigned 30 deputies to America and the Philippines,[30] as against more than 250 for peninsular Spain – though the former comprised some 14 million inhabitants and the latter only ten million. Moreover, as well as being considerably less than that of peninsular Spain, this representation was very unequal from one kingdom to another.

Lastly the form of election imposed on America delayed the electoral procedures of the peninsula. When Spain was preparing to elect most of its deputies by almost universal suffrage and in proportion to the number of inhabitants, America had to have recourse to the same system as that already used for the elections to the Central Junta and entrust its choice of deputies to the aldermen of the main towns. This difference can only be explained by the desire to reduce the number of Americans elected and by doubt in the ability of Americans to participate in mass suffrage. The reaction of the latter was sharpened even more when they observed yet again a glaring contradiction between these restrictive measures and the discourse which accompanied them – the 'Manifesto of the Regency Council' – composed by Quintana in language so radical that it provided the revolutionaries with arguments to reject Spanish tutelage:

> From now on, Spanish Americans, you are elevated to the status of free-men. You are no longer the same, you who lay until recently under a yoke so much the heavier since you were so far from the centre of power, looked on with indifference, wounded by greed, destroyed by ignorance. Remember when you state or write the name of he who will come here to represent you in the national congress that your destinies no longer depend on ministers or Viceroys or governors; your destiny is in your own hands.[31]

From the beginning of 1810 the legitimacy of the future Cortes seemed then to Americans to be sullied by irregularities to such an extent that they were tantamount to absolute illegality. The fictional and inegalitarian nature of this representation, aggravated by the Spanish refusal to allow provincial Juntas to be constituted in America like those of the peninsula – another way of granting America only a limited right of representation – was a decisive factor in the formation of autonomous American Juntas, a first step towards an independence which at that time was not part of the intentions of most Americans.

The attacks against the legitimacy of the Cortes would from then on constitute one of the principal themes in the discourse of the rebels. And for the Americans who would continue to recognise the peninsular government and would designate deputies, the fight for parity of representation would be played out within the Cortes themselves, with a consistency which spoke volumes for the strength of their complaints.[32]

Cádiz, revolutionary town

The crucial elements of the liberal revolution took place well before the arrival of the American deputies in the metropolis, at the time when the loyalist provinces of America were proceeding towards elections. In a few months, the situation was utterly reversed, to the advantage of the most radical groups in Cádiz, a town which was not only host to the liberal revolution but one of its decisive actors.[33]

By virtue of its location – a peninsula out of reach of cannon but accessible to the English ships – and by virtue of its wealth, Cádiz was the town best able to resist the French forces. In January 1810, when Andalucía was invaded, all people of authority took refuge in this town.

Despite the fact it was besieged from 9 February 1810 to 25 August 1812, the town weighed heavily from that time in the political life of the Hispanic world with all the weight of its 'people' and its merchants. Its population had for a long time been more cosmopolitan than anywhere else in Spain,[34] and the war increased its size even more. In the census of 1801 the town numbered 57,837 inhabitants, and 71,697 in 1813, at a time when a section of the immigrants had already returned to their provinces, which had been liberated in the meantime. Certain estimates support the idea that at the meeting of the Cortes, Cádiz had some 100,000 inhabitants. Hence the composition of the town was turned upside down: a plethora of soldiers and refugees from the occupied provinces, many of them belonging to the high administration and the cultural elites of the country.

The weight of public opinion developed considerably; a large number of men of letters, unemployed jurists and officers without a regiment gathered in the *tertulias* and the coffee houses, which had never been so busy. Running parallel to these debates, public intervention had adopted violent forms since the start of the anti-French uprising. There exists no study on the nature and composition of this 'commons' nor on the forms and consequences of its interventions, but it is clear that the uprisings were capitalised on by the merchants who ran the city.

Nevertheless, it was still two years before they could bring to fruition their plans for hegemony. The débâcle of the end of January 1810 gave them an opportunity to take power, based on universal suffrage. Even before the official dissolution of the Central Junta the military governor of the town handed over his office to the town council. And during the night of 27 to 28 January, his *síndico*, Tomás Istúriz, organised public elections in the districts which were electing a new Junta according to the wishes of the *cabildo*.[35]

One may wonder what the atmosphere in the town was like when people did not know which would arrive first in the port, the French army or the Duke of Albuquerque; and one may speculate as to how this night of popular consultation was spent, when all the heads of family of this populous town had to give their opinions. Though under a very democratic guise, the proceedings, which consisted of appealing to the people to set aside a government brought to power by a previous riot, resembled a *coup d'état* on a city scale. Soon after its election the new Junta took over power from the Regency that had been nominated, under pressure from Britain, by the last members of the Central Junta. Between February and March 1810, the trade of the town furnished some 26 million reals to help the Badajoz army and at the end of March, the Cádiz Junta had assumed responsibility for managing the finances of the state.

In fact, as an essential member of the government of resistance Spain, the Junta exercised a decisive influence on the Regency to bring about the meeting of the Cortes within the time specified and according to the forms desired by the liberals. For them it was a question of electing 'men to whom to entrust the sublime responsibility of saving the nation from all oppression, be it internal or external, by forming a political constitution which, by demarcating clearly the respective attributions of legislative, executive and judiciary powers, would ensure the nation's rights to independence and civil liberty'.[36] The main lines of its programme were mapped out: to capitalise on the regime's crisis in order to give the country a constitution which would establish the foundations of a parliamentary monarchy.

Who were the members of this powerful Junta? A count of the Cádiz members present in the three electoral assemblies of the city in 1810, those of the Junta, the *cabildo* and the province – 54 individuals – reveals that they were mainly rich merchants, often members of families which had had a house in Cádiz since the previous century, nobles for the most part of Basque or Navarrese origins,[37] or men who had been made nobles; in some cases they were men whose fathers had been aldermen before them.

There was not a journalist, not a pamphleteer among them; their names do not appear in any of the Cádiz publications. The press, direct influence on public opinion were not their domain. Their power was vested elsewhere: in a transatlantic commercial network (approximately 80 per cent of American trade still passed through Cádiz), bolstered by the common Navarrese origin of those citizens of Cádiz by adoption, and by many American merchants.[38]

These merchants did not comprise a progressive modern bourgeoisie but rather an oligarchy controlling a privileged body, the 'merchant consulate' of Cádiz, the last defender of the commercial monopoly and resolute opponent of any idea of free trade with America which might threaten its power. But at the beginning of the nineteenth century, with the loss of profits from the Indies trade, the economic decline of Cádiz was inevitable and its patriciate stood condemned for lack of audacity. The liberalism of its merchants was not economic, but political. Their activism reflected their progressivist convictions, their values, their sensitivity to modern blandishments. These merchants had a way of life identical to that of the most open elites of Spain; they shared their reading and their taste for learned, cultural, economic and secret societies; they travelled outside the peninsulas, traded with foreigners, spoke English and French, frequented the coffee houses, the theatre and the *tertulias*.

The victory of the revolutionaries

It was in this old-fashioned, besieged and overheated town that the decisive battles for the meeting of the revolutionary Cortes took place. The supplanting of the Central Junta by a conservative Regency Council had represented a defeat for the revolutionaries who were in a hurry to bring together a sovereign national assembly. Cádiz fought against the Regency with all its supporters for change: a good number of the innovators of the preceding years who had taken refuge in the town, young people, newcomers on the political scene, like the Count of Toreno and, in the background, the merchants of Cádiz and the 'commons' whom they controlled. From mid-June 1810 events gathered impetus.

For three months the innovators increased their pressure on the Regency, which was beset by the weight of public opinion: from the press, and from coffee houses and street gossip. The meeting of the Cortes seemed to be the panacea to all problems, including that of the unity of the monarchy which the formation of American Juntas appeared to threaten. In three months the innovators obtained what they wanted: the meeting of the Cortes at Cádiz,[39] the formation of a single chamber gathering together the deputies of the Third Estate, the designation of substitutes from among the residents of Cádiz with origins in America and the occupied provinces; the opening of the sittings as soon as half the deputies plus one were present – including substitutes;[40] the Regency would not act to revise mandates, would not preside over the assembly and would impose on the Cortes neither the subjects to be dealt with nor the order of the agenda. The assembly would be its own master.

If by its nature the new assembly became revolutionary, it followed it would become so also in its composition. This is why the elections of the Spanish and American substitutes which took place in Cádiz assumed a considerable importance. They would determine who would have the majority, not only on the opening of the assembly but beyond it, for the substitutes elected in September 1810 would actually take their seats for three years, assuring the liberals a majority for the duration of the Cortes.

Their number was fixed at 23 for Spain and 30 for America and their election took place between 18 and 22 September, a few days before the opening of the Cortes.[41] The system combined modern criteria – all men who were more than 25 years old and were natives of the province were qualified electors, whatever their status[42] – with the old practice of drawing lots within a *terna* chosen by seven grand electors. The proliferation of new forms of sociabilities added new variables to the vote. As the Count of Toreno wrote, as soon as the selection of substitutes was announced

> ... the spirits of the young rose.... Everything was Juntas, meetings, discussions, debates.... The candidacy of deputies was discussed and people looked not to the dignitaries, men who had grown old in the old court or in the outmoded customs of the councils or other corporations, but rather towards those who were considered the most enlightened, the most passionate and the most capable of freeing Spain from the rust which had sapped its strength.[43]

This comment reflects the two philosophies which opposed each other in the election: on the one hand the old one, which without excluding pacts gave precedence to the maintenance of established dignities; on the other, the modern, product of debates and new forms of social interaction in which the innovators could be found. If the group vote, as a consequence of their meetings, had little effect within the electoral Juntas – as the disappointment of Quintana shows in relation to the *Madrileños* Junta – nevertheless it was decisive in limited voting, as is revealed in the elections of the Spanish American substitutes.[44]

Here one can clearly perceive, by counting the votes, the contrast between a group making its voice heard in a disciplined way[45] and voting for the same names, and the dispersed pattern of voting of others. This first group comprised young radicals, supporters of the autonomy, if not the independence, of Spanish America; several were future leaders of the revolt.[46] The ideological alliances seem to have been decisive; the party gathered together men of far-flung regions – from Mexico to Chile – thus excluding the influence of traditional family or geographical bonds.

The group succeeded in controlling the election of most of the American substitutes, only the Caribbean and Peru escaping their influence. As for the remainder of Spanish America, out of a total of about 93 voters, the 32 members identified as being from the radical group (34 per cent of the electors) managed to get 16 from among their number designated as grand electors (76 per cent) and twelve among the elected (60 per cent). Only the final selection by drawing of lots impeded their vigorous campaign.

The election of substitutes at Cádiz was a master stroke of the innovators, who thus assured for themselves a majority in the Cortes that they doubtlessly would not have obtained otherwise. When one month after the opening of the sessions and at the end of one of the most passionate debates in its history, the Cortes approved the freedom of the press, it was the substitutes and the four deputies from Cádiz who won the day for the liberals: they voted 97 per cent for the bill and provided some 65 per cent of the liberal vote, the elected deputies for the most part voting against.[47]

The status of the substitutes also affected that of the deputies who had been elected in Spain and in Spanish America. From the mass of refugees, the youngest of the cultural elites were chosen – civil servants, soldiers, clerics – that is to say the most progressive in ideological terms who, having been educated after the French Revolution, had been familiar since their youth with modern political principles.

The disparity between this liberal group which extraordinary circumstances brought together at Cádiz and the rest of the Hispanic world is vast, not only with regard to the bulk of the society which had remained almost universally traditional, even archaic, but also in regard to the majority of the elites, both in Spain and Spanish America, as the development of the Cortes showed following the arrival of the elected deputies. The preponderance of the innovators then declined regularly without, however, the liberals losing their majority in the assembly. They maintained this thanks to the safety net formed by the substitutes and owing to their mastery of the mechanisms of modern politics, when confronted by men of less experience. They owed it also to the pressure exerted by the public and to the fact that, since the vote on the nation's sovereignty, any challenge to the powers of the Cortes constituted the crime of *lèse-majesté*. The revolution which began in September 1810 can be rightly called the revolution of Cádiz.

However, the election of substitutes which assured the success of liberal projects in Spain was a stumbling block to the recognition of the Cortes by Spanish America. To the resistance already evinced against the principle of representation by substitutes was added the doubt shown about the electoral conditions. It was soon learnt in America that about a hundred people without a mandate had designated 25 deputies – four electors per deputy elected. The legitimacy of the Cortes, which was already very questionable for many on account of the inequality of representation which Spanish America suffered, was even more weakened.

The revolutionary Cortes and their composition

While waiting for the news to reach Spanish America, the revolution followed its course in Cádiz. On the morning of 24 September, after attending mass together, 101 deputies gathered in the theatre of the Isla de León; after having duly elected a president and a secretary, and heard a speech from the Regency, they were left to their own devices. When the regents had left the room, Canon Diego Muñoz Torrero, a deputy from Extremadura, proposed the proclamation of the sovereignty of the Cortes; he gave way to Manuel Luján, likewise from Extremadura, who had prepared a memorandum on this, a decree of eleven articles: the first declared that the Cortes were the legitimate representatives of the nation and that in them rested national sovereignty; the second recognised Ferdinand VII as King; the third established the separation of the three powers; the fourth, the responsibility of the executive entrusted provisionally to the Regency which was bound to recognise the sovereignty of the assembly (articles five, six and seven). The deputies then refused to leave until the Regency had sworn on oath; fetched at once, four of the five regents came to swear and it was after midnight before everything was concluded.[48]

After this first fundamental victory the revolutionaries still had the task, as masters of the Cortes, to dismantle the old regime, section by section, and to elaborate a constitution which would serve as a basic agreement for a new society.

While these events were unfolding in Cádiz, and well after, the rest of the Hispanic world continued to elect deputies who would be incorporated gradually in the Cortes right up until just before their dissolution in 1813. The delay in many elections was due essentially to the war: in Spain, due to the fighting and the occupation by the French army of a good part of the peninsula; in Spanish America due to the uprisings and the civil war which began in 1809 and which continued until independence. Added to these obstacles was the time lag in communicating the legal measures to Spanish America and the duration of the deputies' journey. These elections thus lacked unity of both space and time. We will content ourselves with a global look at the deputies elected.

The electoral measures of January/February 1810, intended for the election of provincial deputies, were not uniform and different electoral systems had been planned for Spanish America and for Spain – and even in the interior of Spain, for the different provinces.

In Spain, the elections of the deputies to the Third Estate took place according to three systems: a small number of deputies represented the provincial Juntas resulting from the uprising; others were allotted to the towns which had had the privilege of electing a *procurador* to the old Cortes; while most were elected by all the *vecinos*,[49] proportionate to the number of inhabitants.

In the first instance a representative was allotted to the Juntas which had symbolised since 1808 the insurrectionary representation of the people. In the second, the electoral body of the aldermen was increased by the addition of an equal number of electors chosen by all *vecinos*. In the third instance, a modern system of election was employed, with almost universal suffrage, but indirect and in three tiers.[50] The new regime was certainly representative and based on a broad popular suffrage, but indirect suffrage was still given the task of carrying out a sifting process so as to entrust power to the elites; in all three cases the election was concluded by the drawing of lots.

Table 1
The Status of the Substitutes and Deputies

Professions	(A)	%	(B)	%	(C)	%	(D)	%	(E)	%	(F)	%	Totals	%
Local administration	1	5	0	0	0	0	0	0	3	2	0	0	4	1
Tradesmen	0	0	2	7	0	0	0	0	0	0	1	3	3	1
Clerics	3	14	5	17	2	15	3	11	61	33	20	56	94	30
Sheriffs	0	0	0	0	0	0	22	79	0	0	1	3	23	7
Civil servants	13	59	0	0	1	8	0	0	17	9	10	28	41	13
High administration	0	0	3	10	1	8	0	0	22	12	1	3	27	9
Member of provincial Junta	0	0	0	0	8	62	0	0	0	0	0	0	8	3
Soldiers	3	14	14	48	0	0	1	4	16	9	2	6	36	12
Nobility	0	0	1	3	0	0	0	0	7	4	0	0	8	3
University teachers	0	0	2	7	0	0	0	0	0	0	1	3	3	1
Liberal professors	2	9	2	7	0	0	1	4	23	12	0	0	28	9
Landowners	0	0	0	0	0	0	0	0	3	2	0	0	3	1
No data stated	0	0	0	0	1	8	1	4	33	18	0	0	35	11
Totals	22	100	29	100	13	100	28	100	185	100	36	100	313	100

(A) Substitutes for the provinces of Spain. (B) Substitutes for the provinces of America. (C) Deputies designated by the Spanish Juntas. (D) Deputies designated by the towns of Spain profiting from the privelege of being represented in the Cortes of the old regime. (E) Deputies elected by the Spanish provinces. (F) Deputies elected by the American provinces.

Calculations made from the Diario de Sesiones de las Cortes extraordinarias, as well as ACM, *Credenciales*, 1,6; P. Chavarri Sidera, *Las elecciones de diputados a las Cortes generales y extraordinarias (1810-1813)* (Madrid, 1988).

Note: Column totals may not sum to 100% due to rolling errors.

The origin of the deputies who emerged from these three types of election suggests a number of comments (see Table 1). The Juntas and the privileged towns chose the deputies from among their members – essentially nobles, aldermen and some clerics and civil servants. The range of origins of the deputies elected by almost universal suffrage is much broader. Here, with percentages bordering on ten per cent, were members of high administrative office, various types of civil servant, members of the liberal professions, soldiers and, especially, clerics (33 per cent). Here we are dealing with an unexpected consequence of the transition to a modern representative system based on the individual. Once the representative system by corporation was abandoned, society elected dignitaries of all types, of whom the most respected were members of the clergy.

These characteristics were even more marked in Spanish America whose deputies were mainly ecclesiastics (56 per cent) and civil servants (28 per cent). To the explanations already put forward for Spain we should add here the realisation that the deputies would be away for a long time caused the electors to prefer men without family commitments, that is priests and young civil servants.

In both cases, in Spain as in Spanish America, it is proper to add an additional factor to those which we have just enumerated, common to both elected clerics and laymen. A vast majority of them had undertaken higher education to graduate or doctorate level. Clearly the electors wanted to designate distinguished persons, but also members of the cultural elites; enlightened people who seemed to them the most worthy to defend them and to progress towards the reform of the monarchy. And it is amongst the youngest of them that the most militant revolutionaries were to be found.

These were nobles, priests, royal or military officers, but none of them represented a 'revolutionary bourgeoisie': among their number there were only five merchants, of whom none belonged to the revolutionary factions. Unless we distort words from their true meaning, the Hispanic revolution was carried out by members of the intellectual elites of the old regime who had become, through cultural transformation, modern elites.

The perusal of some Spanish-American elections allows us to add some details to this picture. The very broad suffrage which was used for provincial elections in Spain was not introduced in Spanish America; only the *cabildos* of the provincial capitals had the right to vote. Hence the American electorate was the same as that which had participated in the previous elections, for the Central Junta. What, then, was the distinguishing feature of these new elections?

Doubtless the most significant change came from the climate in which they took place. If the elections for the Central Junta took place generally with due respect for the provisional authorities of the peninsula, the following elections were held in an agitated climate. Certain provinces, casting doubt on the legitimacy of the Cortes, were subject to uprisings in favour of independence, which in certain zones[51] became civil wars. Thus, paradoxically, the loyalist regions had to accept the *fait accompli* of the Spanish revolution which the groups favouring independence were challenging.

These elections were also different from the preceding ones in the fact that on this occasion those elected by the *cabildos* had to be natives of their province, which eliminated Spaniards residing in Spanish America and thereby reinforced regionalist tendencies.

In Spanish America, which had remained faithful to the peninsular government, the elections took place for the most part when the sovereignty of the Cortes was already established. The political regime of the Empire had changed, partly due to the American substitutes, but without consultation with the American provinces. The representatives that Spanish America designated had thus as their task to negotiate, within an all powerful assembly, reforms in favour of their provinces. Nevertheless, the uprisings, threat of which could always be invoked by loyalists, furnished a weighty argument in favour of equality of representation between Spanish America and the metropolis – an equality which Spanish America, remaining loyal to the metropolis as it did, tended to impose by adopting forms of representation which were less archaic than the regulations prescribed. Several elections demonstrated the wish to include all *vecinos* in an electorate which was supposed to have been limited to the members of the *cabildos*.[52] All of which suggests too that the regions loyal to Spain were not of necessity the most conservative.

Epilogue: Modern Representation and Traditional Society

When the Cortes of Cádiz promulgated the Constitution of the Spanish monarchy, on 19 March 1812, the Hispanic revolution had completed its first stage. Crucial steps had been made: absolutism had collapsed, multiple elections had allowed the 'nation' to make its voice heard and the nation had proclaimed its sovereignty; a representative regime was being put in place. The new constitution was resolutely modern: national sovereignty, separation of powers, individual freedoms, abolition of corporations and privileged statutes, elective responsibilities at all levels – municipal, provincial and national – and almost universal suffrage.

If we adhere to the texts, the Hispanic world in its entirety adopted the forms and principles of political modernity. The restoration of absolutism in 1814, with Ferdinand VII's return, constitutes an aberration that was swiftly stopped. In 1820 a new Spanish revolution triggered the process again in a still more radical fashion (only the intervention of a French expedition acting in the name of the Holy Alliance halted this development); by means of this, loyalist America started on its way towards independence.

The balance sheet that one can draw up for this process is split. The installation of a new legitimacy was the principal cause of the dissolution of the Empire, the suddenness and brutality of which could in no way have been foreseen. The refusal to accept real equality of representation on the part of the Spanish stirred up old quarrels and gave rise to American independence movements, themselves founded on an idea of the 'nation' – the nation which did not yet exist.

On the other hand, the swift passage to modernity, posed many problems for the future. The triumph of the new principles was assured and, to a great extent, irreversible. But did that mean that both Spanish and Spanish American society had become modern? And that political life had adopted practices consonant with the new ideas proclaimed with so much solemnity?

Nothing could be further from the truth. As we have seen, the victory of the revolutionary minority was due to a combination of exceptional circumstances; the absence of the King, the necessity to give legitimacy to the provisional powers constituted to fight against Napoleon and, above all, the domination of the liberals at Cádiz. In addition, even if the aspiration for representation was very widespread, it is not clear that the majority understood it in the same way as the modern elites who were the principal actors of the Hispanic revolution. Society remained deeply traditional, even archaic, as were a good number of its dignitaries, especially in America. Certainly the elites evolved rapidly after 1808, abandoning principles still held by the old regime, for modern cultural references. But what was possible in the realm of principle was impossible when it became a question of actual behaviour.

Family cliques, clientelist networks, municipal bodies, all these collective participants in the old society remained strong and healthy despite the adoption of new principles. Modern political life and its electoral dimension could not avoid being profoundly changed; electoral competition could not reflect the free opinion of individual citizens, since these were very much in the minority. Only those members of the elites who had subscribed to new political concepts corresponded to the ideal of representative democracy. And it was they who would confront each another in modern elections by mobilising, each in their own way, the old collective actors, that section of the society that the dignitaries 'represented' in the name of traditional authorities. From this moment *caciquismo*, the structure so peculiar to the political life of the Hispanic countries, assumed the place that it was to occupy for a long time to come.

Notes

1. The word 'Liberal' was invented in Spain during the Spanish revolution, before reaching the rest of Europe. It designated at that time a revolutionary who fought against the old regime and for a constitutional regime.
2. Deputies who were appointed to act pending the arrival of elected deputies.
3. The sources used in this study come essentially from the *Archivo de las Cortes españolas* (ACM), the *Archivo Histórico del Ejército* (AHE) and the *Archivo Histórico Nacional* (AHN) in Madrid; from the *Archivo General de la Nación* (AGN) in Mexico, and from many Andean sources. For a more complete and detailed version of this text, see *Caravelle, Cahiers du Monde Hispanique et Luso-Brésilien*, No. 60 (Toulouse, 1993), pp. 5-57. We have also developed the problems of this revolutionary era in Marie-Danielle Demélas, *L'invention politique. Bolivie, Equateur, Pérou au XIXe siècle* (Paris, 1992) and François-Xavier Guerra, *Modernidad e Independencias. Ensayos sobre las Revoluciones hispánicas* (Madrid, 1992).
4. Elements on the composition of Juntas are to be found in Angel Martínez de Velasco, *La formación de la Junta central* (Pamplona, 1972), chap. III.
5. In this sense, the argumentation of Miguel Artola is conclusive: the Juntas are *de facto* revolutionary powers that no precedent could justify. See M. Artola, *Los orígenes de la España contemporánea* (Madrid, 1959) and *La España de Fernando VII* (Madrid, 1968).
6. They had been suppressed by Philip V after his victory in the war of the Spanish Succession and the principal towns of these kingdoms had been integrated into the Cortes of Castile. Only the Cortes of Navarra survived as a separate entity.
7. The installation of the Central Junta in the *Gazeta de Madrid*, no. 129 extraordinary issue, 29 Sept. 1808, and the *Gazeta de México*, no. 133, 29 Nov. 1808, extraordinary issue.
8. Martínez de Velasco, *La formación de la Junta central*, pp. 195-6.
9. The expression, in French in the text, is from Jovellanos in his letters to Lord Holland.
10. Real Orden, Sevilla, 22 Jan. 1809, AHN Madrid, *Estado* D71. The document was published by the authorities of the different regions at various dates according to the various delays caused by the difficulties of communication.

11. The term 'colony' came into current but not official usage in the second half of the 18th century in parallel with the Bourbons' undertaking to modernise, wanting to make America the foundation for Spain's prosperity. The very word was loathsome to the Americans. When Americans did sometimes use it, at the beginning of the 19th century, it was in the old sense, as the new founding of a metropolis, never in the modern sense of colonised country.

12. The Philippines were considered as part of the Indies and in fact they were a far-off dependency of New Spain. Since all the measures alluded to were applied to America, they also applied to the Philippines.

13. See, for example, Camilo Torres, *Representación del cabildo de Santa Fé de Bogotá a la Suprema Junta Central de España*, 1809 (Bogotá, 1960).

14. The city of Guanajuato gave its powers in its name 'and in representation of all the other suffragan, *cabildos* of the cities, towns and places contained within its borders ....' AGN, *Historia*, vol. 417, exp. II, fol. 289 et seq.

15. Real Orden of 22 Jan. 1809, AHN, *Estado*, 54, D71.

16. The *cabildo* of Mexico said, after learning that the drawing of lots in New Spain had confirmed who had finally been elected: 'This *ayuntamiento* has seen its election approved by the powerful hand of the Almighty with great joy ...' AGN, *Historia*, vol. 417, exp. II, fol. 259 et seq. The same reaction was seen in the Andes: the *cabildo* of La Plata (present day Sucre, in Bolivia) recalled that the election of his deputy 'had been confirmed by providence...'. ACM, *Actas*, leg. 3, exp. II.

17. See for Mexico, AGN, vol. 418, exp. V, VI, VII, X and XIII; for Peru, AHN, *Estado*, 58, F, 156; for Chile, Miguel Luis Amunátegui, *La Crónica de 1810* (Santiago de Chile, 1911), t. I, pp. 346-61.

18. See AGN, *Historia*, vol. 418, exp. V.

19. Julio V. González, *Filiación histórica del gobierno representativo argentino* (Buenos Aires, 1937).

20. The essential part of the sources are in AGN Mexico, *Historia*, vol. 417.

21. Powers and orders of the city of Zacatecas, 7 Dec. 1809. AGN, *Historia*, vol. 417, exp. II, fol. 179 et seq.

22. On this question, see especially Federico Suárez, *El proceso de convocatoria de las Cortes, 1808-1810* (Pamplona, 1982).

23. Real Orden of 22 Dec. 1809 – published in Mexico by *bando* of Viceroy Lizana, 14.VIII. 1809, AGN, *Historia*, vol. 445, exp. I.

24. These resemblances reflect as much an institutional parenthood shared between France and Spain as the perfect knowledge of the French Revolution that the principal participants of the Spanish revolutions possessed.

25. Where the absence of press freedom kept the political debate in the narrow framework of elite social circles.

26. The Spanish step recalls the French preparation of the Estates General and the request, through the council of the King on 5 July 1788, for 'memoranda, information and elucidations' on the deportment of the Estates Generals.

27. The *tertulia* is the generic name of the new form of sociability. It included salons with a varied participation, literary or scientific societies and, increasingly, political societies. The venues were various: private houses, university establishments, coffee houses.

28. Decree of 28 Oct. 1809, in Manuel Fernández Martín, *Derecho parlamentario español. Colección de Constituciones, disposiciones de carácter constitucional, leyes y decretos electorales para diputados y senadores, y reglamentos de las Cortes que han regido en España en el presente siglo* (Madrid, 1885), t. II, p. 594 et seq. The decree provided for the convocation of the Cortes on 1 January 1810 and for them to meet on 1 March the same year.

29. See, for example, the letter from the *cabildo* of Guatemala to the Preparatory Commission of the Cortes, 30 Jan.1810, HN, Madrid, *Estado*, leg. 20, E.

30. Decree of the Central Junta of the 29 Jan. 1810 in Fernández Martín, *Derecho parlamentario español*, t. II, p. 614 et seq.

31. *Manifesto of the Regency Council to the Spanish Americans*, 14 Feb. 1810, in Fernández Martín, *Derecho parlamentario español*, t. II, p. 594 *et seq.*

32. See for these debates: Marie-Laure Rieu-Millan, *Los diputados americanos en las Cortes de Cádiz* (Madrid, 1990); Brian R. Hamnett, *La política española en una época revolucionaria, 1790-1820* (Mexico, 1985); and Timothy Anna, *Spain and the Loss of America* (Lincoln, Neb., 1983).

33. For the town at this time, see the classic work of Ramón Solís, *El Cádiz de las Cortes*, illustrated edn. (Madrid, 1987).

34. Within it there was a French colony of some thousands of people: big merchants, but also temporary immigrants, often from the Limousin and engaged in all sorts of small trades.

35. Adolfo de Castro, *Historia de Cádiz y su provincia* (Cádiz, 1858), pp. 685-6.

36. Adolfo de Castro, *Cortes de Cádiz. Complementos de las sesiones verificadas en la Isla de León y en Cádiz. Extractos de las discusiones, datos y noticias, documentos y discursos publicados en periódicos y folletos de la época* (Madrid, 1913), t. I, p.122, Manifesto of 17 July 1810.

37. The inhabitants of many of the valleys of the Basque country and Navarre enjoyed a collective *hidalguía*.

38. This explains the links maintained by the men of Cádiz with certain deputies from overseas. See Rieu-Millan, *Los diputados americanos en las Cortes de Cádiz;* and María Teresa Berruezo, *La participación americana en las Cortes de Cádiz (1810-1814)* (Madrid, 1986).

39. ACM, *Credenciales*, leg. 5, 16. The convocation decree of the Central Junta of 1 Jan. 1810 provided for the meeting of the Cortes at Mallorca.

40. The decree is given in Fernández Martín, *Derecho parlamentario español*, t. II, pp. 600-1.

41. Only one week after the appearance of the order which organised it. The decree is given in Fernández Martín, *Derecho parlamentario español*, t. II, pp. 605 et seq.

42. Only the members of regular orders, state debtors and servants were excluded. The decree clarifies as evidence that 'pure Indians, and their descendants originating from mixed marriage with the Spanish can be elected deputies, as they are equal vassals [of the King]'.

43. Conde de Toreno, *Historia del levantamiento, guerra y revolución de España* (Madrid, 1953), p. 285.

44. Their statements have been largely preserved, with the nominating vote of all the electors. Only those of the electoral Junta of Santa Fé-Caracas are miss-

ing. The others are in ACM, *Credenciales*, 1, 6, in the file on Cádiz.
45. One can identify the members of this group by the protest they made to the Junta prior to the election, on 18 Sept. 1810, against the inequality of representation of Spanish America. We have drawn the 34 names of the members of this group from this document. ACM, *Credenciales*, 1, 6.
46. One finds among them, for example, the Mexican José María Coutto, who had to leave the country for having made anti-Spanish remarks; for New Granada, José Domingo Caicedo, José Mejía Lequerica, the Count of Puñonrostro, or the Venezuelans Palacios and Fermín Clemente Francia who were very close to Bolívar; in Argentina, Carlos Alvear, the future leader of the Argentine revolution.... on the other hand, José Miguel Carrera, a future Chilean radical, figured among those who still voted in the old way.
47. Figures compiled from *Diario de sesiones de las Cortes extraordinarias*, No. 25, 19 Oct. 1810, pp. 53-4.
48. On what was said at that first session we only have the résumé of the interventions which occurred. We do not know the names of all those who spoke. It is only from the 80th sitting, on 15 December 1810, that tachygraphs started to give an account of the total debate. Our reference is to the *Diario de sesiones de las Cortes generales y extraordinarias*, vol. I, pp. 1-4.
49. ACM, *General*, leg. 124, exp. 2, 'Sobre el modo de hacer las elecciones de procuradores de Cortes en los pueblos'.
50. The parish, the headquarters of the *partido* and the capital of the province. The different electoral orders are in Fernández Martín, *Derecho parlamentario español*, t. II, pp. 570 et seq. See also, for the elections, Pilar Chavarri Sidera, *Las elecciones de diputados a las Cortes generales y extraordinarias (1810-1813)* (Madrid, 1988).
51. The *Audiencia* of Quito, Venezuela, New Granada, Río de la Plata and Mexico.
52. This is the case, *inter alia*, for La Plata (Alto Peru) and Maracaibo (ACM, *Credenciales*, exp. 11), Puno and Santa Marta (ACM, leg. 3, exp. 38).

CHAPTER 3

THE BALLOT, LAND AND SOVEREIGNTY: CÁDIZ AND THE ORIGINS OF MEXICAN LOCAL GOVERNMENT, 1812-1820*

Antonio Annino

In 1825, the Minister for Internal and Foreign Affairs of the new federal republic of Mexico, Lucas Alamán, writing with characteristic lucidity, stated:

> now that control has been lost and obedience to all higher authorities has been swept away, there remains nothing to bind together the lesser powers or even to lend them respectability in the eyes of the people, and from this flows disorder, anarchy and civil war.[1]

Lack of legitimacy and of institutional hierarchy: this was the future Conservative leader's perception of the problem of governing the republic. The civil war between insurgents and counter-insurgents was without doubt an influential factor in the destruction of the vice-regal order. This chapter addresses a further aspect of the crisis: the dissemination of early electoral practices of a liberal type in the few years during which the Constitution of Cádiz was applied. It has been stated on many occasions that the Cádiz Constitution failed to be applied in New Spain – as Mexico was known before independence – as a result of civil war and the aversion of the Spanish authorities. However, the real issue is a somewhat different one: the governors of Mexico City were anti-liberal, but they recognised that the Cádiz Constitution was a political instrument which could be used to weaken insurgency. Therefore, they applied it, while failing to implement certain of its more important aspects, such as freedom of the press – but they did bring about elections, in particular those which enabled the establishment of elective local councils in the towns.

This decision had extraordinary consequences for the outcome of the crisis and for the future of Mexico. Local autonomy still figures as an important concept in the collective mentality of the Mexican people. It has been said that local autonomy is an old tradition, of colonial origin,

---

* Translated by Patricia Roberts.

which is in fact not the case, since few towns pre-dating the Constitution of Cádiz possessed a local council – *cabildo* (with the obvious exception of the indigenous *cabildos*). Moreover, throughout the nineteenth century, the people's struggle to defend their territorial rights was in stark contrast to the colonial past, for in the (available) documents reference is often made to 'sovereignty'. The dual concept of land and sovereignty, though apparently of traditional origin, derived from the period of the Constitution of Cádiz, and established the foundations of Mexican local government.

This connection between the provincial world and the liberal constitution reveals a paradox: the Cádiz Constitution was of a centralising character, but once applied to New Spain it unleashed a massive process of political decentralisation which destroyed the institutional hierarchies, bequeathing that doom-laden legacy to the republican future, as Lucas Alamán observed in his letter. And so it was that when Agustín de Iturbide launched the Iguala Plan (1821), the New Spain of the Bourbons had already disappeared and a different political configuration now applied from that of 1808, when a coup in the capital had sufficed to take control of the country. The change in the structure of the political domain was very well depicted by General Gómez Pedraza in his memoirs. Relating the events of 1821, Pedraza asserted that Iturbide's original plan had been 'to post some loyal troops in the citadel of the capital and to effect a rebellion in favour of independence'. However, 'I persuaded Iturbide that the plan was ill-conceived and in conclusion told him that in my opinion the movement should commence *from the periphery and work towards the centre*, and that the occupation of the capital would be the last step in the enterprise'(author's emphasis). The reliability of the account may be in doubt, but the manner in which the Trigarante Army conducted themselves is not. As a result, between 1808 and 1821 the axis around which political power revolved was radically displaced from the centre to the periphery, where it remained fixed throughout the course of the nineteenth century: any change of regime, any military rising, even the Mexican Revolution itself, occurring a century later, would come about in terms of the periphery.

It is clear that the strength of the local societies and their ability to influence national events cannot be explained in terms of permanent weakness at the centre, nor incompatibility between liberalism and Mexican society. The history of Hispanic America is characterised by miscegenation and in this context one must also consider the widely debated problem of the reception of liberal political models. What is at issue here is not the degree to which European liberalism remained 'pure', but the form in which it was disseminated in multi-ethnic societies; whether it transformed power-relations, the political practices of the protagonists, systems of values and if so, in what ways. We must address the question of resources used by local societies to maintain their strength and their autonomy *vis-à-vis* 'national' centres that attempted to impose a new order. This analysis of the Cádiz experience reveals the ways in which the communities used the vote to achieve a form of local self-government, which was, without doubt, much stronger than during the colonial period. The change which occurred had not figured in the plans of the authors of the Constitution, but it is precisely this point which is of greatest interest: the individualistic terms in which the model was cast met with a powerful chain of reasoning informed by the concept of community and corporation. This did not result in conflict between the two, but in interaction, since neither the model nor the communities remained as before.

To this end, it is worth drawing attention to a crucial question which originates with Cádiz: one facet of so-called political modernity is linguistic change. The languages of the old regime were concrete: the nation was a set of territorial structures and organisations, sovereignty was vested in the person of the King but also in the Kingdoms, freedoms were private privileges. The languages of modernity are abstract, they not only invent new words but transform the old: 'nation', 'sovereignty', 'liberty', 'representation' become values, sloughing off their concrete and specific referents. The collective consensus around the new values was obviously not a spontaneous process in any country; it depended on the scope to impose the abstract language upon the multiple languages which were common social currency. If this challenge was not the most important one in the Anglo-Saxon areas, as Edmund Burke emphasised, it undoubtedly was in the Latin areas, where the language of the Enlightenment was of a markedly abstract character, and was the matrix of constitutional and electoral language. New Spain is a particularly telling example, since nobody, in the throes of imperial crisis, managed to monopolise the new language: it was disseminated, untrammelled, in far-flung rural villages, where communities appropriated and moulded it into a different form, adapting it to their own needs and interests. A certain dualism, or more precisely ambiguity, arose from this process: new voting practices enjoyed consensus and were defended by the communities, whilst the new concept of sovereignty, which implied a delegation of power from the bottom upwards, from the *periphery* to the *centre*, was not accepted. For a few years, or perhaps even longer, the constitutional language of liberalism was perceived by these communities as an evolution in colonial language, as a new form of classic Hispanic contractualism.

Elections under the Cádiz Constitution

Nevertheless, the trajectory of early liberalism in Mexico also depended upon the Cádiz Constitution. *Prima facie*, the text is 'long and inflexible', as the constitutionalists would go on to say. A constitution brimming with enlightened optimism, with the will to programme political change of great magnitude: meticulous in its attention to detail, to the point of appearing prolix, the text is much more flexible than at first appears, and provided many openings for local societies and their values. A homage to that Montesquieuean spirit not far removed, as we know, from the Spanish liberals.

The section dedicated to elections, to how the new form of representation could be established, is one of the sections of the Constitution which evinces the greatest flexibility. The imbalance between the abstract concept of sovereignty, which seeks, in the French style, to centralise and to ratify, and the electoral mechanisms, granting as they do great flexibility to those engaged in the voting procedures, in the interpretation of the norms, is striking: a sovereignty which is centralised, but which leaves very little scope to the representatives of the Executive at local level. The Constitution specified three electoral stages: for the Cortes, for the *Diputaciones Provinciales* and for the new *Ayuntamientos* – municipal councils. The nature of the vote depended, however, on the functions assigned to each of the three bodies. The last two were assigned an administrative and consultative role, under the authority of the *jefes políticos*, civil servants appointed by the centre of the empire. Elections for the *Diputaciones* and municipal councils had no political character in the Constitution, but rather were designed to function as a mechanism for the selection of local notables and their transformation into indirect civil servants, constitutionalising a principle which was already extant in the Bourbon era. Further Bourbon characteristics, so to speak, imbued the new idea of political representation: those elected to the Cortes, and to other incumbencies, could not refuse the appointment except for serious personal or health-related reasons, of which the authorities had to be informed. Even the office of deputy was first and foremost a duty to the state, according to principles which were applied to many civil servants elected by *ternas* (short lists) or lots in the Bourbon period, as was the case, for example, with local mayors.

The Cádiz elections were indirect two-tier elections to the Cortes and *Diputaciones* and one-tier elections to the municipal councils, according to the model provided by the French Constitution of 1791. Nevertheless, the definition of the electoral constituency was very different: it was not defined by districts but by parishes, that is to say not by a geometrical concept of territory, but by a communal, social, 'natural' concept, characteristic of the Catholic tradition of natural law, which located society outside the state, as a pre-existing autonomous entity. The point is worth emphasising: although of a modern stamp, the 'iconography' of the Spanish liberals did not break with those absolutely relevant aspects of tradition which were rooted in the mentality of the peoples, both in Spain and in America. In order to qualify for the vote at parish level, aspirants 'must be citizens, over twenty-five years old and resident in the parish' (art. 45); the same prerequisites were necessary, at the next level, for the *electores de partidos*; for that of deputies to the Cortes there was a requirement, in addition, to be in receipt of an annual, private, income (art. 92).

The Constitution excluded different castes from citizenship and from the franchise, but imposed no requirements of literacy at parish level. At the higher level, there was an implicit requirement for literacy because voting was done in writing, whereas in the parish assemblies the vote was public and effected orally.

For the purposes of the present study it is of interest to ascertain the powers of the parish *juntas*. In the first place: what was the actual prerequisite for the vote? The Constitution made a distinction between *Spaniards* and *Spanish citizens*: the former were 'all those men born free and resident *(avecindado)* in the dominions of Spain and their sons' (art. 5); the latter were 'those Spaniards who can by both maternal and paternal lineage trace their origins from the Spanish dominions of both hemispheres, and who are resident in whatsoever community of the same dominions' (art. 18). Further prerequisites can be inferred from the causes which denied citizenship: 'the condition of domestic servant', and 'lack of employment, trade, or an honest livelihood' (art. 25).

In short, in order to vote, a citizen must be settled in a community and be earning an honest living. Two questions arise from this: 'community' *(pueblo)* did not mean simply any settlement in the Hispanic world, but signified an institution with rights and privileges. With regard to having employment, or an honest living, it is clear that eligibility for the vote was based on the classical principle of the individual's reputation within the community. The Cádiz constitution delineated an electoral body which did not correspond to an abstract and universal ideal of citizenship. In order to become a citizen and a voter, it was necessary to be a recognised member of society as organised within territorial institutions, which is to say the *pueblos*. The foundations of liberal representation according to Cádiz were more communitarian, or, it could be argued, associatory, than individual, in that the *pueblo* was a corporation. Notwithstanding the fact that the Cortes of Cádiz destroyed many aspects of the *ancien régime*, the laws of Castile and of the Indies continued to be observed regarding the *pueblos*. Nor did the Constitution include a declaration of the rights of the individual in the French style. This is borne out by the reiteration, in various articles, of the status of *'vecino'*, which constituted the authentic identity of the citizen and the voter. According to tradition, a *vecino* was a head of a family and a landowner. What was the sense of *vecino* in New Spain in 1812? We do not know. The constitution imposed no age-limits, and denied the vote to 'sons of families', who were categorised not by age, but by virtue of their subjugation to *patria potestas* (legal guardianship), with neither trade nor property to their name. It is therefore safe to assume that the authors of the Constitution identified the *'vecino'* with the father of the family.[2] The link between citizenship, voter, local society, was reinforced further by the powers granted to the parish *juntas*, which ruled, without possibility of appeal, on the prerequisites: 'the same *junta* will decide on the instant as it sees fit and its decision will be implemented without any recourse [against it] at this instant and to this sole effect.' (art. 50). This serves as an example of a delimitation that the Constitution imposed upon itself: through the *juntas*, the definition of the electoral college was delegated to the different territorial units which traditionally formed the empire, to a set of different collective codes which the Constitution sanctioned implicitly. As a result, even within an apparently long and inflexible Constitution, the boundary between written norm and collective mentality was manifested as a *continuum*, a link rather than a rupture, between the old and the new order. And since the practices governing voting requirements inhabited this movable boundary between the old and the new, the power of the *juntas vis-à-vis* bureaucracy depended, in America, on the strength and legitimacy enjoyed by the state.

The centralism of the Constitution therefore contained limitations within its very text. The crisis in the colonial state played a key role in the application and interpretation of that article which granted to every community having a minimum of 1,000, or even 500 inhabitants, the right to constitute itself into a town council with constitutional, that is to say, elective, status. In order to assess, at the outset, the prospects that this article opened up, it is appropriate to recall once more that a town was not a settlement but an institution, and that as such it could join with various towns. Furthermore, those who took the final decision as to which people would constitute members of the town were not the authorities but the inhabitants, or rather the inhabitants of a given territory. The true quantitative identity of a town invariably remained a random element, changing according to the interests at work, and this constituted an all-important dimension in the application of the Constitution in New Spain.

The First Elections and the Break-down of the Colonial Town

An early example of what could be expected to occur was the election of the new *cabildo* in the City of Mexico in 1812. From the first it was clear that the vote would be informed by political rather than administrative considerations; the *criollos* triumphed in all the parish elections, resulting in a disagreeable surprise for the authorities. We owe the wealth of information at our disposal to the Viceroy's attempts to cancel the elections, and to the fact that to this end he commissioned a judicial enquiry which left a legacy of data we can use to form a picture of voting practices and the reasons for the break-down of the colonial town. Its structure reflected a society made up of groups and associations, each overshadowed by privileges and immunities, in densely populated and autonomous districts. In 1812, rather than by economic status, residence was still determined by family ties, by professional status and connection with corporations, by the geographical and ethnic origins of the inhabitants.[3] The abortive Bourbon attempt to transform the city into a centralising agency of the state had preserved a social order which had more in common with that of the seventeenth century than with the Enlightenment project. The constitutionalism of Cádiz incorporated this Bourbon concept into its own project.

Formally speaking, the Mexican metropolis was three-dimensional, the administrative, the ecclesiastical, and the Indian dimensions existing on unequal terms. In 1782, the city had been divided into eight larger districts and 32 smaller ones, with the aim of facilitating control over the population, over and above their allegiance to groups, corporations and ethnic communities. Each 'quarter' had a mayor, and his tasks as the 'political father' reveal a clear plan to divest social groups of disciplinary power and to transfer it to the state.[4] Nevertheless, the city notables did not accept their new duties as they had done in Madrid, and the castes appropriated them in order to constitute themselves into a corporation.[5]

The reform of the quarters demonstrated the difficulty of restructuring the metropolis according to the geometric model of enlightenment administration. In the words of one Spanish civil servant, the problem depended on the power of the Church, whose prerogatives over the recoupment of quotas and appointments were such that 'they became inextricably linked with each of the classes which goes to make up the state'. In the parishes, and therefore throughout the whole city, the Crown administration could do nothing without the intervention of the prelates, and 'no-one is unaware of the multitude of positions which the Church can occupy through the parishes, the sacristies and devout works, nor of the blood-ties and other connections exploited by the leading families in order to provide their sons and favourites with careers'.[6] The power of the Church was built on solid material foundations: in 1811 the Church owned 47 per cent of real estate and more than half of the land, largely within the inner city.[7] The most important section of the city was in mortmain and the ecclesiastical charter was more powerful than the bureaucracy of the day.

The identification of the Indian dimension is difficult. The two districts (*parcialidades*) into which the city of Mexico was divided, San Juan Tenochtitlán and Santiago Tlatelolco, constituted a mixture of pre- and post-hispanic peoples, with their distinct quarters and hierarchies: the governor of each *parcialidad* controlled a certain number of district mayors, and these in turn controlled a complex hierarchy of further civil servants, whose jurisdiction even extended to other towns, although, according to Gibson, the two *parcialidades* had, by the end of the eighteenth century, lost most of the rural areas.[8] The old city plan of 1812 no longer made a physical distinction between the white sector and the Indian one because whites and peoples of mixed race and caste had lived for some time within both groups, and in 1772 the distinction between white and Indian parishes had been eliminated. In order to identify the 'authentic' Indian sector, it would be necessary to reconstruct the tax connections, the location of the community funds, and the indigenous *cabildos*.[9] Notwithstanding the fact that we are ignorant of many aspects of the indigenous society of the capital in the days preceding independence, it is probable that it was very different in rural areas: without *calpulli*, with private property which was quite well developed, very commercialised, and predominantly artisan.[10] Furthermore, in 1811, eleven of the fifteen districts counted in a census revealed quite an extended family network, which encouraged kinship ties, together with access to political and religious office.[11]

The first election had the effect of transforming relations between the three political dimensions of the city. To a great extent this depended on the power which the Constitution conferred upon the parish *juntas* in the evaluation of the voting requirements. But who took the decisions? Formally, the Audiencia decided that each electoral table in the outlying areas of each church should be presided over by a member of the old *cabildo*. Nevertheless, the evidence reveals a more complex picture: three of these electoral presidents attested before the Audiencia the full and certain legality of the *juntas*, while the remaining ten affirmed that they had counted upon the declarations of the priests and the ethnic authorities.[12] How was the practice of establishing eligibility to vote determined? First, it is perhaps worth drawing attention to the fact that, although there were various censuses in existence (the last was in 1811), the authorities never thought to use them for the purpose of verifying the legality of the electoral body. There was no article in the Cádiz Constitution, nor any decree in the Cortes, which had taken this possibility into account. As a result there was no existing electoral register. Delegation to the *juntas* was comprehensive. Within this framework, each *junta* was a public representation of parish society. The area around the electoral tables where oral votes were transcribed was covered by an awning, under which were chairs and benches for priests, local notables and ethnic authorities, who decided upon the eligibility of the voters. In reality each electoral *junta* was a small open town council – *cabildo abierto*; this was so much the case that one of its presidents, in recollecting the events, spoke of precisely this, a '*cabildo abierto*', betraying with this usage the 'iconography' of the community.[13] For example: in an 'Indian' parish before 1772, such as Santa María, the table opposite the main square was arranged with three chairs for the priest, the president and the clerk, a bench to the right-hand side for the remaining three clerics and various nobles, a further bench to the left for 'the chief body of the Republic of Indians' (notwithstanding the fact that the Republics had been abolished by the Constitution), and two facing benches for 'the most decent in attendance'.[14] This representation of the estates of the parish community was mirrored in other areas: Santo Tomás, San Pablo, Santa Ana, San Antonio las Huertas, Santa Cruz Acatlán.[15] Moreover, 'ballot papers with the same name' were circulated, according to witnesses, in each of the parishes, and the Audiencia sought to establish how many. In the parishes with an Indian majority, no ballot papers were circulated, nor did they hold a *junta*, properly speaking, because 'the Indians who voted withdrew soon afterwards', 'the majority withdrew immediately after voting'.[16] That is, the Indians voted in accordance with their own customs, and with candidatures manipulated directly by the ethnic authorities.

If the circulation of ballot papers is studied on the basis of the evidence, it is possible to establish that it varies noticeably as a function of ethnic composition and location of parishes, enabling us to identify three forms of circulation. The first corresponds to the most structured Indian dimension, where the circulation was nil, and where, significantly, only clerics and Indian ex-governors were elected.[17] The second is widely disseminated and corresponds to certain parishes with a so-called 'mixed' and fluctuating population, with a strong element of castes, mixed-race peoples and white and Indian artisans, unconnected to ethnic structures or corporations.[18] These were parishes situated in intermediate territory between the native quarters and the central area of the city. Those elected were a cleric and a lawyer in the first parish, two lawyers in the second, a cleric and a lawyer in the third, two clerics in the fourth, one cleric in the fifth, a lawyer and a cleric in the sixth. The third method by which ballot papers were circulated was less rigorous, and was used in the large white parish of Sagrario which occupied virtually all of the inner city, and in three medium-sized parishes within it, of which only one (Salto del Agua) contained native areas. Sagrario, by virtue of having the most inhabitants, selected four *electores*: a canon of the cathedral and a former *criollo* judge (*Oidor*) of the Audiencia, a theologian and a lawyer of distinguished family. The remaining parishes elected two clerics who practised law, one military officer, another cleric and two lay members. Ballot papers were circulated within Sagrario, exclusively with reference to the former *Oidor*.[19]

The data arising from the judicial enquiry demonstrates that lawyers were elected in parishes with the greatest circulation of ballot papers, where the population showed greater social and ethnic variations. The clerics, in contrast, were elected in a relatively consistent fashion, but outside the inner city. The ascendancy in political and electoral terms of the dual concept of lawyer-priest was posited on the existence of a multi-ethnic and mixed social dimension, rather than one characterised by corporations. These figures have frequently been presented as an 'intermediate stratum' in the colony which, by virtue of the crisis and the early liberal experience, succeeded in consolidating itself politically. But Humboldt's statistics reveal that the composition of this 'stratum' was very limited: 517 lawyers and 171 secular clergy.[20] Possibly, a more realistic approach would be to speak of corporations, which as a result of electoral processes, and civil wars, acquired a political weight which outweighs their social composition. Lawyers and clerics did not constitute the 'third estate' which was imposed as a result of the mechanisms of the new form of representation. Moreover, we must bear in mind that their status as the clientèle of the Church and the elite classes, their family dependency upon and indebtedness towards these groups, limited to a great extent the political autonomy of this supposed 'intermediate layer'. In the case of the city of Mexico these limits were even more in evidence: when in April 1813 the voters in the parishes gathered to elect the new town council, they designated eleven landowners, five merchants, and two former Indian governors.[21] None of them, including the two former Indian governors, had been an *elector*, and with the exception of these, all of the remainder evidently lived in Sagrario. In the city of Mexico the new elections in the liberal mould offered an opportunity to lawyers and clerics, but within the bounds of the existing social hierarchies.

The most striking political outcome of these elections was the exclusion of the powerful Spanish merchant corporation which monopolised trade with the Peninsula (the Consulado) and which sustained direct contacts with the Spanish liberals of the constituent body of Cádiz through the Cádiz Diputación. In May of 1811 a secret representation had been sent from Mexico to the Regency, attacking the rights of the *criollos* with all the rhetoric on American inferiority which had been propagated in Europe for a century.[22] In November of the same year the Mexican Diputación had despatched an agent to Cádiz with a handsome sum of money and an assignment to defend the representation thesis.[23] When it became evident, after the elections in the parishes were over, that the Spaniards were not going to secure a place in the new town council, the Viceroy Calleja, in advance of the meeting of the voters in April, sought without success the mediation of the bishop in favour of the members of the Consulado.[24]

There is no doubt about the political significance of the vote, because it formalised the crisis in the colonial regime, on a public level. It is worth pausing to reflect, nevertheless, upon the processes which were unleashed within the social organisation and throughout the urban areas. We have already drawn attention to the high (and unprecedented) level of freedom which the very text of the Constitution of Cádiz had conferred upon the parish *juntas* regarding the criteria used to determine eligibility to vote. Perhaps the most important implication was that the *juntas* would determine the legality of the electoral body, without the intervention of the state, which thwarted the Audiencia's attempts to nullify the vote. This failure was political rather than juridical: the Audiencia could not use the censuses to corroborate the profile of the voters *a posteriori*. In addition, when it *was* attempted, it was clear that the censuses carried out by the Bourbon state registered a very different number of inhabitants from those registered in the parish congregations managed by the priests. In this case the numbers depended upon a kind of joint approach to the two different types of census. In December 1812 the Audiencia had gathered together the 17 books of hearings of the electoral *juntas* with the 31 ledgers registering the names of voters. In January the priests of each parish submitted their data. This resulted in a population figure which was 40 per cent smaller than that which had figured in the census of the previous year conducted by the quarters.[25] The point is that the quarters included in their census thousands of lepers and a fluctuating population which had escaped from the rebellion, but it is precisely this fact which demonstrates the degree to which numbers masked differing concepts of what constituted a '*población*': that of the parishes was a social grouping, and therefore a *vecindad*; that of the 1811 census emanated from the public administration. And the constitution made reference to the *vecindad* in its definition of citizenship. The failure of the authorities governing the capital provides clear evidence that the concept of citizenship derived from Cádiz.

A further fact which remains to be examined is that the distribution of *electores* who were actually elected across the parish and the circulation of ballot papers, demonstrate a marked degree of autonomy in the social, cultural and ethnic dimensions within the city. This autonomy was consolidated by virtue of the indirect electoral system, which in turn reinforced the social hierarchies. The Constitution did not prohibit *electores* from, in turn, being elected to the councils; nevertheless the witnesses spoke of ballot papers with the names of *electores*, not of future members of the town councils. It follows from this that two practices governing candidatures were in operation, at different times and in different places. The dual nature of the vote thus set in train two processes: it drew together the leaders of each socially organised group, and lent the social hierarchies a new political legitimacy. The Cádiz ballot did not throw the corporate organisation of society into crisis, but rather relocated it within a new institutional framework.

The political legitimacy which the vote conferred upon socially organised groups had a considerable effect upon the course of the crisis in the colonial regime. The *criollos* took control of the cities, while the ballot also equipped the indigenous population with a new weapon with which to defend their interests. The Constitution had abolished the

Republics of Indians, but the right for any town with a minimum of 500 inhabitants to constitute itself into a town council gave the indigenous communities an opportunity to administer their assets within a new constitutional framework. This was the belief of the governors of the suppressed *parcialidades* of San Juan Tenochtitlán and Santiago Tlatelolco in Mexico city itself: in May 1820 'the governors, mayors, and other members of the groups' requested the Viceroy that the community funds (*cajas de la comunidad*) remain untouched until the two groups establish their respective constitutional councils. They justified their petition as follows:

> for it is so demanded by all those who constitute these and sundry other groups under the incumbency of the present town council, for we do not wish to suffer the same misfortune as in earlier times, now that we have recourse to the protection granted to us by the Political Constitution of the Monarchy; and in this respect, aspiring, as we solely do, to the retention, increase, security and custody of monies which are the property of our peoples, intended exclusively and solely for the purposes signalled by that learned Code, it would now accord with that same Code that the transfer be effected not merely with our consent, but that the accounts should first be rendered up to us so that, by effecting such audits and calculations as our knowledge of the case demands, Your Excellency, or the Provincial Diputación, having sight of all these things, should mete out such apportionment as you see fit.[26]

The attempt was unsuccessful as a result of opposition from the town council of the capital. Nevertheless, the precedent, with all that it implied, had been set: the indigenous peoples did not remain passive in the face of the liberal transition; they went so far as to contemplate the division of the city into three councils, one to be composed of whites and two of Indians. This would suggest that the sense of belonging to the 'city' did not exist among the indigenous people, a further reason to examine what was signified by the colonial 'city'. Nevertheless, what the indigenous communities failed to achieve in the capital became possible in the rural towns when the ballot had been extended.

The Local Revolution: the Municipal 'Sovereignty' of the Towns

First, it is worth drawing attention to certain figures: the correspondence of the sub-delegates and the governors allows us to estimate the existence of a total of 630 new elective councils in New Spain in 1820. Once again it is important to stress the limited number of colonial *cabildos*. Even taking into account the proliferation of indigenous *cabildos* in the Republics, one revolutionary aspect stands out: under the new constitutional regime all the councils were equal. The territorial distribution of the new councils is therefore significant:

Administrative Divisions	New Councils
Veracruz	6
Zacatecas	13
Guanajuato	15
Tlaxcala	42
México	85
Valladolid	90
Puebla	172
Oaxaca	200

Certain administrative divisions are omitted, and it is clear that the figures are not definitive, but rather those which are currently available in the archives. Notwithstanding this, it is obvious that the ballot was extended in greater measure to the Indian territories. This fact at once poses at least three difficulties. The first is how to explain such a massive extension in the few years during which the Constitution had been applied. As has already been pointed out, the explanation can be found in the minutes of the Electoral *Junta* of New Spain, and in the correspond-ence of the Viceroys Calleja and Apodaca. The *Junta* was composed of the Viceroy, the Archbishop of Mexico, two *criollo* notables and the *Intendente* of Mexico, and it was responsible for the organisation of the elections. There is no doubt that it was the colonial authorities which brought about the elections in the towns in order to cordon off insurgency by political means. The aim was to grant autonomy and self-government, the classic aspirations of the towns, and, as we shall see, this decision accelerated the crisis in the regime. Calleja was a ferocious anti-liberal, but he expedited the elections in spite of the opposition of the Audiencia, which, at the very moment the first election in Mexico City was over, despatched a lengthy, secret report to the Regency, requesting that the Constitution be suspended in the Viceroyalty.[27] In an apparently paradoxical sense, the imperial crisis had an important hand in bringing about the first experience of elections in Mexico: between 1812 and 1814 the problem was the rebels; in 1820-21, when the Constitution had been restored in Spain and America was just one step away from emancipation, liberalism was the last resort of the Peninsula if they were not to lose all. This was the sentiment expressed by the Minister of War in Madrid in a letter to the Viceroy Apodaca in the September of 1821:

> His Majesty is firmly persuaded that once Your Excellency is placed in command of this army and at the head of this province, nothing will remain to be done to appease the spirits of the Americans: by uniting the common vote under the powerful influence of civil liberty.[28]

And thus another of what may be termed the 'paradoxes of Cádiz' is that the first experience of liberalism in Mexico was neither encouraged nor controlled by the *criollo* elites. They accepted the experience, used it and were even divided over it, but the impetus derived from the colonial authorities. And since this was no superficial experience, the fact that the leadership was out of step with the phenomenon itself, signalled a significant challenge for the future governability of the republic.

The second problem posed by the quantity and territorial distribution of the new town councils is the perception of them in the communities. Did the ballot and constitutional values disrupt the 'iconography' of the communities? The answer is that they did not, that there was no discontinuity. The dissemination of the Cádiz Constitution was not based upon a new type of social gathering or collective representation. The only new symbol was the name of the main squares in the towns and cities: *Constitution Square (Plaza de la Constitución)*. The state of civil war undoubtedly had an influence, but it is important to bear in mind two points: the Cortes or parliament did not develop an organic plan for a new political iconography, though this does not mean that no changes took place. The role played by books and pamphlets in America as much as in Spain has been emphasised with some justification.[29] Nevertheless, this kind of change did not of itself affect the whole of society. To attain such an aim, an initiative which would bring images into play would be necessary, and this presupposes a dynamic function in the exercise of political power, as suggested by the now classical studies of the French revolution.[30] A further aspect of no lesser importance is the use of images in modern politics presupposes a level of secularisation sufficiently well advanced to guarantee the visibility *per se* of the change in values. What is lacking in the Cádiz experience overall, and not merely in Mexico, is precisely this aspect. The Cádiz Constitution did not advance secularisation. It provided for the confiscation of property held in mortmain and the abolition of ecclesiastical exemptions and privileges. But these measures already figured in the ideological programme of the enlightened reformists of absolutism. They did not signal *per se* a will to secularise society, which is quite another proposition. These measures could coexist with the religious prerogative of intolerance towards any religion other than Catholicism. And it is well known that the Cádiz Constitution reaffirmed precisely this principle. Possibly this position on the part of the Spanish (Catholic) liberals explains the lack of enthusiasm for a new political iconography.

However, a programmed ritual did exist for the divulgation of the Constitution: the oath and the act of *publication*. As was the case for that part of the Constitution bearing upon elections, these two formal acts reveal even more to us about the bonds between the old and the new experience of Cádiz. The Cortes attempted to destroy the privileges, but did not attack the idea that society was constituted into natural entities. Perhaps for a French liberal of the day privileges and corporations were one and the same thing, but for a Spanish liberal there was a fundamental distinction to be made: there was a place for the former in the political sphere, and not for the latter, for these formed part of 'natural' society, which was pre-state, according to the legacy of the Catholic tradition of natural law. The ordinances sent to New Spain by the Cortes leave no room for doubt: the Constitution had to be sworn in by the corporations: lawyers, officials, doctors, artisans, universities, administrative offices, the Audiencìa itself, etc., and this is in effect what was done. The basis of the act was totally religious, the rite was no different from the past tradition of swearing oaths: at the centre of the scene, the Cádiz Constitution was laid out upon a table next to a crucifix, a copy of the New Testament, a candle, and very often a picture of the king – no new symbols. The traditional nature of the oath raises the problematic question of which type of obligation was at the heart of the Constitution: whether it was classic Hispanic contractualism or the modern bond founded on the notion of will. A recent study has emphasised convincingly how the transformation of the oath in Western constitutionalism perfectly expresses progress towards the secularisation of political obligation.[31] It seems acceptable to express certain doubts about the Cádiz case, particularly if we examine the sense of the word *publication*. The term is not new, it belongs to the tradition of the *ancien régime* and denotes the ritual act by means of which the king made a public representation of his domain, as something superior *vis-à-vis* his subjects, and as something totally different from what is considered to be the modern public sphere.[32]

A discussion of what is 'modern' in the Constitution of Cádiz falls outside the scope of the present study,[33] which aims rather to locate this text as critically as possible within its historical framework, which is an era of changes, but not of rupture at any cost, of aspirations to what was a difficult balance between the old and the new, and which is the most familiar facet of the Hispanic revolutions. Even more so in the light of an evaluation, such as this one, of the perceptions of the text held by the collective protagonists, the towns of New Spain.

Why, then, do we consider that the advent of the Constitution in the towns did not modify the collective iconography? In their letters to the higher authorities, the sub-delegates describe the swearing-in and *publication* ceremonies of the Constitution which were held in the towns. They were in every aspect similar to the traditional community festivals, with Mass, three days of *tianguis* (the Indian market), pealing of bells, rockets, street serenades, and different processions. Among these the 'Constitution procession' stands out: after Mass, during which the priest praised the text, a copy of the Constitution was carried along, physically, on the shoulders of the bearers. The parade followed the corporate organisation of the town: after the Constitution, the clerics, the sub-delegate together with the army chiefs, the 'respectable *vecinos*', the 'chief body of the Republic' (in spite of having been abolished), and finally the *vecindad*, organised into its *cofradías* (lay brotherhoods organised through some church or monastery) and their banners.[34] It is not difficult to imagine that in the towns the text was perceived outside of its cultural autonomy: it was something new, but well integrated into the symbolic communication codes of local tradition. To a certain degree, it was precisely the newness of the 'learned code' which consolidated the legitimacy of the tradition. We know nothing of the ceremonies in Spain, but in New Spain the circumstance of civil war coupled with the authorities' option in favour of the Constitution ensured that the text would be divulged with the official sanction of all the leading powers, ecclesiastical and civil and military. The first liberal charter was not divulged in the midst of open ideological conflict, but it provoked such conflict, which in the first instance could not be made manifest.

The third problem posed by the extent to which new councils became widespread is the possible links between old and new offices. Was there a connection between the hierarchies elected on the basis of the Constitution, and the older ones, which governed the communities, for instance the offices of the *cofradías*? The importance of the question is obvious: since Cádiz had suppressed the Indian Republics – although everyone continued to speak of them – the community assets remained unprotected. If a town succeeded in installing an elective council, it had the possibility of recreating jurisdiction over the assets, by placing them under the category of *'propios'*, that is, belonging to the town. The case of the City of Mexico, which we have cited, demonstrates that this was effectively the intention of the ethnic authorities. Nevertheless, the documentary evidence to date on the connection between the offices is limited. A further question arises from the Oaxaca case: of the 200 Cádiz town councils, 117 had been subject, before 1812, to 'head towns' (*cabeceras*). In Oaxaca there were 90 republics.[35] Although it is impossible to determine the location, the spread of the new *juntas* at least raises the doubt that the Constitution could foster a new phase of fragmentation and re-grouping of the communities under new *cabeceras*, and therefore that after this process there emerged a new layer of chief administrators.

There is no easy answer to these questions, but it *is* possible to develop an hypothesis within the framework of the most important process documented by (available) sources: the spread of councils caused a radical transfer of competences, provoking a crisis throughout colonial rule. The case of the Metepec district in the Intendencia of Mexico is a good illustration of this process. It was the biggest of the districts in the Intendencia: 111 kilometres long and 67 wide. By the middle of the eighteenth century, it had 36 republics representing approximately 300 towns (*pueblos sujetos*), according to Villaseñor and Sánchez.[36]

When the Constitution was implemented, an event occurred which was well described by the sub-delegate in a letter to the Governor on 15 July 1820. In commenting upon the fact that the 'pure' Indians (that is to say from the Republic) of the town of San Lorenzo Huitzilapa had decided there was no reason why the number of *regidores* from the new town council should be proportionate to the 'inhabitants', the sub-delegate painted a very clear picture: *'because these towns wish to be on a par with the city of Toluca, they compare a town with the capitals'.*[37] Toluca was a few kilometres from the district of Metepec and, although it had no *cabildo* in the pre-constitutional era, it was one of the largest towns in the Intendencia. In 1820, the Indians of a much smaller town such as San Lorenzo, decided that the number of *regidores* should be almost, if not exactly, equal to those in the town council of Toluca, and according to the sub-delegate this was not an isolated example. What is the explanation for this voluntary and wholesale transgression of the constitutional norm? The perception of the sub-delegate was inaccurate: in reality the Indians had no interest in 'being on a par with the city', the decision to increase the numbers of *regidores* rested on a concern expressed very clearly by another town, that of Santiago Tlacotepec, when they wrote to the Diputación requesting the installation of a town council:

it should also be borne in mind that all the inhabitants of the *cabecera* as of those others cited speak the mazahual language, thus rendering their prosperity and welfare difficult to oversee, and it is for this reason that the town council should be installed . . . furthermore, the distance of three leagues from Santiago to San Mateo Atenco, where there is a town council . . . all of this would be eased with the installation of a town council in Santiago where with the remaining towns they can proceed to the election of an individual to the aforementioned corporation, from each place, respectively.[38]

The second section of the quotation reveals to us the principle which most probably obtained in the case of many Indian constitutional town councils: the new model of representation was bound to respect one principle of the former model of the republics, that is to say that each indigenous town council should have *regidores* from each town in the territory. Thus, the new liberal model began to be adapted to local values, to the great outrage of the sub-delegates, but with the tacit approval of the higher authorities.

San Miguel Almoloya del Río reveals yet another overlapping element of key significance. As is well known, in the towns of New Spain whites and Indians often co-existed. In San Miguel there were, in 1820, between 600 and 700 *vecinos*, three-quarters of whom were Indian, and one quarter Spanish and castes, distributed across nine small towns and a few villages and districts. In March of 1820 the sub-delegate reported that:

in the *junta de vecinos* in which by common agreement it was decided that two mayors should be nominated, one Spanish and one Indian, each separate from the other in their respective residential districts; one *regidor* to each of the districts so that to immediate effect, and with all haste, they should administer justice in their respective towns, reporting to their mayors as necessary.[39]

And so it was that two mayors, eleven *regidores*, and one *síndico procurador* were elected, which is to say a number of members almost equal to those of the council of Mexico City. This example is relevant to our study because it reveals once again that the new abstract concept of '*habitantes*', as a purely numerical identity, was not accepted by the whites either. On the other hand, we know that the duplication of representative organs where whites and Indians co-existed was a widespread practice in the colonial institutions, such as, for example, in the mixed *cofradías*. As was the case in Santiago Tlacotepec, in San Miguel the new Constitution was interpreted on the basis of the values and practices of local society. However, in the case of San Miguel, the sub-delegate's letter clearly indicates how the new idea of sovereignty was gradually being consolidated in the town councils, because in the small towns the *regidores* were to administer justice, something which was not entirely foreseen by the Constitution of Cádiz.

With the spread of elective councils in the rural areas, there was, therefore, a transfer of powers from the state apparatus to the new organs. Possibly the political circumstances of the day facilitated this process. There is no doubt that what played a major role in it was the failure to implement a major part of the Constitution: the reform of the judicial machinery provided for in a decree of the Cortes or parliament in 1813, which, by removing two of the four functions of the viceroys, governors and sub-delegates, foresaw a new system of judges in both the civil and criminal domains. In 1820 this decree was implemented in New Spain, when the crisis was entering its final phase, and in the absence of financial resources. The result was that when Independence dawned there were only six new judges while the remaining authorities in effect lost two of their four functions.[40] In this context, the new town councils appropriated the judicial function, which represents perhaps the most radical rupture with the Cádiz experience, bearing in mind what the exercise of justice signified for the collective mentality within a multi-ethnic society of the *ancien régime*, such as was the New Spain of the day. The Catholic monarchy succeeded for three centuries in securing the loyalty of the Indians through tolerance in the practice of justice. Terms such as 'impotence' and 'corruption' may be and often have been used, but what is certain is that for the Indians and the *criollos* the weakness of the Crown was always perceived as a signal to practise justice according to local codes. The Bourbon reforms attempted to consolidate the authority of the state to a greater degree, and it is well-known that the outcome of this was the countless rebellions against 'despotism' occurring towards the end of the eighteenth century. The principle of devolution of sovereignty, demanded by the provincial councils in 1808 after the dynastic crisis, legitimised the autonomist tradition in the field of justice too, since one of the characteristics of sovereignty was precisely justice. The Cádiz councils in the towns, and the impossibility of implementing the decree of 1813, produced even more significant consequences: they expedited the territorial fragmentation of the attributes of sovereignty. The process was clear in 1820, it became more radical during the Iturbide period, and significantly, went hand in hand with the loss of the government's power to recoup taxes. There was always a close relationship between the administration of justice and that of taxes. The spread of the elective councils sustained this link, and in a certain sense institutionalised it, but in the teeth of the state, because on acquiring the opportunity and the necessity to cover their own costs, the new elective organs created a tax filter between the central government and the land, monopolising the contributions. In Metepec, there were even town councils which requested the removal of the four functions from the sub-delegate, and one civil servant alerted the Intendente:

> as the constitutional mayor is exercising all of the functions, and as I am now a *vecino*, I duly protest that neither I myself nor my guarantors are responsible for the levy.[41]

Conflicts and complaints of this kind occurred throughout the whole of New Spain. The explanation is that the decree of 1813 on the reform of the tribunals contained an article (art. 7 of chap. 4) which foresaw the possibility that:

> until such time as there is no distribution of the appropriate judges of the district, then the cases and civil and criminal proceedings will continue in the domain of Judges appointed by the Crown, Sub-delegates, and the constitutional mayors of the towns.[42]

Notwithstanding this, in 1820, when the Constitution was restored, and in the throes of imperial crisis, a further decree of the Cortes or parliament sanctioned the interim jurisdiction of the constitutional mayors, solely in the area of litigation. Juridically, the situation was clear, but the real outcome was quite different, because the town councils appropriated all of the prerogatives in the area of justice. It is important to emphasise the fact that in the context of a juridical solution pointing to a joint administration of justice, the real outcome was a conflict betwen old and new jurisdictions. As has already been noted, the town councils, according to the constitutional project of Cádiz, had no remit to become political organs, and even less self-governing bodies, and nevertheless this is exactly what occurred. By means of the elective councils the towns secured a form of self-government which was possibly unprecedented: power over taxes, justice, communal assets, and, where relevant, soldiery. The practices of self-government created a new jurisdiction, which had not been provided for in the Constitution. But the result of this great change in the territorial hierarchies was that in New Spain the separation of powers did not develop at local level.

Conclusions

Our analysis evidently leaves many questions unanswered, chiefly those which bear upon the indigenous communities. As always, we must bear in mind the variations in local circumstances. For example, in her classic study Nancy Farriss indicated that in Yucatán the elections of the new councils favoured the peoples of mixed race, who succeeded in monopolising the offices of mayor. The documentation of the Diputación Provincial of New Spain, which refers to the territory of the former Audiencia of Mexico, and to that of the remaining sections of the General National Archive, demonstrates that in many places the Indian Republics were transformed into town councils, in such a way that the Indians had access to all of the offices.

A further problem of considerable importance, as already indicated, is the possible link between the system of former offices and that of the new, since the new town councils administered the assets of the communities. There are few sources available on this subject: for Metepec we have discovered four cases out of 13 councils: San Jerónimo Amanalco, Santiago Tianguistengo, San Mateo Atenco, Santa María Atlacomulco.[43] In these towns there was a double election when the new town council was established: the first for the *regidores* outside the church, the second inside the church for the purpose of electing the stewards (*mayordomos*) of the *cofradías*. In the first three cases *regidores* were elected to the offices of stewards, and in the fourth a steward was elected *regidor*. In San Mateo a 'citizen's pact' was stipulated for the purpose of moderating the resources of the *cofradías*. In a further case, Santa María Atlacomulco, the priest opposed the town council's control of the *cofradías*, and wrote to the Intendente to protest that the *cofradías* and the town councils belonged to different areas of jurisdiction. The Intendente openly passed the complaint to the mayor, who responded to the bishop to the effect that the *cofradías* of his town had no constitution, and therefore came under the aegis of the civil domain. The case of Santa María is not the only one; many sub-delegates complained in their letter to the authorities, that between 1820 and 1821, the town councils 'amassed assets'.

Notwithstanding the limited scope of our present study, it would appear that the theme of the elections under the Cádiz regime is of great interest for three reasons. First, it is fairly clear that the dissemination of the new model of liberal representation in New Spain deepened the general crisis in the colonial system, while at the same time transforming it to such a degree that it bequeathed a difficult legacy to the republican elites, one which can only be defined as 'colonial' in a partial sense. It was, rather, a legacy formed during the years of crisis in the colony, and which reinforced the rural areas, by virtue of the inter-relationship between the liberal electoral model and the values of the peoples. This type of legacy, in the second place, changed the terms of the liberal problem in republican Mexico: the great problem of the elites was not how to disseminate the liberal model, for this was a consummated fact which had occurred before independence and without the protagonism of the *criollos*. The real problem would be how to ensure that the model for liberal representation would serve to invert the tendency towards territorial fragmentation, towards local autonomy, in order to consolidate political power at the centre. The real problem would, in other words, continue to be that of 1808: where does sovereignty reside? This leads us to the third question: the conflict and tensions between town councils (*pueblos/ayuntamientos*) and governments would not manifest itself, as at times depicted by the elites, in terms of a constitutionalised minority and a constitutionalised majority. The conflict would occur within a single domain, but with different practices and values, equally legitimate in the perception of the protagonists. The force of this double legitimacy would be so powerful that it would never come under official attack, as is proved by recent studies on so-called 'popular liberalism' in Mexico.[44]

Finally, many studies have indicated that in the formative stages of the modern nation-state, one of the crucial cleavages which must be overcome is that between centre and periphery. This first attempt to analyse the Cádiz experience in Mexico suggests that the cleavages which were forged through the course of the colonial crisis were two: not solely, as is well-known, that which throughout the nineteenth century set the province-states against the capital within a federal framework, but that which caused each capital within each province-state to suffer the problem of how to conduct its relations with the town councils, which continued to claim their 'sovereignty' right up to the Mexican revolution. From this a further question arises: how many types of federalism existed in Mexico after the break-down of the colony?

Notes

1. Quoted in M. Bellingeri, 'Conflictos y dispersión de poderes en Yucatán (1780-1831)', in A. Annino and R. Buve (coord.), *El liberalismo en México*, Cuadernos de Historia Latinoamericana, no. 1 (Hamburg, 1993), p. 74.
2. The Madrid Council of State in a meeting of 28 April 1820 when the constitution was restored, calculated the number of American voters and

judged that there were 2 million 'fathers of families', Archivo General de Indias, Indiferente General, Sec, V. exp. 1523.

3. M. Dolores Morales, 'Estructura urbana y distribución de la propiedad en la ciudad de México in 1813', *Historia Mexicana*, vol. 25 (Jan-Mar 1976), pp. 363-402. With the same title, the same author published a more detailed version of this analysis of the 1813 census in A. Moreno Toscano (comp.), *Ciudad de México, ensayo de construcción de una historia*, INAH, Col. científica, no. 63 (1978), pp. 71-107.

4. It was necessary to ensure that there were sufficient teachers and doctors, to send the poor to the hospice and the sick to hospital, to suppress vagabondage, to send the young to work with 'well-known' employers, to offer weaving to poor women, to oversee prices and the movements of the common people, compile a register of *vecinos*, act as judge in marital conflicts, supervise the condition of the pavements, collaborate in the levying of taxes. Each of the mayors (*alcades mayores y menores*) would have carried a staff and have enjoyed criminal and civil legal privileges (*fueros*). See the *Ordenanza de la Nobilísima Ciudad de México en cuarteles, creación de las alcaldías de ellos y regia de su gobierno, dada y mandada observar por el Exmo Señor Don Miguel de Mayaga* (Mexico, 1782).

5. Archivo Antiguo Ayuntamiento, *Policía en general*, vol. 3627, exp. 43, f.8.

6. Ladrón de Guevara, 'Discurso sobre la policía en México', in S. Lombardo Ruiz, *Antología de textos sobre la ciudad de México en el período de la Ilustración (1777-1792)*, INAH, Colección científica, no. 113 (1982), p. 103.

7. A. Lavrin, 'La riqueza de los conventos de monjas en Nueva España; estructura y evolución durante el siglo XVIII', *Cahiers des Amériques Latines*, no. 2 (1973), p. 100. This work demonstrates that half of Church property in 1813 belonged to the convents, but that it was negligible during the previous century, and therefore much of the Church's wealth deriving from landed property had been accrued during the Bourbon period.

8. C. Gibson, *Los aztecas bajo el dominio español 1519-1810* (Mexico, 1967), pp. 372-412.

9. The problem is a complex one because the location of the community funds did not necessarily correspond to the location of the towns and districts, as has been demonstrated by A. Lira, *Comunidades indígenas frente a la ciudad de México. Tenochtitlán, Tlatelolco, sus pueblos, sus barrios, 1812-1919* (Mexico, 1983), Appendix 3.

10. Gibson, *Los aztecas bajo el dominio español*.

11. G. Brun Martínez, 'Las razas y la familia en la ciudad de México en 1811', in A. Moreno Toscano, *Ciudad de México*, pp. 113-23.

12. Archivo General de la Nación de México (AGNM), *Dictamen de la audiencia al Virrey Vanegas del 8 de enero 1813*, Historia, vol. 443, exp.14.

13. AGNM, *Francisco de Urrutia al Intendente Gutiérrez del Maso, 13 de enero de 1813*, cit. exp. 22, f.40.

14. *Ibid.*

15. AGNM, for San Pablo, *Juan Antonio Cobian al Intendente Gutiérrez del Maso, 13 de enero 1813;* for Santa Ana, *Antonio Menéndez Prieto al . . . ,*

12 de enero 1813; for Santo Tomás, *Juan Cervantes y Padilla al . . . ,*
12 de enero 1813; for San Antonio las Huertas, *Augustín del Rivero al . . . ,*
18 de enero 1813; cit. exp. 17, f. 35; exp.15f. 35; exp. 13, f. 31; exp. 25, f. 43.
16. *Augustín del Rivero . . . cit.*; *Juan Cervantes y Padilla . . . cit.*
17. For example, in Santa Ana, to the north of the city, which took in all of the
districts of the Santiago Tlatelolco *parcialidad*, where only one *elector* was
selected, the Indians voted *en bloc* for the priest of the same parish, Ignacio
Sanches Hidalgo. In San Antonio las Huertas the Indians voted mostly for
the Count of Jala [Conde de Jala], a cleric, and son of the famous Count of
Regla [Conde de Regla].
18. According to J. González Angulo Aguirre, *Artesanado y ciudad a finales del
siglo XVIII* (Mexico, 1980), pp. 180 *et seq.*, in the last colonial period there
were very real signs of a progressive crisis in the artisan associations of the
City of Mexico due to the increase in independent and free producers of
goods, a phenomenon apparently tolerated by the authorities.
19. AGNM, *Resumen de las secciones de la parroquia del Sagrario de los votos
que sacaron los 4 electores que eligieron a los feligreses de ella,* Historia,
vol. 447, exp. 4, f. 61; *El Intendente Gutiérrez del Maso al Virrey
Vanegas, 11 de enero 1813, ibid.*, exp. 10, ff. 6-7.
20. A. V. Humboldt, *Ensayo Político sobre Nueva España* (Mexico, 1965), p.
123.
21. L. Alamán, *Historia de México desde los primeros movimientos que
prepararon la Independencia en el año 1808 hasta la época presente,*
México, 1850, 5 vols. Tomo 3, Apéndice, doc. n. 10. ed. facs. (Mexico,
1985).
22. *Representación del consulado de México al Rey Don Fernando Séptimo el 27
de mayo de 1811,* Biblioteca Nacional de Madrid, Sección manuscritos,
Fondo América, f. 404.
23. AGNM, *Operaciones de Guerra,* tomo 31, f. 96.
24. T. Anna, *La caída del gobierno español en Ciudad de México* (Mexico,
1979), p. 185.
25. In its *Dictamen* of 1 April the Audiencia speaks of incomprehensible
figures. Our own calculation on the basis of information submitted by the
priests reveals a population, registered in the parishes, of 78,572
individuals. The census of the recently constituted Council of Police and
Public Order had estimated 168,811 persons in 1811. The discrepancy in
the figures may also result from the fact that in 1811 the city was invaded
by thousands of refugees who were fleeing from the rebels. In 1813 there
was a serious epidemic in the city which caused more than 20,000 deaths.
See K.A. Davis, 'Tendencias demográficas urbanas durante el siglo XIX en
México', in Moreno Toscano, *Ciudad de México*, pp. 372-412.
26. Archivo de la Diputación Provincial de Nueva España (ADPNE), vol. 1,
1820, exp. 17.
27. The entire text was published by J. Delgado, *La Audiencia de México ante
la rebelión de Hidalgo y el estado de Nueva España* (Madrid, 1984).
28. AGNM, *Operaciones de Guerra,* vol. 920, exp. 2
29. F.-X. Guerra, *Modernidad e Independencias* (Madrid, 1992), pp. 227–69.
30. We refer here to M. Ozouf's well-known work, *La fête révolutionnaire,
1789-1799* (Paris, 1976).

31. P. Prodi, *Il sacramento del potere. Il giuramento politico nella storia costituzionale dell'Occidente* (Bologna, 1992).
32. This distinction has been emphasised by J. Habermas, *Strukturwandel der Oeffentlichkeit,* Nuewied, 1962, trad. ital. *Storia e critica dell'opinione pubblica* (Bari, 1971), p. 17.
33. See chapter 2.
34. AGNM, *Operaciones de Guerra,* vols. 30 and 31.
35. AGNM, *Gobernación,* caja [box] 13, 1821-22, E-7, exp. 27. This fact is to be found in a letter of March 1822, from the Governor of Oaxaca to the Emperor Iturbide: 500,000 inhabitants, 930 towns, 200 town councils, 20 *cabeceras de partido,* and 90 republics, notwith-standing the abolition, in the Constitution, of the latter.
36. Villaseñor y Sánchez, *Theatro americano, descripción general de los reynos y provincias de la Nueva España, y sus jurisdicciones* (Mexico, 1748), pt. 2a, chap. 13. This text by Villaseñor is the last which enumerates the republics. The census of the Viceroy Revillagigedo of 1793-94 considers only the towns, and not the republics.
37. AGNM, *Operaciones de Guerra,* vol. 393, 1821, Gutiérrez del Maso, exp. 123.
38. AGNM, *ibid.,* exp., 125.
39. AGNM, *ibid.,* exp., 134.
40. *Exposición de la diputación provincial de Puebla sobre los males de Nueva España,* in J. H. Hernández y Dávalos (ed.), *Colección de documentos para la historia de la guerra de independencia de México* (6 vols., Mexico, 1877-82), vol. V, doc. 158, pp. 550-3.
41. AGNM, *Historia,* vol. 435, exp. 32.
42. AGNM, *Historia,* vol. 404, 1820, f. 80.
43. AGNM, Operaciones de Guerra, vol. 393, 1821, Gutiérrez del Maso, f. 125.
44. G. Thomson, 'Popular aspects of liberalism in Mexico', *Bulletin of Latin American Research,* vol. 10 (1991), pp. 265-92.

CHAPTER 4

THE ELECTORAL REFORMS OF 1861 IN ECUADOR
AND THE RISE OF A NEW POLITICAL ORDER

Juan Maiguashca

Ecuador became an independent nation in 1830. Its first constitution declared that its government would be: 'popular, representative, alternative and accountable'.[1] It was only in 1978, however, that the seventeenth constitution of the country abolished the literacy requirement, thus permitting the bulk of the Ecuadorean population to elect governments which were, in principle at least, truly popular, representative, alternative and accountable. In the century and a half that elapsed between these two dates, there took place a struggle between those who wanted to restrict the system of representation in one way or another and those who worked to expand it. Of the many clashes perhaps the most interesting and decisive of all was that which took place in 1861. Very little however has been written on the subject and that which exists is in need of revision.[2]

There are two interpretations of the electoral reforms of 1861. According to one the reforms were brought into being by an emerging bourgeoisie. According to the other they were put together by the traditional highland landlords.[3] But they both agree that the reforms were used to defend and advance the narrow interests of their proponents, which constituted a tiny section of the population. However, recent empirical research on Ecuadorean economic history and the study of primary sources which have not been used as yet permits us to question these interpretations and to make the following two assertions. The first is that the reforms of 1861 were fundamentally the initiative of the Ecuadorean state, not that of privileged social groups; and the second is that these reforms made a crucial contribution to Ecuadorean political development.

Some preliminary remarks are in order. In current Ecuadorean and Latin American historiography it is common place to regard the state as practically non-existent and, consequently, as a weak social actor until fairly late in the nineteenth century. Because of this the interpretation that we propose may be received at the outset with considerable scepticism. But views on the state in nineteenth century Latin America are changing. New works have appeared which call attention to the fact that in Latin American countries before the state became an agent of social domination, it functioned for a long period of time exclusively as a bureaucratic institution. The authors of these works point out that if one paid attention to this aspect of the state one would get a more positive view of its performance as a social actor during the period in question. Immediately after Independence, for instance, the state as an institution was responsible for setting up political and administrative machineries to replace those of the colonial powers. It also promulgated constitutions and laws in order to lay the foundations of a new social and political order. Finally, given that, with the exception of Brazil, the Latin American nations adopted the republican form of government, the state formulated the rules and procedures for political participation.[4]

Convinced that there is much to be gained from studying Latin America from this perspective, I have written elsewhere about the state as an institution in Ecuador during the nineteenth century.[5] I concentrated on three sets of activities – political and administrative penetration, normative standardisation and incorporation of new social actors into the political system. This allowed me to show how the Ecuadorean state invented itself as an administrative entity, how it set the terms for the development of a new society and, last but not least, how it conditioned the process of class formation and national integration. The purpose of this chapter is to contribute to this new perspective, the practitioners of which, in my opinion, are rewriting nineteenth century Latin American political history. In particular, what I intend to do now is to focus on the third type of activity mentioned above, namely, that which has to do with political incorporation, and explore in more detail the role of the state in the formation of the Ecuadorean political community. To this end, I have chosen to deal with a concrete case: the electoral reforms of 1861.

The Reforms of 1861: A Critique of Current Interpretations

The prerequisites for citizenship and political participation when Ecuador started its republican life in 1830 were the following: to be married or be at least 22 years old; to own property worth 300 pesos, or practise a profession or a trade (domestics and labourers were excluded because they were seen as not having independent political judgement); and to know how to read and write.[6]

The vote was obligatory for all citizens who, at the parish level, elected the members of the cantonal electoral assembly. It was the task of this assembly to meet in the capital of each of the seven provinces every four years and elect municipal counsellors, mayors, deputies and senators. Deputies and senators constituted the national representation. An equal number of them were elected for each of the three departments in which the seven provinces were divided, namely, the departments of Quito, Guayaquil and Cuenca.[7] It was the prerogative of these representatives to elect the President and Vice-President of the country. The economic prerequisites to be elected deputies and senators were higher than those needed to be a citizen, while those required to be elected President and Vice-President were even higher. Women were excluded from citizenship and from the electoral process altogether. In short, the electoral process that was set up in the 1830s excluded from the emerging political system the vast majority of the population. The various mechanisms of exclusion were the following: economic prerequisites, literacy test, equal representation of departments regardless of population, indirect elections and public elections, and finally gender.

This state of affairs, however, changed drastically in 1861. First, the economic requirement for citizenship and political participation was abolished. Second, proportional representation replaced equal representation for the election of deputies. Third, the province, a much smaller territorial unit, replaced the department as the territorial unit for elections. Finally, the electoral process became direct and secret. The only features of the old system that were kept in place were the gender and the literacy requirements. The former was abolished in 1929 and the latter, as already stated, in 1978. The reforms of 1861 amounted to a repudiation of the exclusionary republic of the 1830s. Yet current interpretations have not adequately recognised this fact.

According to M. Medina Castro, the reforms of 1861 were brought about by a rural bourgeoisie which had emerged in the coastal lowlands of Ecuador. Given that these reforms reflected the interests of this class, he argues, they had two salient characteristics. On the one hand, they were progressive in that they did away with the economic prerequisite for citizenship and for political participation, thus allowing more Ecuadoreans to be part of the political system. On the other hand, their inclusionary potential was really quite limited since they were meant to serve the interests of an emerging bourgeoisie which was quite small. Thus, for Medina Castro the reforms of 1861, while important in theory, were not particularly significant in practice.[8]

A more complex account of the reforms of 1861 is offered by Quintero in an article devoted to examining the system of political representation in nineteenth century Ecuador. Armed with data gathered from the archives of the Legislative Palace, this author attempts to demonstrate (see Table 1) that the voters that controlled the electoral process throughout the century were those located in the highlands.

Table 1
Size of the Ecuadorean Electorate and percentage of Regional Voters over National Voters, 1848-1894

Region	1848 electores		1856 electores		1888 sufragantes		1894 sufragantes	
	X	Y	X	Y	X	Y	X	Y
Highlands	159	83%	509	63%	21,887	72%	21,241	60%
Coast	33	17%	297	37%	8,444	28%	14,257	40%

Source: Elaboration by the author of data taken from R. Quintero, *Revista Ciencias Sociales*, vol. 2, nos. 7-8, 1978, pp. 89, 97 and 100.

X	=the number of voters
Y	=percentage of regional voters over all national voters
electores	=members of electoral assemblies who participated in indirect voting
sufragantes	=direct participants in universal and secret voting

Given these statistics, the inevitable conclusion is that the reforms of 1861 could only have been the work of the landowning class. He suggests that they were offered as a concession by this social group in order to reduce class conflict and thus maintain its hegemony. Indeed it could not have been otherwise. Democratic institutions, he argues, were a mere fiction in a country whose economic structure was precapitalist in nature. The best evidence that this was the case was the fact that the Indian population, which comprised the majority of Ecuadoreans, was kept in bondage in caste-like relations until 1918.[9]

As for the impact of the reforms of 1861, Quintero maintains that they did not significantly affect the process of enlargement of the electorate in the nineteenthth century. Whereas 2,827 voters or 0.3 per cent of the national population participated in the elections of 1830, only 17,709, 1.7 per cent of the population, voted in the elections of 1899, the last of the century.[10]

A close examination of the empirical data, however, permits us to challenge both interpretations. I do not think that it is possible to demonstrate that the reforms of 1861 reflected the interests of the rural coastal bourgeoisie, as Medina Castro argues. Although the economic history of Ecuador is yet to be written, some progress has been made of late. This research shows that two regional economies, not one as he contends, were energised by an expanding European market in the 1850s. The first was the cocoa economy in the coast (Guayas) and the second the cascarilla economy in the southern highlands (Azuay).[11] The new economic elites were a handful, and their fortunes were modest. More importantly, there is no evidence to suggest that they had formulated at this time a political project of their own. Their primary concern seems to have been to establish their hegemony over the old rich in their respective regions. To this end they sought external allies, the central government among them. When the electoral reforms were proposed in 1860 by the government of Gabriel García Moreno, which was an administration closely connected with the landlords of the northern highlands, some of the new rich did support this initiative. In so doing, however, they did not see themselves as making an alliance with these landlords. Rather, their intention was to strengthen the power of the central government. One can argue, of course, that their preference for strong government was consistent with their class interest. The fact remains that they were not the proponents of the reforms and only some of them supported them.

Turning to Quintero's interpretation, let us begin by reflecting on the empirical material summarised in Table 1. The division of the Ecuadorean electorate in terms of Highlands versus Coast assumes that highland landowners constituted a solid electoral block throughout the nineteenth century. In fact, this was not the case. According to B. Malo, one of the most prominent figures in Ecuadorean political life in the 1850s and 1860s, the highlanders of the northern provinces tended to follow the lead of the city of Quito, while the highlanders of the southern provinces often voted with the city of Cuenca. These two cities saw themselves as rivals and often the principal city of the southern highlands sided with that of the coast against Quito. A more accurate picture of the voting patterns in nineteenth-century Ecuador, therefore, can be obtained by putting aside the coast/highland dichotomy and adopting instead a tripartite division which takes into account the politics of the period. (See Table 2).

Table 2
Size of the Ecuadorean Electorate: percentage of Regional Voters over National Voters, 1848-1894: A Reinterpretation.

Regions	1848 electores	1856 electores	1888 sufragantes	1894 sufragantes
Quito	63%	33%	48%	41%
Cuenca	20%	30%	24%	19%
Guayaquil (Coast)	17%	37%	28%	40%

Source: Elaboration by the author of data obtained from R. Quintero, *Revista Ciencias Sociales*, vol. 2, nos. 7-8, 1978, pp. 89, 97, 99 and 100.

If Malo's description of electoral behaviour in the Ecuadorean highlands is correct, that is, if it is true that Cuenca and Guayaquil banded together against Quito, then one cannot speak, as Quintero does, of the electoral dominance of the highland landowners throughout the nineteenth century. Nor can one interpret the reforms of 1861 as an effort on their part to keep in check an emerging coastal bourgoisie. These reforms will simply have to be explained in a different manner.

Why does Quintero lump together the highland vote? In our opinion he does so because he assumes that the northern and southern highlands had a similar economic structure.[12] However, the cascarilla trade was responsible for the capitalisation of a new social group interested in foreign trade and financing rather than in the exploitation of the traditional *hacienda*. Nothing equivalent took place in the northern highlands, not at least until the 1870s. The diversified voting behaviour of northern and southern highlanders, therefore, could be explained not only in political terms, as Malo does, but also in economic ones.

Also at issue is Quintero's assessment of the impact of the reforms of 1861 on the Ecuadorean electorate. Whether or not the primary aim of those who passed the reforms was to expand political participation, the fact is that they did so, thus initiating a new period in Ecuadorean history. (See Tables 3 and 4).

Table 3
Size of the Electorate: percentage of Voters over Departmental* Population, 1848-1856

Departments:	Population	1848 Actual Voters	% of Population	Population	1856 Actual Voters	% of Population
Quito	483,000	121	.02	703,506	262	.04
Cuenca	152,000	38	.02	243,459	247	.1
Guayaquil	141,730	33	.02	141,730	297	.2
Total	768,000	192	.02	1,108,082	806	.07

Source: Compiled by the author from material obtained by R. Quintero, *Revista Ciencias Sociales*, vol. 2, nos. 7-8, pp. 89, 97, 99 and 100.
* The territorial unit for elections between 1830 and 1860 was the department.

Table 4
The size of the Electorate: percentage of Voters Relative to Provincial* Population, 1888-1894

Provinces:	Population	1888 Actual Voters	% of Population	Population	1894 Actual Voters	% of Population
(Old Dept. of Quito)						
Carchi	28,453	1,225	4	28,967	851	3
Imbabura	53,744	2,214	4	54,716	1,689	3
Pichincha	162,122	3,965	2	165,053	3,770	2
Leon	86,622	1.836	2	8,189	2,307	3
Tungurahua	81,406	2,526	3	82,878	2,494	3
Chimborazo	96,423	1,859	2	98,166	2,651	3
Bolívar	33,985	1,064	3	34,600	1,133	3
(Old Dept. of Cuenca)						
Cañar	50,582	1,682	3	51,496	1,618	3
Azuay	104,642	3,770	4	106,534	3,029	3
Loja	52,163	1,746	3	53,106	1,699	3
(Old Dept. of Guayaquil)						
Guayas	77,533	3,940	5	98,000	8,115	8
Los Ríos	25,923	876	3	32,000	1,393	4
Manabí	50,661	2,781	5	64,100	3,520	5
El Oro	25,765	648	3	36,600	1,006	3
Esmeraldas	11,539	199	2	14,553	223	2
Total	1,004,791	30,332	3	1,073,329	35,498	3.3

Source: Compiled by the author from material gathered by R. Quintero, Revista Ciencias Sociales, vol. 2, nos. 7-8, pp. 89, 97, 99 and 100.
* The territorial unit for elections from 1861 onwards was the province.

As Table 3 shows, the percentage of participation relative to population during the first half of the nineteenth century remained stationary (from .02 – i.e. one fifth of one per cent – in 1848 to .07 in 1856). In the second half, however, it jumped to 3.3 per cent in 1894 (see Table 4). In absolute terms, the numbers of voters increased from 192 in 1848 to 35,498 in 1894. This may be a conservative estimate. The election of 1894 was for a vice-president and, as such, did not have the full characteristic of a presidential election. More revealing of the extent of political participation in Ecuador is, in our opinion, the presidential election of 1892, the last of its kind in the nineteenth century. The number of voters at this date was 62,878, which amounted to roughly six per cent of an estimated population of one million.[13] Accordingly, it could be argued that the real expansion of political participation throughout the nineteenth century was from .02 per cent in 1848 to 6 per cent in 1892 in proportional terms; and from 192 in 1848 to 62,878 in 1892 in absolute terms.

Other trends that reveal increased political participation are qualitative rather than quantitative in nature. The growing regularity of elections as the accepted mechanism for the transmission of power is a case in point. In the first half of the nineteenth century Ecuadorean presidents were for the most part elected by national conventions. But in the second half, as Table 5 shows, this mechanism was increasingly replaced by direct presidential elections.

Table 5
The Presidents of Ecuador in the Nineteenth Century and their Form of Election.

	President	Year	Convention	Congress	Direct Elections
1.	J.J. Flores	1830	..		
2.	V. Rocafuerte	1835	..		
3.	J.J. Flores	1839		..	
4.	J.J. Flores	1843	..		
5.	V.R. Roca	1845	..		
6.	D. Noboa	1851	..		
7.	J.M. Urvina	1852	..		
8.	F. Robles	1856			..
9.	G.García Moreno	1861	..		
10.	J. Carrión	1865			..
11.	J. Espinosa	1868			..
12.	G. García Moreno	1869	..		
13.	G. García Moreno	1875			..
14.	A. Borrero	1875			..
15.	I. de Veintemilla	1878	..		
16.	J.M.P. Caamaño	1884	..		
17.	A. Flores	1888			..
18.	L. Cordero	1892			..
19.	E. Alfaro	1897	..		

Source: material collected by the author from Tribunal Supremo Electoral, *El Proceso Electoral Ecuatoriano* (Quito, 1989), pp. 131-4.

Was the increase in the number of direct presidential elections a consequence of the electoral reforms of 1861? The evidence points in this direction. A possible explanation is that in the 1840s and 1850s, when the electorate was minute, the national conventions had no problem claiming and securing legitimacy. After 1861, however, with the enlargement of the voting public, this became increasingly difficult, because national conventions came to be seen as the expression of a political faction rather than that of the national will – hence the need to resort more and more to direct elections.

Yet another conspicuous characteristic of Ecuadorean political life in the second part of the nineteenth century, which suggests increased participation, is electoral corruption. Complaints of irregularities on the part of the representatives of the state or of local potentates at this time increased significantly. There can be no doubt that these irregularities took place and that they obstructed and quite often made a mockery of the electoral process. Yet, these very complaints are an indication that the electoral process was becoming the accepted means for resolving matters of political succession rather than *coups d'état* and national conventions.[14]

So far I have identified the inadequacies of the current interpretations of the reforms of 1861. In the remainder of the chapter I shall argue that the reforms in question were a response on the part of the Ecuadorean state to the political crisis of 1859. At the heart of this crisis were the strained relations between centre and periphery, together with the exacerbation of social conflict, both of which caused the successful revolution of March 1845, known as the *Marcista* revolution after the name of the month during which it took place.

The Marcista Revolution and the Political Crisis of 1859

Ecuador in the 1830s found itself in a state of acute economic, social, political and cultural fragmentation. This was the result, among other reasons, of factors related to the process of Independence, and to the passage from colony to nation. The wars against Spain disrupted traditional patterns of economic activity and ruralised the population. When the time came to organise the new state, there was a proliferation of local leaders and an erosion of authority even at the parish level. Placed between Peru and New Granada, the new state was threatened by two powers who proclaimed very early the necessity of doing away with what they regarded to be a purely 'artificial' political entity. Since this idea found proponents in Guayaquil and Cuenca, the dangers of an invasion were compounded with threats of secession. Then throughout the 1830s and 1840s there emerged within the national territory new political centres such as Guayaquil and Cuenca, formerly mere outposts of Quito, the old colonial capital. We have already seen how these three cities, as capitals of the three departments, began to compete in electoral and other ways, making the 'internal equilibrium' of the country the most important political issue for much of the nineteenth century. In the meantime, the main cleavages of the colonial period between the hispanic and the indigenous peoples remained as glaring as ever.

Under these circumstances, the only centripetal force within Ecuador was the state as an institution. It provided a scaffolding which permitted the structuring of political life. Moreover, it gave society a sense of direction. The goals to achieve were: a republican form of government, republican values and a republican political system. Much less clear were the means necessary to achieve these goals. As the 'national elites'[15] attempted to extend their state-building efforts over the national territory, they met with the resistance of 'peripheral elites', both at the departmental and provincial levels. A partial indicator of this phenomenon was a process of political differentiation which began in the 1840s. In 1845 Guayaquil had two provinces, Cuenca two and Quito three. By 1860 Guayaquil had four and Quito five. Only Cuenca remained unchanged. Except in the southern highland, therefore, the provincial elites were on the move in the 1850s. While it is true that this mobilisation was in some cases a reaction against the departmental capitals, it is also true that it had to do with gaining some control over the process of centralisation unleashed by the state.

Closely interconnected with the territorial conflict, Ecuador experienced a social conflict that saw the 'aristocrats' pitted against the 'people'.[16] As we have said above, the Constitution of 1830 excluded from citizenship the vast majority of Ecuadoreans. A decade or so later, in 1843, General Juan José Flores, representing the aristocrats, managed to impose a new constitution which was even more exclusionary. The reaction against the Charter of Slavery, as it was called, was widespread and was one of the main forces behind the *Marcista* revolution of 1845. The wars of Independence had been fought by the common people and they simply would not be excluded from a political system for which they had worked and died.[17] The revolution of 1845 permitted the popular classes, which had remained at the margin of political life until then, to make their presence felt and become a factor to contend with for the rest of the century.[18]

Both of these conflicts, the territorial and the social, became inextricably connected during the 1850s. This had to do with the nature of the Ecuadorean governments during this period. The revolution of March 1845 toppled General Flores and brought to power 'national elites', led by newcomers to the political stage, namely, Generals J.M. Urvina and F. Robles. Variously described by the foreign representatives in Quito as people of mixed ethnic origin or as members of the middle classes, the so called *Marcistas* remained in office until 1859.[19] This political takeover was not the consequence of economic changes: a small bourgeoisie made its appearance in Ecuador for the first time only in the late 1850s and early 1860s. Instead, what propelled the *Marcistas* to power, besides the push from the popular classes, was a sudden vacuum of leadership among the aristocrats. Rocafuerte, the outstanding liberal leader of Guayaquil, had left Ecuador in protest against the enactment of the Constitution of 1843. As already seen, Flores was eclipsed by the revolutionaries of 1845.[20]

For a few years, until the early 1850s, Urvina and Robles operated behind the scenes and allowed straw men to take turns in the presidential office. But when it became clear that they had no rivals of stature, they took over the reins of government by merely threatening the use of arms.[21] Determined to remain in office, Urvina and Robles decided to use as a social base the popular forces which had been mobilised in 1845. To this end, they surrounded themselves with people from all walks of life sympathetic to a more democratic republic. Little by little the new political elites put into place a political project that could be characterised as populist.[22] With regard to political and administrative matters, the *Marcistas* proposed a unitary state which, however, would be tempered by a decentralised administration, responsive to local interests. As for normative standardisation, they were critical of previous administrations for making the idea of 'liberty' the sole foundation of their legislation. Just as important, the *Marcistas* argued, was 'equality', a principle without which there could not be a true republic. Finally, with regard to political incorporation, the *Marcistas* wanted an electoral system that would permit a more direct participation on the part of the Ecuadorean citizenry.

The administration of General Urvina (1852-1856) and, to a lesser extent, that of General Robles (1856-1859) worked hard to implement the *Marcista* platform. Although a definitive assessment of their accomplishment has not yet been produced, one thing is clear: these administrations exacerbated the territorial and social conflict as never before and set the stage for the crisis of 1859.

Although the *Marcistas* made an effort to use the popular classes as their social base, they did not succeed. One thing was to mobilise them, and quite another to weld them into an organised political force. In the end they did manage to put together a grouping they called the 'democratic' party.[23] This entity, however, was no more than a loose conglomeration of political clients. Thus, lacking a reliable following, the *Marcistas* sought the support of the army, which was perceived as a natural ally. A branch of the Executive since 1845, the Ecuadorean army had removed foreign officers who had come to Ecuador at the time of the wars of independence, and had opened its doors to Ecuadoreans of modest origins. According to British and US representatives in Ecuador, the chiefs and officers were 'almost all persons of low station in society'.[24] This was true of Generals Urvina and Robles, who were nevertheless connected with the upper classes. Having been faithful to the interests of the army throughout their careers, however, they were liked and respected by the members of this institution. Thus the *Marcista* administrations and the army came to count on each other.[25] This explains the appointment of military types as political representatives of the central government in key areas of the periphery. Not surprisingly, as the *Marcista* administrations extended their control over the length and breadth of the country, the 'peripheral elites' began to protest against the 'invasion of militarism'.[26]

Besides centre-periphery conflict, the *Marcista* administrations, in their efforts to implement their ideas of normative standardisation, heightened the level of the social conflict already present. It will be recalled that the *Marcistas* were critical of the aristocratic republic of the 1830s because, among other things, it had kept intact the ethnic cleavages in Ecuadorean society. Determined to implement the principle of 'equality', the *Marcistas* abolished the institution of slavery in 1853 and that of the Indian tribute in 1857.

Widely approved in principle by Ecuadoreans at large, these laws had in practice an unsettling effect on the highland and lowland upper classes. In general terms, they saw these laws as a veiled effort on the part of the government to woo the popular classes and to foster among them a mood of insurrection. It is not a coincidence that at this time some Indian groups declared themselves 'urvinistas' and participated in rural uprisings.[27] The highland elites, in particular, considered themselves the victims of the abolition of the Indian tribute. Carried out without any provision to replace it with other local taxes, the highland area, where the vast majority of the Indian population lived, was left without a much needed source of income.

State penetration of the periphery and normative standardisation in favour of the popular classes created a difficult situation for the peripheral elites, particularly in the highland area. The reaction against the government was first evident in Cuenca. Then it manifested itself in Quito. By 1858 the peripheral elites took their grievances to the Senate where they launched an attack against the Robles administration.[28] From this moment on the political situation became very tense and the probability of a crisis increased with each passing day.

The crisis of 1859 was triggered by two events. First, the Robles administration suddenly fell apart. President Robles was taken ill and temporarily abandoned his post in 1858. At the same time, for reasons still unclear, two of his ministers (Finance, and War and Marine) failed to attend their duties on a regular basis. As the machinery of the state ran into a standstill, the political opposition began to regroup led by a new generation of politicians, the fiery García Moreno among them.[29] Thus the enemies of *Marcismo* were given the opportunity to take the initiative and to start preparations for the possible takeover. The second event that triggered the crisis was a diplomatic dispute between the governments of Ecuador and Peru. Formally it had to do with territory that Ecuador had pledged in 1857 to the British bondholders in partial payment of its debts to them and which the Peruvian government claimed as theirs. Informally, the dispute was a quarrel among various factions of the Ecuadorean and Peruvian political elites. General Castilla, the Peruvian president, had irritated Robles by allowing General Flores to use Lima as a launching pad for an invasion against Ecuador. Robles, on the other hand, had provoked Castilla by meddling in Peruvian domestic affairs and by siding with Castilla's main political opponent.[30]

By then, Robles had resumed office in a vain attempt to control the unfolding crisis. By the end of 1858, he had closed Congress, which was increasingly controlled by a revitalised opposition. He then transferred the seat of government from Quito to Guayaquil. But the municipality of Quito saw in this measure the removal of the capital of the country to the coast on a permanent basis and protested loudly. The government's response was to put the municipal officers in gaol. The escalation of the confrontation was now inevitable and on 1 May the Quito regional elites rose in revolt, repudiated the Robles administration and set up in its place a Provisional Government.[31]

Ecuadorean historiography has tended to see this revolution as a regional, conservative reaction against *Marcismo*.[32] The participants themselves, however, thought of it differently. The May revolution for them was a political movement led by a new generation of public men with a proactive rather than a reactive political programme. Their concern was to question not just the Robles government, but the whole Ecuadorean political system, and what they proposed to do was to create a new one based on the reformation of political representation.[33]

Quito's revolt was not the end of the Robles presidency. He fought back, now supported by his friend and ally General Urvina. But although they were able to recapture Quito, they did not have the strength to keep their gains. When the Quito elites regrouped and reorganised their Provisional Government, both *Marcista* leaders finally gave up and left the country.

Immediately after the disappearance of the constitutional order, the peripheral elites took over the political scene. In addition to the provisional governments of Quito, there appeared one in Guayaquil and two more in the southern highlands (Cuenca and Loja). Thus at the end of 1859 the Ecuadorean state was literally in pieces. It was replaced by four formally constituted entities, '...all with different views and without any prospect of their coming to an understanding as to the future state of the republic'.[34] The only thing they seemed to agree on was that the political 'pact' that brought them together in 1830 when the Ecuadorean state was born had been broken and had to be renegotiated.

The crisis lasted for another year as the four regional centres struggled to remove the Peruvian forces still present in Guayaquil and to rebuild a new national consensus. In the end, it proved easier to accomplish the former than the latter. Confronting four different governments simultaneously, the Peruvian invaders found it difficult to make war. And as time passed and expenses rose, the Peruvian Congress began to question the wisdom of the exercise. Thus, under pressure to get things done, General Castilla entered into negotiations with the head of the Guayaquil provisional government. In the Treaty of Mapasingue, which was formalised on 25 January 1860, General Franco, the head of this government, accepted the Peruvian territorial claims in the Amazon region in exchange for military assistance. Castilla's victory, however, was short-lived. News of the treaty travelled fast and had the magical effect of uniting the rest of the country against Franco. Confronting this sudden turn of events General Castilla gave up and returned to Peru on 10 February, abandoning Franco to his own devices.[35]

With the Peruvian forces gone, the attention shifted to the domestic power struggle in which Quito had a head start. Not only had it been the first to rise against the discredited Robles, it had also been the only provisional government that had consistently maintained a national rather than a regional perspective. Keeping up this stance, a few days after Castilla returned to Lima, it took it upon itself to publish a manifesto formally condemning the Treaty of Mapasingue and proclaiming itself the defender of the Ecuadorean nation. This had the effect of securing for Quito the allegiance of Cuenca and Loja and of polarising the internal struggle between the provisional government of Guayaquil and that of Quito.[36] In the next phase of the conflict Quito made overtures to Guayaquil in an effort to obtain a negotiated peace. But Guayaquil would not hear of it. Probably still counting on Castilla's help, Franco demanded that García Moreno, the leader of the Quito government, be expelled from the country; that Cuenca and Loja accept the authority of the Guayaquil government; and that the Treaty of Mapasingue be fully recognised. Unfortunately for Franco, General Flores, the ablest

Ecuadorean commander at the time, returned from his exile in Lima and offered his help to the Quito government. García Moreno accepted it without hesitation and, scraping material and human resources here and there, managed to organise a strike force which, led by Flores, took Guayaquil on 24 September 1860.[37]

The National Convention of 1861

No sooner was the civil war over than the political leaders and interest groups throughout the country began positioning themselves to participate in the process of national reorganisation. The old order, the pact of 1830, had been built on the balance of power among the three regional centres: Quito, Guayaquil and Cuenca. This balance, in turn, rested on the principle of equal representation according to department. In September 1860 the issue that Ecuadoreans had to face was whether to renew the old pact or put together a new one. The first to engage in the debate was Guayaquil. Soon after its surrender to the forces of General Flores, the municipality of this city published a manifesto arguing for the preservation of the principle of equal representation.[38] Anxious to keep the initiative, Quito responded immediately. In a letter to Pedro Carbó, the governor of Guayaquil, García Moreno denounced the *status quo* and attacked the principle of equal representation as contrary to the fundamentals of 'representative government'... which 'is based on the respect of the will of the majorities...'. And García Moreno concluded:

> My opinion as a member of government, as a citizen and as a *Guayaquileño* is that the Republic should be treated as one family; that the borders of the old districts should disappear in order to contain the pretensions of the provinces; that the vote should be direct and universal...; that the number of representatives should be proportional to the number of electors to be represented.[39]

Fearful that the position of the municipality of Guayaquil would be adopted by other sections of Ecuador, García Moreno countered it with a proposal of his own. He took advantage of the fact that it was up to the Quito government to restore legality and that the accepted mechanism for this purpose was a National Convention, in order to present Guayaquil with a *fait accompli*. In December 1860 García Moreno decreed that the voting for the members of the Convention had to be proportional to population. In addition he ordered the elections to be direct, secret and free of economic conditions.[40] In one bold move García Moreno had gained the initiative. The outcry in Guayaquil and Cuenca was immediate. Had it not been that Quito was in control of the army and that the head of this army was General J. Flores, Ecuador would have plunged once more into anarchy.[41]

To the surprise of most people, the elections were held in an orderly and efficient manner and, as a result, a National Convention met in Quito from January to July of 1861. The Provisional Government entrusted this body with the task of producing a new constitution. To this end, the Convention broke into committees and one of them, the Constitutional Committee, was given the task of producing a draft of the new charter using as a model the constitution of 1852. This Committee worked under the shadow of imminent conflict. Although, as noted, the elections for the Convention took place without any incident, García Moreno's decree was hotly debated throughout the country before and after the elections.[42] It took the Committee a fortnight or so of intense work to complete its constitutional project, which was then submitted with a covering report. In this report, the members of the Committee made a point of informing the Convention about the pressures that had conditioned their work. They had focused their attention on reorganising the political institutions of the nation. However, given the prevailing climate of opinion, they also made an effort to harmonise the conflicting views and interests of the main political forces of the country. The report went on to state that the members of the Committee had worked hard to adapt the republican form of government to the concrete circumstances of Ecuador in 1861. It concluded by identifying in some detail the reforms the Committee had introduced in their constitutional project. Among these reforms two were singled out as the most important ones: the reforms in the system of representation and those in the system of administration.[43]

Concerning the first, the report recommended the adoption of the principle of population for the election of the members of the House and that of equal representation for the Senate. In the Committee's opinion, this would create an equilibrium between the two chambers and, just as important, it would conciliate two views of representation which were dividing the country. In addition, the report proposed adopting secret and direct suffrage for the elections of deputies, senators, provincial governors, municipal and parish officials. This, the Committee claimed, was bound to secure the interest of Ecuadoreans in participating in political life and in electing their own representatives. It is interesting to note that nothing was said concerning universal suffrage.

The second main reform recommended by the committee was the decentralisation of the administration. The purpose of this proposal was twofold. On the one hand, it sought to create a balance between central and local government, something which was deemed indispensable in a republican form of government. On the other hand, the proposal was a response to a very strong current of opinion that had developed in the periphery against centralism throughout the 1850s, as we have seen in the previous section, and which had peaked in the crisis of 1859.

On 31 January, the discussion of the draft of the new constitution began in earnest, article by article, 149 in all. We shall here concentrate only on those which are related to the two sets of reforms the Constitutional Committee singled out for attention. The debate ran smoothly until it reached article nine, the article on citizenship. At this point, Huerta, one of the representatives from Guayaquil, tabled a motion that the economic requisite for it should be abolished.[44] He argued that the exercise of political rights should be governed by independence of mind and culture, not property as hitherto. Additionally, he claimed that it was time to remove the obstacles that restricted the number of citizens to so few. He then reminded his peers that the Provisional Government had already done away with this requisite in the electoral decree that set the rules for the election of the Convention. He concluded by urging them to build on this precedent.[45]

Huerta's motion upset the members of the Constitutional Committee. As already noted, there was not a word about universal suffrage in their report to the Convention. Indeed, there was not a word about it in the constitutional project itself either. Given that it probably was the most salient and controversial aspect of García Moreno's electoral decree of December 1860, it seems that the Committee had ignored it in an effort to avoid conflict. After Huerta's intervention, however, the clash was inevitable.

Those in favour of the motion were for the most part new names in Ecuadorean politics and came from all parts of the country. A good representative of this group was Felipe Serrade, a young physician from the northern highlands. In the course of his interventions he presented two types of argument in support of Huerta's motion. The first dealt with principles. There was a contradiction, he claimed, between the principle of sovereignty and the economic prerequisite for citizenship. Whereas the latter reduced citizenship to the propertied classes, the former granted this privilege to the people as a whole. He was for the expansion of political participation and urged his colleagues to adopt the principle of sovereignty as the foundation for political life. Sarrade's second type of argument was historical. He reminded the members of the Convention that many of them were there representing the political movement that had started in Quito in May 1859. It was their task, he urged them, to implement the platform advocated by this movement. Otherwise, he said, 'the sacrifices of the May revolution would have been in vain.... . If we do not abolish [the economic restrictions]... we would be accountable to the people'.[46]

The opposition to Huerta's motion was led by the elder statesmen in the Convention such as J. J. Flores, Pedro José Arteta, Vicente Sanz and Mariano Cueva, all highlanders like Serrade. They argued that property guaranteed independence of mind and a free vote, that the abolition of the economic prerequisite would create inequalities among large landowners, favouring those with the greater number of dependents, and that universal suffrage was not a practical principle but a theoretical one which would lead the country to chaos, as in New Granada. Vicente Sanz even went so far as to remind his opponents of the dangers of incorporating the Indian masses into 'civilised' political life.[47] All to no avail. Following the rules for constitutional debates, after the third reading, Huerta's motion passed by a clear majority. Thus, somewhat unexpectedly, universal suffrage became part of the Constitution of 1861,[48] which is not to say that it was an accident. As Serrade stated, it was an important part of the programme of the revolution of 1859.

Current historiography, as already discussed, characterises the electoral reforms of 1861 in class terms: the coming of age of the bourgeoisie (Medina Castro) or the defensive strategies of highland landowners (Quintero). A careful examination of the debates points to a different interpretation. The supporters of Huerta's motion came from all parts of the country. Moreover they belonged to different social groups. Pedro José Arteta (Pichincha), Miguel Albornoz (Ambato), and Ramón Borrero (Cuenca), for example, were members of the upper classes. Luciano Moral (Guayaquil), Manuel Villavicencio (Esmeraldas), Juan León Mera (Ambato), Felipe Serrade (León), and Vicente Cuesta (Cuenca), belonged to the middle sectors. What most defenders of universal suffrage had in common was that they belonged to the same age group. Conversant with the democratic reforms that swept Latin America from Mexico to New Granada throughout the 1850s, only some of them were doctrinaire liberals.[49] They all shared, however, the determination to succeed where their fathers had failed, that is, in the institutionalisation of a republican order based not on the privileged few but on the majority of the people.[50] The social actor behind universal suffrage, therefore, was a new generation which was transformed by the Revolution of 1 May 1859 and by the election of December 1860 into agents of the Ecuadorean state.[51]

With the question of universal suffrage settled, the Convention turned its attention to proportional representation. As mentioned above, at the beginning of the Convention the Constitutional Committee had recommended the adoption of a mixed system for the election of congressional representatives: equal representation for the Senate and proportional representation for the House of Representatives. The first point did not generate much discussion. The second, however, just like the motion for universal suffrage, provoked a spirited debate.

Again, two positions defined themselves. The most eloquent spokesman of one of them was T. Mora, one of the representatives from the southern highlands (Loja). For Mora, the principle of population was not applicable to a country like Ecuador, owing to the 'moral nullity of the indigeneous classes'.[52] In a society where the vast majority of the population was ignorant and poor, argued Mora, proportional representation should be based on citizenship, not nationality pure and simple. Whereas the first required literacy, the second was automatically granted to all born in the country. After all, Mora concluded, 'sovereignty was not born from the masses but from illustration'.

Mora's position was opposed by, among others, M. Nájera from the northern highlands (Chimborazo). He reminded the Convention that they had already approved articles one and two of the new Constitution which explicitly stated, on the one hand, that the Republic was composed of all Ecuadoreans and, on the other, that sovereignty resided in the people, not just in citizens. This being the case, Nájera concluded, the Convention had no alternative but to make sure that proportional representation encompassed all Ecuadoreans: 'adults, children, women, etc'.[53] He did not mention explicitly the 'Indian masses' but, given the drift of his argument, it was clear that they were also to be included.

Nájera's position prevailed comfortably. This was obviously not an unexpected outcome. As we have seen above, proportional representation conceived in the largest sense of the term had been the banner, so to speak, of the Quito Provisional Government ever since García Moreno wrote his famous letter to the governor of Guayaquil in October 1860. It was also that of the majority of the members of the Convention. Even those who argued against it, like T. Mora, ended up adopting it and recognising its significance.[54]

It is important to underscore at this point that proportional representation was adopted not just for the sake of expanding the electorate, but ultimately to replace the political pact of 1830. As noted, there was a national debate on equal representation shortly after the promulgation of García Moreno's decree for the election of the

Convention of 1861. One of the most distinguished participants in this debate was the highland political leader B. Malo. In January 1861, just as the Convention was preparing to meet, Malo, an old political leader of the southern highlands, wrote a famous newspaper article in which he accused García Moreno of unilaterally undoing a political arrangement freely arrived at by Quito, Guayaquil and Cuenca in 1830. Far from being unjust and the cause of so many misfortunes, Malo argued, equal representation for the three departments was fair, beneficial and a guarantee of peace and order. In his opinion it was proportional representation which was dangerous. The reason for this was the fact that Quito had more population than Cuenca and Guayaquil put together. Under this system Quito's interests were bound to prevail, to the detriment of those of the other two regions. Thanks to equal representation, however, an 'internal equilibrium' had been achieved in Ecuadorean political life. Malo concluded by warning that the adoption of proportional representation would disrupt the internal balance of power and would exacerbate inter-regional and centre-periphery relations.[55]

Malo's article did not have much influence in the deliberations of the Convention. On the contrary, the members of this body disagreed with him almost to a man. To them the crisis of 1859 had to do in great part with the departmental system. Even after the crisis was over, the departments had provoked the odious quarrels of 'equality and inequality of representation' throughout the country.[56] The only way of preventing another débâcle from happening was by replacing the departments with provinces as the main territorial unit for electoral purposes. This change involved a democratisation of power because the provinces were smaller and more numerous than the departments. Two consequences would follow from this replacement. First, the polarisation between the central power and the three departments would become a thing of the past. Secondly, new life would be given to the localities. For these localities to flourish, however, it was urgent to protect them from state interference. Hence the importance of the second great reform submitted by the Constitutional Committee to the Convention: administrative decentralisation.

After the revolution of May 1859, the Quito Provisional Government had published a proclamation pledging to decentralise the national administration as soon as the normalisation of political life made it possible. This may come as a surprise to those who associate García Moreno with extreme centralism. But, as head of the Quito Provisional Government, García Moreno sometimes had to voice ideas which were not precisely his own, but those of his supporters.

The idea of decentralisation surfaced again, as already noted, when the Constitutional Committee submitted its recommendations to the National Convention.[57] Once the Convention began its deliberations, however, decentralisation became one of the leitmotifs of the debates. Many of the Convention's members insisted on discussing it at the very beginning, in the parts of the constitution where the concept of national power was defined. Next to the legislative, the executive and the judicial powers, Borrero and other southern highlanders proposed the creation of an entity called 'sectional power' which would be 'supreme' within the jurisdiction of each province. Borrero's motion was not well received by a number of northern highlanders. The adjective 'supreme', argued Arteta, applies only to 'national' institutions. The notion of sectional powers contradicted the idea of Ecuador as an indivisible polity, a principle already approved by the Convention. Most alarmed of all was Flores. What Borrero and his followers were really after, he said, was a federal form of government. Borrero's motion was put to the vote and was rejected. This, however, was just the first round of a contest that lasted throughout the Convention.

Other skirmishes between the defenders and the opponents of 'sectional powers' followed. But the frontal clash took place when the members of the convention reached article 102, which had to do with internal administration. This article established that henceforth provincial governors, political chiefs (canton authorities) and political lieutenants (parish officers), would be elected by direct and secret suffrage. Given that all these officers had been, at least from 1845 onwards, appointed directly by the executive,[58] article 102 was truly revolutionary.

The debate this time took the following form. Having failed to persuade the Convention to recognise the existence of 'sectional powers' in that part of the Constitution devoted to the powers of the State, the defenders of this idea saw an opportunity to get their way by amending article 102 to include the creation of Provincial Assemblies. Elected by popular vote, like the governors, political chiefs and political lieutenants, these bodies would have legislative powers within their jurisdictions. The justification for this was that of all Ecuadorean territorial units only the provinces had developed into a 'commonwealth of customs, habits and interests'.[59] Thus, the provinces were the appropriate site for an entity capable of ensuring the effectiveness of administrative decentralisation. For the same reason, the Provincial Assemblies had also the potential of becoming the only countervailing force capable of diluting the monopoly of power in departmental centres and in the capital of the country established by the pact of 1830. The 'provincialists' concluded their argument by insisting that only through empowering the provinces could a new political order be built.

Those who were against the creation of Provincial Assemblies were very effectively led by General Flores. In his view, the 'provincialists' had spoken vigorously in favour of the new bodies, but they had failed to distinguish administrative from political matters. Given that the Provincial Assemblies would have legislative faculties, they were not really administrative organisms but 'sectional powers'. As such, they did not make much sense, since power could only be an attribute of national entities; this proposal therefore meant the adoption of a federal state. If that was what the 'provincialists' were aiming at, Flores concluded, they were sadly mistaken: federalism had been the ruin of many a Latin American country.

Turning to article 102 as such, Flores said that the discussion of the election of the territorial agents of the executive had also been marred by failure to distinguish administrative from political matters. According to Flores, failure to distinguish administrative from political questions was also responsible for another confusion. Administrative decentralisation, he said, had to do with the municipal system, not with the apparatus of the state. It was a mistake, therefore, to interfere with the appointments of governors and other 'immediate agents' of the executive. It was fine for the municipal officers, whose tasks were predominantly administrative, to be chosen by the locality they served. However, the appointment of, say, a governor, was another matter. Because a governor formed part of the executive's team, it was the president's responsibility to select him directly. Otherwise, the unity of action of the executive could be destroyed and he could not be properly held accountable for his performance.

The charges hurled by Flores and his followers against the 'provincialists' proved effective. Little by little the latter abandoned the idea of Provincial Assemblies. Something similar happened with article 102. For a while the 'provincialists' argued that the task of a republican executive was to work with local officials selected by the people. Flores and his followers, however, argued forcefully against the idea and defended the right of the executive to select its immediate agents so that the president could have good collaborators. When the time came to the vote, it was clear that the 'provincialists' were having second thoughts.

Article 102 was voted twice. The first time, it passed with only three 'nays'. But the second time it was rejected by 18 votes to 16. Fortunately for the 'provincialists', an article could be revoked if and only if two thirds of the votes had been cast against it. Since this was not the case, article 102 survived and became the law of the land. But the article was stillborn. No sooner were the results known than Egas (Imbabura) put forward the following motion: 'That in the section for temporary measures (of the new Constitution) an article be included allowing the executive to appoint provincial governors for the time being.' Seconded by Noboa (Los Ríos) and J. Aguirre (Pichincha), the motion was passed without much discussion.[60] It was a very curious way of concluding such an important debate.

When the Convention was over, the only evidence of administrative decentralisation were articles 101 and 103 which created municipalities at the provincial, cantonal and parish levels.[61] Even with regard to this point Flores prevailed. He argued that Ecuador needed administrative, not political, decentralisation and that the key institution for this was the municipality. There could be, Flores conceded, provincial, cantonal, and parish municipalities, but the natural focus for administrative decentralisation was the canton, not the province. Clearly, unlike universal suffrage and proportional representation, administrative decentralisation was not an unqualified success. Even so, together with the electoral reforms, it is an indicator of efforts on the part of the National Convention to lay the foundations of a new political order.

The debate on administrative decentralisation concluded the work of the Convention. A few days later the revised draft of the constitution was unanimously approved and García Moreno was elected president and Mariano Cueva vice-president of Ecuador. Religious ceremonies were organised in the Cathedral of Quito for 2 and 3 April, at which time the president and the vice-president respectively were scheduled to be sworn in. On the first date, García Moreno's acceptance speech was brief, forceful and packed with ideas. He pledged himself, among other things, to 'reestablish the rule of morality', 'to respect and protect the sacred religion'; 'to replace the dangerous and absurd theories that diminish patriotism among the youth with the peaceful achievements of hard work and wealth'; and 'to defend the honour and the rights of the state'.[62]

Many members of the Convention were probably puzzled by this speech. There was no reference whatsoever to the constitutional reforms. Worse still, there seemed to be more than a touch of disapproval. Yet, as shown, the Quito Provisional Government, of which García Moreno was the undisputed leader, was the main proponent of universal suffrage, of the vote according to population and of administrative decentralisation. How do we explain this apparent contradiction?

The answer has to do, as already suggested, with the way García Moreno conducted himself as head of the Provisional Government. In this connection, in 1861, he wrote to his brother-in-law: 'in the difficult and painful situation I have found myself since May 1859, everybody has tried to use me as an instrument... ignoring... my will... and my convictions. I have been ... forced to ... serve passively, while at the same time being held alone responsible'.[63] Although García Moreno was not a man given to playing second fiddle, it seems that, owing to the critical state of the country in 1859-61, there were times when he allowed himself to be used by the revolutionaries of May 1859. So it is not surprising that he found in the Constitution of 1861 things he agreed with as well as things to which he objected strenuously.

Judging from his pronouncements shortly after he took office, we know that García Moreno found articles 101, 102 and 103 establishing a decentralised system absolutely misconceived. He could not imagine having in his government provincial governors who had not been chosen by him. This, I think, explains the peculiar conclusion of the debate on article 102. Representative Egas's motion to the effect that a clause should be added at the end of the Constitution 'allowing the Executive to appoint provincial governors for the time being' was, in my opinion, García Moreno's doing. Reasonably sure that he was going to be elected to the presidency, he worked behind the scenes to formulate Egas's motion and to have it passed. The fact is that García Moreno was never personally in favour of decentralisation of any kind, political or administrative.

On the other hand, García Moreno was very much in favour of universal suffrage and proportional representation. Consequently he approved this part of the constitution of 1861. Whereas decentralisation fragmented political power, these two electoral reforms could be used to obtain the opposite effect – by diminishing the impact of the three regional elites. In the aftermath of the crisis of 1859 García Moreno saw the urgent need of strengthening the power of national government. Hence his references to law and order, to religion as a moralising force and to the honour and right of the state in his acceptance speech. Moreover, beyond the short term, García Moreno shared the idea of the May 1859 movement that the exclusionary republic that had prevailed from the 1830s could only be defended and managed by might, not right. From this perspective the electoral reforms of 1861 were one way of addressing the horizontal and vertical social mobilisation that took place in the 1850s and of institutionalising a process of political incorporation that would, in due course, produce a more inclusionary political community.

Conclusions

When the National Convention closed its doors, the political order organised in 1830 had been replaced by a new one. As we have seen in this chapter, this change involved two moments. In the first, which took place in the 1850s, the *Marcista* administrations released forces – the conflict between centre and periphery and that between the aristocrats and the people – that resulted in the crisis of 1859 and in the collapse of the old political structure. In the second, which lasted about three years, from 1859 to 1861, a new generation of political leaders led by García Moreno put into place a new political edifice. The most important tools the new generation used in this endeavour were the 1861 electoral reforms. It is the contention of this chapter that they did so as representatives of a national rather than a regional or a class perspective.

But in what sense was the new order of things to contribute to Ecuadorean political development? To begin with, universal suffrage and proportional representation incorporated for the first time into the Ecuadorean political system the different social groups mobilised or stirred up by the *Marcistas*. Whereas universal suffrage affected the middle and the popular urban sectors who had been marginalised during the first thirty years of the republic, proportional representation included, in principle at least, blacks and Indians, as we have seen in the discussions on the subject which took place in the National Convention.

There was also something progressive at the territorial level. Although the department was abolished as the administrative unit in 1835, the electoral system based on 'equal representation according to departments' brought it back into prominence in the 1840s and 1850s. Its role, Malo's arguments notwithstanding, was very divisive because it made Ecuador a multi-centred polity with Quito, Guayaquil and Cuenca. Moreover, it excluded the provinces from sharing power. Yet judging from what was said in the National Convention, it was at the provincial level that there developed between 1830 and 1860 a 'community of interests' which was simply ignored by the prevailing political order. The adoption of 'proportional representation' in 1861 changed this state of affairs. By making the province the key political unit in Ecuadorean political life, a greater distribution of power at the territorial level was achieved. At the same time, this brought about a higher degree of 'territorial incorporation'.

Notes

1. F. Trabucco, *Constituciones de la república del Ecuador* (Guayaquil, 1975), p. 34.
2. The literature on the Ecuadorean electoral process in the 19th century is extremely thin: J. Tobar Donoso, 'El sufragio en el Ecuador', *Revista de la Asociación de Derecho* (1949); R. Quintero, 'El carácter de la estructura institucional de representación política en el estado ecuatoriano del siglo XIX', *Revista Ciencias Sociales*, vol. II, nos. 7-8 (1978); M. Medina Castro, 'Proceso evolutivo del electorado nacional', in E. Ayala (ed.), *La historia del Ecuador, ensayos de interpretación* (1985); and E. Albán Gómez, 'Evolución del sistema electoral ecuatoriano', in *Tribunal Supremo Electoral, Elecciones y democracia en el Ecuador,* vol I. *El Proceso electoral ecuatoriano* (Quito, 1989).
3. See respectively, Medina Castro, 'Proceso evolutivo del electorado', and Quintero, 'El carácter de la estructura institucional'.
4. See, in particular, M Kossok, 'Revolución, estado y nación en la Independencia', in I. Buisson *et al.* (eds.), *Problemas de la formación del estado y la nación en Hispanoamérica* (Bonn, 1984), p. 169, and S. Valenzuela, *Democratización vía reforma: La expansión del sufragio en Chile* (Buenos Aires, 1985).
5. J. Maiguashca (ed.), *Historia y región en el Ecuador, 1830-1930* (Quito, 1994).
6. Trabucco, *Constituciones de la república*, p. 35.
7. The Department was abolished as a territorial unit in 1835 but it was kept in existence for the administration of some activities of the central state such as elections.
8. Medina Castro, 'Proceso evolutivo del electorado', p. 316.
9. Quintero, 'El carácter de la estructura institucional', pp. 85, 102-4.
10. *Ibid.*, pp. 86-7.
11. See Maiguashca, *Historia y región*, particularly Palomeque's chapter, pp. 69-142.
12. For a criticism of Quintero's approach, see J. P. Deler and Y. Saint-Geours, *Estados y naciones en los Andes* (Quito, 1986), vol. 2, pp. 419-34.
13. Quintero, 'El cáracter de la estructura institucional', pp. 86-7.
14. On electoral corruption, see comments by Tobar Donoso, 'El sufragio en el Ecuador', p.14.
15. From 1830 to 1884 there were economic prerequisites to holding office. As a result, the political and administrative elites of Ecuador throughout this period naturally belonged mostly to the propertied classes. From this fact current historians have inferred that these elites were governed by their class and/or territorial interests in the exercise of their public duties, thus rendering useless a distinction between 'national' versus 'peripheral' elites. This inference, however, has not been checked empirically. The evidence available suggests that the people who manned the state apparatus, irrespective of their territorial or social origins, tended to adopt what could be called an 'institutional point of view'. It is perfectly in order, therefore, to speak about the 'national elites' as a distinct social actor in Ecuadorean public life.

16. These terms, 'people' and 'aristocrats', were used by contemporaries, including foreign diplomats in Ecuador.

17. G. Ramón, 'Los indios y la constitución del estado nacional', *Ponencia al IX Simposio Internacional de historia económica: las comunidades campesinas de los Andes en el siglo XIX* (Quito, Mar. 1989), p. 31.

18. Public Records Office (PRO), FO 25, vols. 9:53; 11:45; 16:63; 22:55, 83; 24:15.

19. PRO, FO 25, vol. 24:15; and American Diplomatic Correspondence, National Archives of the United States (henceforth ADC), Quito, 4 Dec. 1849.

20. The 'liberal' and 'conservative' label in Ecuador were used to distinguish the two main political factions of the upper classes.

21. PRO, FO 25, vols. 24:15 and 26:32.

22. Maiguashca, *Historia y región*, pp. 377-83.

23. PRO, FO 25, vol. 26:48.

24. PRO, FO 25, vol. 24:15, and ADC, Guayaquil, 12 May 1851.

25. PRO, FO 25, vols. 24:49; 26:48; 30:84; and ADC, Quito, 1 June 1857.

26. Foreign representatives in Ecuador took sides during the 1850s. Walter Cope, the British Chargé d'Affaires, sympathised with the aristocrats in Quito and in the departmental capitals. Cope came to the conclusion that the *Marcistas* had established a system of 'despotic militarism' as early as 1851. See FO 25, vols. 22:69, 83; Cope to Foreign Office, Quito, 20 Jan. 1852, vol. 24, and Guayaquil, 1 Oct. 1852, vol. 26. Aware that the *Marcistas* regarded the United States as the 'model republic', North American representatives were less critical. They also acknowledged that the *Marcistas* were interested in advancing democracy in Ecuador. ADC, Cushing to Secretary of State, Guayaquil, 6 Apr. 1852; 30 July 1852; 2 Mar. 1853; and White to Secretary of State, Quito, 18 Jan. 1854.

27. With regard to Indian mobilisation in the southern highlands from the 1850s onwards, see M. A. Vintimilla, 'Luchas campesinas en el siglo XIX y la Revolución Liberal de 1895', *Revista del IDIS*, No. 8 (Cuenca, 1980), pp. 83-94. For a general account of the phenomenon of 'urvinismo', see E. Ayala, *Lucha política y origen de los partidos en Ecuador* (Quito, 1982), pp. 94-107.

28. See Malo, *Escritos y discursos*, p. 218; ADC, Quito, 10 Apr. and 1 June 1857, and 10 Jan. 1858.

29. ADC, Quito, 1 June 1857, 10 Jan. and 24 Aug. 1858.

30. PRO, FO 25, vol. 32:118.

31. See L. Robalino Dávila, *García Moreno* (Puebla, 1967), p. 211; R. Patee, 'La época crítica de la historia ecuatoriana, 1857-1861', *Boletín del Centro de Investigaciones Históricas de Guayaquil* (1941), pp. 17-18; and FO 25, vol. 34:41.,

32. Ayala, *Lucha política y origen de los partidos en el Ecuador*, pp. 107-12.

33. Robalino Dávila, *García Moreno*, p. 211.

34. PRO, FO 25, vol. 34:111.

35. Patee, 'La época crítica', pp. 23-4.

36. ADC, Quito, 22 Mar. 1860.

37. M. Van Aken, *King of the Night: Juan José Flores and Ecuador, 1824-1864* (Berkeley, 1989), p. 255.
38. Tobar Donoso, *El sufragio en el Ecuador,* p. 12.
39. Quoted in Tobar Donoso, *idem,* pp. 12-13.
40. Robalino Dávila, *García Moreno,* pp. 296 and 300; and Tobar Donoso, *El sufragio en el Ecuador,* p. 13.
41. Van Aken, *King of the Night,* pp. 256-9.
42. *Diario de los trabajos de la Convención Nacional reunida en la capital de la república en el año de 1861* (Quito, 1861), p. 111 (hereafter quoted as *Diario*). This source, a daily record of all the debates that took place in the convention, has hitherto been largely neglected by historians. This document is not easily available as there are very few copies left. I had access to the *Diario* thanks to the generosity of Enrique Ayala and Malcolm Deas.
43. *Diario,* pp. 53-5.
44. In 19th century Ecuador, the right to vote without economic prerequisites was called 'universal suffrage'. In this chapter I have kept the contemporary meaning of the term.
45. *Diario,* pp. 100-101.
46. *Diario,* pp. 168, 192, 205 and 300; Robalino Dávila, *García Moreno,* p. 211.
47. *Diario,* p. 102. See also *ibid.,* pp. 102, 165, 168.
48. Mera, one of the youngest members of the Convention, made a move to do away with the literacy qualification as well; *Diario,* pp. 107, 171. But few rallied to his cause. Thus the only two qualifications that remained in place for citizenship in the Constitution of 1861 were gender and the proof of literacy.
49. All the evidence suggests that the only doctrinaire liberals in the Convention were the two young representatives from Loja: Toribio Mora and Francisco Arias. Mora published his views in an influential paper in that province, which he himself established, *La Federación.* See A. Mora Reyes, *Don Manuel Carrión Pinzano y el gobierno federal de Loja y tres maestros lojanos* (Loja, 1959).
50. *Diario,* pp. 193, 300; Robalino Dávila, *García Moreno,* p. 211; and G. García Ceballos, *Por un García Moreno de cuerpo entero* (Cuenca, 1978), pp. 41-5.
51. For the use of the concept of 'generation' in Ecuadorian cultural history, see J. Valdano, *Ecuador: cultura y generaciones* (Quito, 1985), p. 87. Political historians could emulate cultural historians and use this concept to their great advantage. It acknowledges a phenomenon of social life. It allows the historian an opportunity to avoid falling victim either to the notion of 'the great man' or to class determinism.
52. *Diario,* p. 111.
53. *Diario,* p. 251.
54. See Mora's comments after the reform was passed, in *Diario,* p. 192.
55. B. Malo, *Escritos y discursos* (Quito, 1940), pp. 214, 216-7.
56. *Diario,* pp. 111, 180-1.
57. *Diario,* pp. 181 and 55.
58. *Diario,* p. 379. See also R. Borja y Borja, *Derecho constitucional ecuatoriano* (Madrid, 1950), vol. I, pp. 602-4.

59. *Diario*, pp. 359 and 408.
60. *Diario*, p. 480.
61. Trabucco, *Constituciones de la república*, p. 201.
62. *Diario*, p. 497.
63. Robalino Dávila, *García Moreno*, p. 213.

CHAPTER 5

PRIESTS AT THE HUSTINGS:
ECCLESIASTICAL ELECTIONEERING IN
NINETEENTH-CENTURY IRELAND

K. Theodore Hoppen

The nineteenth-century Irish electoral system was largely modelled upon that of England. The Act of Union of 1800 abolished the Dublin parliament and provided instead that at first 100 and later slightly more Irish representatives be sent to Westminster where they henceforth constituted about one sixth of all members of parliament. Constituencies were (as in England) divided between predominantly rural counties and more urban boroughs, while voting rights were generally confined to men aged at least 21 who possessed (or in some cases merely occupied) property to a certain value. Again, as in England, voting was public until 1872 and complex registration mechanisms existed to establish precisely who could and who could not proceed to the poll.[1]

However, significant national peculiarities in the social and political spheres meant that the general culture of electoral life often followed distinctively Irish patterns. And because the balance of power within Irish politics shifted substantially during the nineteenth century, and did so in a manner not experienced in England, deviations grew more marked as time went on. While, therefore, Ireland's electoral landscape in, say, 1820 represented no more than a hibernicised version of that of contemporary England, by 1900 the differences had become more striking than the similarities.

As in most countries the nature of electoral life in Ireland was ultimately shaped by social, economic, and political considerations of the broadest kind. Thus, Ireland's failure to industrialise meant that electoral processes continued to function within a predominantly rural environment where the characteristic clashes of the countryside, rather than disputes between factory workers and capitalist employers, constituted the chief medium of political exchange. At the same time religion permeated almost all aspects of politics and electioneering not only because it represented a kind of epitome of three centuries and more of Irish history, but because the privileges of the Protestant minority eventually created so much resentment among Catholics that an entirely new form of popular electoral politics was brought into being.[2]

Given that such was the situation it is not surprising that elections in nineteenth-century Ireland revolved around the tensions between a Protestant elite seeking to retain as much power as possible and predominantly Catholic voters attempting, sometimes energetically, sometimes not, to secure advantages for themselves. Elections provided the theatre within which much of this conflict was played out, not because electoral processes were (until the very end of the century) notably democratic,[3] but because they supplied the most readily available constitutional mechanism for assessing, even if only inexactly, the relative state of power relationships within society as a whole. Not only that, but in the Irish case the electoral system also supplied both a crucial instrument of influence to the various elites of the time *and* an environment within which contemporary social processes could make themselves politically manifest.

Before the Great Famine of 1845-9 rural society was made up of three broad groups, none of them entirely uniform, but all sustaining a degree of political and cultural coherence and identity. At the top came an elite of about 10,000 persons who owned (but in general did not farm) the land. A few possessed enormous estates like the Marquess of Downshire's 100,000 acres. More typical were men with about 4,000 acres or so, though many had less and an increasing number in the early nineteenth century were finding themselves in severe financial difficulties.[4] Far more important numerically were the other two social and economic groups of the time: the tenant farmers and the labourers. Although farmers enjoyed comparatively little formal security of tenure, in practice, and particularly after 1850, evictions were considerably less common than has sometimes been supposed.[5] Reasonably reliable estimates suggest that in 1841 the number of adult males engaged in agriculture was about 1.7 million. Of these some 400,000 can be called 'farmers', 50,000 being prosperous operators with average holdings of 80 acres, 100,000 middle-size farmers with about 50 acres, and the majority (250,000) men with 20 acres or so worked entirely by themselves and their families, though a substantial proportion had of course much smaller holdings still. This left 1.3 million adult males (plus their dependants) for whom labour mattered more than the occupation of land. About 300,000 of these were 'cottiers', which in Ireland meant that they worked for payment but also held very small plots of potato ground rented from tenant farmers rather than directly from the landlords themselves. The remaining one million were labourers pure and simple.[6]

One of the chief effects of the Great Famine was a dramatic reversal of these proportions, so that by 1891 farmers and their relatives had come to constitute more than three-quarters of Ireland's total occupied male agricultural population. In other words, a sharp demographic collapse had taken place among the landless labourers, with the result that, by the end of the century, the non-landlord sector of rural Ireland had come to be dominated, demographically as well as economically, by farmers of various kinds. Indeed, already by the late-1860s more than three out of every four voters in the 32 county constituencies were farmers, the rest being chiefly small-town artisans, professional people, and so forth.[7]

The Clergy and their Flocks

Although Catholics in Ireland obtained the vote on the same terms as Protestants in 1793, it was not until the 1820s that a distinctly Catholic electoral bloc began to emerge.[8] Two related developments brought this about. In the first place, the activities of the Catholic Association founded in 1823 by the lawyer and minor landowner, Daniel O'Connell, to secure the admission of Catholics into parliament (what became known as Emancipation) created entirely novel organisations dedicated to electoral intervention. In the second, O'Connell's ability to build a mass following by using the network of local influence possessed by the Catholic Church had the effect of incorporating the clergy into the electoral sphere in an altogether new and dramatic way.[9] From then onwards priests and bishops provided one of the chief forces in constitutional politics and electioneering. Having first been mobilised in connection with an issue that could be regarded as a 'religious' one (Emancipation), they gradually extended their activities into areas that were religious only very loosely or not at all (repeal of the Union, agrarian reform, Home Rule, and so on).

By the middle of the century the electoral activities of the clergy had become matters of common report and equally common exaggeration and misunderstanding. Already by the 1830s *The Times* was painting lurid pictures 'of disciplined hordes of Catholic voters, completely submissive to the commands of their spiritual and secular masters, the priests and the agitators'. A Catholic MP in 1852 declared that 'you will find that every election [since 1826] was gained mainly by the aid of the clergy; every election that was lost was because they did not zealously co-operate'.[10] More confident still was Sir Francis Head, an English Protestant who came to Ireland in 1852 to collect ammunition with which to denounce the electoral 'power of the priests', and who, after a fortnight's tour, had no doubts at all that 'every poor, illiterate, honest Irishman, living with his pig and donkey in a chimneyless cabin, is completely in the hands and at the mercy of his spiritual master'.[11]

Now, of course, many priests had been extremely busy electorally well before the Famine. Among the few educated Catholics living in rural parishes, they had canvassed, organised, signed petitions, acted as informal agents, collected money, even spoken from the hustings.[12] Yet, at the same time, their involvement had been neither constant nor – on the whole – self-generated. It was O'Connell who had approached the clergy in the 1820s, not the other way about.[13] At the general election of 1826 when the clergy had first made a significant impact in perhaps half-a-dozen constituencies, it was generally the priest, according to Thomas Wyse (O'Connell's chief election expert at the time), who 'was hurried along with the torrent, and had only to decide whether he should ride on its surface, or be buried altogether beneath the stream'.[14] And once Emancipation had been granted in 1829, clerical electioneering for a time declined as priests proved reluctant to involve themselves so fully in O'Connell's next campaign for repeal of the Union, an issue which, at least to begin with, they saw as sitting less closely to their own religious and sectarian concerns.[15] Small wonder that English observers generally, and politicians in particular, could never quite make up their minds whether priests controlled the Catholic electorate or whether, as the Viceroy Lord Clarendon argued in October 1847, the clergy had in fact 'become the slaves of the people'.[16] Hence the frequent suggestions throughout the century that the government should follow continental practice and actually pay a salary to the priests in order to 'free' them from popular control,[17] a curious notion if in reality they possessed the enormous powers so often ascribed to them.

In truth the relationship between the clergy and their flocks was a complex one fashioned by a common history of disadvantage, mediated through filters of mutual dependence, and never precisely aligned as to either methods or aims. The so-called penal laws of the first half of the eighteenth century had institutionalised the inferior and oppressed state of all Catholics, rich as well as poor, clerical as well as lay. And while it would be wrong to exaggerate the strength of the solidarity which this created, the fading presence of a wealthy Catholic gentry certainly helped to produce – partly by necessity, partly by choice – a closer relationship between priests and people than was the rule in continental Europe. In 1835 Alexis de Tocqueville dined at Carlow with a party of Catholic ecclesiastics (including five bishops): 'the conversation turned on the state of the country and politics, the feelings expressed were extremely democratic. Distrust and hatred of the great landlords; love of the people, and confidence in them. Bitter memories of past oppression'. On another occasion Bishop Kinsella of Ossory told him how shocked he had been to see, on a recent visit to France, sentries posted outside the archbishop's palace at Rouen: 'I don't like that sort of guard of honour; they make people think of your Archbishop as the representative of the King much more than that of Jesus Christ'.[18] But while to some extent such feelings were indeed generated by a congeries of experiences common to all Irish Catholics, the fact that the clergy depended entirely for financial support upon their flocks clearly gave the latter a degree of influence over the former which they might otherwise not have possessed. This, as has been noted, worried many outsiders. What, however, was even less widely understood was that an increasing proportion of this support was coming from the growing farmer community and from the Catholic middle classes of the towns – precisely the groups from which the bulk of the priesthood was itself recruited.[19] And it was the resulting alliance between reforming ecclesiastics anxious to suppress the often chaotic, backward-looking, and populist attitudes of pre-Famine rural Catholicism (with their emphasis on holy wells, exotically-celebrated local patron feasts, and alleged 'survivals' from pagan times) and the increasingly literate agrarian and urban middle classes which constituted perhaps the most significant aspect of nineteenth-century Irish Catholicism's transformation from a demotic folk religion into the ultramontane, clericalist, and altogether more religiously formal church characteristic of more modern times.[20]

What, among much else, this process of transformation made manifest was a growing disjunction between a clergy whose closest social sympathies lay with tenant farmers[21] and the aspirations of the large but shrinking landless elements within the rural population. Thus, open and effective clerical action on behalf of desperately poor labourers was rare. Two Kildare priests found themselves totally isolated among their brethren when, in July 1832, they tried to organise a meeting 'for the avowed purpose of increasing the wages of the labourers and compelling every farmer and landowner ... to give up one acre for the benefit of the poor'.[22] Rural priests were to be found telling labourers to 'obey the law' and not cause trouble for farmers burdened by having to pay tithes to the established church. In 1847 the 'principal farmers' of Limerick joined the local clergy in demanding strong coercive action to reduce the disorder of a famine-stricken countryside.[23]

As a result of such developments, two connected trends become evident in the middle third of the nineteenth century. In the first place, the increasing clericalisation and modernisation of Catholicism gave the priesthood a growing monopoly of spiritual and theological power. And the more autonomous the priests' role became, the more successfully were the clergy able to sustain an identity as religious specialists amidst the powerful national and secular political movements that were to appear later. In the second place, increased lay acquiescence as regards clerical views of what constituted moral (especially sexually moral) behaviour was not accompanied by a similar deference in the field of politics, which henceforth became the one major area in which reciprocal criticisms remained not only possible but endemic. More notably still, post-Famine politics offered one of the very few forums in which priests could still behave as if the distinctions between the 'religious' and 'profane', which ecclesiastical modernisers had been so anxious to make, had achieved neither effective definition nor widespread implementation. And by tying themselves so closely to the farmer classes, the clergy also often seemed to act primarily as spokesmen for sectional interests rather than articulators of the political feelings and economic aspirations of rural society as a whole. In the strictly religious and moral spheres priests achieved greater and greater dominance; in politics they were never more than one powerful group among many.

Of course, in an important sense, the clergy were merely swimming with the social and economic currents of the time. The absolute and relative post-Famine decline in the number of landless labourers shifted the power centre of rural politics ever further towards the tenant farmers. While before the passing of the Irish Franchise Act of 1850 the vagaries of electoral law had meant that significant numbers of those with such small holdings that they approximated economically to little more than cottiers had been able to vote,[24] for the thirty-five years thereafter the county electorate was strictly confined to those occupying property with a poor law valuation of at least twelve pounds. Such people paid a minimum of fifteen pounds a year in rent and certainly did not include those smallholders adventitiously enfranchised before 1850.[25] Indeed, the way in which electoral politics were so commonly placed within the context of the struggle between landlords and tenant farmers reflected above all the priorities of the latter. Landless labourers had little direct contact with landlords and felt themselves exploited, not by the remote proprietors of broad acres, but by the farmers who employed them and provided them with expensive potato ground. The Devon Commission enquiring into the Irish land question was told again and again in 1844 how labourers were 'opposed by farmers', made 'dependent as slaves', 'more wretched than the Fellahs of Egypt or the blacks of Cuba', how the jealousy between farmers and labourers was 'much stronger' than that between landlords and tenants.[26]

When, therefore, priests pictured themselves and were pictured by others to be electorally active principally in order to counteract the political power of the landed proprietors, this was by no means the precise equivalent of fighting for the people, rather it amounted, first and foremost, to fighting for the medium-size and large tenant farmers. In 1835 an inspector of police noted how, during the Kerry elections, priests and landlords constituted the chief *forces de frappe* in a particular kind of economic struggle, the one armed with 'excommunications' the other with 'ejectments'.[27] During the 1852 general election popular papers like the Nation argued that 'the sole political power able and adequate to resist' landlordism was that of the priests, while Conservative organs like the *Londonderry Sentinel*, by looking through the other end of the same telescope, could regard it as 'a duty on the part of the landlords to exert influence, in order to counteract the machinations of ... the priests'.[28] And it is significant that, having once become involved in Irish electoral politics on the 'religious' issue of Catholic Emancipation in the 1820s, thereafter the priesthood tended to mount its most substantial interventions more often on land questions directly related to the interests of tenant farmers than on anything else. The comparative post-Emancipation lull in clerical electioneering was reversed, not initially by O'Connell's campaign to repeal the Union, but by the growing concern of farmers over the tithe payments they were required to make for the support of the Protestant Church of Ireland. Agriculturalists, noted a Cork priest in 1832, 'understood about tithes very well; but they were not so clear about repeal ... on the question of tithes they would go with him against their landlord, but he was afraid he could not drag them out on repeal so readily'.[29] Again, the dominant electoral issue in the 1850s revolved around the demands of the Tenant League for land reform, while the engine which eventually drove Parnell and the Home Rule Party to prominence in the 1880s was, above all, an agrarian one.[30]

The Limits of Clerical Influence

While land issues constituted the political nexus which bound tenant farmers and priesthood most closely together, their primacy casts revealing light upon both the strengths and weaknesses of the clergy's electoral interventions. Tenurial questions were, above all, secular phenomena, however much the clergy's interests and social backgrounds may have been involved. In this respect they bear comparison with

O'Connell's repeal movement of the 1830s and 1840s and with the Home Rule movement of the 1880s. In each case the ultimate object was at best indirectly connected with the imperatives of Catholicism and the Catholic Church. The initiative came from laymen concerned about secular ends such as devolved government, land reform in favour of tenant farmers, or a combination of the two. The political systems created to achieve these ends, while heavily reliant upon clerical support, were, therefore, secular both in nature and in the character of their operations.[31] The result was that the priesthood never succeeded in developing a coherent, independent, and self-generated form of political or electoral behaviour which could function reliably without the guidance of a powerful lay leadership. O'Connell and Parnell provided such leadership and it was only under overall control of this kind that priests found themselves able to deploy their electoral influence to sustained and national effect. At other times, notably during the confused periods of fissiparousness and localism which marked both the years between 1847 and 1875 and again after 1890,[32] the Church, while extremely active and energetic electorally, tended to flounder like a ship without captain, compass or maps.

Paradoxically, therefore, periods of weak or almost non-existent lay control witnessed not only the most active clerical electioneering (as the priesthood sought to fill what amounted to political vacuums), but also the least effective. Thus the general election of August 1847, which took place three months after the death of O'Connell and at a time when his movement had clearly fallen apart under the impact of famine and the defection of the Young Irelanders, was marked by the busiest and most high-profile intervention by the clergy since 1829.[33] And similar, indeed even more intense, levels of activism characterised the two decades that followed, with the general election of 1852 constituting perhaps the acme of rudderless and ultimately futile electioneering on the priesthood's part. At 19 of the 23 contested county elections outside Ulster, priests either proposed, seconded or spoke for candidates on the hustings.[34] Even cursory minimum counts reveal that crucial individual meetings attracted large numbers of local priests: 18 in Mayo, 24 in Westmeath, 14 in Carlow, 18 in Tipperary, 23 in Meath, 36 in Queen's County. In Limerick (and elsewhere) the clergy completely controlled the selection of candidates on the popular side.[35] Yet throughout the 1850s and 1860s priests, rather than acting as effective lieutenants to powerful lay politicians, found themselves merely one interest group among many others seeking local advantage or sectional goals: the gentry, shopkeepers, artisans, farmers, merchants and many others. As a result, it was never entirely clear what precisely was being aimed at, much less being achieved. The weak Independent Irish Party of the 1850s, which succeeded O'Connell's repeal movement, was always deeply suspect in the eyes of important clerical leaders like Paul Cullen, appointed Archbishop of Armagh in 1849 and of Dublin in 1852.[36] The Tenant League, which agitated during the 1850s to improve the tenurial position of farmers, was supported by some priests and vociferously opposed by others. The Catholic Defence Association, founded in 1851 to counter the British government's anti-Catholic Ecclesiastical Titles Bill of that year, proved attractive to clerics but much less so to laymen.[37]

Cullen, who soon became the dominant Catholic ecclesiastic in Ireland, specialised in trying to suppress the electioneering of priests of whom he disapproved by issuing general orders to stay aloof while, when it suited him, advising others to work for the return of candidates 'who will respect our civil and religious rights'.[38] The result was confusion. In 1859 a significant number of anti-Cullen priests actually supported the overwhelmingly Protestant Conservative Party (which had promised some minor concessions), with the result that – for the only time in the post-1832 period – Conservatives won a majority of the Irish seats (55 out of 105). More striking still was the total failure of the National Association set up in 1864 under tight ecclesiastical auspices to campaign politically and electorally for Catholic objectives.[39] When left to themselves, as it were, bishops and priests, however politically engaged, were rarely able either to set the agenda or control the character of political life at the national level. The engine, indeed, strained, a great deal of noise was made, but the progress forward proved disappointingly slow.

It was, therefore, weakness and confusion rather than unity of purpose that encouraged the efflorescence of clerical electioneering so characteristic of the 1850s and 1860s. At Louth in 1854 and 1857 priests savaged each other on the hustings. At New Ross in 1852 parish priest and curate violently supported opposing candidates. Meath priests were involved in open fisticuffs at Navan in 1855. Bishop O'Brien of Waterford noted in 1857 how 'our clergy, unfortunately, are as much divided as those of Cashel and Kildare'. At Kilkenny in 1859 the priests were again bitterly split.[40] Equally destructive were those inter-diocesan conflicts encouraged by local particularism Here individual bishops seemed sometimes positively to relish the clash of rivalry and distrust. Archbishop MacHale of Tuam and Bishop Gillooly of Elphin, whose responsibilities overlapped in the Galway and Roscommon constituencies, were locked in permanent conflict. In King's County wrangling broke out between the clergy of the Killaloe, Ardagh, and Meath dioceses.[41] What became known as 'spiritual intimidation' reached its peak in these years. Disappointed candidates and voters could appeal to parliamentary select committees (after 1868 to judges) against electoral returns they considered invalid and the number of petitions alleging spiritual intimidation rose from nine between 1832 and 1851 to 18 between 1852 and 1881, with six MPs being unseated in the later and only two in the earlier period.[42] Divided, frustrated, and without clear political guidance, the clergy wielded their religious weapons during election campaigns as never before: refusals to administer the last rites, unvarnished cursing, providing spiritual sanction to what often amounted to little more than local rivalries and mundane disputes. Priests in Kilkenny pointedly reminded their parishioners that 'you cannot give half your soul to God and the other [half] to the Devil. It is a moral essence; it is indivisible; it will all go to Hell or to Heaven'. In Limerick they locked the chapel doors and urged captive flocks to 'keep their baptismal vows and ... renounce the Devil' by voting for one Catholic Liberal rather than another. In Mayo Father Conway could be heard announcing 'My curse as a priest, the curse of God, the curse of the Church and people be upon you if you vote for Colonel Higgins'.[43] Priests threatened to withhold the sacraments from recalcitrant voters, certainly in Kerry, Louth, Cork, Tipperary, Mayo, Longford and Dublin, and almost certainly in many other places also.[44] Longford priests expressed the hope that obstinate electors would rot 'till the maggots and worms eat you and after that you may go to Hell'.[45]

Clerical involvement in electioneering was, indeed, never more prominent than in the years which followed the Famine: for example in 1859 over two-thirds of the priests in County Kilkenny and four-fifths of those in County Louth signed their names to electoral placards, flysheets, and manifestos. Not only, however, did contemporary commentators differ about the impact of such things, but endemic disagreements and disputes diminished the Church's importance as a national vehicle of political influence. For every fear that the Church's power was growing, there were suggestions that it was diminishing and that, 'people think, and act, much more for themselves than they did'.[46] Observers pointed to the failure of specific electoral interventions: in County Cork and Queen's County in 1852, Cashel throughout the 1850s, County Sligo in 1857, Limerick City in 1858, Queen's County in 1868.[47] Priests, it was widely remarked, were only successful when articulating the implicit preferences of their flocks or when canvassing topics (denominational education is an obvious example) upon which the mass of the laity had few burning convictions. But such views, even if true, ignored the distinction between political influence upon a broad national stage, on the one hand, and local influence, on the other. The former was achieved only in alliance with dynamic secular movements or as a kind of sub-text to gradually increasing spiritual authority, the latter could exist even during the most confused and chaotic periods in Irish political life. While in the eighteenth and early nineteenth centuries the rural priest had still faced a degree of rivalry within the local community from such comparatively independent figures as traditional poets and schoolmasters, thereafter he was to stand virtually alone until the arrival of shopkeeper allies in the later nineteenth century (products of a growth in retailing) produced a sharing, though not notably a diminution, of status.[48]

Amidst the confusions of the mid-century period certain prominent priests succeeded, more than ever before, in becoming what amounted to local electoral 'bosses', reputedly capable of 'delivering' voters to almost any candidate they chose. Yet, interestingly, such figures flourished more often in the hot-house atmosphere of the smaller borough constituencies than in the counties. Thus the historian, Sir John Acton (later known for his sea-green views on the corruption of power), was returned in 1859 for Carlow Borough through the good offices of Father James Maher whose support more than outweighed Acton's transient presence in the constituency and exiguous public programme.[49] Elsewhere too individual priests built up impressive electoral connections which depended for their effectiveness more upon the patterning of local conditions – employment levels, a desire for better drains, kin relationships, mercantile rivalries – than upon any governing ideas of a more general kind. When the Catholic lawyer, Thomas O'Hagan, arrived to canvass for the Kinsale Borough by-election of 1863 he found the parish priest and his curate claiming to 'control' 34 of the 130 voters on the register, a bloc rivalled only by that of Captain Heard, a substantial local landowner and himself MP for the borough between 1852 and 1859.[50] In Galway Town at about the same time Father Peter Daly owed his undoubted influence not so much to his clerical office as to the firmly secular base of chairmanship of the corporation and the gas company, presidency of the Mechanics' Institute and the Commercial Society, and ownership of the Lough Corrib Steam Company.[51] Again, in Dungarvan, Father Jeremiah Halley made himself indispensable by the opportunist manoeuvring of a small faction devoted to him by ties of kinship, sympathy, and dependence. After some free-wheeling preliminaries in the late-1840s he pursued a breathtaking course, supporting now Whigs, now Tories, now

Independent Oppositionists. Amidst the enthusiastic local game of political musical chairs, Halley retained a central importance.[52] In 1857 he stopped supporting the interest of the Whig Duke of Devonshire (who owned large estates in the district) and was roundly abused by his grace's agent, only to be wooed again in 1859 when, however, he secured the return of a pro-Tory Independent by means of an alliance with the Conservatives arranged personally with the government's principal Irish minister, the Chief Secretary himself.[53]

By isolating one element – clerical influence – in a complex equation, it is of course possible to beg rather than to answer questions. However, the results of two by-elections in County Cork (a constituency divided between the jurisdictions of the Bishops of Cloyne, Cork, Ross, and Kerry) show how, even in the mid-century period, the *local* impact of the clergy could still be very great indeed. When in 1852 the Cloyne priests 'imposed' their candidate upon the Liberal machine, the effect upon the polling figures was dramatic, with the Liberals obtaining 65 per cent of the vote in the Cloyne districts but only 41 per cent elsewhere. Eight years later, when the Cloyne priests supported a Conservative and the other dioceses a Liberal, the proportions were reversed, with the Liberal candidate receiving 47.3 per cent of the vote in the Cloyne areas but 86.5 per cent in the remaining parts of the constituency.[54]

Not that the overall electoral effectiveness of the clergy, whether on the local or the national level, was fashioned entirely by uncontrolled internal divisions or collaborations, important though these could be. Thus, from time to time, bishops, individually or collectively, tried to restrain the lower clergy's electoral interventions either because they feared that disunity would ultimately undermine the Church's influence over things other than politics or because they were worried by the extremism of some of their subordinates. In 1830 a joint pastoral letter enjoined a withdrawal from politics after the granting of Catholic Emancipation. Another joint resolution followed in 1834.[55] Between 1850 and 1854 a series of regulations along the same lines was issued both by the national episcopate and (more locally) by the bishops of the four ecclesiastical provinces into which Ireland was divided. As usual, however, they had little effect. On the one hand, priests were 'strictly' forbidden from discussing 'merely secular' matters such as elections within chapels; on the other, enormous loopholes were opened up by exhortations to condemn bribery and perjury, to maintain the rights of the Church, and to be 'solicitous' in seeing that both parliament and local authorities were stocked with 'men of integrity and favourable to the Catholic religion'.[56] Already by 1857 even those bishops who had most strongly supported the resolutions were admitting their virtual ineffectiveness.[57] Other bishops who had never had much faith in 'rules' made it publicly plain that electoral activity by the clergy would evince few episcopal condemnations from them, as when Archbishop MacHale of Tuam stonewalled with virtuoso dexterity when asked by the Mayo election committee of 1857 whether he would condemn a priest who, 'standing in his vestments at the altar' had loudly declared that 'the curse of God would come down upon anyone voting against his country, and his country's cause, and voting for Colonel Higgins was doing so'.[58] Even less effective, because coming from outside Ireland, were Rome's efforts – most notably in the 1840s and 1880s – to set strict limits to the clergy's politicking. While the British government consistently displayed a naive faith in the power of a conservative Vatican over Irish politics and regularly brought diplomatic pressure to bear to encourage its exercise, by the end of the century few others took a similarly sanguine view.[59] Just as, therefore, Irish Catholic laymen and women deferred to the clergy on political and electoral matters only to a very circumscribed extent, so Irish priests and bishops paid very limited regard to Rome's pronouncements on what was or was not politically acceptable.

What neither London nor Rome understood was that the power as opposed to the energy of the clergy's electoral actions was invariably limited more by the balances inherent in the Irish political and social systems than by formal rules or external commands. Voters were seldom simply inert entities to be pulled this way or that by either landlord or priest. As the laity became more educated and articulate and as the better-off farmers became more and more dominant politically, so priests increasingly found themselves attacked and criticised when their electoral wishes failed to coincide with strongly-held opinions in particular localities. Again, it is notable that this kind of electoral disjunction was especially pronounced during the 1850s and 1860s when priests, on occasion, had their windows smashed, were offered violence in the streets, were reported to their bishops for abusing laymen, were manhandled by election mobs, had to face open defiance, and even had to plead with landlords for protection against politically recalcitrant parishioners.[60]

Lord Palmerston, not usually an acute observer of the Irish scene, rightly pointed to the confusions inherent in the opinions of those like the Viceroy Lord Clarendon who, in 1847, prepared a memorandum for the Russell administration in one part of which 'he assumes that the priests have no influence in Ireland and in another part [of which] he assumes that they have a great deal'. In reality, Palmerston insisted, 'they have influence and they have not, they have it in some things and not in others'.[61] To put it another way, the clergy's political and electoral power fluctuated in response to changing local conditions as well as in response to the relative coherence or distintegration of popular politics at the national level. When in the 1880s Parnell's Home Rule movement came to dominate nationalist and agrarian politics the short-term effect upon clerical electioneering was profound. Parnell's main organisation, the National League, while granting the clergy a prominent formal role in the selection of parliamentary candidates and the conduct of elections, in practice exercised tight centralised lay control in a manner not seen before. Ostensibly Home Rule candidates were chosen at county conventions which all local priests were free to attend. This, however, was a mere sham because such conventions invariably selected persons presented to it by the party's central apparatus meeting privately in Dublin.[62] But while in one sense this obliged the clergy to accept what seemed like the shadow rather than the substance of power, in reality, by returning priests and bishops to the auxiliary status they had occupied under O'Connell (and doing so with unwonted firmness and clarity), the National League directed ecclesiastical electioneering into such fruitful channels that the clergy were able to help the Home Rule movement to achieve unprecedented triumphs at both national and local levels.[63] Just as a skilfully pruned apple tree soon yields more fruit than before, so the skilfully restricted priesthood of the 1880s was soon seen to be having more real electoral impact than the luxuriantly untramelled clergy of former times.

But despite frequent assumptions to the contrary, nothing is forever in Irish history. Once Parnell's power was broken after the famous O'Shea divorce case of 1890, the clergy reverted to the type of undisciplined behaviour that had characterised the three decades before 1880. Once it had become clear that Gladstone and the Liberal Party would have nothing to do with Parnell, the Catholic clergy swung overwhelmingly behind the anti-Parnellite faction which now constituted much the larger part of the Home Rule movement. Bishop Nulty of Meath produced a pastoral to be read in all his diocesan churches on Sunday 3 July 1892 (just as the general election of that year was about to start) which left nothing to the imagination. Parnellism, he declared,

> strikes at the very root and saps the foundations of Catholic faith ... Like pagan-
> ism [it] impedes, obstructs and cripples the efficiency and blights the fruitful-
> ness of the gospel ... The dying Parnellite himself will hardly dare to face the
> justice of his creator till he has been prepared and anointed by us for the last
> awful struggle.[64]

Outside the Protestant North-East, priests once again became initiators of action rather than simple auxiliaries. They collected money to support favoured candidates. They chaired and guided selection meetings. They acted as electoral aides and coordinators. On polling day they escorted voters to the booths. At few public meetings was one not to be found presiding, or at least speaking. They had seldom been busier. It was almost as if the 1880s might never have happened.

Yet, once again, the more one probes beneath the surface the less unambiguously effective all this activity becomes. In some constituencies, such as East Clare and North Galway, Parnellite candidates triumphed despite the most energetic efforts on the part of local clergymen. Though priests were widely thought to enjoy particularly despotic power over illiterate voters, no direct correlation emerges between constituency figures for the Parnellite share of the combined Parnellite and anti-Parnellite vote and the relative presence of illiterate electors. Especially revealing is the set of elections held in the North and South Meath constituencies. At the general election in 1892 the priests were extremely busy and the anti-Parnellites won. Then, on petition, new elections were called precisely because of undue clerical interference: the priests calmed down, but the results were almost exactly the same.[65] Nor did the group within the anti-Parnellite party that most clearly appealed to clerical attitudes on political questions – that led by T. M. Healy – succeed during the 1890s in ever becoming more than a comparatively small, though loud and factious, minority.[66] While, therefore, it undoubtedly suited Parnell and his adherents to emphasise the extent of clerical opposition to them so as to foster the notion that his defeat had been obtained by unfair and illegitimate means, it 'may be doubted that the Church, however gross its incursions into nationalist politics, bore so high a degree of responsibility for Parnell's defeats'.[67] This is not, of course, to deny importance to the role of the clergy in the political life of the 1890s, merely to say that the effects were general rather than particular and that the atmosphere created counted for more than particular actions undertaken before or during the times when voters actually went to the poll.

Conclusions

What, in the end, differentiated the Catholic clergy from their Protestant counterparts in terms of electoral power in particular and political power in general was, indeed, precisely their ability to shape, mould and direct the broad cultural mores of the great majority of the Irish people. Of course the priesthood had sectional affiliations, and the final campaign against Parnellism can be seen, at least in part, as an expression of that socially and economically conservative alliance between prosperous farmers and the Catholic Church which had characterised Ireland for fifty years and more. Nevertheless, the increasing homogenisation of late-nineteenth-century rural society, together with the deferential religiosity of the rural poor, gave the clergy a very wide leverage over both the countryside and the many towns where agricultural migrants formed a large proportion of the population.

'Clerical influence' over elections must, as a concept, remain imprecise both as to nature and degree. It cannot only mean the simple alteration of votes, but must also be related to the gradual moulding of opinion. It did not rise and fall in neat chronological patterns. Its impact depended not only upon the carrots of popular identification and sympathy, but upon the sticks of outright intimidation and spiritual coercion. It functioned most effectively when constrained and directed by powerful external political forces like those led by Daniel O'Connell and Charles Stewart Parnell, and most weakly when allowed to go its own way. Amidst the hyperactivity of the 1850s, 1860s and 1890s it is easy to mistake energy for effectiveness. And even effectiveness can be calibrated according to different scales. While in the years immediately after the Great Famine the priests could often provide the crucial impetus behind the return of particular candidates, they entirely failed to shape politics in a manner that was either ultimately congenial to clergymen or popular among Catholics as a whole. By adopting (or being obliged to adopt) a less independent stance in the 1880s and to a lesser extent in the 1830s and 1840s, the priesthood may – almost certainly unconsciously – have undertaken a series of tactical retreats while, nonetheless, contributing mightily to strategic advances along a very broad front indeed.

Notes

1   C. Seymour, *Electoral Reform in England and Wales: The Development and Operation of the Parliamentary Franchise, 1832-1885* (New Haven, 1915); J. Prest, *Politics in the Age of Cobden* (London, 1977); K. T. Hoppen, 'Politics, the Law, and the Nature of the Irish Electorate, 1832-1850', *English Historical Review*, vol. 92 (1977), pp. 746-76; and 'The Franchise and Electoral Politics in England and Ireland, 1832-1885', *History*, vol. 70 (1985), pp. 202-17.

2   During the nineteenth century Roman Catholics constituted a little over 75 per cent of the population. Although they included some wealthy merchants and landowners, the great majority were of lower status. The Protestant minority (heavily concentrated in the North-East) was not, however, denominationally united. Just over half belonged to the (Anglican) Church of Ireland while most of the rest were Presbyterians of various kinds. For details, see W. E. Vaughan and A. J. Fitzpatrick (eds.), *Irish Historical Statistics: Population 1821-1971* (Dublin, 1978), pp. 49-68.

3   As late as 1871 only 15.9 per cent of adult males in Ireland possessed the vote as compared to 33.6 per cent in England and Wales: see Hoppen, 'The Franchise and Electoral Politics in England and Ireland', p. 215.

4   J. S. Donnelly, Jr., *The Land and the People of Nineteenth-Century Cork: The Rural Economy and the Land Question* (London, 1975), pp. 9-72; K. T. Hoppen, *Ireland since 1800: Conflict and Conformity* (London, 1989), pp. 33-59; *idem*, 'Landownership and Power in Nineteenth-Century Ireland: The Decline of an Elite', in R. Gibson and M. Blinkhorn (eds.), *Landownership and Power in Modern Europe* (London, 1991), pp. 164-80.

5   B. L. Solow, *The Land Question and the Irish Economy, 1870-1903* (Cambridge, Mass., 1971), pp. 51-7; W. E. Vaughan, *Landlords and Tenants in Ireland, 1848-1904* (Dublin, 1984), pp. 15-17.

6   J. S. Donnelly Jr., 'The Social Composition of Agrarian Rebellions in early Nineteenth-Century Ireland', in P. J. Corish (ed.), *Radicals, Rebels and Establishments: Historical Studies XV* (Belfast, 1985), pp. 151-69.

7   K. T. Hoppen, *Election, Politics, and Society in Ireland, 1832-1885* (Oxford, 1984), p. 105.

8   For scattered earlier electoral interventions by the clergy, see P. J. Jupp, 'Irish Parliamentary Elections and the Influence of the Catholic Vote, 1801-1820', *Historical Journal*, vol. 10 (1967), pp. 183-96.

9   J. A. Reynolds, *The Catholic Emancipation Crisis in Ireland, 1823-1829* (New Haven, 1954); F. O'Ferrall, *Catholic Emancipation: Daniel O'Connell and the Birth of Irish Democracy, 1820-30* (Dublin, 1985).

10 A. Macintyre, *The Liberator: Daniel O'Connell and the Irish Party, 1830-1847* (London, 1965), p. 111; *Minutes of Evidence taken before the Select Committee on the Cork City Election Petition*, H[house of] C[ommons Paper], 1852-3 (528), xi, p. 436.

11 F. B. Head, *A Fortnight in Ireland* (London, 1852), p. 265. Head's researches were partly based on official files: see Lord Eglinton to Lord Derby, 4 Aug. 1852, Scottish Record Office (Edinburgh) Eglinton Papers MS 5333; also Head to Lord Naas, 2 Oct. 1852, N[ational] L[ibrary of] I[reland, Dublin] Head Letters MS 18513.

12. J. H. Whyte, 'The Influence of the Catholic Clergy on Elections in Nineteenth-Century Ireland', *English Historical Review*, vol. 75 (1960), pp. 239-59.

13. F. O'Ferrall, '"The Only Lever..."? The Catholic Priest in Irish Politics, 1823-29', *Studies* (Dublin), vol. 70 (1981), pp. 308-11.

14. T. Wyse, *Historical Sketch of the late Catholic Association of Ireland*, 2 vols. (London, 1829), vol. 1, p. 283.

15. Whyte, 'The Influence of the Catholic Clergy', p. 241.
16. Bodl[eian Library, Oxford] Clarendon Deposit (Irish) Letter-Book I: Memorandum for Lord Minto.
17. D. A. Kerr, *Peel, Priests and Politics: Sir Robert Peel's Administration and the Roman Catholic Church in Ireland, 1841-1846* (Oxford, 1982), pp. 64-5; E. R. Norman, *The Catholic Church and Ireland in the Age of Rebellion, 1859-1873* (London, 1965), pp. 300-3 and 337-8. On clerical finances generally, see D. J. Keenan, *The Catholic Church in Nineteenth-Century Ireland: A Sociological Study* (Dublin, 1983), pp. 226-39; Hoppen, *Elections, Politics, and Society in Ireland*, pp. 224-32.
18. A. de Tocqueville, *Journeys to England and Ireland*, edited by J. P. Mayer (London, 1958), pp. 130 and 145-6.
19. Hoppen, *Elections, Politics, and Society in Ireland*, pp. 174-83; Keenan, *The Catholic Church in Nineteenth-Century Ireland*, pp. 61-6.
20. E. Larkin, 'The Devotional Revolution in Ireland, 1850-75', *American Historical Review*, vol. 77 (1972), pp. 625-52; S. Connolly, *Religion and Society in Nineteenth-Century Ireland* (Dublin, 1985), pp. 42-60; Hoppen, *Elections, Politics, and Society in Ireland*, pp. 211-24.
21. For example, of the 378 priests coming in the nineteenth century from the Kilmore diocese (most of County Cavan and parts of County Leitrim), all but half-a-dozen were from families with farms of more than 35 acres: see D. A. Kerr, 'Under the Union Flag: The Catholic Church in Ireland, 1800-1870', in Lord Blake (ed.), *Ireland after the Union: Proceedings of the Second Joint Meeting of the Royal Irish Academy and the British Academy, London, 1986* (Oxford, 1989), p. 34.
22. Lord Melbourne to Lord Anglesey, 25 July 1832, Royal Archives (Windsor) Melbourne Papers 94/32 (cited with the gracious permission of H. M. Queen Elizabeth II); Major Tandy to W. Gossett, 22 and 29 July 1832, N[ational] A[rchives] D[ublin] Outrage Papers Private Index 1832/1341.
23. *Dublin Evening Post*, 24 Jan. 1837; Report of Chief Constable Hutton, 13 Feb. 1832, NAD Outrage Papers 1832/255 Box 2175; Lord Clarendon to Lord John Russell, 3 Dec. 1847, Bodl. Clarendon Deposit (Irish) Letter-Book II. O'Connellite organisations were notably unsympathetic to labourers: see *Pilot*, 26 Apr. 1837.
24. Hoppen, 'Politics, the Law, and the Nature of the Irish Electorate', pp. 746-76.
25. Hoppen, *Elections, Politics, and Society in Ireland*, pp. 18-21 and 89-116.
26. *Appendix to the Minutes of Evidence taken before Her Majesty's Commissioners of Inquiry into the State of the Law and Practice in respect to the Occupation of Land in Ireland*, part iv, HC, 1845 [672], xxii, p. 130; *Index to Minutes of Evidence taken before Her Majesty's Commissioners of Inquiry...*, HC, 1845 [673], xxii, pp. 233, 234, 236, 242, 243, 251, 252, 254.
27. *Report from Select Committee on Bribery at Elections; together with the Minutes of Evidence*, HC, 1835 (547), viii, p. 272.
28. *Nation*, 21 Aug. 1852; *Londonderry Sentinel*, 25 June 1852. See K. T.

Hoppen, 'Landlords, Society and Electoral Politics in Mid-Nineteenth-Century Ireland', *Past & Present*, no. 75 (1977), pp. 62-93.

29. Cited in M. Murphy, 'Repeal, Popular Politics, and the Catholic Clergy of Cork, 1840-50', *Journal of the Cork Historical and Archaeological Society*, vol. 82 (1977), p. 41; see also K. B. Nowlan, 'The Catholic Clergy and Irish Politics in the Eighteen Thirties and Forties', in J. G. Barry (ed.), *Historical Studies IX* (Belfast, 1974), pp. 121-2.

30. J. H. Whyte, *The Independent Irish Party, 1850-9* (Oxford, 1958), pp. 1-17, 37, 86-8; *idem*, 'Political Problems, 1850-60', in P. J. Corish (ed.), *A History of Irish Catholicism*, vol. 5, fascicule 2 (Dublin, 1967), pp. 12-38; S. R. Knowlton, *Popular Politics and the Irish Catholic Church: the Rise and Fall of the Independent Irish Party, 1850-1859* (New York, 1991), pp. 29-52; S. Clark, *Social Origins of the Irish Land War* (Princeton, 1979), pp. 107-245; P. Bew, *Land and the National Question in Ireland, 1858-82* (Dublin, 1982), *passim*.

31. O. MacDonagh, 'The Politization of the Irish Catholic Bishops, 1800-1850', *Historical Journal*, vol. 18 (1975), pp. 37-53.

32. K. T. Hoppen, 'National Politics and Local Realities in Mid-Nineteenth-Century Ireland', in A. Cosgrove and D. McCartney (eds.), *Studies in Irish History presented to R. Dudley Edwards* (Dublin, 1979), pp. 190-227.

33. Whyte, 'The Influence of the Catholic Clergy', p. 243.

34. Head, *A Fortnight in Ireland*, pp. 281-3. See also newspaper cuttings on the 1852 election collected by the British government and presented to the Vatican, in Vatican Secret Archives, Seg. di Stato 1852/278.

35. Head, *A Fortnight in Ireland*, pp. 285-324; Vatican Secret Archives, Seg. di Stato 1852/278.

36. E. D. Steele, 'Cardinal Cullen and Irish Nationality', *Irish Historical Studies*, vol. 19 (1975), pp. 239-60; Whyte, 'Political Problems, 1850-1860', pp. 12-38.

37. Whyte, *The Independent Irish Party*, pp. 28-31. The bill (which later became an act) was part of a hysterical British reaction to the restoration of a Roman Catholic hierarchy in England and Wales in 1850. It (ineffectively) forbade Catholic bishops from naming their sees after places in the United Kingdom.

38. Steele, 'Cardinal Cullen and Irish Nationality', p. 248; Cullen to Rev. Tobias Kirby (Rector of the Irish College in Rome), 9 Dec. 1853, P. J. Corish, 'Irish College Rome: Kirby Papers', *Archivium Hibernicum*, vol. 31 (1973), p. 50; E. Lucas, *The Life of Frederick Lucas MP*, 2 vols. (London, 1886), vol. 2, p. 124; Hoppen, *Ireland since 1800*, pp. 158-9.

39. P. J. Corish, 'Cardinal Cullen and the National Association of Ireland', *Reportorium Novum: Dublin Diocesan Historical Record*, vol. 3 (1962), pp. 13-61.

40. Rev. J. Powderley to Kirby, 25 Feb. 1854, Irish College Rome: Kirby Papers, 1377; Archbishop Dixon to Kirby, 13 Apr. 1857, *ibid.* 1925A; *Dublin Evening Post*, 15 June 1852; Cullen to Kirby, Nov. and 2 Dec. 1855, Corish, 'Irish College Rome: Kirby Papers', *Archivium Hibernicum*, vol. 31, pp. 56-7;

O'Brien to Cullen, 2 Mar. 1857, D[ublin] D[iocesan] A[rchives] Cullen Papers; C. B. Lyons to Cullen, 19 Apr. 1859, *ibid.*

41. Gillooly to Kirby, 26 Oct. 1862, Corish, 'Irish College Rome: Kirby Papers', *Archivium Hibernicum*, vol. 30 (1972), p. 31; Bishop Power to Cullen, 9 Aug. 1868, DDA Cullen Papers.

42. The number of petitions presented (and pursued) and the number of those resulting in voidance amounted to 55 and 28 in 1832-51, and 54 and 19 in 1852-81 – calculated from information in the relevant parliamentary papers on individual petitions; various legal handbooks; anon., *The Franchise and Registration Question* (London, 1841); *Return of the Election Petitions alleging Bribery and Corruption*, HC 1866 (77), lvi, pp. 515-28; *Return of all Election Petitions alleging Intimidation or Undue Influence*, HC 1866 (114), lvi, pp. 529-36; *Returns of the Number of Petitions complaining of Undue Returns*, HC 1880 (69), lvii, pp. 63-8.

43. Report on Kilkenny, 18 July 1852, NLI Mayo Papers MS 11184; J. Ball to Lord Dunraven, 21 Feb. [1858], P[ublic] R[ecord] O[ffice of] N[orthern] I[reland, Belfast] Dunraven Papers D3196; *Telegraph or Connaught Ranger*, 24 Feb. 1858; *Minutes of Evidence taken before the Select Committee on the Mayo County Election Petition*, HC 1857 (182 Sess. 2), vii, pp. 7-8 and 41.

44. *Londonderry Sentinel*, 30 July 1852; Dean Kieran to Archbishop Dixon, 26 Feb. 1854, Armagh Diocesan Archives Dixon Papers VII/2; *Cork Constitution*, 15 July 1852; *Daily Express* (Dublin), 24 July 1852; Cullen to Kirby, 5 Feb. 1858, Corish, 'Irish College'; Kirby Papers, *Archivium Hibernicum*, vol. 30, p. 66; Report on Longford, 7 Aug. 1852, NLI Mayo Papers MS 11037; J. Lord, *Popery at the Hustings: Foreign and Domestic Legislation* (London, 1852), p. 40.

45. *Copy of the Shorthand Writer's Notes... and the Minutes of Evidence taken at the Trial of the Longford Election Petition*, HC 1870 (178), lvi, p.301.

46. Clarendon to Russell, 29 Nov. 1851, Bodl. Clarendon Deposit (Irish) Letter-Book VII.

47. Lord Shannon to Lord Derby, 31 Mar. [1852], Liverpool Record Office Derby Papers 150/11; R. Miller to E. Staples, 29 Apr. 1852, Draper's Hall (London) Drapers' Company Archives Letter-Book Irish 1850-60; Rev. P. Leahy to Cullen, 8 Mar. 1857, DDA Cullen Papers; *Dublin Evening Mail*, 8 Apr. 1857; J. Ball to Dunraven, 21 Feb. [1858], PRONI Dunraven Papers D3196; *Freeman's Journal*, 15 and 17 Aug. 1868.

48. T. Ó Fiaich, 'Irish Poetry and the Clergy', *Léachtái Cholm Coille*, vol. 4 (1975), pp. 30-56; L. M. Cullen, 'The Hidden Ireland: Re-assessment of a Concept', *Studia Hibernica*, no. 9 (1969), p. 23; Hoppen, 'National Politics and Local Realities in Mid-Nineteenth-Century Ireland', pp. 195-8.

49. J. J. Auchmuty, 'Acton's Election as an Irish Member of Parliament', *English Historical Review*, vol. 61 (1946), pp. 394-405.

50. See the list of Electors in H. E. O'Donnell to O'Hagan, 29 Dec. 1862, PRONI O'Hagan Papers D2777/6; also M. Barry to O'Hagan, 14 Mar. 1862, *ibid.*; Rev. Dr Coveny to O'Hagan, 24 Dec. [1862] and M. Barry to O'Hagan, 20 Mar. 1862, *ibid.*

51. Norman, *The Catholic Church and Ireland*, pp. 16-17; J. to M. J. Blake, 4 and 12 Feb. 1859, NAD Blake of Ballyglunin Papers 6936/81.
52. F. E. to W. Currey, 13 May 1852, NLI Lismore Papers MS 7191; F. E. Currey to F. J. Howard, 29 Mar. 1857, *ibid.*; F. E. Currey to Duke of Devonshire, 22 Apr. 1859, *ibid.* MS 7190; also *Cork Constitution*, 17 and 31 Mar. 1857, 12 and 21 Apr. 1859, 24 June and 7 July 1865.
53. F. E. to W. Currey, 4 Apr. 1857, NLI Lismore Papers MS 7188 and 10 Apr. 1859, MS 7190; also Halley to Lord Naas, 28 Nov. 1858, NLI Mayo Papers MS 11023 and 15 Apr. 1859, MS 11036; J. F. Maguire to Disraeli, 4 Apr. 1859, Bodl. Disraeli [Hughenden] Papers B/XXI/M/69.
54. *Cork Southern Reporter*, 23 Mar. 1852; also *ibid.*, Feb and Mar. 1860, *passim*.
55. J. F. Broderick, *The Holy See and the Irish Movement for the Repeal of the Union with England 1829-1847* (Rome, 1951), pp. 45-6, 48-9, 58-9; MacDonagh, 'The Politicization of the Irish Catholic Bishops', pp. 44-5.
56. For the crucial Latin text, see E. Larkin, *The Making of the Roman Catholic Church in Ireland, 1850-1860* (Chapel Hill, 1980), p. 498, also pp. 170-274.
57. Bishop O'Brien to Cullen, 8 Mar. 1857, DDA Cullen Papers; Archbishop Leahy to Cullen, 3 Apr. 1857, *ibid.*
58. *Minutes of Evidence... Mayo County Election Petition*, HC 1857 (182 Sess. 2), vii, pp. 227-8.
59. On the 1840s, see Broderick, *The Holy See and the Irish Movement for the Repeal of the Union, passim;* on the 1880s, E. Larkin, *The Roman Catholic Church and the Creation of the Modern Irish State, 1878-1886* (Dublin, 1975), pp. 185-94, and *idem.*, *The Roman Catholic Church and the Plan of Campaign, 1886-1888* (Cork, 1978), *passim*.
60. *Dublin Evening Post*, 15 June 1852; University College Dublin Folklore Commission Papers, MS 1194, folios 360ff.; C. S. Farrell to Bishop Cantwell, 29 Nov. 1855, DDA Cullen Papers; A. C. O'Dwyer to Cullen, 10 Mar. 1857, *ibid.*; *Minutes of Evidence taken before the Select Committee on the Clare Election Petition*, HC 1852-3 (595), pp. ix, 179 and 201; E. O'Brien to W. Crowe, [4] May 1859, NLI Mayo Papers MS 11063; *The Times*, 2 May 1859; Sir R. Lynch Blosse to Lord Naas, 18 Nov. 1858, Mayo Papers MS 11021.
61. Palmerston to Lord Minto, 29 Oct. 1847, National Library of Scotland (Edinburgh) Minto Papers MS 12073.
62. C. C. O'Brien, *Parnell and his Party, 1880-90*, corrected impression (Oxford, 1964), pp. 128-32.
63. See, for example, J. O'Shea, *Priest and Society in Post-Famine Ireland: A Study of County Tipperary, 1850-1891* (Dublin, 1983), pp. 200-5; Larkin, *The Roman Catholic Church and the Creation of the Modern Irish State, passim*; and Larkin, *The Roman Catholic Church and the Plan of Campaign, passim*.
64. Cited in C. J. Woods, 'The General Election of 1892: The Catholic Clergy and the Defeat of the Parnellites', in F. S. L. Lyons and R. A. J. Hawkins (eds.), *Ireland under the Union: Varieties of Tension: Essays in Honour of T. W. Moody* (Oxford, 1980), p. 300.

65. *Ibid.*, pp. 310-12.
66. D. W. Miller, 'The Roman Catholic Church in Ireland: 1898-1918', *Eire-Ireland*, vol. 3 (1968), pp. 75-91; F. S. L. Lyons, *The Irish Parliamentary Party, 1890-1910* (London, 1951), pp. 42-57.
67. F. Callanan, *The Parnell Split, 1890-91* (Cork, 1992), p. 264.

CHAPTER 6

CLERICAL ELECTION INFLUENCE AND COMMUNAL SOLIDARITY: CATHOLIC POLITICAL CULTURE IN THE GERMAN EMPIRE, 1871-1914

Margaret Lavinia Anderson

In 1863 Franz Josef Hergenröther, Professor of Church History in Würzburg, subjected the question of the clergy's role in elections to careful analysis. Hergenröther was no liberal. His defence of papal infallibility in 1870 would soon gain him notoriety. Yet in his discussion of the propriety of clerical participation in electoral politics, Hergenröther proved to be anything but an ultramontane hotspur. He pointed frankly to the pitfalls of both abstinence and 'engagement'. Engagement encouraged the impression that the clergy pursued worldly ends. Yet the priest was a citizen, and if, in constitutional countries, where elections were so important, he failed to make use of his political rights, he neglected his duty to the Church and set a bad example for others. Even so, a priest must not campaign, he must not harangue crowds, he must not become involved in party battles. It was a thin line the Reverend Professor was drawing, and he conceded that mistakes would be made. But 'the clergy will be ignored if it ignores the conditions of present society', he concluded. A 'mute onlooker ..., risks losing the confidence of the people'.[1]

Hergenröther was joining a debate that had been simmering throughout Catholic Europe for a decade.[2] References throughout his analysis to struggles in Poland, to clerical demagogues in Italy, to the fate of Lammenais and Lacordaire in France suggest that the German clerical elite, like their Liberal and later their Social Democratic counterparts, viewed contemporary public life, if not *sub specie aeternitatis* then at least *sub specie europeana*. His international perspective pushed Hergenröther to the conclusion that there was 'today no actual Catholic politics; on the contrary, there is only a politics of individual Catholics. The Church offers us no set political system...'. Such a minimalist reading of Catholic political theory was considerably 'ahead' of clerical practice in many Western countries. The Vatican adopted it only in 1888.[3] Yet the fact that Hergenröther was able to cite authorities ranging from the liberal canon lawyer Johann Friedrich Ritter von Schulte to the conservative publicist Georg Phillips – German Catholics on opposite sides of the infallibility question and soon to be on opposite sides of political questions as well – suggests a broad consensus for such minimalism within the mainstream of German Catholic letters, clerical and lay, liberal and ultramontane.

Minimalism in theory became quietism in practice as the German civil war and Austria's defeat in 1866 led to the near collapse of clerical intervention in elections. The Catholic party that had existed in the Prussian Landtag since 1852 disappeared. Deputies from the clerical estate, who had held seventeen Landtag seats in the late 1850s, were reduced to two.

Yet in less than a decade this situation was reversed. The cautious reserve of the hierarchy, the uncoordinated, largely individualistic interventions of the lower clergy, both features of German elections since 1850, as well as the emerging consensus of the early sixties that there was no such thing as an 'actual Catholic politics, but rather only a politics of individual Catholics' – all were transformed into their opposites: the shared understanding from episcopal *Residenz* to rural rectory that the safety of the Church depended on election outcomes and that only someone who supported a particular party – the Centrum – with word and deed was a 'true Catholic'. With the taboo on partisanship, the taboo on campaigning also fell. 'Priests came to see politics as...inseparable from the religious order they wished to preserve', as Helmut Smith has noted. Elections became an extension of religious life.[4] Contrary to most changes in *mentalité* and political behaviour, this one can be given a precise date. The reversal began in South Germany with elections to the Zollparlament in 1868. It spread to Prussia during the Landtag and Reichstag elections of winter 1870-71. Its main features would endure until the end of democratic politics altogether in 1933.[5] The result was a phenomenon known, and not only to its opponents, as 'political Catholicism'. And for much of German opinion, 'clerical influence' became *the* sin against free elections.[6]

Electoral Politics and Catholic Culture

The clergy's reversal was not the result of the victory in 1870 of infallibilists in the Vatican, though the timing made it look that way. It was the product of the convergence of two processes, the first universal throughout the West, the second peculiar, at least in its form and intensity, to Central Europe.

The first, and universal, process was the sacralisation of political conflict that accompanied enfranchisement. Politics, which distributes power, and religion, which provides meaning for communities, inevitably came together wherever extensions of the suffrage gave communities access to power and the means of validating their own meanings against those of others. The emergence of the parson as a political force, though felt by many contemporaries to be a mark of backwardness, occurred precisely when, as an Austrian liberal noticed with surprise, politics had begun to move 'into freer paths'. This process, and the involvement of the clergy in elections, was remarkably similar across state and denominational boundaries, as witnesses from nineteenth-century Iowa to Besançon, from England to Spain, from Colombia to Canada attest.[7] The sudden introduction of direct manhood suffrage in the constitution of the new North German Confederation in 1867, its extension to South Germany during the Zollparlament elections, and its nationalisation in the constitution of the German Empire in 1871, set the stage in Germany for wider participation in elections – and clerical prominence.

The second, more local, process leading to the clergy's *volte face*, one more visible to contemporaries, was rising anti-Catholicism. Hostility to the Church of Rome was certainly not confined to Germany. But in Catholic countries, such as Austria or France, it was easier to distinguish between attacks on the institutional Church and hostility to the population at large; in Protestant countries, it was easier either to ignore the Catholic population or to discriminate against it without incurring political penalties. The wars of the seventeenth century had left Germany neither Catholic nor Protestant but roughly in balance. And now the war of 1866, and the defeat of Austria, reduced the Catholic population of what had once been the German Confederation to a minority of 36 per cent in the German Empire. Thus anti-Catholicism in Germany triggered, and overlaid, tensions between what we might today call minority and majority ethnicities. Moreover, in Germany anti-Catholicism was the flip side of a nationalism that had suddenly, after 1866, become both loud and popular with success. In the national narrative of German history increasingly touted as Germany's collective memory, the Roman Church was figured as villain, and the autonomy guaranteed it in Prussia's 1850 constitution became a dangerous concession to a perennial national enemy. Cultural aims that in a different context might have been merely secularising or even modernising (reform of the marriage law, transfer of school supervision from church to state) were re-defined as 'national' – and understood as anti-Catholic

In the midst of this nationalist rush, the new democratic suffrage increased the Church's vulnerability at the same time that it suggested the remedy: popular political action. In late 1870 prominent lay Catholics moved to resurrect the Centrum Party, the defunct champion of Prussian Catholicism, on a new and national basis. The bishops rallied. And in many districts throughout Germany the parish clergy made sure that the party came to the attention of the faithful. When the ballots were counted in 1871 the revived and now national party had managed to capture about a third of the Catholic electorate. Protestants, especially Liberals, responded with fear and loathing – and legislation.

Here is not the place to describe the Kulturkampf, the German cultural wars of the 1870s and 1880s that began with legislation against the politicking priest, re-wrote the legal position of the Catholic Church, and ultimately shaped the political culture(s) of Germans for generations. From the standpoint of Catholic political culture, three consequences of the Kulturkampf stand out. Most immediate was Catholic mobilisation. Voting came to be regarded as a 'test' that Catholics 'passed' by party loyalty.[8] Even in districts whose demography made the Centrum's victory a foregone conclusion, turnouts averaged more than 70 per cent, rates the Empire as a whole would not reach until 1903.[9] Second, as bishops and priests resisting the Kulturkampf went into jail or exile, the prestige of the clergy rose to unprecedented heights.[10] The third consequence, which flowed naturally from the persecution that produced the second, was to shift the initiative in Catholic affairs from the Church to an elected *party* leadership, and to habituate the Catholic laity to looking towards that leadership for direction.[11] But this tacit shift of authority from Church to Centrum gave those priests who were not incarcerated or on the run an enormous incentive to involve themselves in the party in every way possible. Which they did.

Here Germany seems unique. Although the intertwining of religious with political issues was a universal feature of electoral politics during the development of Western democratic institutions, automatically giving the clergy a leading role, nowhere else in Europe or America did clerical influence on elections become so widespread, so continuous, and so effective as in Catholic Germany. Nowhere else was it institutionalised in a powerful party. Although only a few priests – Canon Christoph Moufang and Bishop Wilhelm Emanuel von Ketteler of Mainz come to mind – were prominent Reichstag speakers, no fewer than 91 of the Centrum's 483 deputies during the course of the Empire were clergymen. In Silesia, West Prussia and Posnania, Catholic and Polish parties would have been hard put even to find sufficient candidates had they not been able to call on their priests. This exigency was even more true in Alsace-Lorraine, where sentiment for boycotting the German elections was so strong that Moufang had to press the Bishop of Strasbourg to take the initiative, with the result that of the ten Alsatian deputies in 1874 of 'Catholic' persuasion, seven were priests and two of these were bishops.[12]

The clergy's real political weight, however, lay outside of parliament. Some, barely known to the wider public, were 'insiders', funnelling information and advice on an almost daily basis between the party leadership in Berlin and selected bishops and cardinals.[13] Many were organisers – of semi-political clubs, co-operatives, trade unions, legal aid societies. By 1913 nearly 70 per cent of all the parishes in the Archdiocese of Freiburg, the region most resistant to political Catholicism, were equipped with a branch of the 'People's Association for Catholic Germany', a multi-purpose support group for the Centrum, and each branch was either largely or entirely under clerical direction.[14] Some priests were journalists. Not just major Centrum publications, but also the entire Sunday press and most of the local 'cheese sheets' in Catholic regions were written, managed, and edited in the spare time of some over-worked priest. And dynamos like Pastor Theodor Wacker of Baden and Chaplain Georg Friedrich Dasbach of Trier managed to combine in one person the offices of popular tribune, labour leader, journalist, publishing entrepreneur and regional party boss.

Did this make the Centrum a 'clerical' party? On issues of national policy, even policy affecting the Church, these clerics took their marching orders from a democratically elected party, whose leaders were laymen– a remarkable phenomenon in a religious culture in which the clergy were defined, in theology textbooks, as 'the Church', the laity only as 'in' the Church.[15] In state politics, on the other hand, the record is more complicated. In German-speaking (but not in Polish-speaking) Prussia, and perhaps even in Württemberg and Hessen, policy decisions also remained largely in lay hands. In Bavaria, however, from the 1890s on, and in Baden from the very beginning, the party's leadership was clerical.

Priests also forged the links between the various levels of electoral politics. Sometimes this network was explicit and established early. Already for the 1871 election the deaconates (diocesan sub-divisions encompassing nine to twenty-two parishes) of Trier had become *de facto* party precincts, composed of wards (the ecclesiastical term was 'definitions') of several parishes each, and the diocesan paper published a detailed plan showing how precinct captains and ward-bosses (parsons all) could produce the desired election results.[16] In areas where such formal organisation did not appear until later, or where the laity took the initiative, the clergy were still the indispensable brokers of the political process, and not just during the actual campaign. In Baden, the pastor was the invariable recipient of 'inquiries and assignments from the district and central party leadership, leaflets and election newsletters to be distributed, requests for funding these and other campaign activities'.[17] The situation was no different in the Emsland.[18] Priests were automatic members (called 'born members') of district nominating committees, where they nearly always made up the largest single group. As such they were buffers between warring economic factions, and since their own interests were above all in winning, they were responsible for forcing through compromises, either by the power of their arguments –or of their power.[19] In constituencies where the leadership of the parliamentary party in Berlin picked the candidate, these leaders would still consult first with the parish clergy. If local demography meant that the Centrum had no chance of winning, should they put up their own man anyway – a symbolic 'candidate for the count' *(Zählkandidat)*, whose totals would at least reveal the party's strength – or should they throw their support behind another party? Lay notables could not be trusted to decide these issues. More vulnerable to government pressure and susceptible to government promises than the clergy, they were apt to make the kind of muddy compromises that risked losing the high turnouts and militant loyalty of the voters on which the party's long-term power ultimately rested.[20]

Given the fact that in Imperial Germany ballots were not issued at the polls by the government, but had to be obtained by the voter, from the candidate or his agents, the parish clergy's most important task was to make sure that the Centrum's 'secret' ballot got distributed. The Centrum's dependence on them for this task, though it varied locally, was always high. A table constructed in the 1880s for Meppen-Lingen, one of the 'blackest' (for the number of cassocked ecclesiastics) constituencies in Germany, reveals that more than 67 per cent of the contact men responsible for ballot distribution were priests. Even in Baden, at the other end of the (Catholic) scale, an investigation in the early 1890s revealed that of the 800-odd parishes in the state, 160 pastors were, contrary to the desires of their government, working for the Centrum.[21] Priests distributed ballots through their communion classes if possible; by standing at the door of the polling place if necessary. Pastor Gotherr of Eschbach roused the farmers out of their beds at 4 a.m. on election day to give them Centrum ballots before they departed for work. Pastor Schäfer in Liptingen went out into the fields, pressed a ballot into a tardy peasant's hand, and watched his horse and plough for him while he went off to the polls.[22] In a letter to the *Kölnische Volkszeitung* a rural pastor passed on a tip to his fellow clerics:

Approximately twenty voters from my little village have for some time lived in the industrial region. It was easy for me to inquire after their addresses. I will send each an exhortation to vote for the Centrum in the run-offs.

This kind of networking, he suggested, could be done 'generally and systematically'.[23]

The role of the priest was of course different in the economically depressed villages of the Eifel than in big cities like Cologne; in the South than in the North; in confessionally or ethnically homogeneous districts than in those with mixed populations. But in the eyes of the ordinary small-town Catholic, the priest *was* the Centrum Party. Germany's laws of assembly practically forced the priest to the fore. Every public meeting had to be registered in advance with the police and, in most states, the sponsor was required to reside in the community in which the meeting was to be held. In small towns and villages where the people who counted were either Conservatives or Liberals and supporters of other parties were their dependants, the pastor was often the only Centrum adherent who dared put his name on such a request. Campaign rallies thus depended on the priest. Not only was he the indispensable chairman of the rally (and voters could pick up their admission tickets at the rectory), as often as not he was the principal speaker.[24] Rallies were usually held on Sundays, and it excited little wonder when a pastor, still riding high after a long afternoon of campaigning, inadvertently began his evening sermon in church with '*Meine Herren!*'[25]

Inevitably these *Hochwürden*, especially where lay notables were few, exercised authority not only by virtue of their ascribed social or spiritual position but by amassing specifically *political* power, including a kind of patronage. *Their* decision to sponsor him for elective office could turn a clodhopper into a notable – a transfiguration hilariously, but not entirely inaccurately, depicted in the 'correspondence' of the immortal Jozef Filser, Ludwig Thoma's peasant who suddenly found himself travelling first class to Munich's 'barliament' to take up the burdens of 'governing'.[26] The clergy's sponsorship was even more important for local office. Catholic mayors and councilmen, *ex officio* members of local Centrum election committees, found that if they wanted to keep their positions and the economic perks that went with them, they had better stick close to their clerical patrons. As a nobleman noted ruefully to a compeer whose parliamentary aspirations had been frustrated by a Würzburg nominating committee: local Centrum leaders were what they were only through the clergy; the withdrawal of clerical support would mean their fall.[27]

The Power of the German Priest

Because it was visible to everyone, because it was essentially a particular
– if peculiar – form of party infrastructure, the 'chaplainocracy', as contemporaries dubbed it, could not be *ipso facto* grounds for invalidating an
election.[28] Election 'influence', if it meant anything, had to refer to violations of the voter's freedom, not through the performance of a public
task, but through explicit or implicit pressure from the clerical office itself. When the Progressive deputy for Koblenz exclaimed that he would
'rather have *one* chaplain working for me in an election then ten headmen
or mayors, …*one dean* is more effective than ten county commissioners
[Landräte], and the influence of a bishop far outweighs that of Herr
Count zu Eulenburg or any other Minister of Interior', he was not referring to the superior staffing of the Centrum's bureaucracy. He was
pointing to the spiritual power of the priest.[29]

How was this power made 'operational'? The German Church considered it bad form to mention names from the pulpit, whether for praise or
for blame. The necessity of disarming election challenges and avoiding
prosecution under the various imperial and state laws regulating the clergy's political speech also insured that commentary from the altar was
usually couched in generalities.[30] Thus the prayers at mass before the
elections in the 1870s called for a good outcome; in the 1880s the so-
called general prayer at the end of the mass was dedicated to 'an important
matter'; rosaries were requested 'so that the up-coming very important
day will proceed favourably'; election day masses were celebrated with
the special intention of a 'result pleasing to God'. But since these remarks
– and especially the injunction to vote 'according to your conscience' –
were immediately quoted in the Centrum press, more explicit endorse-
ments were hardly necessary. (Bavarian nuns, however, were more
outspoken, instructing their schoolchildren to say Paternosters for a
Centrum victory.)[31]

Rarely (Bavaria in the 1870s is an exception) was failure to vote,
much less voting against the Centrum, explicitly termed a 'mortal sin'.
The episcopate, unlike its French counterpart, avoided the word 'sin' altogether, preferring to emphasise the 'voting obligation' (which, however,
might take precedence – as the Archbishop of Cologne announced in
1919, when polling fell on Sunday – over the Sabbath obligation).[32]
Theological terminology, with its implied penalties, was always an em-
barrassment for Centrum laymen, many of whom were more than a little
ambivalent about the clerical company they were obliged to keep.
And the clergy themselves – ever aware of Catholics' minority status –

were willing, within broad outlines, to employ the euphemisms that their party's officially 'non-confessional' designation required. Thus, while Catholic voters were warned that they were 'responsible' to God for how they voted, they were also admonished, over and over (in 1907, even by the Pope) to 'vote your conscience'. In an era in which politics were conceived, in the words of Gladstone, as 'morality writ large', and morality was confessionally-defined, for the officiating clergy to drape their partisanship in the universal and individualist language of conscience, transparent veils at best, was less a sign of hypocrisy than of a kind of political prudery. Yet it maddened the Centrum's liberal opponents to see how easily the ultramontanes assimilated liberal lingo to their own political appeals.[33]

The clergy's role in elections and Centrum politics did not diminish over time. In fact, as the waning of the Kulturkampf began to reduce communal pressures for conformity and the Catholic nobility began to shift to the conservative parties, the clergy's relative weight within the Centrum grew. The movement of Germany's populations into the cities depleted the Centrum's lay cadres in the smaller towns and countryside that formed the bastions of the party and made it, especially in Southern Germany, even more dependent on its 'black' armies. In Bavaria, they acquired a weight in electoral and parliamentary politics that would have been inconceivable in the 1860s. In Hessen, the clergy reached the apogee of its influence within the party only in the Weimar Republic – after the Centrum's own hold over the allegiance of Catholics had itself considerably loosened.[34] And where ethnic and economic issues divided the Catholic vote, as in Upper Silesia in the early twentieth century, when the Polish National Democratic challengers finally wrested five seats from the Centrum in 1907, three of the new party's victors were priests.[35] Liberal slurs about clericalism, the cartoons of *Simplicissimus* featuring cassocks swarming like bees, all of the apparent exaggerations of the Centrum's opponents should not mislead us; it is scarcely possible to exaggerate the degree to which these figures in cassocks *were* the Centrum Party.

Did clericalism in politics encourage authoritarian habits of mind? The Church's own teachings about the structure of legitimate authority, which can be documented from any theology lexicon, any seminary handbook, would seem to support this supposition.[36] So strict was the ultramontane conception of hierarchy that the idea that suggestions might come from below, even within the clerical caste itself, had been condemned by the pope as 'mad fantasy'. In 1887 Bishop Karl Klein of Limburg demanded from his diocesan priests 'loyal, childlike attachment' to his own election instructions – as if only fractious children might have other views. As late as 1906 a papal encyclical affirmed that 'the majority has no other right than to allow themselves to be led and to follow their shepherds like a docile herd'.[37] Language such as this was impossible to square with the independence ('maturity', in the contemporary idiom) that all parties agreed was essential for a voting public.

Yet when one moves from lexica to practice, particularly electoral practice, these 'mad fantasies' that those at the bottom had a legitimate say in clerical politics kept re-appearing. The German clergy proved more than willing to break the chain of command when the instructions from their superiors offended their *party* loyalties. 'The bishop himself', proclaimed a Trier pastor in 1907, 'if he were to come here and put himself up against [Chaplain] Dasbach [a local politician], wouldn't get a single vote'.[38] Massive disregard of papal wishes occurred in 1887 when Leo XIII demanded that the Centrum disavow its platform and support the government's military bill. When the party twice refused, Pope Leo leaked his instructions to its arch-enemy Bismarck, and allowed the Chancellor to use them against the Centrum for election purposes – causing enormous scandal.[39] In this conflict between the Pope and the political party, the clergy, beginning with the Bishops of Cologne, Osnabrück, and Trier, decided for the party. And those prelates, such as Bishop Klein of Limburg, who (for political reasons of their own) did side with Rome, were deserted by their (woefully un-childlike) diocesans. At a rally in Baden, when asked by a heckler what he would do if his own (wavering) bishop issued the same election instructions as Bishop Klein, Pastor Bauer of Münsterthal shouted back, 'Then I would still vote no!' His vicar became so passionate on the subject that the police had to threaten to dissolve the rally. Throughout the archdiocese of Freiburg, even in districts where a loyal Centrum man had no hope of winning, the lower clergy showed their colours by repeatedly supporting Democrats or Radicals rather than the National Liberals that the pontiff favoured. As Pastor Dieterle reminded his flock in Dogern : 'in secular matters the pope was just as much a sinner as humans [sic!] are'. Pastor Eble in Minseln had only sarcasm for a heckler who threw up to him Pope Leo's instructions to support the military bill: 'Now all of a sudden the pope is infallible!' In the district [Amtsbezirk] of Achern, Pastor Bronner was reported as declaring that 'the current pope' (!) was 'by no means as beloved by him as he is by the "gentlemen" and their ilk'. More privately (though not privately enough, apparently, for he was arrested afterwards for violating article 166 of the imperial penal code) Vicar Vögtle opined in a tavern in Ballrichten: 'The pope is an old grandmother. Old grandmothers have many wishes that can't be fulfilled – I can prove that to you out of the catechism!'[40] The defiance of papal wishes in 1887 and then again in 1893 were only the most spectacular occasions when electoral politics subverted ecclesiastical hierarchy.[41] In lesser cases it happened over and over again. Government officials were shocked to learn of a run-off election between a Conservative and a Social Democrat in which the rector of a parish supported the Conservative, his chaplain, the Social Democrat![42] It is worth remarking that when Max Weber reflected on political Catholicism he referred not to the 'hierarchy', but to the '*chaplain*ocracy'. It was not a term anyone used for Ireland or for France. Here too, the German experience seems unique.

Not every Catholic liked a politicking priest, but Germany presents us with few instances comparable to Ireland, where the conspicuous campaigning of the clergy was met with equally conspicuous examples of Catholic defiance. Irish election mobs smashed rectory windows and roughed up pastors on the hustings, crying 'mind your own business', 'no priest in politics', and, tellingly, 'Hurrah for Bismarck...'. They staged dramatic walkouts from church. They rose in their pews to denounce the election advice being offered from the altar. When the seventy-five year old bishop of Meath attacked Parnell's supporters in a sermon in his cathedral, a worshipper shouted out, 'You are a liar!'[43]

In Germany, Catholic voters had been known to defend their hearths against the importunities of door-to-door clerical canvassers, as when a Trier businessman forcibly removed the young Chaplain Dasbach from his premises. But such instances were so few as to become legendary.[44] *Public* Catholic objections to clerical intrusiveness, when they occurred at all, were likely to be collective, well-organised, and themselves political. In Liptingen an unpopular pastor, who had conducted a one-man campaign in 1906 to end his village's long tradition of National Liberal voting, ran up against such a wall of resistance that he appears to have come close to a nervous breakdown, losing control of himself in the middle of a sermon. When he then denied communion to a woman whose husband distributed the liberal newspaper, the village revolted. One hundred and fifty Catholic men, close to Liptingen's entire voting population, signed a declaration announcing their resolve to avoid Pastor Schäfer's 'outrages' by not entering the church so long as 'this gentleman officiated; alternatively we will bring in a pastor with different beliefs' – i.e., a schismatic Old Catholic. But Baden, where this protest occurred, was exceptional in the tenacity with which the tradition of Liberal voting within certain Catholic communities resisted the advances of the clergy-sponsored Centrum.[45] And I have found no resistance, even in Baden, to priestly politicking by members of the congregation *within* a church: no fists shaken, no cries of outrage, no huffy walkouts. Outside Baden, we have to scour the landscape for open signs of Catholic anger at clerical electioneering, at least before the twentieth century.[46]

Was this silence because, as Liberal proponents of the Pulpit Law regulating clerical speech argued, holy *spaces* enjoyed special legal protections against disruption? Perhaps. Legal protection hardly seems to have been necessary, however, given general cultural attitudes in which the 'the peace' [*Hausfrieden*], even of secular buildings, went largely unchallenged by the public and, on the rare occasions when disturbance threatened, was strictly enforced by the secular arm.[47] Indicative of the widespread German assumption that a citizen's best protection was the state is the case of a teacher in Meßkirch, who felt that a sermon attacking liberalism contained an allusion to him personally. He simply contacted the public prosecutor.[48] Could the 'juridification of social conflict', posited by Winfried Schulze for the early modern period, have continued even in imperial Germany, leading dissenters simply to report (*'anzeigen'*) politically obnoxious pastors to the authorities? A recent study of the clergy in Baden suggests that this may have been the case.[49] But probably more important for explaining the quiet in the Church was the fact that the clergy themselves, thanks to the Kulturkampf legislation, were both more revered and more restrained than their Irish counterparts.

The fact that, under the pressures of electoral politics, chaplains might defy rectors, pastors ignore bishops, and bishops cleave to party over pope, while it points to the incongruence between ultramontane theory and political practice, does not prove that at the very bottom of the chain of command, the voter felt the same freedom 'to take away degree, to untune that string'. If Pastor Thröne's confident remark in a tavern in Rosenberg that the pope 'can't mix in political things; the farmer will listen to the pastor first' supports scepticism about the hierarchy's political authority, it should make us equally careful about jumping to conclusions about the voter's independence.[50] But we cannot ignore the possibility that, in the face of pastors who behaved like party agents, the silence of German congregations, in such marked contrast to the unruly Irish, meant consent – although consent of a non-individualistic, communal sort.

At its most basic level, the power of the priest lay in his ability to define community, or at least to articulate the community's own view of itself. And what was the community's view? Voters apparently did not conceive themselves as 'German men' so much as 'Catholic men', who did things in 'Catholic ways'. However discreetly the pastor himself might behave at the polling place, his bell-ringer, his bookkeeper, and his vestry-men, any or all of whom might be sitting on the election panel, had little compunction against telling a dissenter that if he continued along Liberal (or Conservative, or Social Democratic) paths, then he was 'no longer a Catholic man'. When a voter in a Mosel pub sounded off against the Centrum, the party stalwart at the next table could be counted on to call over to him: 'Sure! and we all know *you* have lost your faith!' 'Reading only liberal papers and always wanting to be the government's "good boy"', were among the sins included in the *Prayer and Instruction Book for the Catholic Men's World,* published under the archdiocesan *imprimatur.* The person committing them demonstrated his lack of solidarity and 'on election day would be a weathercock and a traitor'. Little wonder that the generation of Catholic Liberals born before 1840 was not replenished. Liberals along the Rhine and Mosel complained that even when they found Catholics who shared their views, they would not run for office, fearing that their neighbours would say 'he has no religion' and that they would be boycotted by the entire population.[51] In a country where confessional homogeneity within small communities was the rule, and as late as 1907, 122 of the Reichstag's 397 electoral districts were made up of populations whose confessional homogeneity was greater than 95 per cent, the social penalties for dissident behaviour could be severe.[52] When Catholics were watching Catholics, the terrors of the confessional, which played such a large role in liberal polemic, were hardly necessary.

The kinds of pressures for conformity that existed spontaneously in the village were replicated artificially in urban areas in an extensive associational network that gave any priest who wanted to weigh in politically an inestimable advantage over notables of rival persuasions. Catholic club life, especially in northwestern Germany, was socially even more inclusive than the electoral constituency, encompassing all sorts and conditions of men, and women as well. And presiding over each one of these clubs, vetting its speakers, determining its agendas, was a priest. In the Westfalian part of the diocese of Paderborn, 46 per cent of the entire Catholic population, of all ages, belonged to at least one association, and in some areas the numbers reached two-thirds. In the historical literature this network of religious practices, feast (and fast) days, social clubs, and, eventually, business and political organisations has come to be known as the 'milieu', with inevitably narrow connotations. Its own publicists were pleased to call it 'Catholic Germany', a counter-world that might be only a subset of any given geographical community, but was also, with its trans-local connections, as broad as the nation itself (and therefore escaping the identification with a single class that so crippled Catholic politics in France and Spain).[53] This Catholic '*Vereinskosmos*', as Josef Mooser has dubbed it, established a safe zone that was all the more welcome after the war of 1866, that is, after representatives of the 'national' culture, defined as Protestant by both Liberals and Conservatives, felt increasingly free to speak of Catholics as intruders in their own country.[54] The pattern of the milieu's finely meshed grid might appear devotional when viewed from one angle. But with only a slight shift in perspective the same pattern resolved itself as social, and with another slight shift, as political. Before the founding of the Empire in 1871 the knots in this web of associations had been common participation in sacramental rituals. After 1871 these knots were made tighter by rituals of solidarity with their clergy (especially on their release from prison) and in rituals of opposition at the polling place.

Solidarity was not equality. '*Das katholische Deutschland*' was egalitarian only at the communion rail – and at the ballot box. Its components were distinct (with different functions assigned to clergy and lay, male and female, and every conceivable vocation) and hierarchical.[55] There was no promiscuous mixing, for each was expected to take pride in his or her own estate. The nobility joined the mass demonstrations paying homage to their persecuted bishops, but they marched in separate delegations with their own insignia, and they contributed to the Catholic cause through their own organisations, such as the Knights of Malta.[56] The university graduate gloried in belonging to the *Bildungsbürgertum*, but, as a member of the Görres Society, he not only remained a Catholic in good standing, his pen was enlisted on Catholic Germany's behalf. Worker and journeyman took part in activities appropriate to their own occupational cultures, indeed under certain circumstances might even find their radicalism encouraged: all while remaining within the 'fold' of their black-clad shepherd. The participation of the Catholic woman – maid and married – within this Catholic public sphere insured that even without the franchise she too would eventually be assigned a role in elections – preparing the way for strong female support for the Centrum during the Weimar Republic. Clerical leadership encouraged these separate self-understandings. But along with differentiation, Catholic culture set an equally high valuation on mutual dependence. Political Catholicism's election clubs were not called 'Freedom', much less 'Equality'; instead they sported names like 'Concordia' and 'Harmonia'.

The power of this language of solidarity, which harmonised differences and latent (and not-so-latent) social hostilities, did not depend upon theology, the universality of the salvation message. Nor on the re-activation of medieval corporativist ideology, although its haze (but no more than a haze) still hovered over the language and habits of the late nine-teenth century. The solidarist vision was given its vitality by the democratic suffrage, which brought all Catholics, *as* Catholics, together on election day in their own kind of political corporate communion.[57] The Emsland's *Katholische Volksbote* apostrophised its readers in 1878: '...You farmers blessed [*versehen*] with a team [*Gespann*] equalise the differences between the estates, and if necessary hitch up your wagons and drive the old and weak to the election urn; the deed will be its own reward.'[58] In Trier support for the Centrum eventually reached higher levels than participation in Easter communion.[59]

Conclusions

The result of the culture wars that emerged almost immediately in the wake of the re-drawing of the map of Europe between 1866 and 1871 was a tectonic shift in Germany's political landscape.[60] As far back as the 1830s, German public life had been organised into two camps: those who supported the Government versus those who criticised it; Right versus Left. Beginning with the Prussian Landtag election in late 1870, this con-stellation had begun to give way. By the second imperial election in 1874, Left and Right had been re-configured to make room for a third grouping that included the Centrum along with regionally-based protest parties: the Bavarian Patriots, the Poles, and the 'clericals' of Alsace-Lorraine, all of which were Catholic, although they were usually joined by the Protes-tant Hanoverians and Danes. Each of these groupings represented constituencies which preferred to collaborate with other permanent mi-norities, regardless of ethnicity or confession, than with the *national* alternatives of Left and Right. Locally, however, wherever such dissent-ers stood a chance of winning, Left and Right would join hands in a politics of national concentration (*Sammlungspolitik*).[61] Thus, deeper than the three-group constellation was a more fundamental divide: two political nations whose voters were forever lost to each other. Contempo-rary polemic figured them as the 'national' parties and the 'enemies of the Reich' (*Reichsfeinde*). Our own political science maps them as 'cen-tre' and 'periphery'. The simplest labels – for all the exceptions one might make for specific individuals, regions, or elections – is simply Protestant and Catholic, descriptions referring less to different confes-sions (though in the case of the 'Catholic' label, it often was that) than to two political cultures.[62]

  In their depth and in their extent these fault lines were genuinely new.

As Karl Rohe has shown, they delimited what was, in spite of the familiar names of liberal, conservative, and even Centrum, a new party system.[63] The Catholic camp was not merely the expression of higher turnouts from a pre-existing, but previously unmobilised plebeian constituency. It represented a genuine *re*-alignment among Catholicism's upper strata as well. Imperial elections nationalised these allegiances even when the local situation bore little relationship to the slogans of the national parties. Thus in 1878, the campaign manager for the unsuccessful 'national' candidate in a Württemberg district complained that their election, with a turnout of 75 per cent, demonstrated 'how far the power of the ultramontane party extends even into our land – which hasn't been touched by the Kulturkampf '.[64]

Once the re-structuring had taken place, the new constellation had extraordinary durability. In industrial regions with a strong Catholic presence it retarded the emergence of a third camp, Social Democracy, by nearly two decades. In the Ruhr, after remarkable progress between 1867 and 1870, the Socialist movement collapsed in the face of the re-alignment. Protestant Duisburg and Catholic Essen, both with large industrial proletariats, now became showcases for the 'national' (usually Liberal) and the Catholic camps, respectively. On the basis of a worker's confession, railroad officials in Bochum knew to which of their employees it was safe to issue leave on election day: Protestants could be counted on to vote National Liberal.[65] 'Not to put too fine a point on it', writes Karl Rohe, 'before it could be a victim of the Socialist Law,... [the socialist movement] was already victim of political Catholicism and of the two-camp formation that its rise created.'[66] Even in the 1890s, after Social Democracy had pushed large sections of the liberal constituency over to the right and captured a considerable part of the rest, the confessional marker delimiting German political allegiances endured. Having survived the upheavals of rapid industrialisation, it would persist even after the collapse of the Reich itself. It overrode the crises of hyper-inflation in the 1920s and depression in the 1930s. After 1945 it reappeared, and traces survive still. The choirs are bare, the clergy are dying of old age, but the confessional divide remains the strongest predictor of voting behaviour in the Federal Republic even today.[67]

The salience of 'clerical influence' in public discussion about elections should not be read univocally as a sign of German political 'backwardness'. By becoming agents of a political party, the Catholic clergy had acquired a 'modern', practical usefulness to their congregations enjoyed by few of their counterparts in other countries.[68] In the process they had also acquired a pragmatic, but nonetheless real, commitment to democratic elections, parliamentary procedures, and party politics – commitments in which they schooled their flock, by their practice as much as by their preaching.[69] But the very success of the clergy's party as a vehicle for the minority's desire for cultural validation and political power, a success that legitimated democratic forms of conflict among this one part of the population, undermined the legitimacy of these forms among the Protestant majority. By embedding an ancient confessional divide in modern party conflict, the very existence of the Centrum had made the reconciliation of a significant number of Germans to party and parliamentary conflict unusually difficult. One should not be surprised therefore that efforts to invalidate elections allegedly tainted by 'clerical influence' showed little regard for freedom of speech as the foundation upon which all free elections depend. Not that such challenges implicitly denied that Catholic voters were mature enough to make genuine choices. But the consequences were neverthless heavy ones. Edmund Morgan has suggested that the political fiction of a wise and independent yeomanry was essential to the ability of the British parliament (and later, the American colonies) to wrest sovereignty from the Crown. If 'inventing the people' with qualities sturdy enough to entrust them (fictionally) with power is a necessary precondition for parliamentary sovereignty, then the fateful topos of manipulative priest and childlike people elaborated during Germany's cultural wars worked in the opposite direction. And it helps explain why so many modern citizens tolerated a less-than-parliamentary monarchy so willingly, so long.[70]

Notes

1. F. J. Hergenröther, 'Ueber die Betheiligung des Klerus an politischen Fragen', first printed in *Bamberger Pastoralblatt*, 1863, nos. 3, 5, 7, 9, then in *Archiv für katholisches Kirchenrecht, mit besonderer Rücksicht auf Oesterreich und Deutschland*, vol. 15, Neue Folge 9 (1866), pp. 67-84, quotes from pp. 68-9, 71.
2. The stimulus came from Austria: Dr. T. Pachmann, 'Ueber politische Clerikal-Vertretung – ein altes Thema neu bearbeitet', *Österreichisches Vierteljahreschrift für Rechts-und Staatswissenschaft*, vol. 10 (1862), pp. 106-20, soon reprinted in the daily press; Dr. G. Clericus, 'Die Theilnahme des Klerus an der Gemeinde-und Volksvertretung', in Moys, *Archiv für katholisches Kirchenrecht*, vol. 10, Neue Folge 14 (1863), pp. 75-93. For the debate on a more popular level, see E. Müller, 'Darf der Seelsorger Politik treiben?' in *Märkisches Kirchenblatt* (MK), 16 Jan. 1869, no. 3.

3. Encyclical 'Libertae' in Wolfgang Graf, *Kirchliche Beeinflussungsversuche zu politischen Wahlen und Abstimmungen als Symptome für die Einstellung der katholischen Kirche zur Politik* (Mainz, 1971), p. 103.

4. H. S. Smith, 'Nationalism and Religious Conflict in Germany, 1887-1909', unpubl. PhD diss., Yale University, 1991, p. 54.

5. My argument about the clergy's reversal in mentality and behaviour does not dispute the transformation of Catholic sensibility in a more ultramontane and 'clerical' direction, underway for some time. See J. Sperber, *Popular Catholicism in Nineteenth-Century Germany* (Princeton, 1984).

6. M. L. Anderson, 'The Kulturkampf and the Course of German History', *Central European History*, vol. 19 (March 1986), pp. 82-115; 91ff.

7. Pachmann, 'Ueber politische Clerikal-Vertretung', p. 106. For the convergence of religious with electoral politics in a variety of settings cf. R.J. Jensen, *The Winning of the Midwest. Social and Political Conflict, 1888-1896* (Chicago, 1971), pp. xii, viii, 57-9, and *passim*; J. P. Charnay, 'L'église catholique et les élections françaises', *Politique. Revue Internationale des Doctrines et des Institutions*, Nos. 19-20 (July-Dec. 1962), pp. 257-306; N. Gash, *Politics in the Age of Peel. A Study in the Technique of Parliamentary Representation. 1830-1850* (New York, 1953), p. 175; K. T. Hoppen, *Elections, Politics, and Society in Ireland 1832-1885* (Oxford, 1984), p. 37; E. Posada-Carbó, 'Elections under the Conservative Hegemony in Colombia, 1886-1930', Paper presented at the Latin American Studies Association, XVIII International Congress, Atlanta, 10-12 March 1994, esp. pp. 25-6.

8. Thus the Canon of the Paderborn cathedral, C. Stamm, in his *Dr. Conrad Martin Bischof von Paderborn, Ein biographischer Versuch* (Paderborn, 1892), p. 368.

9. In districts where Protestants were dominant but under 75% of the population, turnouts averaged only 50.3%. I am aware of the 'ecological fallacy' of deducing the voting behaviour of individuals from the social characteristics of election districts, but even as a rough guide the contrast is illuminating. Whatever the mathematics, it is unlikely that Protestants disposing of fewer than 25% of the votes could have produced district-wide turnouts of 70% and more. See G. A. Ritter and M. Niehuss, *Wahlgeschichtliches Arbeitsbuch. Materialen zur Statistik des Kaiserreichs 1871-1918* (Munich, 1980), pp. 99-100.

10. Examples in Ä. Ditscheid, *Matthias Eberhard, Bischof von Trier im Kulturkampf* (Trier, 1900), pp. 100, 104-6.

11. Anderson, 'The Kulturkampf and the Course of German History', pp. 109-15.

12. Twenty-two per cent of the Centrum's deputies during the Reichstag's first legislative period (1871-4; some elected in by-elections) were priests, 20% in 1903, 11% in 1912. In the Prussian Landtag, 8% and 16% of the Centrum and Polish delegation, respectively, were clerics in 1883, as were 14% and 20% of the delegation to the Baden and Bavarian parliaments, respectively, in 1906. Calculations are my own. See R. Morsey, 'Der politische Katholizismus

1890-1933', in Anton Rauscher (ed.), *Der soziale und politische Katholizismus. Entwicklungslinien in Deutschland 1803-1963* (Munich, 1981), vol. I, pp. 110-64, 119; *Jahrbuch für die Amtliche Statistik des Preußischen Staates* (Berlin, 1883), p. 222; S. Suval, *Electoral Politics in Wilhelmine Germany* (Chapel Hill, 1985), pp. 69-70; H. Bodewig, *Geistliche Wahlbeeinflussungen in ihrer Theorie und Praxis dargestellt* (Munich, 1909), p. 12; H. Neubach, 'Schlesische Geistliche als Reichstagsabgeordnete 1867-1918. Ein Beitrag zur Geschichte der Zentrumspartei und zur Nationalitätenfrage in Oberschlesien', *Archiv für Schlesische Kirchengeschichte*, vol. 26 (1968), pp. 251ff, 265, 276; Graf, *Beeinflussungsversuche*, p. 195.

13. As is made clear in the papers of Alexander Reuß, Abteilung 105, folders 1490-1660, and Bishop Michael Korum, Abteilung 108, Folder 817, in the Bistumsarchiv Trier.

14. I. Götz von Olenhusen, 'Die Ultramontanisierung des Klerus. Das Beispiel der Erzdiözese Freiburg', in Wilfried Loth (ed.), *Deutscher Katholizismus im Umbruch zur Moderne* (Stuttgart, 1991), p. 59.

15. On the Centrum as a 'clerical' party, see my 'Inter-denominationalism, Clericalism, Pluralism: The *Zentrumsstreit* and the Dilemma of Catholicism in Wilhelmine Germany', *Central European History*, vol. 21, no. 4 (1990), pp. 350-78.

16. H.-W. Steil, *Die Politischen Wahlen in der Stadt Trier und in den Eifel- und Moselkreisen des Regierungsbezirkes Trier 1867-1887* (Bonn, 1961), pp. 97-8. The equation of deaconates and *Definitionen* with precincts and wards is my own gloss.

17. H. Köhler, quoted in C. H. E. Zangerl, 'Courting the Catholic Vote: The Center Party in Baden, 1903-1913', *Central European History*, vol. 10, no. 3 (1977), pp. 220-40; 227-8.

18. Windthorst to Forstinspektor Rudolf Clauditz, 15 Nov. 1882, Niedersächsisches Staatsarchiv, Osnabrück, Dep. 62-b, 2379. My thanks to Dr. Joseph Hamacher of Haselünne for these documents.

19. Examples are found in K. Müller, 'Politische Strömungen in der Rechtsrheinischen Kreisen des Regierungsbezirks Köln (Sieg, Mühlheim, Wipperfürth, Gummersbach und Waldbröl) von 1879 bis 1900', unpubl. PhD diss., Bonn, 1963, pp. 84, 353, 358, 361, 363, 371. For the protest of the Kraus Society, see 'Memorandum to the Bishops of Germany on the Political Agitation of the Clergy', *Zwanzigsten Jahrhundert*, No. 11, 17 March 1907.

20. Windthorst to a priest, 25 and 29 Oct. 1876; 5 and 9 Oct. 1879; a priest to Windthorst, 30 Aug. 1882; Baron W. von Schorlemer-Vehr to Herr Ziner, 13 Aug. 1889: Bundesarchiv Koblenz (BAK) Kleine Erwerbung No. 596; Chaplain Kurtz to Baron Fechenbach, 28 Feb. 1882, BAK Fechenbach papers.

21. 'Vertrauensmänner', Oct. 1884, Niedersächsisches Staatsarchiv Osnabrück, Dep. 62-b; Smith, 'Nationalism and Religious Conflict', pp. 53-4.

22. Pastor Gotherr, Amtsvorstand Staufen to Ministerium des Innern, Baden, 1 July 1893, Generallandesarchiv Karlsruhe (GLA) 236, No. 14901, p. 4/a; Pastor Schäfer, on religion classes: Bodewig, *Wahlbeeinflussungen*, pp. 89,

109. My thanks to Helmut Smith for the documents from the general state archives at Karlsruhe and Koblenz.

23. Bodewig, *Wahlbeeinflussungen*, p. 143.

24. Zangerl, 'Courting the Catholic Vote', pp. 227-8; Bodewig, *Wahlbeeinflussungen*, p. 146.

25. Anon., 'Religion und Politik', *Das Neue Jahrhundert*, vol. 3, no. 47 (19 November 1911), pp. 556-61; 557. For rallies on Sundays see Müller, 'Politische Strömungen', p. 196.

26. Ludwig Thoma, *Jozef Filsers Briefwexel* ([1912] Munich, 1981), paperback edition.

27. Von Schauensee to Baron von Fechenbach, 18 Oct. 1884, BAK Fechenbach papers.

28. For discussion of the 'Chaplainocracy' see J. Most, SD: *Stenographische Berichte über die Verhandlungen des...deutschen Reichstags* (SBDR), 10 Apr. 1878, p. 875. The term was of course made famous by Max Weber's 'Beamtenherrschaft und politisches Führertum', in 'Parlament und Regierung in neugeordneten Deutschland', *Gesammelte Politische Schriften* (Tübingen, 1971), pp. 320-9.

29. L. Berger, SBDR, 21 Jan. 1875, p. 1177.

30. For example, 'Katholischer Wähler', *Katholischer Volksbote*, no. 29, 21 July 1878; V. Campe, 'Die geistliche Wahlbeeinflussung und das neue Strafgesetzbuch', in *Nationalliberale Blätter*, vol. 24, nos. 40 and 41 (1912), p. 36.

31. Priests in St. Ulrich, Murg, and Rickenbach, quoted by Minister Turban to Grand Duke Friedrich, 31 March 1887, GLA 60, No. 494, p. 2 (hereafter: 'Turban Report'). On nuns see Bodewig, *Wahlbeeinflussungen*, p. 149; on prayers see Steil, *Die Politischen Wahlen*, p. 121. For reports by government agents on the clergy's circumspection in politicking see Regierungs-Rat von Horn to the Governor in Koblenz, 'Report on the Election Activity of Clergy and Beamten', 24 Feb. 1907 (hereafter, Horn Report), Landeshauptarchiv Koblenz (LHAK), Signatur 403, No. 8806, p. 3.

32. *Kirchlicher Anzeiger* (Köln) 1919, in Graf, *Beeinflussungsversuche*, p. 166. 'Todsünde', *ibid.*, p. 183; similar cases, pp. 172-3, occurred in the 1920s (for the Bavarian People's Party), 1930s (against the Nazis), the 1940s and 1960s (against Communists and Social Democrats).

33. On being 'responsible to God' see Ketteler, *Mainzer Journal*, 1871, no. 49, p. 1. This practice continued as late as 1950. Apparently the only bishop to use the word 'sin' for failing to do everything one could to bring about the election of defenders of the Church was Prince Bishop Förster of Breslau, in 1872. Graf, *Beeinflussungsversuche*, p. 173. The papal admonition of 1907 was addressed to Spaniards, but was read by Pastor Roth to his congregation in County Prüm. 'Horn Report', p. 15. Though 'voting your conscience' was assumed to mean voting Centrum, some pastors really meant it. Reyscher, SBDR, 18 Apr. 1871, p. 270.

34. Cf. H. G. Ruppel and B. Groß (comp.), *Hessische Abgeordnete 1820-1933*.

Biographische Nachweise für die Landstände des Großherzogtums Hessen (2. Kammer) und den Landtag des Volksstaates Hessen (Darmstadt, 1980); Graf, *Beeinflussungsversuche*, p. 197.

35. I. Schwidetzky, *Die polnische Wahlbewegung in Oberschlesien* (Breslau, 1934), pp. 78-9.

36. And has been used to do so: cf. C. Weber, 'Ultramontanismus als katholischer Fundamentalismus', in W. Loth (ed.), *Deutscher Katholizismus*, pp. 20-45. C. Dardé, 'Fraud and the Passivity of the Electorate in Spain (1875-1923)', in this volume, also implies that Catholicism had a deleterious effect on political culture.

37. As late as 1960 the *Osservatore Romano* asserted that '...every Catholic in every area of his life must conform his private and public behaviour to the ...instructions of the hierarchy'. Only in 1966 did the German Church, via the Bishops of North-Rhein-Westfalia, affirm that no one might any longer claim ecclesiastical authority for himself alone in the ordering of earthly matters – which may be considered the Catholic equivalent of the Social Democrats' Godesberg Declaration. On the 'docile herd' see *Vehementer nos* (1906); On the 'mad fantasy', see *Mirari vos* (1832); Graf, *Beeinflussungsversuch*, pp.157-8, 159, 161-2, 271.

38. 'Horn Report', p. 4v.

39. On the 'Septennat Election' of 1887, see my *Windthorst. A Political Biography* (Oxford, 1981), pp. 335-58.

40. All of these quotations come from the 'Turban Report', *passim.*

41. E.g., Müller, 'Politische Strömungen', pp. 309-10.

42. Amtsvorstand Ettlingen to Innenministerium, 25 June 1893, GLA, 236, no. 14901, p. 9/a.

43. Hoppen, *Elections, Politics, and Society*, pp.240-42; Woods, 'The general election of 1892', pp. 300-1; J. H. Whyte, 'The Influence of the Catholic Clergy on Elections in Nineteenth-Century Ireland', *English Historical Review*, vol. 75, no. 295 (Apr. 1960), pp. 239-59, esp. pp. 247-9.

44. Anon, 'Der katholische Geistliche auf der politischen Arena. (Von einem römisch-katholischen Priester)', *Das Neue Jahrhundert*, vol. 1, no. 8 (12 Feb. 1909), pp. 90-4; esp. 93.

45. Conversely, Badenese Catholics expressed their disapproval of unpopular pastors by voting against the Centrum. Amtsvorstand Bonndorf to Minister of Interior, 30 June 1893, GLA 236, no. 14901; Bodewig, *Wahlbeeinflussungen*, p. 89.

46. The silence on disruptions in O. Elble, *Der Kanzelparagraph (§130a St.-G.-B.)* (Heidelberg, 1908), and Bodewig, *Wahlbeeinflussungen*, who otherwise scrape the bottom of the barrel for evidence against the clergy, has to be taken as conclusive. A pastor who backed a non-Centrum party was subjected to irritated disapproval. Graf, *Beeinflussungsversuche*, pp. 189-90.

47. Cf. the bemused comments on the peacefulness of German electioneering in 'The Working of a German General Election', *Blackwood's Edinburgh Magazine*, vol. 181 (Feb. 1907), pp. 266-81.

48. Amtsvorstand Meßkirch to the Baden Ministry of Interior, 17 July 1893, GLA 236, no. 14901, p. 1/h; Bodewig, *Wahlbeeinflussungen*, p. 89. A similar case occurred in Alsace when a pastor's offhand refusal to intercede at an election rally on behalf of a liberal teacher led the teacher to sue both pastor and Centrum candidate for libel. 'Momentbild aus der Zentrumsagitation', *Das Neue Jahrhundert*, vol. 2, no. 2 (9 Jan. 1910), p. 21. But evidence of open disapproval of politicking priests is rare. E.g., *Görlitzer Anzeiger*, 8 Jan. 1874, no. 6 , p. 33.

49. Baden: Götz von Olenhusen, 'Die Ultramontanisierung des Klerus', esp. pp. 60-3. Schulze's 'juridification' concept was argued most fully in 'Peasant Resistance and Politicization in Eighteenth-Century Germany', address delivered to the American Historical Association, December 1987. W. Hagen has also drawn attention to the use of the court system by the agricultural poor in 'The Junkers' Faithless Servants: Peasant Insubordination and the Breakdown of Serfdom in Brandenburg-Prussia, 1763-1811', in R. J. Evans and W. R. Lee (eds.), *The German Peasantry: Conflict and Community in Rural Society from the Eighteenth Century to the Present* (London, 1985).

50. 'Turban Report'.

51. Dr. Anton Keller, Pfarrer in Gottenhein bei Freiburg, *Das Gebet-und Belehrungsbuch für die Katholische Männer* (Kevelaer, 1902); for 'Catholic men', 'lost your faith', see Bodewig, *Wahlbeeinflussungen*, pp. 62, 92, 140, 143; for 'Catholic ways', see Smith, 'Nationalism and Religious Conflict', p. 81.

52. Smith, 'Nationalism and Religious Conflict', p. 35.

53. See F. Borkenau's sharp contrast between German 'social' and Spain's very un-social Catholicism in *Spanish Cockpit* ([London, 1937] Ann Arbor, 1963), pp. 9-10.

54. E. Müller, 'Dann laß ich fünf Fuß tiefer Graben', *Bonifacius Kalender* (1883), p. 3. For accounts of the Catholic milieu, see Sperber, *Popular Catholicism*; Smith, 'Nationalism and Religious Conflict'; J. Mooser, 'Das katholische Vereinswesen in der Diözese Paderborn um 1900. Vereinstypen, Organisationsumfang und innere Verfassung', in *Westfälische Zeitschrift*, vol. 141 (1991), pp. 447-61; 452 ('Vereinskosmos'), 455. K. Rohe, *Wahlen und Wählertraditionen in Deutschland* (Frankfurt a. M., 1992), p. 54, points out that before 1871 a *politically relevant* milieu was by no means ubiquitous; cf. also Rohe, 'German Elections and Party Systems in Historical and Regional Perspective: An Introduction', in Rohe (ed.), *Elections, Parties and Political Traditions. Social Foundations of German Parties and Party Systems, 1867-1987* (New York, 1990), pp. 1-26.

55. As Rohe warns, 'Parochialitäten sind kein herrschaftsfreie Idylle'. 'Konfession, Klasse und lokale Gesellschaft als Bestimmungsfaktoren des Wahlverhaltens. Überlegungen und Problematisierungen am Beispiel des historischen Ruhrgebiets', in L. Albertin and W. Link (eds.), *Politische Parteien auf dem Weg zur parlamentarischen Demokratie in Deutschland. Entwicklungslinien bis zur Gegenwart* (Düsseldorf, 1981), pp. 109-26; esp. 121.

56. Stamm, *Conrad Martin*, p. 369; H. Rust, *Reichskanzler Fürst Chlodwig zu Hohenlohe-Schillingsfürst und seine Brüder* (Düsseldorf, 1897), pp. 621-2, 826.
57. The Centrum delegation to the Prussian Landtag held a corporate communion every Saturday. *MK*, 21 Jan. 1871, no. 3, p. 24.
58. 'Katholischer Wähler', *Katholischer Volksbote*, 21 July 1878, no. 29.
59. Smith, 'Nationalism and Religious Conflict', p. 32.
60. I have argued for such a shift, with graphs, in 'The Kulturkampf and the Course of German History', pp. 82-115, esp. 82-9, in 'Piety and Politics: Recent Work in German Catholicism', *Journal of Modern History*, vol. 63 (December 1991), pp. 681-716; 682-9, and in *Windthorst*, pp. 192-8; and against the static picture made famous by M. R. Lepsius, 'Parteiensystem und Sozialstruktur: zum Problem der Demokratisierung der deutschen Gesellschaft', in G. A. Ritter (ed.), *Deutschen Parteien vor 1918* (Cologne, 1973), pp. 56-80. A more thorough criticism of Lepsius, with a penetrating analysis of the caesura in the party system is Rohe, *Wahlen und Wählertraditionen*, esp. chap. 2 and pp. 81-3.
61. 'Sammlung' was first employed against Catholics; see M. L. Anderson and K. Barkin, 'The Myth of the Puttkamer Purge and the Reality of the Kulturkampf', *Journal of Modern History*, vol. 54, no. 4 (Dec. 1982), pp. 647-86, esp. 679-80.
62. This cleavage structure produced new understandings of 'confession'. Thus in 1907 a campaigning cleric disputed that the government's claim that it had appointed 'Catholics' to high positions was 'false...since the *Oberpräsident* is, admittedly, Catholic, but *leider Gottes*, national'. Horn Report, p. 6.
63. Although in some Prussian districts, in Baden, where the culture wars had began in the sixties, and in Bavaria, where elections to the Zollparlament raised questions of national identity, this bi-polarism was already evident by 1867. Replacing many other earlier discussions, see Rohe, *Wahlen und Wählertraditionen*, esp. p. 63, 65, 71-2.
64. Oberamtspfleger Haaf to Herbert Bismarck, Gaildorf, 6 Aug. 1878, Bundesarchiv Potsdam, Reichstag, no. 14693, pp. 58-61. I differ with Sperber's *Popular Catholicism*, p. 255, which sees the change in Catholic representation as almost entirely a function of changes in turnout, and with D. Blackbourn's *Class, Religion and Local Politics in Wilhelmine Germany. The Centre Party in Württemberg before 1914* (New Haven, Ct., 1980), which dates the confessionalisation of Württemberg politics only with the economic changes in the 1890s. Even without a state-wide organisation in Württemberg, the Centrum still won a large share of the vote in most Catholic districts in Württemberg national elections in the 1870s.
65. Wahlprüfungskommission, Report for Fifth Arnsberg, SBDR, 20 Apr. 1885, p. 1771.
66. Rohe, *Wahlen und Wählertraditionen*, pp. 85-6; Rohe, 'Konfession, Klasse und lokale Gesellschaft', *passim*; J. D. Hunley, 'The working classes, religion and social democracy in the Düsseldorf Area, 1867-78', *Societas*, vol. 4, no. 2 (Spring 1974), pp. 131-49.

67. Quoted in K. Rohe, 'Forward', in Rohe (ed.), *Elections, Parties, and Political Traditions*, p. vii; cf. also his 'German Elections and Party Systems', *ibid.*, p. 3; J. Falter, 'The Social Bases of Political Cleavages in the Weimar Republic, 1919-1933', in L. E. Jones and J. Retallack (eds.), *Elections, Mass Politics, and Social Change in Modern Germany. New Perspectives* (Washington, D. C., 1992), pp. 371-97; J. Falter, *Hitlers Wähler* (Munich 1991), p. 350. This is not to say that in some places, e.g., in Dortmund from 1893 on, class and ethnic identities did not weaken the confessional marker. H. Graf, *Die Entwicklung der Wahlen und politischen Parteien in Groß-Dortmund* (Hanover and Frankfurt a.M., 1958), p. 27.

68. E. Weber, *Peasants into Frenchmen* (Stanford, 1976), pp. 359-64, attributes the priest's loss of authority in the Third Republic to the spread of newspapers and the frequency of elections as well as to the fact that the modern state took over more and more of the functions for which people had previously depended on him. In Germany these signs of modernisation, as newspapers and elections, in fact strengthened the Church.

69. Cf. the similar conclusions reached by Posada-Carbó: 'Elections under the Conservative Hegemony in Colombia', p. 29.

70. E. S. Morgan, *Inventing the People. The Rise of Popular Sovereignty in England and America* (New York, 1988).

CHAPTER 7

THE ROLE OF THE CHURCH, THE ARMY AND THE POLICE IN COLOMBIAN ELECTIONS, c. 1850-1930

Malcolm Deas

Colombia has a long electoral history, it has enjoyed the reputation of being a republic where the Church was powerful and politically active, and it has persistent problems of public order. These themes are beginning to attract more patient attention from some historians primarily interested in the history of the republic, but they also provide material for reflections that perhaps have wider implications. This chapter will explore the electoral role of three institutions, the Church, the army and the police, but must first outline the political and electoral history of the country.[1]

Colombia has never been subjected to long periods of authoritarian rule. The pattern of how the country was to be governed can be seen practised by its first President, Francisco de Paula Santander, and it consisted of basically civilian alliances held together across the regions by correspondence and journalism. Though this system was inevitably dominated by notables, Colombia was predominantly a mestizo society where there were no clear racial bounds to political participation, a phenomenon noted by more than a few nineteenth-century travellers.

By the middle of the last century two political currents had emerged, the Liberal and the Conservative, which survive to this day, or which are at least clearly visible to the discerning eye behind recent changes in nomenclature.

A conventional backgound chronology (and conventional chronology is what matters in political memory) would show Liberal dominance in the 1830s giving way to Conservative until 1849, Liberal again until 1854, a Conservative interlude replaced by Liberal rule 1863-1885, Conservative hegemony 1885-1930, Liberal 1930-1946.

Nineteenth-century changes were accompanied by civil war. Liberals and Conservatives came to be antagonised by this history, which has to be studied in detail if one wishes to determine the particular reasons for any personal or geographical allegiance – it has long been recognised that simple sociological categories are not much help in explaining political affiliations.

Electoral Politics, Anticlericalism and the Liberal Cause

One prominent divider was the religious question.[2] Colombia was by no means a uniformly catechised country, and a close examination of late colonial society reveals many areas whose temper already rejected any church control in a manner that anticipates later republican anticlericalism.[3] Nonetheless, in the highlands inhabited by the majority of the native population that had survived the conquest, and where most of the population of the republic was still to be found, the Church had much more than a rhetorical claim to be the founding institution of society. Under the republic it met with a series of persecutions at Liberal hands, during the course of which it lost property and suffered various spectacular indignities: the abolition of tithes, the expulsions of bishops and regulars, state supervision of worship, a constitution that failed to mention God. After 1885 a rapprochement was arranged that restored official recognition to a degree unknown elsewhere in Spanish America, and until 1930 the Conservative rulers of the country could regard Colombia as an island of orthodoxy beset by a sea of heresy and indifference. So could their opponents, though with a different choice of words.

It is not therefore surprising that the late-nineteenth-century Colombian Church was politicised. It always had been. Not only would an indifferent or neutral Church have been entirely strange to the ruling notions of the Spanish Empire, it would have been strange to its practice. It was the Archbishop, Caballero y Góngora, who deftly put down the Comunero Rebellion of 1781. Moreover, in the internal affairs of the colonial Church there was much politics. It held internal elections, for example, and its own experience with elections was therefore older than the republic itself.

The first half-century of republican rule naturally intensified its involvement, both through its local difficulties and through the vicissitudes of the Church in Italy and in the rest of Europe.[4] Along with the government's employment of force and fraud, undue clerical influence lead Liberal complaints of electoral injustice after the party's fall from power in 1885.

Fear of clerical influence had been of long standing. When universal suffrage was introduced in the Constitution of 1853, many Liberals had regarded it as folly, likely to smother the infant Liberal republic at birth: it was seen by some commentators as counter-revolution in remote New Granada just as much as in some parts of Europe.[5] In a society still overwhelmingly rural and illiterate, they pictured the electorate as dependent and deferential, directed by the trio of priest, landowner and mayor. This argument has been less questioned since than it was at the time. Leaving aside the question whether this trio was always in harmony, it is still believed by many that the Church was the consistently effective electoral arm of the Conservative party, perhaps its principal electoral resource. '¿Cuantos votos puso?', the Archbishop of Bogotá Bernardo Herrera Restrepo was said to ask about every candidate for preferment put before him, 'How many votes did he put?' And in legend the inability of his successor Archbishop Ismael Perdomo to decide between rival Conservative candidates is seen as the decisive element in the party's downfall in 1930, rather than any decline in the Church's electoral influence.[6]

Yet there are many reasons for doubting this simple picture. One doubter was Manuel Murillo Toro, the leading Liberal ideologue of the middle of the last century, who defended universal suffrage in a remarkably direct and sanguine manner after rehearsing, citing many French arguments, the case against it: that it handed power to a clergy that manipulated the poor and ignorant. Critics, he wrote, should be patient; the illiterate were not stupid, and indeed on many matters were better informed than the uselessly educated; in some parts of the country they were more than usually enlightened: ' ... the masses of the coastal regions and the hot valleys understand political questions better and judge them more impartially than many of the bosses, lawyers and clerics of the cold country'. He doubted the power of priests and landowners:

In my opinion their power in elections under universal suffrage has been exaggerated. It is true that they can take advantage of their respective positions, but fortunately there are motives that hold them back. In the one case and in the other there exists over and above the desire of wielding influence the desire to get rich, to get the most out of the parish or the land and that runs counter to influencing. A priest who wants to have influence has to begin by making himself loved and respected, and in order to do that he has above all else to show himself disinterested, generous, charitable; if he does not, he will be disliked, he will get into conflicts with the other local powers and will end up not being able to exert influence. The same happens to the landowner. If he wants to dispose of a lot of votes in the elections, it is necessary that he should not charge high rents, that he should open his waste to tenants, that he should pay wages on election day; with the current scarcity of labour in agriculture, the proprietors cannot take advantage of the tenants, without great inconveniences. And as the majority of the priests and proprietors are not men for whom it matters very much to exercise influence in elections, as doing so would imply them making sacrifices they abandon them altogether... Looking at this situation in the abstract, and applying it to the parties, influences balance out. If it is true that the majority of priests belong to the Conservative party, the majority of landowners are Liberals, especially the small proprietors who are the most numerous. From this it follows that though the priests under universal suffrage carry the elections in Bogotá, Tunja and Antioquia, they still will not get anywhere in Vélez, Socorro, Pamplona, Casanare, Mariquita, Ocaña, Mompós, nor on all the Atlantic Coast.

Moreover there are many Liberal clerics, and they are precisely the most intelligent, the most sociable, the most generous and the most noble characters, the ones who are best able to exert influence, they follow the party without personal interest and consequently lend it great support.[7]

Murillo was an optimist, and his judgements naturally favour his own party. Yet he did not write as an idle spectator, but as a leading practical politician who knew his country well. He was twice to be its President. It would be foolish to dismiss the views of such a man as naive, even though this article dates from before the era of Conservative rule after 1885 in which the most notorious examples of clerical political intervention are to be found.

They are to be found exposed extensively in Liberal political writing. One of the fullest collections is contained in the volume of protest compiled by the Liberal party after its presidential candidate General Benjamín Herrera lost the election of 1922, *Los Partidos Políticos en Colombia.*[8]

There is no doubt at all that the clergy overwhelmingly favoured the Conservative party. After the Conservatives and their allies had captured the government in 1885, they had conscientiously restored God to the Constitution and many privileges to the Church, and negotiated a generous Concordat with the Vatican. The native clergy were reinforced by ultramontane regulars from Europe, who had no inhibitions about carrying on their struggles locally, and who provided the more extreme anti-liberal leadership.[9]

Early on, the Liberal protest of 1922 states its case against the clergy's behaviour:

The Liberal Party, through the mouth of its Chief, has declared that it professes absolute respect for the religious beliefs of the majority of Colombians.

Having made this sincere declaration, Liberalism cannot understand the vehement campaign against it that has been carried on by the immense majority of the clergy, a campaign in which precisely those priests who are not sons of the country have distinguished themselves by their fury. In the last electoral struggle not only Liberals but also their wives and children have been cruelly outraged by rabid insults and ferocious malice, and the multitude has heard Liberalism accused from the pulpit of professing immoral and subversive doctrines and of committing atrocious crimes. These accusations have reached unbelievable extremes.[10]

The dossier contains a number of cases of denunciations from the pulpit – 'Liberal dogs, sons of bitches', allegedly from the priest of Gachetá – and a number of examples of other kinds of clerical hostility and interference: clergy distributing voting papers stamped with parochial approval and giving other precise directions; excommunications; denials of the sacraments to unrepentant Liberals and denial to them of access to parish registers for the certificates necessary to register to vote; denunciations of Liberal leaders; regular clergy voting *en masse*; the organisation of village mobs by priests against Liberal speakers and the ringing of church bells to disrupt their meetings; threats of the pains of eternal damnation – the priest of Tocaima, using a sugar-boiling image, announced that Liberals would burn in the fifth vat of Hell, which God had already enlarged to contain them; the priest of Espinal was accused of firing on Liberals from the *casa cural*.[11]

The conduct of the higher clergy is also scrutinised, and falls short of the standards enjoined by the Pope. A Jesuit in the smart Bogotá suburb of Chapinero had the bad taste to preach against Liberals, 'leaving the good and pious ladies who heard him quite stupefied. At that same hour His Holiness Benedict XV was dying in Rome, the author of that memorable encyclical which prohibits making the pulpit a party platform, an encyclical which, sad to say, has never been obeyed, nor is now obeyed, by the Colombian parish priest.' The pastoral letter of the Arcbishop of Medellín instructs that it is a mortal sin to vote for someone whose religious ideas either inspire suspicion or are unknown: 'the circular is ingeniously worded and contains no express recommendation. Naturally it is an attack on the candidature of General Herrera.' Altogether less prudent was the response of the Bishop of Tunja to an enthusiastic Conservative reception: 'The prelate replied to the speeches with an inflamed political harangue exciting their zeal, and ended by shouting out a *viva* to the Conservative party and General Ospina, according to *El Nuevo Tiempo*.[12] This is, as we understand it, the first occasion on which a Prince of the Church, from the balcony of his palace, has adopted such an attitude and presented such a spectacle to his flock, the vast majority of whom are Liberals.'[13]

There is a prurient pleasure and amusement in reading of such examples in the formal tones of this distant republic seventy years ago, which only the most austere or humourless or Catholic will deny. But then one begins to suspect that this pleasure might be shared in some degree by the compilers.[14] Then one comes to doubt not the whole matter, but the particular focus that it has been given.

It would be rash to try to revise too far the received view of a politically involved Church, one that certainly exercised a great deal of political power in some parts of the country. Some well documented examples can be found, from Boyacá, Santander, Antioquia, Caldas, Nariño. Certain Bishops – Miguel Angel Builes of Santa Rosa de Osos, Ezequiel Moreno Díaz of Pasto are the best known – have left both a memory and a record of their anti-Liberal activity, and there is plenty of evidence attesting the involvement and influence of 'Carlist' priests in Conservative parts of Santander.[15] Such men were a part of the sectarian political machinery in the Conservative armoury, and some of them showed little restraint in setting it in motion, or little resistance to being set in motion themselves. But in Colombia, as in Ireland, Italy or Spain, it is still necessary to ask to what degree the Church was an effective political organisation.

The degree to which the population was catechised and pro-clerical varied, as has been noted.[16] The Colombian Church was not particularly rich, even before it lost its properties at mid-century, and it was not particularly strong in numbers: my guess would be that the Church was far less present in the lives of the population than it was in Ireland, for example.[17] Antioquia, which at the end of the century had come to be regarded as the Department possessing the best organised and most dynamic clergy, had surprisingly few priests at the time of Independence. The basic ecclesiastical geography of the country has always to be borne in mind. One finds it reflected in the Liberal catalogue of complaints of 1922, which records instances of clerical interference, with, as one would anticipate, more from some parts of the country than from others.

But even here the record of 1922 contains some surprises. For example, Liberalism kept its end up in Chiquinquirá, the country's foremost place of pilgrimage, which one would have thought to be more dominated by the Church. In general, Liberalism is strong in the towns, confirming Colombia's broad adherence to the common correlation of urbanisation and secularisation, loosely defined, even though most of the towns are small and unindustrial – the pattern even holds for Tunja, the old clerical centre where the Bishop had been so singularly indiscreet.

The impression one is left with at the end of the document, and it is the most thorough compilation of its sort that the Liberals made in the Conservative era, is that clerical influence and involvement is not the prime cause of their defeat. Both the weight of the argument and the statistical exercises in the book show that the main enemy is fraud, usually in the form of inflated numbers of Conservative votes in what were considered the 'governmental' departments, those in which government influence was easiest to exercise. The examples given here are Nariño and Boyacá: 'In Nariño and Boyacá, Conservatism has the majority among the illiterate peasants, friends of any government not for ideological reasons, which they do not have, but out of fear, servility, wretchedness. Recruiting, prison, arbitrary taxation, those are the causes.'[18]

There were various ways in which numbers could be inflated in rural areas where there was little supervision or possible opposition. Some of these required people actually to cast their votes, and in such cases persons who had neither the property nor the literacy qualifications required by law were permitted and encouraged to vote. There are some allegations of this being done with the help of priests, interesting instances of the *de facto* widening of the suffrage by the Conservatives who in 1886 had restricted it. A probable incidence of such excessive voting is provided by Gramalote, Norte de Santander, a town founded by Conservative refugees from Liberal persecution and one much ruled by its priests. The pertinent figures are these:[19]

	No. of inhabitants
Census of 1918:	9,637
Census of 1912:	8,633
Literate:	789
Over 21:	1,720
Conservative votes:	3,147

Nonetheless much fraud must have been less conscientious and more direct, the simple *canastada*, or basketful, the fictitious inflation of numbers.

In those cases clerical assistance may have been welcome, but it was hardly necessary. There were plenty of lay Conservative party men skilled in such affairs who were perfectly capable of working on their own. It may well be that in Colombia, as in Ireland, Church involvement was much more ancillary than has subsequently been supposed.

Further doubt on the clergy's effectiveness comes from awareness of political division within the Church. Colombian parties were always loose and factious, and hierarchical authority was also weak in the Church. Miguel Antonio Caro, Vice-President and acting President for most of the 1890s, who had begun his political career as a hyper-ortho-dox ultramontane and who remained a fervent believer all his life, was all the same driven to despair by the crudity and indiscipline of priests in politics at the end of his government, and made them the subject of one of his bitter Latin anathemas. Division and insubordination were appar-ent again at the end of the 1920s.[20]

Disinterested descriptions, or even detailed descriptions, of Colom-bian elections are not all that easy to find, though much detail is certainly still buried in the press and in the surviving archives of the Ministry of Government. One such description is given by Eduardo Rodríguez Piñeres, who in 1918 was a member of the joint commission defining the frontier between Colombia and Ecuador, and a detached witness of the elections in Pasto, the capital of the clerical and 'governmental' Depart-ment of Nariño:

I was present at the presidential elections of 1918 in Pasto, which were characterised by the order and composure you would expect of a city ... Long before voting opened, the partisans of Señor Suárez (the eventual Conservative winner) were going about some with broad blue ribbons in their hats, others with blue rosettes on the chest, useful emblems for gaining them admission to the voting tables without difficulty. The supporters of Valencia, the Conservative dissident, got round this trick by wearing the same signs and so enjoyed the advantage of the same 'open sesame'. The coalitionists (the dissidents) had distributed voting papers with the name of their candidate to the indians of the neighbouring village of La Laguna, with instructions to keep them carefully and to be sure to vote with them, but always to accept the voting papers that the capuchin friars would distribute among them when they escorted them to vote. The indians followed instructions, and were arriving with their two votes each when someone let out a *viva*, and the cry was interpreted by them as signifying every man for himself, and they ran off. Very few were held back by the friars, who believed that they were all going to vote for their candidate, when in reality those who managed to vote voted with the paper they had brought with them hidden. In truth, nobody in this world knows who he is working for.

At five in the afternoon the result was already known: the coalitionists had been defeated by roughly three hundred votes, those of the Army, which did vote in Pasto, and those of the religious orders. There was a lot of deafening shouting as the victors, led around by a band, celebrated a victory that they would not have won without those reinforcements. At night there were some violent incidents that might have turned out worse. A few days after the voting, as a result of a drunken brawl in Chapal in which politics got mixed up, some *indios* and *indias* were thrown into gaol, and one of the *indias* was barbarously put in a cell even worse than the worst that the Bogotá police is said to use. The politicians saw some possible party advantage in this, and in their telegrams to Bogotá they described it as happening before the elections, and done to deter the coalitionists, which gave the capital press the pretext for firing off red-hot articles about 'distinguished matrons put in the stocks' and 'barbarous commotions heralded by mystic processions and infernal brass bands' ... and other expressions from the sectarian repertoire, rich in its abundance and cheap because it costs nothing.[21]

It is strangely easy to overlook how intensely political all post-election polemic inevitably is, and to read it with insufficient scepticism. Again, it is only gradually that one becomes aware of how necessary anticlericalism was to the Liberal cause at this time, as one sees how avidly the Liberals seized upon every chance to publicise the political activities of the clergy, many of them trivial, such as the *párroco* of Cocuy donating a calf for a celebration barbecue. Something more than whistle-blowing is involved.

There is a clue in a party communication from Manizales: 'From the pulpits and in the fly-sheets the anti-Liberal insult campaign is being intensified, using expressions unimaginable. This increases Liberal enthusiasm.'

Liberal enthusiasm, identity, autonomy, identification with freedom and progress, assertion of citizenship, of non-servile status, of un-indianness – all these were reinforced by denunciation of the Church, and denunciation from the Church.[22] In the Colombian context this all had a powerful attraction, of great assistance in maintaining the morale and cohesion of the party. In ways that Voltaire had not foreseen, if the Church had not existed, the Colombian Liberals might have found it necessary to invent it.

The Liberals, with some frequency, appealed to the teachings of the Pope against the local bishops and clergy, sometimes seeking to involve the Nuncio. The most famous example of such coat-trailing was General Rafael Uribe Uribe's lengthy and erudite pamphlet, *De cómo el liberalismo político colombiano no es pecado,* widely distributed, sometimes free, in the first decades of the century, and full of references to the encyclicals and the most reputable European authorities. It was the object of a number of more lengthy rebuttals in Colombia and was eventually formally condemned by the Holy Office, none of which can have harmed its prestige.[23]

Another skilful exploiter of clerical hostility was the journalist Enrique Santos Montejo, who edited *La Linterna* to lighten the darkness of Tunja, Boyacá, from 1911 to 1919. His delight in being denounced by name from the pulpit by the Bishop is hardly concealed, nor is his pride that *La Linterna* has been formally condemned by the Church: 'We cannot find words to express the pleasure it is to have a contender of such illustrious calibre as Bishop Maldonado ...'.[24] The Bishop's denunciations are laughable, they will have no effect on the Liberals, 'who constitute the majority of decent society, and who seeing themselves painted in such fierce colours by señor Maldonado will only do as we do, smile indulgently and carry on'.[25]

Why does the Church persist in such futile courses? The answer is summed up by Santos Montejo:

> In Colombia, unfortunately, it has not been possible to reach an agreement that will once and for all end the conflicts between the Church and the parties. There are two reasons for this: the first is the exaggerated concept that the Prelates and the Clergy in general have of their own power and influence over the masses. This exaggeration gives them that proud confidence that makes them underestimate the dangers of extreme courses of action. The second reason is the self-interested adhesion of the Conservative party to the Church, and the support the Church consequently gives it in all its enterprises.[26]

Elections and Public Order

In a moment of frustration in the confused period preceding the changes of 1885, their chief architect Rafael Núñez had quoted a North American diplomat: 'In Colombia there are only two things in order, the Army and the Church.'[27] The Army too had a long history of electoral activity. The remainder of this chapter will briefly examine that role, that of the police, and the government's use of force. When looked at closely, these phenomena too, like clerical influence, turn out to be quite different one from another, to evolve distinctly and to have surprising limitations.

The Army voted from the early days of Independence. Not unnaturally in a republic newly emancipated by force of arms, soldiers were considered at least as worthy of full citizenship as anyone else. The early debates on military status, on the desirability of the *fuero* or separate military jurisdiction, favoured the close integration of the citizen soldier with the rest of society. That implied that he could vote. Even if the suffrage was to be restricted by income or literacy, some soldiers, even sergeants and corporals, might still vote. Soldiers were certainly keenly aware of their political interests.[28]

Civilians were as keenly aware of the unrepublican aspects of this procedure. How could the soldier's vote be regarded as free? How was the free exercise of political choice compatible with military discipline? How could the civilian citizen be confident that he could cast his own vote freely if soldiers were voting too?

Colombian governments had scant resources of patronage, and were reluctant to discard the electoral advantage offered by control of even the small military forces the country could customarily afford to maintain. These forces, in the face of a more or less constant possibility of civil war, were commanded by officers who were inevitably government partisans. Their electoral usefulness took several forms. One was the direct vote of the troops, generously assumed by those who controlled the lists of electors to fulfil the conditions required by successive laws. Another, practised occasionally in the weaker states under the federal constitution of 1863, was the forcible re-arrangement of local political situations to suit the central government, which sometimes involved carrying out some sort of election. A third was to overawe the voters. One of the commonest ways of doing this, which involved no direct use of force, seems to have been to put about the rumour that recruiting would coincide with polling. Forcible recruiting was widely resented and feared until well into the twentieth century, and such a rumour could effectively persuade a not very enthusiastic electorate to stay away.

The Liberal *Guardia Colombiana* of the federal period was replaced after 1885 by a purged national army, but it continued to be put to electoral use. The military vote was not finally abolished until 1930. The Constitution of 1886 merely forbade the army 'deliberating'; it did not say anything against it voting. Nonetheless, the practice attracted increasing criticism in the 1890s, from Conservatives as well as Liberals, and from soldiers as well as from civilians. The government was criticised for augmenting troop numbers at election time, subjecting the troops to *transhumancia electoral*, electoral nomadism, moving them from place to place according to political need, and for letting political loyalty shown in electoral services influence promotions. It was attacked for voting the troops in formation; at least, said the critics, soldiers should be allowed to vote individually, or in small groups, so that they could have a chance of voting freely. The government replied with lame circulars implausibly prohibiting officers from directing their men how to vote, and defended the voting in formation as dictated by the need to maintain public order at election time, usually a time of some stress. Military voting from time to time was itself a cause of street disorders.[29]

The abandonment of the military vote in the twentieth century took the following course. After the disastrous War of the Thousand Days, Colombia's last formal civil war which culminated in the loss of Panama, President Rafael Reyes pursued with unprecedented vigour the creation of a nonpartisan professional army, contracting a Chilean military mission for that purpose in 1907.

The change was gradual, and frequently resisted by officers of the 'old army'. But the new force complained increasingly that involvement in elections, even keeping public order at election time, was not a proper military concern. It was bad for discipline, the expenses incurred ate into scarce military funds, it interrupted training, it damaged the national standing and prestige of the army. Police matters should be handled by the police.

The expansion of the franchise in national elections might have been supposed to make the military vote irrelevant, as the army remained small. However, competition was at times keen even under the Conservative hegemony, for the ruling party was far from monolithic and was constantly divided by faction. The temptation to use the vote of the army was still a lively one in the decade of the 1920s.

A remarkable evolution had none the less taken place in the wake of the Reyes professionalisation. In the circumstances of Colombia, with its extensive territory, widely scattered population highly politicised on 'sectarian' lines, and skeletal forces of order, keeping the peace and offering minimal guarantees posed acute problems in the practical conduct of peaceful elections that have not received their due attention. Over the two decades after Reyes's rule ended in 1909, it became increasingly common for local authorities to request detachments of the army to help keep the peace at election time. It is clear from the archives of the Ministry of Government that these requests were not for troops to vote or to coerce: the requests are clearly for the presence of a recognisably neutral force. It is often obvious that what is wanted is symbolic, even a sergeant or a corporal and two or three men will do. Despite initial resistance from the military, the government often does its best to comply.[30]

There are lapses in virtue, occasions for example when such requests were ignored because it was seen to be politically expedient to keep the troops elsewhere where their votes were needed. All the same, public opinion had come to see the army as an institution that was not part of the electoral machinery that governments had at their disposal. Its hierarchy and its chain of command were distinct. It represented the nation. There was some point in appealing to its neutrality.

The contrast was the police, predominantly local forces under the patronage of local political figures, extensively used in elections and frequently got together solely for electoral purposes. The pattern in the literature on elections and in the Ministry of Government archive is clear. The local and departmental police cannot offer any guarantees of neutrality or safety. On the contrary, they are the heart of the problem. The exiguous national police – there was such a force; its members are usually referred to as detectives – enjoys somewhat more confidence, but what peaceful citizens request is above all the presence of the army.

This can be clearly seen in the conflictive department of Santander in the aftermath of the change of government in 1930. The Conservative author of a diary that records the results of that change to Liberal dominance in the region of García Rovira is careful to distinguish between departmental police and revenue (drink monopoly) guards, national police and detachments of the army. The departmental police and guards are overtly political, agents recruited for 'liberalising' the region. The national police are somewhat preferable, but the only real prospect of 'guarantees' is offered by the army. This perception does not appear to owe much, if anything, to any supposedly Conservative allegiance among its officers, but to its divorce from the local political machinery, its national status, its sense of honour and *patria*.[31]

The diary also shows that the army is too small for the task of keeping the peace. It cannot maintain its precarious presences for long enough, and it too tends to get corrupted by the local political antagonisms when it is broken up into small units scattered around the divided and sectarian countryside. All the same, it is the only national institution that offers a hope of neutrality. The intense involvement of the police, all too apparent in the 1922 election on the Conservative side, is held up in contrast. At times the Liberal police have to be escorted through the district by the army. A careful student of this document and of the 1922 Liberal protest can also begin to reconstruct in detail just how the police were deployed in elections, how frequently the mere threat of directed trouble was enough to keep unwanted voters away, what sort of harrassment was employed, how on occasion real force could be applied with impunity.

This chapter should not conclude with what the reader may have been led to expect, some sort of balance between Conservatives and Liberals, with the army holding the ring at election times. The late 1940s were to see electoral violence much more intense than that experienced around the change in party hegemony of 1930.[32] The Church continued to give its support to the Conservatives, the army remained incapable of controlling numerous local conflicts, the police were re-politicised all over again. Of these three institutions, the first still retained its illusions of power, the second remained weak, and the third had no defences against sectarian manipulation until it was placed under the Ministry of War by the brief military government of 1953-1957. Colombia's electoral apprenticeship was particularly long and painful. Precisely for that, it shows certain facets and problems of electoral evolution, common to many other polities, in particularly acute form.

Notes

1. The pioneering studies are D. Bushnell, 'El sufragio en la Argentina y en Colombia hasta 1853', *Revista del Instituto de Historia del Derecho*, no. 19, Buenos Aires (1968), 'Voter participation in the Colombian election of 1856', *Hispanic American Historical Review*, vol. 51 (May 1971); 'Aspectos de historia electoral colombiana del siglo XIX', *Política y Sociedad* (Tunja, 1975); 'Las elecciones presidenciales, 1863-1883', *Revista de la Universidad Nacional de Medellín*, no 18 (Nov. 1984). See also the remarks on elections in his *The Making of Modern Colombia* (Berkeley, 1993), and 'Las Elecciones en Colombia: siglo XIX', in *Credencial Historia*, Bogotá (Feb. 1994). On related matters, see my 'Algunas notas sobre el caciquismo en Colombia', *Revista de Occidente*, Madrid, (Oct. 1973), reprinted in *Del poder y la gramática* (Bogotá, 1993), and my chapter 'La política' in B. Castro (ed.), *Historia de la vida cotidiana en Colombia* (Bogotá, 1995). See also studies of Colombian electoral history by the editor of this volume, E. Posada-Carbó, including 'Elections under the Conservative Hegemony in Colombia, 1886-1930' paper presented at the LASA conference, Atlanta, 1994, and 'Electoral Violence in Colombia: A Comparative Perspective, 1830-1930' paper presented at the Instituto Universitario Ortega y Gasset, Madrid, Feb. 1995. See also his 'Elections and Civil Wars in Nineteenth-century Colombia: The 1875 Presidential Campaign', *Journal of Latin American Studies*, vol. 26, pt. 2 (1994). I have much benefited by numerous discussions with him. An official compilation of electoral statistics is 'Colombia, Registraduría Nacional de Estado Civil', *Historia electoral colombiana, 1810-1988* (Bogotá, 1988). For readers unfamiliar with Colombian history, Bushnell's introductory work can be read in conjunction with my chapters in L. Bethell (ed.), *Cambridge History of Latin America*, vols. III and IV (Cambridge, 1985, 1986) and the relevant parts of A. Tirado Mejía, J. O. Melo and J. A. Bejarano (eds.), *Nueva Historia de Colombia*, 6 vols. (Bogotá, 1989).

2. The best and most accessible introduction to Church-State relations in Latin America remains J. L. Mecham, *Church and State in Latin America*, revised edition (Austin, 1966). For Colombia, see J. P. Restrepo, *La Iglesia y El Estado en Colombia* (London, 1885). There is a great deal of political information in the republican parts of Mons. J. Restrepo Posada, *Arquidiócesis de Bogotá. Datos biográficos de sus prelados*, 3 vols. (Bogotá, 1961-66). Useful summaries of the history of relations in republican times and of the

backgound to the Concordat of 1888 are in C. Valderrama Andrade, *Un capítulo de las relaciones entre el estado y la iglesia en Colombia*. *Miguel Antonio Caro y Ezequiel Moreno* (Bogotá, 1986), chap. 1, and F. González, 'Iglesia y estado desde la Convención de Ríonegro hasta el Olimpo Radical, 1863-1878', *Anuario colombiano de historia social y de la cultura*, Bogotá, no. 15 (1987).

3. V. Gutiérrez de Pineda, *La Familia en Colombia*, 2 vols. (Bogotá, 1963 and 1968), vol. I, *Trasfondo histórico*, chap. 17. See also for late colonial local politics M. Garrido, *Reclamos y representaciones*. *Variaciones sobre la política en el Nuevo Reino de Granada, 1770-1815* (Bogotá, 1993).

4. As elsewhere in the catholic world, papal instructions were disseminated among the clergy in an effort to define the limits of legitimate political involvement. These came to be set wider in a country with a history of what the church naturally regarded as persecution, where one of the two main parties developed a strong anticlerical strain. There are scattered examples from a wide choice over many decades: *Deberes de los católicos en las próximas elecciones* (Bogotá, 1848) includes approving mentions of the Irish success in gaining Catholic Emancipation, and of French catholic organisation; indifference a sin, voting a duty: X.X.X.(pseud.), *Por la Iglesia* (Bogotá, 1909), restates the papal position and defends recent clerical involvement in a number of local questions, including temperance campaigns and opposition to Japanese immigration; P. A. Brioschi, Archbishop of Cartagena, *El clero y la política* (Cartagena, 1918) approves a just and moderate intervention: 'God is Lord and Master of the elections and it is He who one day will judge electors, candidates and elected, each according to his works, and he will no more pardon those who sin in elections than those who sin elsewhere.'

5. Though universal manhood suffrage was abandoned for national elections in the Constitution of 1886, it persisted for local ones. The reader should also be aware that despite their advantages, factions in power did not always win. For the details of suffrage history, see the works cited in note 1.

6. For a sympathetic account of the difficulties of these two Archbishops, in the face of clerical and lay Conservative division and the many real limitations of their authority, see Mons. J. Restrepo Posada, *La Iglesia en dos Momentos Difíciles de la Historia Patria* (Bogotá, 1971). The habitual question asked by Archbishop Herrera comes from information from family descendants. See also my 'Algunas notas sobre la historia del caciquismo' for Perdomo's difficulties in guiding the hierarchy in 1929. Landowner influence in Colombian elections was generally weak, and is far less conspicuous in the record than 'government machinery' or the activities of the clergy. The reasons are explored in the same essay. It should also be stressed that though prominent Conservative politicians were usually willing to accept the electoral support of the clergy, they frequently resisted any attempts at clerical guidance.

7. M. Murillo Toro, 'El Sufragio Universal', *El Tiempo*, no. 39, 25 Sept. 1855. Reprinted in G. España, prologue, *Los radicales del siglo XIX. Escritos políticos* (Bogotá, 1984). The anonymous Conservative pamphlet *Elecciones de la Provincia de Neiva* (Bogotá, 1853), offers some support for Murillo's views. Among much other detail, it denounces the coercion of local indians

by the Liberals who threaten to impose fines on them for not voting, and the involvement in fraud and coercion of a Liberal priest, Presbítero Juan de la Cruz Cala, who presides over the electoral jury. The Conservative party, to confuse matters further, is described in this pamphlet as 'un partido altamente liberal' – 'a highly liberal party'. For further details of Liberal electoral abuses (and for Liberal persecution of the Church) see the relevant chapters of J. J. Guerra, *Viceversas liberales* (Bogotá, 1923).

8. *Los partidos políticos en Colombia* (Bogotá, 1922). The book, compiled by eminent Liberals, runs to 472 pages and makes its accusations in some detail. The government replied with *Memorial del señor General don Benjamín Herrera. Respuesta del Excelentísimo señor Presidente de la República* (Bogotá, 1924).

9. See, for example, the compendium written by the Spanish Agustinian, Nicolás Casas, *Enseñanzas de la iglesia sobre el liberalismo por el Ilmo. Sr. Obispo T. de Adrianópolis, Vicario Apostólico de Casanare* (Bogotá, 1901). This guide contains instructions on the distinct 'grades' of liberalism and their treatment in the confessional, and an entire chapter on elections and 'Sufragio popular'. It ran to a second edition in Spain: (Madrid, 1902). There is as yet no systematic historical study of the Colombian clergy in republican times, nor of its social origins or its social influence, nor of the important role of foreign clergy after 1885. For many aspects of the Church's political activity, see C. Abel, *Política, iglesia y partidos en Colombia* (Bogotá, 1987).

10. *Los partidos políticos*, p. 16.

11. All examples here and in following paragraphs are from *Los partidos políticos*, unless otherwise indicated.

12. The leading Conservative newspaper.

13. *Los partidos políticos*.

14. And not only by the compilers: 'The pastoral of the Archbishop señor Caicedo has caused great hilarity on account of the instructions it gives the parish priests on how they are to proceed in the elections.' *El Gráfico*, an early illustrated paper, carried an amusing article on the conduct of priests in a Bogotá election, with photographs. The photographer was set upon by priests and *beatas*, much to his satisfaction.

15. For Miguel Angel Builes, see M. Zapata Restrepo, *La Mitra Azul* (Medellín, 1973); for San Ezequiel Moreno, canonised in 1992, see my 'San Ezequiel Moreno: "El liberalismo es pecado"', *Credencial Historia*, no. 46 (Oct. 1993); C. Valderrama Andrade, *Un capítulo de las relaciones*, and his edition of *Epistolario del Beato Ezequiel Moreno y otros Agustinos Recoletos con Miguel Antonio Caro y su familia* (Bogotá, 1983). For clerical power in parts of Santander, see E. Bayona Posada, *Memorias de un ochentón* (Bogotá, 1984).

16. Details for the parishes of Cundinamarca at the beginning of the 1880s are given in A. M. Amézquita, *Defensa del clero español y americano y guía geográfico-religiosa del Estado Soberano de Cundinamarca* (Bogotá, 1882).

17. A brief comparison with Ireland: Theodore Hoppen, *Elections, Politics and Society in Ireland, 1832-1885* (Oxford, 1984), p. 171, gives the following figures for Irish *parochial* clergy and the ratio to Catholic population:

Ireland:	total parochial clergy	Catholics per clergyman
1851	2,368	2,214
1871	2,813	1.476
1901	2,938	1,126

The following are figures for *total* Colombian male religious, regular and secular (taken from Patricia Londoño, thesis in progress on social history of Antioquia, Oxford University):

Colombia:	total male religious	inhabitants per religious, approx.
1851	1,672 (295 regulars)	1,100
1870	1,565	2,000
1912	2.138	2,500

These proportions clearly do not favour Colombia – note that the Irish figures exclude regulars – and the trends run in opposite directions.

18. *Los partidos políticos*, p. 26. The statistical conclusions are in the analytical essay 'Prestidigitación electoral', by Dr Jorge Rodríguez, pp. 398-401: 'The Ospinistas (the victorious Conservatives) overdid it. Fifty or sixty thousand fraudulent votes would have been enough to ensure their candidate's victory; they had to exaggerate to the extent of two hundred thousand.'
19. Figures from *Los partidos políticos*, p. 42. For an account of Gramalote, see R. Ordóñez Yáñez, Pbro, *Selección de Escritos* (Cúcuta, 1963), pp. 135-78.
20. See above, note 5. The course of Caro's disenchantment can be followed in Valderrama Andrade, *Un capítulo en las relaciones*. The poem *In clericos quosdam seditionibus permixtos*, pp. 141-2.
21. E. Rodríguez Piñeres, *Por Tierras Hermanas. De Bogotá, por Quito, a la frontera del Sur. Impresiones de un viaje* (Bogotá, 1918), pp. 127-8. Rodríguez Piñeres was a Bogotano liberal, a distinguished lawyer and the author of valuable works of political history. His account of the society of Nariño is generally sympathetic.
22. For confirmation of this from clerical sources, see N. Valencia López, 'Periodismo panfletario y excomunión en el suroccidente colombiano (1912-1930)', *Historia y Espacio*, no. 14, Cali (June 1991). Why, Archbishop Herrera asks himself, are prohibited newspapers so widely read? The answer: 'Out of the cowardice, curiosity and culpable indolence of the catholics, who despite ecclesiastical prohibitions and the voice of conscience think little of disobeying laws human or divine. These enterprising people who glory in their success to the dishonour of catholicism know this very well.' The authorities of the Diocese of Cali deplore the quantity of anticlerical papers, unopposed by any effective clerical response, 'harmful, altogether damaging for simple people, who unfortunately are their most avid readers'. For the Colombian tradition of anticlerical journalism, see my 'José María Vargas Vila', an account of its most successful exponent, in *Del poder y la gramática*.

A surprising proof of resistance to clerical political guidance is given by the manuscript diary of Sofía Durán Do of Suaita, Santander (copy in the author's possession). The authoress is a devout lady in humble circumstances, very much a *beata*, but in her political annotations an unshakeable Liberal. One suspects that the Church had some success in enthusing and marshalling Conservative voters, and negligible success in converting Liberals.

23. Rafael Uribe Uribe was, together with his rival Benjamín Herrera, the most prominent Liberal leader to emerge from Colombia's last civil war, the War of the Thousand Days, 1899-1902; he was assassinated in 1914. The Colombian Church always found it hard to maintain a prudent silence about the sins of the enemy. One is tempted to conclude that a Colombian was much more likely to learn of such systems as communism, socialism and anarchism by way of clerical denunciation than through supporters of such causes, who were certainly far fewer in number in the country than were priests.

24. E. Santos Montejo (Calibán), *Danza de las Horas y otros escritos* (Bogotá, 1969), p. 89.

25. *Ibid.*, p. 132.

26. *Ibid.*, p. 124.

27. Article 'La Paz' in R. Núñez, *La reforma política en Colombia* (Bogotá, 1888), p. 608. The following section on the army and the police owes much to Patricia Pinzón de Lewin, whose *El ejército y las elecciones* (Bogotá, 1994), is part of a wider study on the Colombian army carried out under my direction.

28. See the detailed correspondence between General Mariano Montilla and the Swedish mercenary Count Frederick Adlercreutz about the need in 1829 to make 'good elections' in Cartagena and Mompox, and the use of the controlled military vote to that end, in C. Parra Pérez (ed.), *La cartera del Coronel Conde de Adlercreutz* (Paris, 1928), pp. 70-106.

29. A forceful Conservative criticism is 'El voto del ejército' in F. de P. Muñoz, *Escritos y discursos* (Medellín, 1897), pp. 292-6.

30. The archives of the Ministerio de Gobierno for the decades of the 1910s and 1920s are partially available in some order in the Archivo General de la Nación, Bogotá. The annual *Memorias* of the Ministerio de Guerra detail the performance of electoral duties.

31. B.N. Muñoz, *Crónicas de Guaca. La ruina de un pueblo* (Cúcuta, 1937).

32. For some details see *Sangre y fraude. Testimonio de la tragedia boyacense* (Bogotá, 1949). Even allowing for partisan exaggeration it is clear that the conflict has by then become more violent than in the 1920s. Contrast *Los partidos políticos*.

CHAPTER 8

VOTING IN BUENOS AIRES (ARGENTINA) BEFORE 1912

Paula Alonso*

The electoral reform of 1912 made the vote secret and compulsory in Argentina for all males over 18 years of age. The reform has been thought of as a dramatic turning point in the country's political development, as the turning of Argentina into a modern democracy. Previous reference to the electoral life of the pre-reform period has primarily concentrated on describing fraud and violence and, therefore, little is known about many aspects of the pre-1912 elections.

Focusing on the city of Buenos Aires, this chapter attempts both to enhance our understanding of pre-reform elections and to cast some doubts on the standard interpretations of the city's electoral and political developments. It should be stressed, however, that, given the profound differences between Buenos Aires and the rest of the country, generalisations about elections in the city cannot be applied to the rest of the country.[1] The first section briefly describes the history of the franchise in the province and city of Buenos Aires and analyses the received views on its electoral development. The chapter then concentrates on the voters of Buenos Aires. New findings of the nature of the electorate and the size of the voting population before 1912 offer an alternative account of the city's electoral life. As we shall see, these findings are closely related to socio-economic changes and the development of electoral practices over the decades preceding the 1912 reform.

* The author would like to thank the Leverhulme Trust for financial support during the course of this research and Ezequiel Gallo, Eduardo Zimmermann, Natalio Botana and Ana María Mustapic for commenting on an earlier draft.

An Early Start

In 1821 the constitution of the province of Buenos Aires established male universal suffrage. The only qualifications required to vote were to be male and over 20 years of age. Buenos Aires was not the only province which adopted universal suffrage; at least three other provinces also established it at the time, although after a few years they abandoned it and followed the more common pattern of introducing professional or educational restrictions.[2] In 1852, after several years of anarchy and dictatorship, Argentina became a unified nation and adopted a Constitution drafted according to the North American model. The constitution of 1853 said very little about elections. Paradoxically, although the constitution did establish some requirements for becoming a representative, it said *nothing* about who would be entitled to vote. Regulation of the franchise and of the electoral system was left to Congress.

By then the principle of male universal suffrage had a long history in Buenos Aires, the country's leading province. Although most provinces had restricted voting to the literate or maintained professional qualifications for the franchise, these requirements were soon abolished by the National Congress following the example of Buenos Aires. By 1856 all Argentine males over 17 years of age had the right to vote in national elections. Between 1862 and 1930, when the first military *coup* took place in Argentina, national elections took place with the frequency established by the National Constitution and according to the regulations determined by national laws.

The question of the franchise was resolved in Argentina at a very early stage in its national organisation. Perhaps because of this, it never became a significant issue in the frequent debates about the electoral system in the National Congress. Congressional debates on elections generally revolved around the allocation of votes, the size of wards, the registration of voters and the improvement of the system, but not around the franchise.[3] This does not mean that there was unanimous agreement about the benefits of universal suffrage. Isolated voices were raised from time to time against the absence of restrictions in a new and underdeveloped country. In 1886 for example, a prominent young lawyer published a treatise arguing for the introduction of at least literacy restrictions for those under 21 and for disenfranchising criminals and the unemployed. He expressed with horror:

No other country where popular suffrage is regularly exercised has an electoral body composed of such malleable and unaware elements. The Argentine law has not only happily given the right to vote to the ignorant, the criminal, the beggar and the tramp, but it has also given it to the weak and inexperienced adolescent, whose will is only that of his father or tutor.[4]

He was not alone in disputing the merits of unrestricted suffrage. In 1911, in the first opinion poll conducted in the country, a majority favoured restricting the vote.[5] Nevertheless, demands for restrictions to the franchise never received much political support and were never introduced.

Despite the fact that universal suffrage was adopted at a very early stage in Argentina – there are few parallels – the electorate was reluctant to go to the polls. In the first elections in the province of Buenos Aires in 1821 only 328 men voted out of a population of 60,000.[6] The turnouts for the 1876 election are estimated to be no more than 11.5 per cent of the electorate.[7] Many explanations were given, both by contemporaries and later by historians and social scientists, for the high levels of abstention. They all suggest that indifference, corruption and the predominance between 1880 and 1916 of one political party (the Partido Autonomista Nacional), were the main obstacles to electoral parti-cipation. The high levels of abstention were one of the principal considerations in the introduction of compulsory and secret voting in 1912. The reform was intended to increase the levels of participation (and hence of political involvement), put an end to electoral corruption, and promote the formation of opposition parties.[8] The first presidential elections under the reform (1916) were won by the opposition party.

The small turnouts of the pre-reform period have been one of the main factors upon which historians have based the standard interpretation of Argentina's electoral and political development. The predominant view has been that Argentina's early adoption of male universal suffrage makes her electoral development no different to those of countries which maintained literacy and property restrictions until the first half of the twentieth century. The political and electoral predominance of the landed oligarchy, which continued until 1916, the innumerable accounts of electoral repression, and the small turnouts, have been seen as evidence that, until 1912, elections were simply an exercise in repression and manipulation by the landed elite. Elections prior to 1912 have been understood as one of the many mechanisms employed by the oligarchy to keep the reins of power in its hands.[9]

Accounts of the elections of the pre-reform period tend to an exclusive focus on violence, becoming little more than anecdotes of various fraudulent activities. The electoral reform of 1912 is then compared to the granting of universal suffrage in Western democracies; it is seen as the achievement in Argentina of a full democratic system. However, unlike Western democracies where the transition towards modern democracy was gradual, it has commonly been argued that in Argentina the transition was an excessively abrupt one. One of the main pitfalls of the pre-reform system is thought to have been its failure to provide for the gradual development of political parties and the gradual improvement of the electoral system. It is claimed that, overnight, turnouts for national elections more than tripled, new social forces were included in the political system, elections were abruptly transformed from exclusive to inclusive affairs, and parties for the first time had to appeal to an electorate for votes instead of just relying on corruption and manipulation. Furthermore, many argued that the suddeness of this transition was responsible for the failure of the country's new democracy that, unable to cope, was curtailed by a military *coup* in 1930.[10]

The Voters of Buenos Aires

There has been wide agreement among historians and social scientists that the pre-reform elections did not mean the competition of political parties for the votes of the citizens. This interpretation is largely based on certain views of the nature and size of electoral participation before the vote became secret and compulsory. The traditional view has been that the voting population was composed of members of the elite who, by extensive use of electoral repression, kept the new social forces away from the polls. According to this view, the reform of 1912 meant the expansion of the vote from the top to the bottom of society.[11]

However, in recent analyses of the city of Buenos Aires between 1850 and 1880, it has been argued that voters did not belong to the enlightened elite but to the least qualified sectors of the population (the peons, the journeymen and the railway workers) who were marched to the poll by party factions on election day. It was the early granting of universal suffrage that made possible the manipulation of an unqualified electorate. The reform of 1912, the argument follows, did not mean the expansion of the vote from top to bottom, as had been traditionally argued, but the *creation* of the citizenry as the well-to-do had previously remained indifferent to the country's electoral life.[12]

However, if the electorate of Buenos Aires between 1850 and 1880 was composed of the 'marginal sectors' of the city's population, by the 1890s the situation had significantly changed. Data on the electorate drawn from the Electoral Register of the city of Buenos Aires in 1896 shows that, in the 1890s, the electorate was neither restricted to members of the elite, nor was it composed of the least qualified workers deployed for street fighting on election day.[13] An analysis by professions shows that all sectors of the population were broadly represented on the electoral roll. While the lower and middle sectors of the population represented 45 per cent and 42 per cent of the registrations respectively, the upper sectors composed a significant 13 per cent.[14] Furthermore, 92.5 per cent of the potential voters did know how to read and write, a remarkably high percentage considering the literacy standards of the time.[15]

Current interpretations of pre-reform elections have been based not only on the nature of electoral participation, but also on its size. The undoubtedly small size of the voting population of the city of Buenos Aires before 1912 has led to the dismissal of the electorate as unworthy of serious consideration. It is time, however, to re-think two basic questions: how small was the voting population of Buenos Aires before 1912? And, more importantly, was its size static or were there strong trends over the pre-1912 period?

A first response to these two questions is revealed in Figure 1, which displays the turnout figures and the total population of Buenos Aires from 1890 up to 1910, the last election before the 1912 reform.[16] When comparing the turnouts to the total population, it should be remembered that for six decades after 1869, immigrants comprised two thirds to three quarters of the total adult population. Immigrants could only participate in national elections after acquiring citizenship, which they seldom did. As a result, in the city of Buenos Aires, as in most other areas of high immigrant concentration, between 50 and 70 per cent of adult males could not vote.[17]

It is undoubtedly the case that the numbers actually voting were a minority. However, what has generally remained unnoticed is the strong upward trend in the absolute number of people voting.[18] From as early as 1895, the turnout in Buenos Aires was increasing very rapidly indeed. The figures are rather volatile; this is due to the inclusion of *all* the national elections of the period. The graph includes by-elections (1893); uncontested elections (1890, 1891, 1892); elections that took place in only half the city of Buenos Aires after a temporary change in the electoral system (1904); and elections which, although contested, displayed little competition given the comfortable predominance of one of

Figure 1
Turnouts in Buenos Aires 1890-1910

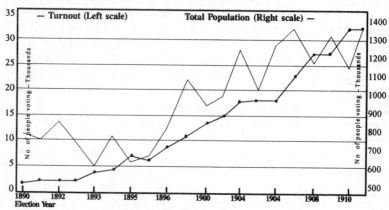

Sources: Population figures are taken from national and municipal cencuses, years 1865; 1887; 1895; 1904; 1909; 1914. The numbers of voters are taken from the electoral results published by *La Prensa* in each election.

the parties (1900, 1908, 1910).[19] However, even taking these elections into account, the trend after 1895 is clear; it does not suggest a static electoral participation, but a strongly growing interest in elections. The graph also shows that turnouts grew fast in a city where the population was also growing at high speed. Indeed, between 1904 and 1909, the city of Buenos Aires grew at an annual rate of 5.8 per cent; the second highest annual rate in the Western world.[20] However, as the graph shows, from 1895 to 1910 the growth in the turnout kept pace with the total population growth.

In a city where the adult population was predominantly composed of foreigners who were reluctant to acquire Argentine nationality and therefore could not vote, the turnouts are best related to the electorate, that is to the adult Argentine males over 17 or 18 years of age rather than to the total population.[21] However, before doing this it is best first to consider a significant characteristic of the electorate of Buenos Aires before 1912 that has been previously overlooked. Table 1 illustrates the size of the electorate in relation to the total population.[22]

In a city whose growth has generally been attributed to the high level of immigration, the rapid growth of the electorate has generally remained unnoticed. However, Columns 1 and 2 in Table 1 show that as the population grew, so too did the electorate, particularly between 1904 and 1914. Column 3 shows that the electorate as a percentage of the total population remained roughly constant, or in other words, the growth in

Table 1
Total Population and the Electorate of Buenos Aires 1887-1914

	(1)	(2)	(3)	(4)	(5)	(6)	(7)
1887	43,867	433,375	10.1				
1895	51,089	663,854	7.7	1.9	5.5		
1904	81,436	950,891	8.6	5.3	4.1		
1914	156,366	1,575,814	9.9	6.7	5.2	4.8	4.9

(1) Electorate   (2) Total population   (3) Electorate as % of Total Population   (4) Annualised Growth Rate Electorate (%)   (5)Annualised Growth Rate Population (%) (6) Annualised Growth Rate Electorate Whole Period (%)   (7) Annualised Growth Rate Population Whole Period (%).
Sources: As for Figure 1.

the electorate kept pace with the growth in the population. In terms of annual growth rates, Columns 4 and 5 show strong rates of 4.1 to 5.5 per cent. More significantly, however, they also show that although growth in the electorate was relatively slow between 1887 and 1895, it outpaced population growth in subsequent years. Admittedly, the growth rates for the electorate are faster from a small base, but the general point remains: the electorate grew strongly during the period. The average annual growth rates across the whole period displayed in the two final columns are roughly equal again, showing a dynamic electorate within a dynamic population.

What, then, was the relationship between the electorate and the turnouts? Although this could be analysed in every election year, for clarity of presentation two representative two-year periods at the beginning and at the end of the sample (1890-1892 and 1908-1910) are discussed in Table 2.[23] In each of these two-year periods there were four elections and in Column 2 of the table the average turnout over the four elections is presented.

Table 2
The Electorate and the Turnouts

	(1)	(2)	(3)	(4)	(5)
1890-1992	49,245	10,840	22.0		
1908-1910	115,467	28,155	24.4	4.8	5.4

Source: As for Figure 1

The first column of Table 2 gives an estimate of the electorate in each period,[24] while the third column shows that the turnout did not decrease as a percentage of the electorate even though the electorate was growing strongly. The annual growth rates displayed in Columns 4 and 5 show that the annual rate of growth of the turnout was actually faster than that of the electorate. Again, it must be noted that this rapid growth of the turnout is from a small base but again the general point is that turnouts as a percentage of the electorate remained roughly constant even though the electorate was growing strongly.

One of the reasons why the rapid growth of the pre-1912 voting population has remained overshadowed relates to its frequent comparison to the turnouts under compulsory voting. When analysing the impact of the 1912 reform on the number of voters, it has been argued that the size of the voting population more than tripled.[25] This argument is based on the comparison of the turnout in 1910 (with an average of 23 per cent across the two elections) with that of the 84 per cent in the first election of 1912. However, Table 3, which presents data on national elections in an extended period from 1890 to 1930, offers a slightly different picture.[26]

Table 3
Turnouts in Buenos Aires 1890-1930 (%)

1890	21.3	1908	28.5
1891	20.1	1910	20.1
1892	27.9	1910	25.7
1892	19.6	**1912**	**84.0**
1893	9.8	1914	84.0
1894	22.4	1916	76.2
1895	11.3	1916	75.6
1895	13.6	1918	72.8
1896	22.0	1920	73.0
1898	36.1	1920	73.0
1900	25.0	1922	73.6
1902	25.1	1922	71.0
1904	34.2	1924	65.3
1904	24.5	1926	63.8
1904	34.6	1928	91.6
1906	33.4	1930	86.1
1908	23.3		

Sources: The electorate between 1890-1910 inclusive is estimated from the census data in 1887, 1904 and 1914. From percentages of the electorate over the total population, a linear trend is used to estimate the percentage eligible to vote in the intervening years. This number is then multiplied by the total population in the actual year to obtain the estimate of the electorate. The estimates between 1912 and 1930 are taken from D. Cantón, *Materiales para el estudio de la sociología política en la Argentina* (Buenos Aires, 1968).

As Table 3 shows, the average turnout of 23 per cent for the elections of 1910 is one of the lowest in the 20th century before 1912, while 84 per cent for 1912 is the highest turnout under secret and compulsory voting (until 1928). In similar fashion the highest turnout under 'free voting' (36 per cent in 1898 or 34 per cent in 1904) could be compared to the lowest under compulsory voting (63 per cent in 1926); it could thus be argued that after 1912 the turnout did not even double.

While it is clear that the impact of the 1912 reform on mobilisation of the electorate has been exaggerated, it is more important to look at the overall trend. The average turnout for the ten elections before 1912, including low turnouts in by-elections and in uncontested elections, was 27.4 per cent. After 1912, the turnout grew rapidly for the first election of 1912 (84 per cent), but then gradually declined. The average turnout for the ten elections after 1912 was 71.8 per cent. In other words the turnout did double but certainly did not more than triple.[27] The impact of 1912 on the electoral mobilisation of the city, although undoubtedly significant, was less dramatic than has been assumed. This makes the expansion of the Argentine electorate due to the reform of 1912 a less exceptional case than has commonly been thought.[28]

The City of Buenos Aires and its Electoral Culture

One of the main pitfalls of most analyses of different aspects of the pre-1912 elections has been in treating the pre-reform period as a single block, as if there had been no changes in the nature of the electorate or in the electoral practices of the city in the more than sixty years prior to the passing of the 1912 reform. Anecdotes of fraud and violence in the 1860s or 1870s have been used to characterise the electoral practices of the whole pre-reform period and randomly quoted turnouts have been thought to be representative of the electoral participation of the period as a whole. There are two main reasons for this. The first and most obvious one is the preliminary stage of the research on pre-reform elections. The second and more surprising reason is the reluctance to link the topic of electoral politics with other areas studied in more depth, such as the development of the city of Buenos Aires or the development of political parties. As a result, we tend to think about the electoral politics of a modern city, which by 1911 had almost one-and-a-half million inhabitants, in the same terms as those of the city of the 1860s, whose population was only 180,000.[29] Similarly, electoral practices for the 1860s and 1870s are assumed to be no different from those of the first decades of the twentieth century.

Furthermore, the failure to take into account the rapid changes that took place during the pre-reform decade has caused historians to exaggerate the impact of the 1912 reform on the political development of the country. The analysis presented above on the nature of the electorate in the 1890s and on the rapid growth of turnouts can be better understood when placed in the context of a growing and modernising city where electoral politics changed more gradually over the years.

The great speed at which Buenos Aires grew has been documented above. Less than 1,000 men and women were concentrated in each square kilometre of the city in 1869; 3,300 in 1895, and almost 8,000 in 1914.[30] However, the transformation of Buenos Aires was not only in terms of numerical expansion; the population also experienced a rapid development in its living standards. In 1884, for example, free and compulsory primary education was introduced, and, 25 years later, illiteracy had been reduced from a third to 14 per cent of the population.[31] The rising standard of living was reflected in other related factors, such as the proliferation of newspapers and periodicals in the city. By the end of the 1870s, 83 newspapers and periodicals circulated in Buenos Aires. Twenty years later, 334 periodicals and newspapers were published in the city, 26 of them were dailies and more than 100 appeared weekly. There were publications in seven different languages.[32] The rapid growth of the population and the general economic expansion stimulated the internal market, which resulted in a great increase in the number of industrial and commercial enterprises and the growth of public services. These activities resulted in the growth of a substantial middle class. According to the available data, the middle layers of society increased from 11 per cent of the population in 1869 to 25 per cent in 1895 and to more than 30 per cent in 1914.[33] It is then not surprising that the rapid socio-economic changes of the city were reflected in the changing nature of the electorate. As we have seen, while in the 1860s and 1870s the voters of Buenos Aires were the less qualified sectors of the society, by the 1890s the electorate was almost entirely literate and represented all the different socio-economic segments of the population.

The transformation of the city of Buenos Aires undoubtedly had significant political effects. Three interrelated aspects of the city's life were of crucial importance: the rise of new political parties; the changes in party organisation; and the changes in electoral practices. During the 1860s and 1870s two political parties contested elections in the city of Buenos Aires. During those years political parties were loose groupings that rallied behind a well-known leader who was generally the presidential candidate. The parties were known by the names of these leaders, who had complete control over electoral strategy (such as the formation of coalitions), over the party candidates, and over the electoral campaign itself. The campaign had different stages. It generally began with a banquet where the leader launched his own candidature. Then a committee would be appointed, composed of the leader's closest friends who were in charge of setting up the list of party candidates for the forthcoming election. The candidates were appointed, not elected; the choice was not questioned by other party members, but needed the final approval of the party leader.[34]

The next stage was the formation of clubs. These clubs adopted different names, such as '25 of May' or 'Electoral Club'. They were of a transitory nature and were formed a few days before each election. Their meetings were small and informal, taking place in the private house of a club member. The electoral campaign was mainly conducted through the press. Each party owned newspapers and before the elections their editorials intensified attacks on the rival party and printed party platforms – all of these were remarkably similar. The campaign generally finished in one of the few theatres of the city, where the party leader delivered a speech and the list of candidates was read out to the cheers of the spectators.

The most important role of the clubs was performed on election day. Elections took place on Sundays, from 9 a.m. to 4 p.m.[35] Polling stations were placed in the local churches of each of the electoral districts into which the city was divided. The polling stations were supervised by randomly chosen local citizens, although party members were also at the polling tables to check for irregularities. In the 1860s and 1870s, elections were generally a violent affair. Commercial enterprises, the theatre and public places closed several days before the election.[36] On election day, voters, who were generally armed either with guns or knives, were guided and guarded on their way to the poll stations by the members of the party clubs.[37] Often the event ended in shootings and deaths which took place either at the time of voting, when opposition groups met at the polling tables, or when the votes were counted at the end of the election day.

There is, unfortunately, no comprehensive study of the turnouts of the 1860s and 1870s. An estimate of the number of voters in the election of 1876, which was a particularly violent one, shows a participation of over 11 per cent of the electorate.[38] As mentioned above, the voting population of the city in the 1860s and 1870s, was composed of the lowest sectors of the population – the peons, the journeymen and railwayworkers, most of whom were foreigners.[39]

In the 1890s, however, significant changes began to take place. The most obvious was the rise of new political parties to compete against the Partido Autonomista Nacional (PAN), consolidated in the 1880s. The National Civic Union and the Radical Party were created in 1891, the Socialist Party was organised in 1896, and the PAN itself faced a series of splits in the early twentieth century. The rise of new political parties had a significant impact on the city's electoral life. Elections in the city now became a highly competitive affair. Against the received view that the PAN dominated the country's electoral life, making it almost impossible for the other parties to compete in elections, it has been shown that elections in each electoral district of the city of Buenos Aires had to be furiously contested by each party.[40]

The political parties also underwent important changes in their internal organisation. By the 1890s, the old style of sporadic party organisation created around a leader had become increasingly unpopular and it became clear that political parties had to be modernised. Modernisation meant adopting the model of the United States and, without exception, all political parties adopted the US system of committees and conventions. Parties became permanent organisations with internal written rules for the selection of candidates and for the functioning of the committees. These committees were different from the old clubs. They had elected authorities, they were permanent, and they had headquarters where meetings were held. There were as many committees as electoral wards of the city. Their members had various functions, but the major one was to promote the party in order to increase the list of affiliations in their district. This was done through different means, such as inviting the leaders of the party to speak at local meetings, or organising 'popular dances' or free barbecues.[41]

Funds were provided by the wealthiest party members or were raised by collecting contributions or by organising local sales of objects donated by members and sympathisers.[42] The committee had frequent sessions; during electoral campaigns they met at least once a week. The authorities of these committees had to take minutes of the discussions and the resolutions taken were published in the party's newspaper. Parties generally began their preparations for the electoral campaigns two or three months before election day; the Socialist Party spent as much as six months preparing for elections. Party candidates, who were elected by party conventions, attended local committee meetings where they delivered speeches during the campaign. As the election approached, the parties' offerings of barbecues, dances and *empanadas* (a local dish) intensified.[43]

As the committees became permanent and began to function regularly throughout the city, their authority gradually increased. Sometimes the presidents of these committees were well-known party members or university students (generally law students) taking their first steps in political life. Most often, however, they were thought of as the 'men of action' of the party, men 'whose importance [was] related to the number of votes they could deliver on election day by legal or semi-legal means'.[44] It was here that the local presidents of the committees found their strength as agents of the electoral contests in their locality.

The territorial electoral control given to these local presidents by the committee system also provided them with considerable power *vis-à-vis* the higher ranks of the party. The presidents of the local committees gradually began to make their voices heard within the party ranks. They often challenged decisions taken by the central committee about electoral strategies and coalitions.[45] At times, they challenged the list of candidates elected by the party conventions, refusing to contest the forthcoming election in their own district.[46] At other times they made deals with the presidents of local committees of the opposition, defying directions from the central committee.[47] Sometimes, these local presidents had to be brought to order. In 1896, for example, the authorities of a local committee were sacked because the party had lost the election in their district. The election day had been sunny, and they had preferred to enjoy an *asado con cuero* (barbecue) rather than organise their local forces to contest the election.[48] The committee system, therefore, provided the city leaders with formal authority over electoral districts and, although the system proved electorally successful, as it permitted the new political parties rapidly to gain electoral power, the party's higher ranks sometimes feared their autonomy and often attempted to weaken their power.[49]

As party organisation gradually changed over the decades, so did the electoral practices in the city. By the 1890s, violence on election day was remembered as a feature of the 'savage' electoral practices of the past, of the 1860s and the 1870s.[50] As was repeatedly stated at the time, the fact that elections ended 'without bloodshed, or without a couple of dead bodies being left near a poll station'[51] was viewed as a sign of progress in the country's political life. In the 1890s, election day had ceased to be feared for its violence by the inhabitants of the city; elections were generally reported as 'peaceful' and 'without incident' by the contemporary press. Shops and theatres stayed open, and only seldom did disturbances interrupt the voting in the polling stations placed in the local churches. 'The ladies attending Sunday mass', *La Nación* reported in

1891, 'would not have realised that an election was taking place in the same church, had it not been for the officers who guarded the entrance.'[52]

However, as was pointed out at the time, the absence of violence in the elections did not mean that the vote had become 'clean'. It only meant that more ingenious tricks had gradually replaced the electoral violence of the past.[53] The lists of complaints drawn up by the parties after the elections provide endless examples of electoral manipulations: false registrations, false voters, men voting several times.[54] In the first years of the twentieth century, particularly after the election of 1904, a market for votes developed in the city, particularly in the poorer neighbourhoods.[55] Many had thought that the absence of violence in elections was a significant step forward; they also thought that the development of a market for votes was a further sign of the gradual pacification of the country's electoral practices. If people could sell their vote, that meant they could not be intimidated.[56]

By the 1890s there was no mention of guns, violence or deaths, and disturbances in elections were limited to occasional fist-fights.[57] By the first decade of the twentieth century the disorders reported were the occasional exchange of 'whistling and insults' between members of contending parties on their way to the polls.[58] It is hardly surprising, therefore, that, over the years, elections involved increasing numbers of voters, as shown by the rapid growth in turnouts. Violence rapidly diminished and practically disappeared, while all sorts of incentives were used to encourage the electorate to participate. Barbecues, dances and cash were increasingly used to tempt the electorate into abandoning their political apathy on election day. By the twentieth century, cars were placed at the disposal of the local committees by affluent party members and, after being decorated with party flags and symbols, were used to transport party voters to the polling stations.[59] Increasingly long electoral campaigns, the pacification of electoral practices and the new means of mobilisation rapidly transformed the nature and size of the city's voting population.

Conclusions

Analysis of pre-1912 elections has tended to rehearse time and again the electoral malpractices of the time. As a result, important characteristics of the voting population and of the electoral practices of the period have remained largely unnoticed.

The electorate of Buenos Aires experienced significant changes over the years of the pre-reform period. Qualitative descriptions of the voting population of the city in the early decades of national organisation show that the 'socially marginal' were the main participants in the elections. By the 1890s, the electoral registers displayed a varied social composition and a predominantly literate electorate. The characteristics of the electorate of the 1890s were not very different to those of the electorate of 1918, six years after compulsory voting had been introduced.[60]

Not only did the electorate of Buenos Aires change markedly in nature, it also grew dramatically in numbers. The impact of immigration in the city of Buenos Aires has commonly overshadowed the important fact that the electorate of the city also grew at incredible speed. One of the most remarkable features of the electorate of the pre-reform period was that the turnouts kept pace with the strong growth of the electorate. Turnouts were small, but they were also growing fast before the 1912 reform. Indeed, their growth is remarkable if we take into account the fact that, between 1898 and 1910, the Radical Party abstained from elections. The Radicals returned to electoral competition only in 1912, after the reform was introduced, winning the first elections they contested in the city of Buenos Aires and the first presidential elections held under the new system in 1916.[61] Despite the fact that a political party with such power of mobilisation abstained in the elections of the early twentieth century, the turnouts grew dramatically.

The population's increasing involvement in the city's electoral life was due not only to the transformation of the city of Buenos Aires, but also to changes in the city's electoral culture. The rise of new political parties and the changing nature of electoral practices provided a series of incentives which attracted the electorate in growing numbers. As has been pointed out, this does not necessary mean that elections were the only means of political participation at the time. But it shows that they became increasingly important.

Evidence on the nature of the electorate in the 1890s, the growing size of the voting population of the city, the changes in the political parties, and the gradual transformation of electoral practices point to a gradual development of the political system over several decades. If to this we add the competitive nature of the elections, it is apparent that the political development of the city was more gradual than has been assumed.

Notes

1. For the peculiarities of the city of Buenos Aires, see Paula Alonso, 'Politics and Elections in Buenos Aires, 1890-1898: The Performance of the Radical Party', *Journal of Latin American Studies*, vol. 25 (1993), pp. 465-87.

2. On the early history of the suffrage in Argentina, see David Bushnell, 'El sufragio en la Argentina y en Colombia hasta 1853', *Revista del Instituto de Historia del Derecho*, no. 19 (1968), pp. 11-29; Hilda Sábato and Elías Palti, '¿Quién votaba en Buenos Aires?: Práctica y teoría del sufragio, 1850-1880', *Desarrollo Económico*, vol. 30, no. 119 (Oct-Dec. 1990), pp. 407-22; Diana A. Tussie and Andrés M. Federman, 'La larga marcha hacia las urnas', *Todo es Historia*, vol. 1, no. 71 (March 1973), pp. 9-47.

3. At least until discussion about the extension of the franchise to women in the 1930s and 1940s.

4. J. N. Matienzo, *La práctica del sufragio popular. Breve estudio sobre la ley electoral argentina* (Buenos Aires, 1886), p. 5.

5. N. Botana, *El orden conservador. La política argentina entre 1880 y 1916* (Buenos Aires, 1977), p. 295.

6. Bushnell, 'El sufragio', p. 24.

7. Darío Cantón, 'El Sufragio Universal como agente de movilización', Documento de Trabajo, Instituto Torcuato Di Tella, no. 19 (1966) p. 5.

8. See R. Sáenz Peña, *Escritos y discursos* (Buenos Aires 1935), vol. II, pp. 72-6; 111-4. For the most compelling analysis of the reform, see Botana, *El orden conservador*, pp. 217-345.

9. For this standard interpretation and its main pitfalls, see Alonso, 'Politics and Elections'. For a critique of the standard argument from a different perspective, see Hilda Sábato and Ema Cibotti, 'Hacer Política en Buenos Aires: Los Italianos en la escena pública porteña 1860-1880', *Boletín del Instituto de Historia Argentina Dr. E. Ravignani*, Tercera Serie, no. 2 (Sept. 1990); Sábato and Palti, '¿Quién votaba en Buenos Aires?' and Hilda Sábato, 'Citizenship, Political Participation and the formation of the Public Sphere in Buenos Aires 1850s-1880s', *Past and Present*, no. 136 (Aug. 1992).

10. This argument is fully developed in K. Remmer, *Party Competition in Argentina and Chile. Political Recruitment and Public Policy, 1890-1930* (Lincoln and London, 1984), pp. 24-34; 221-2.

11. For an analysis of this argument, see Alonso, 'Politics and Elections'.

12. Sábato and Palti, '¿Quién votaba en Buenos Aires?', pp. 402-7; Sábato, 'Citizenship', pp. 142-8.

13. The Electoral Register of the city of Buenos Aires for 1896 – the only one available prior to 1912 – contains the names, addresses, level of literacy, ages and professions of those enrolled.

14. The relatively small percentage of 13% for the upper sectors should not be underestimated, as in 9 of a total of 16 electoral wards the upper sector amounted to more than 10% of the registrations. Alonso, 'Politics and Elections', p. 479.

15. For analysis of the Electoral Register and its wider implications in the understanding of the country's political development, see Alonso, 'Politics and Elections'.
16. The following analysis on turnouts aims to complement the single work on the subject developed by Botana, *El orden*, pp. 189-213.
17. For the impact of immigration in the country see Germani, 'Mass Immigration and Modernization', pp. 289-330; and his *Política y sociedad*, pp. 222-5.
18. As has been pointed out by Botana, *El orden conservador*, pp. 189-97.
19. In the election of 1900, for example, the opposition obtained a total of 135 votes.
20. E. Zimmermann, 'Liberals, Reform and the Social Question: Argentina, 1890-1916', unpubl. PhD diss., Oxford University, 1990, p. 82. (This is now published as *Los liberales reformistas. La cuestión social en la Argentina, 1890-1916* (Buenos Aires, 1995). For the development of the city, see also pp. 79-89.) The most complete study on the population growth of the city is Zulma L. Recchini de Lattes, *La Población de Buenos Aires. Componentes demográficos del crecimiento entre 1855 y 1960*, Instituto Di Tella (Buenos Aires, 1971); for annual rates of growth see p. 31.
21. In 1904 the age restriction for voting rose from 17 to 18 years of age.
22. Figures on the electorate over this period have been taken from the national and municipal censuses of 1887, 1895, 1904 and 1914.
23. Table 3 below provides figures for every year and shows that the turnout as a percentage of the electorate remains roughly constant throughout the whole period.
24. This estimate is calculated using the figures in Table 1 for the four years when numbers are available (1887, 1895, 1904 and 1914). It is then assumed that the electorate as a percentage of the total population (Column 3 of Table 1) adjusts between these years in a linear fashion; in other words, that this percentage declines from 10.1% in 1887 to 7.7% in 1895 by steady annual reduction. Hence an estimate of the percentage of Argentine males relative to the total population is made. This percentage is then multiplied by the total population in any particular year to get an estimate of the size of the electorate.
25. Cantón, 'El sufragio universal', pp. 12-6; and his *Elecciones y partidos políticos en la Argentina. Historia, interpretación y balance, 1910-1966* (Buenos Aires, 1973), pp. 42-8.
26. Table 3 shows that estimates for the elections of 1910 are 25 and 20%. Cantón does not specify how he arrived at the estimate of 23% in 1910; it must be assumed that an average of the two elections of that year was taken.
27. After 1912, turnouts for the rest of the country followed a similar pattern of decline. After a sharp increase in the first election of 1912, they declined to an average of 40% in the 1920s. Anne L. Potter, 'The Failure of Democracy in Argentina, 1916-1930', *Journal of Latin American Studies*, vol. 13, pt. 1 (May 1981), p. 84.
28. *Ibid.*, and Oscar Cornblit, 'La opción conservadora en la política argentina', *Desarrollo Económico*, vol. 14, no. 56 (1975), pp. 635-9.

29. F. Korn has convincingly argued that by 1895 Buenos Aires already enjoyed the features of a modern city.
30. *Censo General de la República Argentina*, 1947, vol. 1, p. 1.
31. For the development of the city of Buenos Aires, see Zimmermann, 'Liberals, Reform and the Social Question', pp. 79-103; J. Scobie, *Buenos Aires. Plaza to Suburb, 1870-1910* (New York, 1974); C. Sargent, *The Spatial Evolution of Greater Buenos Aires, Argentina 1870-1930* (Tucson, 1974); F. Korn, *Buenos Aires. Una ciudad moderna* (Buenos Aires, 1981); J. Scobie, 'The Argentine Capital in the Nineteenth Century', in S. R. Ross and T. F. McGann (eds.), *Buenos Aires: 400 years* (Austin, Texas, 1982), pp. 40-52.
32. *Boletín Demográfico Argentino*, Buenos Aires (1901), no. 5, Año II, pp. 5;13.
33. Germani, 'Mass Immigration and Modernization', pp. 303-4. Although these figures are for the whole country, this pattern was most pronounced in the large cities, particularly in the largest, Buenos Aires. This is also analysed in Germani, 'Hacia una democracia de masas', in T. Di Tella, G. Germani and Jorge Graciarena, *Argentina, sociedad de masas* (Buenos Aires, 1965), pp. 208-17.
34. Félix Luna, 'Los hábitos políticos después de Caseros', *Todo es Historia*, Año XVII, no. 197 (Oct. 1983), pp. 22-4; Paula Alonso, 'Historia del comité, 1890-1898', unpubl. mimeo, Aug. 1991; Cárcano, *Sáenz Peña*, pp. 51-75. For the reports of the contemporary press on the campaigns and elections, see for example *La Nación*, 13 Mar. 1877; *El Nacional*, 7 Feb. 1872; Apr. 1873; Sept. 1878, where these events are described in detail.
35. The hours changed over the years; at times the election day was from 8 a.m. to 4 p.m.
36. Cantón, *Elecciones*, pp. 41-2
37. Cárcano, *Sáenz Peña*, pp. 52, 75
38. Cantón, 'El Sufragio Universal', p. 5.
39. As argued by Sábato and Palti, '¿Quién votaba en Buenos Aires?', pp. 402-7; Sábato, 'Citizenship', pp. 142-8.
40. Alonso, 'Politics and Elections', pp. 480-2.
41. For the development of the committee system, see P. Alonso, 'The Origins of the Radical Party, 1889-1898', unpubl. PhD diss., Oxford University (1992), pp. 114-28, and Alonso, 'Historia del comité'; see also *Archivo General de la Nación* (AGN), Archivo del Dr. Juan Angel Farini. Papeles del Dr. Adolfo Saldías: President of Santa Lucía (no name) to Adolfo Saldías, 23 Sept. 1891, 3-6-3 no. 276.
42. *AGN*, Farini (Saldías): Rufino Pastor to Adolfo Saldías, 12 June 1893 3-6-3 no. 276; *AGN*, Archivo del Dr. Próspero García: P. Argerich to Próspero García, 29 Aug. 1892, 30-3-12.
43. Accounts of the electoral campaigns have been based on the contemporary press, mainly *La Prensa*, *La Nación*, *Tribuna*, and *El Argentino*, during the days preceding the elections. For the campaign and organisation of the Socialist Party see also N. Repetto, *Mi paso por la política* (Buenos Aires, 1956), pp. 86-8.

44. *Tribuna*, 12 Oct. 1894. Presidents of these committees were always male, with the exception of Luisa Mitchel who presided over a local committee of the Radical Party between 1895 and 1898.

45. See for example, *La Prensa*, 16 Feb. 1896; *Tribuna*, 13 and 26 Feb. 1896; 21 Aug.; and 8 Sept. 1897.

46. See for example, *La Prensa*, 9 Jan. 1896; *Tribuna*, 13 and 14 Feb. 1896.

47. *Tribuna*, 7 Feb. 1894.

48. *El Argentino*, 14 March 1896.

49. This was the expressed purpose of the reform of the committee system introduced by the Radical Party in 1895. *La Prensa*, 6 June 1895.

50. There was a very wide consensus about this analysis of the electoral practices. See for example the opinions expressed by *Tribuna*, 19 Mar. 1895; *La Nación*, 5 Apr. 1897.

51. *La Nación*, 5 Apr. 1897.

52. *La Nación*, 16 Mar. 1891.

53. *Ibid.*; see also Sáenz Peña's 'Manifiesto al Pueblo', 28 Feb. 1912, in R. Sáenz Peña, *Escritos y discursos*, vol. II, p. 111; Cantón, *Elecciones*, pp. 41-2; Cárcano, *Sáenz Peña*, pp. 131-2.

54. See for example the list of complaints raised by Francisco Barroetaveña (of the Radical Party) in Congress, *Diario de Sesiones de la Cámara de Diputados*, (5 May 1896); pp. 33-41.

55. Juan Carlos Torre, 'La primera victoria electoral socialista', *Todo es Historia*, no. 76, (Sept. 1973). For the market of votes in previous and later years see also the analysis of each election published by *La Prensa*, 10 May 1902; 6 Mar. 1904; 13 and 14 Mar. 1904; 11 Mar. 1906. The market for votes seems to have declined around 1908, see *La Prensa*, 8 Mar. 1908.

56. This was for example the outspoken view of ex-president Carlos Pellegrini. L. Sommariva, *Historia de las intervenciones federales en las provincias* (Buenos Aires, 1910-1931), vol. II, pp. 314-5.

57. The only exception was one death that took place in an election in 1896; this greatly shocked contemporary opinion. See *La Prensa*, 9 Mar. 1896.

58. See for exmple *La Prensa*, 14 Mar. 1910.

59. See the descriptions of the election day offered by *La Prensa*, 14 Mar. 1910.

60. Using the Electoral Register of 1918, Richard Walter has found that working–class voters represented 37.7% of the registered voters, the middle class 46.3% and the upper class 15.9%. Middle- and upper-class registrations grew slightly in comparison with those of 1895, while the working-class registration shrank. The differences in the social composition of the registers of 1895 and 1918 are, in any case, far from significant. Richard Walter, 'Elections in the city of Buenos Aires during the first Yrigoyen administration. Social Class and Political Preferences', *Hispanic American Historical Review*, vol. 58, no. 4 (Nov. 1978), pp. 595-624.

61. For the electoral results and its causes, see Natalio Botana, 'La reforma política de 1912', in M. Giménez Zapiola (comp.), *El régimen oligárquico. Materiales para el estudio de la realidad argentina (hasta 1930)* (Buenos Aires, 1975), pp. 232-45.

CHAPTER 9

FRAUD AND THE PASSIVITY OF THE ELECTORATE
IN SPAIN, 1875-1923*

Carlos Dardé

This chapter does not provide a comprehensive study of the Spanish electoral system in the period 1875-1923. It only deals with one of its most important and specific characteristics: fraud, particularly the falsification of electoral results. It first indicates the broad historiographic consensus over the extent and importance of electoral fraud. Then it analyses the mechanisms which allowed results to be rigged. Finally, a review is made of the explanations given by historians for electoral fraud, and stress is laid on the passivity of the electorate resulting from the almost total lack of electoral culture, a topic that has received scant attention.

During the period 1875-1923 – which in Spanish historiography is known as the Restoration – there was a series of different electoral laws. The first elections, after the Bourbon dynasty had been restored to the throne in 1876, were held in accordance with the laws previously in force, that is, with universal suffrage. In 1878 a new electoral law was passed establishing a restricted property franchise that remained in force until 1890, when universal male suffrage was introduced; this meant that the electoral roll increased sixfold, rising from about 800,000 voters to just under five million, 24 per cent of the population. In 1907 came further reform and its most important innovation, through the famous article 29, was that 'in those districts in which the number of candidates nominated does not exceed those to be elected, presentation of candidature shall be equivalent to election and shall relieve candidates of the need to be subjected to the same'. Despite the variety of electoral laws and despite the social and economic changes that Spain experienced in this period, constitutional continuity, and the fact that both the territorial distribution of representation and the electoral procedure remained basically unchanged during this period allow us to take an overall view of the Restoration in terms of elections, although the introduction of universal suffrage meant significant changes in political life.[1]

---

* Translation by Ian A. Williams.

The history of elections in this period is of interest not only to see how the system of representation evolved in Spain, but it is also important in explaining the central political process. The failure of liberal monarchy – which ushered in a long period of instability, violence and dictatorship in the history of Spain between 1923 and 1975 – was closely related to electoral corruption, which in turn brought discredit upon the political class and parliament.

Apart from a few contemporary studies, research into Spanish elections in the nineteenth century and the first third of the twentieth is a recent phenomenon, dating from the mid-1960s. The next decade, particularly the last years of Franco's dictatorship, saw electoral history placed at the forefront of Spanish historiography for obvious political ends. According to one of its most assiduous exponents: 'if we studied elections, it was because they didn't exist and they were what we wanted'. The 1980s witnessed an authentic boom in studies of this type both at the provincial and local level, but more recently they have begun to decline.[2]

All this research has borne its fruits: we now have a fairly accurate picture of the election results, of the people who made up the political class, and of their social background. However, there are notable deficiencies because of the mainly descriptive character of most of these studies, which have failed to ask fundamental questions concerning the nature of political life. For example, they frequently list the various fraudulent means used in elections, without considering that such means were mutually exclusive and represented essentially different forms of political life. Thus, they mention the faking of election results, the purchase of votes, the concession of favours, and coercion, all based on the power exercised by those who controlled the administrative machine or economic life, and on the practice of physical violence. However, they fail to specify where and to what extent such means were used, so that we do not know whether we are faced with a predominantly apathetic and indifferent electorate, since it allowed fraud and vote buying, societies controlled by politically or economically-based networks of clients, or a politically mobilised but systematically repressed population.[3]

Since studies of elections in the Restoration period are mostly unsatisfactory, the last part of this chapter, the explanation of fraud, is very general and mainly speculative in character, and consists more of hypotheses, which will have to be confirmed by research at local level, than of firmly drawn conclusions.

The Importance of Fraud in Elections

In November 1933, for the first time in Spanish history, a Minister of the Interior was defeated in a general election. This was also the first time that the result of democratic elections genuinely reflected the opinion of the country (on this occasion victory was for the right-wing parties). The previous elections, held in June 1931, which created the Constitution of the Second Republic, have been considered 'transitional' elections since 'there was only one official candidate, only partial mobilisation and blatant intervention by the civil governors in the electoral process'.[4]

It seems reasonable to assert, therefore, that all democratic elections hitherto held in Spain – and those held with the restricted property franchise between 1876 and 1890 – were fraudulent in overall terms. This does not mean that there were not whole districts and sections where voting was authentic and whose results were genuine – this did occur. But it does mean that the nationwide results did not reflect the freely expressed will of the voters – in accordance with individual perception of their personal or collective interests or with values they identified with personally. Either the results were rigged or electors, when voting, were decisively influenced by the government's representatives or those of particularly powerful people known as *caciques* (local political bosses).

There is an indicator that proves this statement beyond all question: it was invariably the Conservative and Liberal parties that were called in by the Crown to form a government and to call elections. They, alternately and at regular intervals, continued to obtain a majority in the elections, even though this was in no way parallelled by changes in public opinion.[5] Rather than Governments being made by elections, elections were 'made' by Governments called in by the Crown, which was the real source of political power. Representation of the opposition parties was always small – a maximum of 36 Republican deputies in 1903 and seven Socialist deputies in 1923, a representation far less than their true social footing – but even this was occasionally achieved by fraudulent means. Those monarchist politicians such as Canalejas who tried to mobilise opinion were quickly forced to abandon this policy when they saw the meagre electoral rewards it afforded them.[6]

Nevertheless, although governments always obtained overall majorities, these became smaller and smaller. This was partly caused by divisions within the monarchist parties and the rise and development of nationalist parties. Above all, it was due to the tendency to create districts that remained permanently under one individual's control whichever party was in power. This indicates a process in which regions acquired autonomy, that is, a consolidation of local as against central power.

> I need a person in Molledo – of greater or lesser importance there –
> who is willing to accept my representation and who will demand in my
> name seventy or eighty votes, so that no vote will be required. I am
> told I shall be given them. Otherwise, I shall have to send a notary.[7]

This is what one candidate standing for election as deputy wrote in a
private letter to his electoral agent in 1893. The situation it reveals – a
small village for which the results are to be invented without an election
taking place – is, of course, an extreme case. We do not know how often it
occurred, but what we are sure of is that results were faked, whether voting
took place or not, and this was the predominant feature of Spanish elections
during the Restoration.

Of the abundant contemporary accounts I shall cite that of the
Republican Emilio Castelar, who also explains one of the specific
mechanisms used: it was often not necessary to rig the results of all sections
in a district; it was sufficient to do so in a few by giving all possible votes
– or even a few more – to one candidate.[8]

> As a general rule, in rural districts in Spain no voting takes place; mayors,
> who fight to the death over local matters that interest them, show no desire to
> fight over election issues, which interest the Nation; ... a section where
> normally nobody votes is left; and it is only when the results of the other
> sections are known that a candidate, from the majority party or the opposi-
> tion, but usually the majority party, is given all the votes from the section
> where there was no election.[9]

Historiographic agreement on this question is practically unanimous. Even
those, like Raymond Carr, who assert that the regeneration of the regime
was beginning when Primo de Rivera's *coup d'état* occurred, base their
arguments, above all, on the most critical and independent voices in
parliament – as was seen over the issue of military responsibility in
Morocco – and on the principles that spurred the new liberal
Concentration. Only Shlomo Ben-Ami mentions in passing 'an
increasingly independent electorate ... far less manageable than in the past'.
Yet the only evidence he presents to justify his statement is a decline in the
Minister of the Interior's influence on the elections; this, however, is
perfectly compatible with the existence of other influences that had nothing
to do with the ministry or civil governors.[10]

José Varela Ortega in *Los amigos políticos*, a book which remains
indispensable for an understanding of the political system of the

Restoration, reaches the same conclusion:

> ... in Spain, instead of making a list of illegalities, the great revelation is that illegality was the norm; for, in Spain, 'the cleanest certificates of election were the dirtiest'. In other words, where there was no violence but fraud was the rule and involved 'falsifying the certificates of election, seizing them and drawing up doubles'.[11]

Raymond Carr has expressed the same idea: 'It was not a parliamentary regime with abuses: the abuses were the system itself.'[12]

Finally, Gabriele Ranzato, in a recent article, shows total agreement with the above opinions:

> What distinguishes the Italian from the Spanish case is the incidence of another kind of deviation from the model of correct running of elections in a democratic liberal system ... The basic factor in the elections in southern Italy was the typical clientelist exchange: favours for votes ... In Spain, this was not true, not because this type of exchange did not exist or because it was a totally insignificant factor, but because, in the end, the decisive factor in the elections was predominantly, and almost necessarily, fraud.[13]

This does not mean that in certain places – basically large cities – elections were not fair and results genuine. Even if political mobilisation was not really intense in these places, it was intense enough for the will of the people to impose itself, at least the will of those who turned out to vote.

This is what happened in the capital, Madrid, where one cannot speak of a systematic supplanting of the will of the electorate. Although participation was low, between 30 and 40 per cent (in this case the figures for participation are fairly reliable) public opinion played a decisive role. Even with the system of restricted property franchise it required an enormous outlay and great organisation by the monarchist parties to win the elections. In 1893, the Republican opposition won a majority of seats for the first time. In six of the ten elections held between 1903 and 1923, the opponents of the system, Republicans first and later the Socialists, obtained most of the certificates of election.[14]

In Barcelona, the 1901 elections saw the end of monarchist domination, with the entry of the Catalan regionalist and of a new Republican party into Spanish politics. What is most striking is just how little mobilisation was required to achieve this. Although it is impossible to obtain accurate figures, participation is estimated not to have reached 20 per cent, perhaps not even 15 per cent of the registered electors. The Catalan regionalists obtained a majority of seats with the support of less than eight per cent of the electoral roll; the Republicans won the representation of the minority groups with six per cent.[15]

In Valencia, after universal suffrage had been introduced, 'increasing mobilisation of the middle classes' occurred. A new Republican party, modern in character, with a radical reformist programme, was formed around the charismatic figure of the novelist Vicente Blasco Ibáñez and became the dominant political force in the capital between 1898 and 1911. The Catholics also created new social and political initiatives.[16]

Lastly, in Bilbao the repeated victories of the Republicans and Socialists both in local and national elections – although they often needed to resort to fraudulent practices, like 'volcar el censo', that is that the whole electoral roll voted in favour of one candidate, as happened in the working-class districts of the city – further indicate the decisive role of public opinion.[17]

Mobilisation was not limited to the largest cities; in others, figures for general elections, when analysed by sections, and the results of local elections show that there were groups, larger and smaller in number, that were politically active and participated freely. At times of intense political upheaval, as in 1903 and 1910, these groups managed to win the general elections, but usually, because of the reigning political mood, their votes were swamped by those of the rural sections, where fraud was prevalent.

The definition and boundaries of the electoral constituencies were established by the law introduced by the Conservatives in 1878 and, as already mentioned, respected by subsequent electoral reforms. There were two types of constituencies: uninominal rural districts – the vast majority, 280 out of 394 seats (excluding those of the colonies) – and '*circumscripciones*' that elected one deputy for every 50,000 electors, and comprised the main cities and broad rural belts around them. This procedure might be interpreted as a compromise between traditional moderate opinion, favouring the small uninominal districts, and progressive opinion, which defended the large *circumscripciones*. What this in fact meant was that in most of the medium-sized cities, the urban vote – the only genuine vote – was stifled by the rural vote, which was won by *cacique* tactics; in other words, it tended to deter the nation's already scant political mobilisation. This was in spite of the established form of voting in these *circumscripciones* – namely that of writing on the voting slip a smaller number of candidates than deputies to be elected – which sought to guarantee a degree of minority representation.[18]

Finally, there were a few rural districts where the Republican and, particularly, the Carlist opposition were victorious. These results, however, do not seem to be an expression of authentic change in political life, a product of real mobilisation of the electorate, but rather were due to the persistence of personal influence and fraudulent practice.[19]

How Elections Were, and Were Not, Held

There is little or no canvassing in the sense in which canvassing is understood in England; the public meetings and speeches, the posters and colours, the flow of drink among populace, the cabs charged with beribboned and hilarious voters, are unknown. Such demostrations indeed if attempted might end in rioting, and would certainly be used by the authorities as a pretext for arresting, in the name of public order, the supporters of the opposition candidate. Here and there some leading public man ... takes advantage of the elections to proclaim his policy to the world in the shape of an electoral manifesto; here and there a candidate will perhaps arrange to meet a small number of leading voters, and endeavour on personal rather than general grounds to obtain from them promises of support. But the house to house visits, the paid agents and the rest, play but little part in a Spanish election; the individual voter is too insignificant and the chances of his actually voting too uncertain to repay the trouble of securing him.

For Arthur H. Hardinge, civil servant at the British Embassy in Madrid and author of an extensive and invaluable Memorandum on elections in Spain, from which the paragraph quoted is taken, the factor that decided the result of an election in Spain was the part played by the local authorities:

The power of the Ayuntamientos is very great; indeed except in the large cities, where advanced views are common among the working classes, and in some of the strongly clerical provinces of the north, it is they who virtually decide the elections.

The Memorandum is dated 1884, but these statements could be held as generally true for the whole period, although occasionally rural districts witnessed livelier and more competitive election campaigns.

The electoral procedure described by Hardinge can be summarised as follows: mayors controlled political life and, therefore, elections;[20] civil governors (government representatives in the provinces) controlled the mayors, thanks to their great power, which was susceptible to a loose, elastic interpretation; hence the government controlled elections.[21]

We now have good overall analyses of the electoral process during the Restoration, which fully bear out the above description, and which give us a fairly detailed picture of the importance of different electoral operations such as the *encasillado* (designation of official candidates), manipulation of the electoral roll, substitution of mayors and judges, acts concerning the election proper, the subsequent counting of the votes and the declaration of the deputies elect and, finally, review of those elections where complaints were lodged.[22]

In what follows I shall attempt to explain only how fraud was actually carried out. The secret, as everybody knew, consisted in controlling the *mesa electoral,* the board entrusted with the task of receiving and counting the votes, for the different sections into which a district was divided. The *mesa* was composed of the mayor of the most important village in the section, who presided over it, and of certain assessors, not less than four or more than six, who were called *interventores,* and were appointed as scrutators by the electors themselves. Those electors who succeeded in collecting the highest number of signatures proposing them for the position were appointed as scrutators in a duly legalised paper. Sometimes appointment to this position proved more competitive than the election itself, which took place seven days later.[23] Hardinge observed:

> It is easy to see that this arrangement must tell strongly in favour of the Ministerial candidate. The absence of secrecy, the necessity for having recourse to legal assistance, the greater facilities for canvassing possessed by the alcaldes with a large staff of official voters at hand to sign and obtain signatures for their list, these are all so many advantages to the party which counts with the administrative hierarchy; and accordingly the scrutators are almost invariably persons upon whom the Government can rely.

Once the *mesa* of a section was controlled, all its votes could be attributed with impunity to whichever candidate one wished regardless of the number of voting slips deposited in the urn.

An Explanation of Fraud

So far we have seen the importance of fraud and the procedures used to bring it about. The question that remains is why it existed. In the first place, it should be said that electoral fraud was not a by-product of the political system, unforeseen by its creators – principally Antonio Cánovas del Castillo – but its very point of departure. It was the price that had to be paid for Spain to have the political system of civilised nations. Constitutional monarchy was not based on the opinion of the people; many thought that if public opinion were really to prevail, Carlism with its proposal of a theocratic traditional monarchy, or a communist republic, would triumph in Spain. For Cánovas, experience of how the liberal regime had worked following its implantation in Spain proved to him that not even a liberal minority culture could serve as the basis for constitutional government. The norm had hitherto been complete political instability because of the tendency for a party to remain perpetually in power, which meant that those excluded had to resort to the army as a means of attaining it. The solution devised by Cánovas was to remove the military from the political scene by organising a fictitious political game, which involved the parties alternating in power, under the arbitration of the Crown and through elections rigged from above. Cánovas himself recognised that neither before nor after universal suffrage was there in Spain an electorate that was free from governmental influence.[24]

The most famous statement of the artificiality of the Canovite system belongs to José Ortega y Gasset: 'The Restoration ... was a parade of phantoms and Cánovas the great impresario of the phantasmagorical show'. The main consequence of this, according to Ortega y Gasset, was the complete and absolute separation of the 'official Spain' from the 'vital Spain', the lack of authenticity and vitality of everything related to politics, not only to elections:

> It is not a question of a Government that has removed itself over a transitory issue ... from public opinion, not at all; rather, it is that whole parties ..., the entire Parliament, all those Corporations which influence or are directly influenced by the world of politicians, the newspapers themselves ... all of this ... is placed outside and away from the central currents of Spain's soul of today ... All these organisms of our society from Parliament to newspapers and from the country school to the University, all of this which, put together under a single name, we shall call official Spain is the huge skeleton of an organism that has evaporated, has faded away ...'.[25]

It was not only Spanish intellectuals that were aware of this atmosphere. The most widely-read political history of Europe of the time, written by a French author, echoed the idea:

> In appearance, the government was ruled by civilian ministers recruited from those elected by the nation, as they were in countries under a parliamentary system, ... but elections and parliamentary debates remained a theatrical set. The mass of electors, illiterate and indifferent, voted little or voted according to the indications of the clergy and the government's officials, in accordance with local notables, landlords and often usurers ... Spain gives the impression of a people that has received from outside political institutions alien to its customs and foreign to the mass of the nation. The small number of men entrusted with running them, do not feel that they are supported by any real force, they use the formulas and imitate the acts of foreign countries, without being able to turn them into effective action.[26]

Why did most of the population consent to a political game in which their opinion was manipulated and falsified? One factor that must be borne in mind is the influence of anarchism, whose antipolitical doctrine was against participation in elections and parliamentary institutions, and which became widely and deeply, though unevenly, rooted in Spain in the period under study. Anarchism, in fact, justified the remoteness from the parties of a substantial part of the population – at its height, in 1919-1920, the anarcho-syndicalist union, the *Confederación Nacional del Trabajo* (CNT) had over 700,000 members. Since its influence was limited both socially and geographically – to labourers and workers in Cataluña, Levante and Andalucía, in particular – it cannot, however, be considered a valid explanation for electoral fraud, which affected all regions over the whole period and which can be said to have been caused by all social classes.[27]

For some authors, the explanation of the lack of popular reaction to electoral fraud lies in the repressive and violent means to which the dominant political forces resorted.[28] It is true that the anarchists were subjected to continuous and often severe repression,[29] but the other political forces that opposed the system did not suffer such systematic and constant repression as to explain the failure of their goals. It is also true that there are many examples of violence against electors, but only a small number of seats were decided by such methods. As Romero Maura put it:

> it is impossible to understand how repression could be exerted for decades without a ban having to be placed, definitively and for the whole country, on elections and the freedom of the press, freedom of speech and on the right to hold meetings ... No regime has ever managed to preserve them and at the same time perpetuate itself.[30]

The answer most commonly given by contemporaries, especially after the publication in 1901 of Joaquín Costa's work, *Oligarquía y Caciquismo como la forma actual de gobierno en España,* and even more so in current historiography, is that electoral fraud was possible because of the existence of *caciquismo,* a form of control, not only electoral but also political and social, exercised by a few powerful individuals, the *caciques.*

Two general interpretations of *caciquismo* have been given and these can be identified most clearly and concisely with Richard Herr, on the one hand, and Joaquín Romero Maura and José Varela Ortega, on the other.[31] The two interpretations can be distinguished by differing opinions concerning the basis on which *caciquismo* was founded – economic or political – and concerning the nature of its inherent relationship – coercive domination or fairly harmonious patronage.

The interpretation of *caciquismo* as an economically-based phenomenon has a number of important earlier exponents: Manuel Azaña, Gerald Brenan and Antonio Ramos Oliveira.[32] But it is Richard Herr who has provided the most systematic account in an article which analyses how Spanish landed elites 'coped with the new and alien forces of the nineteenth century', among which were the establishment of parliamentary government and universal suffrage. In the 18th century, according to Herr, these elites, from their local enclaves, resisted the rationalising offensives of reformist monarchy; but:

> ... once royal absolutism was replaced by parliamentary government, the elites of the country ... discovered that their power was better guaranteed by controlling the central authority than by resisting it locally. In the process they developed the institution known as caciquismo.
>
> Neither the state administrative and judicial hierarchies nor the political parties offered a reliable instrument for the elites to use in keeping the country running as they wished ... Thus a third parallel hierarchy of authority and administration arose that had no constitutional or legal role, but became the effective network for enforcing the policies of those with social and economic power.

It is not correct, according to Herr, to establish a functional connection between the public role of *caciques* and their membership in the *cacique* hierarchy:

> Membership in the three hierarchies – state, party and *cacique* – frequently overlapped. Both party leaders and local civil servants could belong to the *cacique* network, but they fulfilled functions of that network in their role as *caciques* and not those of their public positions.[33]

The second group of interpretations, on the other hand, stress the relative independence and novelty both of the system and of the political elites with regard to economic structures. Thus, for Romero Maura, the key element was the *cacique*'s appropiation of political resources. The *cacique*, according to this view, always obtains his arbitrary and interested executive power from administrative functions; the path followed to reach the position occupied, whether or not he is the wealthiest man in the village – although if he is, access will have been that much easier – is only secondary; the essential thing is that he should remain there handing out political favours, using public administration in a discriminatory manner.

Varela Ortega has expressed a similar opinion, denying the correlation between economic and political structures, and seeing the key to the system as lying in the control of the administration.

As for the nature of the relationship between *caciques* and the people under their control, those who defend the economy-based *caciquismo* do not raise this issue; it seems that, once the principle of economic domination is established, all else is superfluous; the relationship can be no other than absolute coercive subordination. In contrast, those who identify *caciquismo* basically with political and administrative control explicitly state that it was a form of patronage.[34]

Although both interpretations present difficulties, as their authors themselves recognise, they are in general convincing from a theoretical point of view. We require local research aimed at verifying the interpretations in the areas under study by analysing the composition and the power bases of the political elites, their relation with the economic elites, and the nature of social relations. The two interpretations need not be mutually exclusive: the two types of influence may reach, at one and the same time, different people within a community, and economic control does not preclude patronage. It would also be important to distinguish between the situation before and after the introduction of universal suffrage: it can be foreseen that this weakened the clientelist foundations of the system and increased the weight of economic factors.[35]

Be that as it may, what I think should be emphasised is that the *caciques* could not possibly integrate the whole of the country's adult male population into their networks and, therefore, that economic and political *caciquismo* is not the ultimate reason why most of the country consented to electoral fraud. From the economic standpoint, most regions had significant largely independent sectors of population. If we consider political patronage, both Romero Maura and Varela Ortega have pointed out that, by definition, only a minority can have benefited from administrative favours. The main problem of Costa's thesis that *caciquismo* was the 'present-day form of government in Spain' is that it gives a picture of an excessively organised and structured society in Spain.

Moreover, in a free country where fraud was outlawed and wide freedom of the press existed, nothing would have prevented most people from taking an active part in politics, if they had so wished. What was so striking, as we saw earlier in the case of Barcelona, was the ease with which a determined minority broke *cacique* control over the elections. Even in Andalucía, where 'a man's job depended on his vote', as Malefakis has written, '*cacique* action alone was not able to nullify the potential of the votes of the rural masses'.[36]

It is true that the *caciques* also attempted to satisfy collective needs – such as roads, railways and universities – or to meet the demands of organised groups with specific opinions and interests (protection for industry and agriculture, for example) – what Romero Maura has called 'indivisible benefits'. However, it seems too optimistic to consider, as this author does, that *cacique* control was based on a conscious and complacent acceptance by the majority of the political and economic order.[37]

There is, therefore, another component which must be borne in mind in order to complete the picture of the attitudes of Spanish people to elections in the Restoration, and which must be added to conscious participation in favour of, or against, the system; rejection of politics rooted in anarchism; economic control; and membership of a clientelist group with either an economic or an administrative basis. This component is political apathy, indifference towards democratic institutions: 'so strong is the government organization, so feeble the interest felt by the general public in political questions', complained Hardinge in the aforementioned Memorandum. This attitude would also have been favourable ground for vote-buying by candidates, on those occasions when this occurred. To attempt to quantify each of these attitudes is far beyond our capabilities at the present time, given the current state of research into this topic.

What is clear is the lack of any kind of electoral culture in broad sectors of the Spanish population of the time; not only lack of a democratic electoral culture, understood as the exercise of sovereignty, but also of other forms of electoral culture, e.g. those based on a sense of community, or on deference, whose existence and persistence in other countries throughout the nineteenth century has recently been pointed out.[38] Going to vote, whatever the significance of this act, was not a habit for a good many Spaniards during the Restoration.

Conclusions

The problem of political apathy has been paid scant attention by recent Spanish historiography, which has been concerned almost entirely with the economic and political dimensions of *caciquismo*. Analysis of mentalities has not yet reached this field in the history of Spain. Contemporary observers, however, did perceive intensely this lack of interest in politics on the part of large sectors of the population. The reasons for this indifference were believed to lie either in the nation's psychological traits, or the lack of a developed general and political culture.

Today in a country where, in less than a generation, radical changes have occurred in attitudes and behaviour that were previously considered constituent parts of the national character, explanations based on hypothetical psychological peculiarities of the Spanish people hold little or no water. Thus, Gerald Brenan's opinion that 'the deeper layers of Spanish political thought and feeling are oriental' is considered more a belated expression of the romantic stereotype of Spain than a judgement to be taken seriously.[39]

Hence, it is in the scant cultural development that the roots of the phenomenon seem to lie. Evidence in favour of attributing the people's political indifference to lack of culture is to be found in the statistics for illiteracy for the country in the period under study, which were among the highest in Europe, and only dropped from 72 per cent (of the total population in Spain) in 1877 to 52.23 per cent in 1920. According to the novelist Emilia Pardo Bazán:

> The cause of our backwardness must be sought ... in the intellectual condition of the mass; in the infancy of the people, simple and docile or untamed, but enlightened and conscious never.[40]

This theory was, moreover, defended by important contemporary intellectuals who considered that Spain's main problem was lack of citizens, and proposed, as their major political goal, extending knowledge and education. The lack of success of the political undertakings they promoted may appear logical to us, given the excess of intellectualism and idealism in their theories. Nevertheless, when their ideas are stripped of their polemical or exclusivist character, they are important for their perception of fundamental aspects of the mental state of the country.

It was not just a question of a general lack of culture; it was also a question of a lack of political culture, as stated by the author of the pamphlet on *The causes of the backwardness in the political education in Spain*.[41] That the latter affected not only the masses but also political leaders is clear if one considers the way in which the 1890 law on universal suffrage was passed. The debate took place in the midst of absolute indifference on the part of the nation. The leaders of the monarchist parties recognised and accepted the falseness of the entire electoral process, the basis of the system of representation. The opposition parties – most of the republican and socialist parties – scorned the new law and put their trust in revolution to achieve by force what they in no way expected to attain by pacific and democratic means.[42]

Of the components that made up the mentality of the people and which worked against democratic political culture, one conservative author cited the customary respect and obedience inculcated constantly in country people:

> There is one social circumstance which stamps its character on the political conditions of the peasant. For him life is always on the side of respect and obedience ... In all stages of his life, the one experience whose rewards he reaps is that of submission. In the home, at school, in domestic service, under arms, he has gained no prizes or benefits but through obedience; and, by contrast, the slightest resistance has sufficed for him to be subjected to cruel punishment. To anyone who has been taught by life in this way ... there can be no interest so patently clear in election battles as that of not falling out with those that give orders, because he has ample experience that failure to obey is translated into fines and prison.[43]

One factor which we should keep in mind in order to account for the remoteness of the people from liberal institutions is the influence of the Catholic religion. The difficult relations, both theoretical and practical, between liberalism and Catholicism in Spain are well known. Yet the influence of Catholicism on the creation of the political attitude towards democratic and liberal institutions has surprisingly not been studied. At first sight, of course, Catholicism does not seem to have exerted a positive influence on the development of a liberal and democratic culture; rather, the opposite is true. Some testimony is very explicit in this respect.[44]

The role of the Catholic church in the isolation of Spain's rural masses from politics would also be compatible with the intense mobilisation of its followers led by the ecclesiastical hierarchy on various occasions to defend certain aspects of Church-State relations.[45] Moreover, we should be able to distinguish whether the political passivity of the masses was due to the acceptance of the existing social order – where the influence of religion would be decisive – or whether it was the result of the awareness that any attempt to change things was futile.

In conclusion, we need to investigate further the lines of research that have been opened up and to broaden the field of study with respect to political life in Spain during the Restoration. Contributions on *caciquismo*, which started twenty years ago, had the virtue of replacing the general condemnation of the system with an analysis that provides much more accurate information about it. Compared with earlier explanations which practically only took account of economic factors, the new studies pointed out the importance of specifically political factors. However, there are fundamental aspects related to mentality, to how most of the population perceived political institutions, which have been left aside. These are aspects that we should attempt to understand and research into them calls for new approaches.

Notes

1. On the content and effects of electoral reform, see José Varela Ortega and R. López Blanco, 'Historiography, Sources and Methods for the Study of Electoral Laws in Spain', in S. Noiret (ed.), *Political Strategies and Electoral Reforms: Origins of Voting Systems in Europe in the 19th and 20th Centuries* (Baden Baden, 1990); Carlos Dardé, 'El sufragio universal en España: causas y efectos', *Anales de la Universidad de Alicante. Historia Contemporánea*, no. 7 (1889-90), pp. 85-100; and Javier Tusell, 'Para la sociología política de la España contemporánea: el impacto de la ley de 1907 en el comportamiento electoral', *Hispania*, vol. XXX, no. 116 (1970), pp. 571-631.

2. Javier Tusell, 'El sufragio universal en España (1891-1936): un balance historiográfico', in J. Tusell (ed.), *El sufragio universal, Ayer*, no. 3 (Madrid, 1991) p. 15.

3. Of the period which has most benefited from the study of elections in Spain – the Second Republic (1931-36) – it has been said that 'there is no general study of the political life of the time into which our increasing knowledge regarding election results can be integrated and this is all the more regrettable since it is no longer a question of determining who won the 1936 elections, but of deciding to what extent the democratic experience of the Republic constituted a revolution in Spanish political life'; Tusell, 'El sufragio universal', p. 47. There is even less knowledge of such matters in the period of the Monarchy.

4. Tusell, 'El sufragio universal', p. 48.

5. The failure of the Maura government in the 1919 elections, although indicative of the limitations to the electoral power of the Minister of the Interior in the final stages of the system, was merely a consequence of the split in the Conservative ranks and of the lack of organisation by the Mauristas (followers of the head of the government), and not of a change in the country's ways, as the successive election victories of the Conservatives and Liberals, in 1920 and 1923, respectively, were to prove.

6. On the republican use of fraudulent means, see Carlos Dardé, 'La larga noche de la Restauración, 1875-1900', in N. Townson (ed.), *El republicanismo en España, 1830-1977* (Madrid, 1994), pp. 113-39. On Canalejas, see Salvador Forner Muñoz, *Canalejas y el partido liberal democrático* (Madrid, 1993), pp. 116-29.

7. José del Perojo to Buenaventura Rodríguez Parets, 23 Jan. 1893 *Biblioteca Menéndez Pelayo. Fondos Modernos* (Santander) Manuscritos, 1461, no. 94.

8. In the 1886 elections, the number of votes cast exceeded the number of electors in 10 districts; in one extreme case, by 171.9 per cent. See Carlos Dardé, 'Las elecciones de diputados de 1886', *Anales de la Universidad de Alicante. Historia Contemporánea*, no. 5 (1986), p. 254.

9. *Diario de Sesiones del Congreso*, legislature 1879-80, p. 111. According to the 19th century journalist, Andrés Borrego, the practice of leaving the official election papers blank so that they could be filled in later according to a candidate's particular needs dates from the period 1837-1845; in 1891, the Republican

Gumersindo de Azcárate declared before Congress that 'in many places, in whole areas, *elections are not held, they are written'*. Quoted by Práxedes Zancada, *Las elecciones legislativas en España* (Madrid, 1914), pp. 17 and 52. Proof of the rigging of results with no election taking place as late as 1919 and 1923 is given by Juan Carlos de Lara Ródenas, 'Política y lucha de partidos en la Huelva de la Restauración: las elecciones a Cortes de 1919', *Espacio, Tiempo y Forma,* Serie V, Historia Contemporánea (1990), vol. 3, p. 313, and Ana Rodríguez Ayala, 'Elecciones y élites parlamentarias de Cádiz, 1903-1923', *Espacio, Tiempo y Forma* Serie V, Historia Contemporánea (1990), vol. 3, pp. 274-5.

10. Raymond Carr, *Spain, 1808-1975* (Oxford, 1982), pp. 516-23. Shlomo Ben-Ami, *Fascism from Above. The Dictatorship of Primo de Rivera in Spain, 1923-1930* (Oxford, 1983), pp. 15-6. For one further testimony of the importance of fraud after the electoral reform of 1907 was applied, see Teresa Carnero Arbat, 'Élite gobernante dinástica e igualdad política en España, 1898-1914', *Historia Contemporánea* (1992).

11. José Varela Ortega, *Los amigos políticos. Partidos, elecciones y caciquismos en la Restauración, 1875-1900* (Madrid, 1977), p. 419.

12. Carr, *Spain*, p. 367.

13. Gabriele Ranzato, 'La forja de la soberanía nacional: las elecciones en los sistemas liberales español e italiano', in Tusell, *El sufragio universal*, pp. 129-32.

14. See Juan Pedro Pérez Amoros, 'Sociología electoral de Madrid, 1891-1901', unpubl. M.A. diss., Universidad Complutense de Madrid (1985); Rogelio López Blanco, 'Madrid antes y después del sufragio', in Tusell, *El sufragio universal*; and Tusell, *Sociología electoral de Madrid* (Madrid, 1969) and 'El comportamiento electoral madrileño revisitado', in A. Bahamonde Magro *et al.* (eds.), *La sociedad madrileña durante la restauración* (Madrid, 1989), vol. II.

15. Joaquín Romero Maura, *La rosa de fuego. Republicanos y anarquistas: la política de los obreros barceloneses entre el desastre colonial y la semana trágica, 1899-1909* (Barcelona, 1975), pp. 124-5.

16. Teresa Carnero Arbat, 'La modernización del país valenciano durante la Restauración', in J. L. García Delgado (ed.), *España entre dos siglos, 1875-1931. Continuidad y cambio* (Madrid, 1991), pp. 269-71.

17. Juan Pablo Fusi, *Política obrera en el país Vasco, 1880-1923* (Madrid, 1975), pp. 377-82.

18. Varela Ortega and López Blanco, 'Historiography, Sources and Methods'. For examples of how this procedure worked in medium-sized cities, see S. Forner and M. García, *Cuneros y caciques* (Alicante, 1990), and Carlos Dardé, 'El sufragio universal en la práctica: la candidatura de José del Perojo por Santander en 1891 y 1893', in *Estudios de Historia Moderna y Contemporánea. Homenaje a Federico Suárez Verdeguer* (Madrid,1991), pp. 111-23.

19. For the region of Navarra, see María Cruz Mina, 'Elecciones y partidos en Navarra, 1891-1923', in José Luis García Delgado (ed.), *La España de la Restauración. Política, legislación y cultura* (Madrid, 1985), pp. 111-29.

20. 'Concentrating as they do in their hands all the local administration, and possessing the right to appoint and dismiss the holders of the numerous small

municipal posts (secretaries, desks, tax-collectors, postmen, gardes-champêtres and so on) the importance of the Ayuntamientos and Alcaldes is naturally very considerable. In the rural districts their power and influence is probably greater than that of a squire or large landowner in England. It is true that this power is derived from the popular vote – but in Spanish elections of any kind the official element plays a large part; and on the side of non-official element there is a deep-rooted reluctance to oppose the authorities in possession, which, combined with a certain distrust of the secrecy and efficiency of the ballot-box, operates strongly in favour of the power that be'. In Foreign Office 72/1705, no. 42. Morier to Granville, 28 Apr. 1884.

21. Government control dated from the moderate legislation of 1845, which Cánovas del Castillo called 'an election-winning machine'. Antonio Cánovas del Castillo: speech to Congress, 14th Dec, 1854, *Idem* (1987), p. 4.

22. Javier Tusell, *Oligarquía y caciquismo en Andalucía, 1890-1923* (Barcelona, 1976), pp. 29-211; Varela Ortega, *Los amigos políticos*, pp. 401-32. Gabriele Ranzato, 'Natura e funzionamiento di un sistema pseudo-rappresentativo: la Spagna "liberal-democratica", 1875-1923', in *Suffragio, rappresentanza, interessi. Instituzioni e societá fra '800 e '900*, Annali della Fondazione Lelio e Lisli Basso-Issoco (Rome, 1989), vol. IX, pp. 194-229, The only recent study of an election during the Restoration is that of Dardé, 'Las elecciones de diputados'.

23. This is what happened in Madrid in 1886. See Dardé, 'Las elecciones de diputados', p. 239.

24. Cánovas complained of the lack of free voters but, in fact, was not overconcerned by this for he believed that the apathetic passivity of the majority was an old and respectable source of political power. He also considered that a ruler's legitimacy stemmed more from his dedication to the public good than from the manner in which he had obtained power. See Antonio Cánovas del Castillo, Speeches to Congress, 15 Mar. and 3 May, 1876, and 12 Nov. 1878, *Idem* (1987), pp. 225-9, 280-1 and 330-9. Speech to the Ateneo in Madrid, 6 Nov. 1889, *Idem* (1981), pp. 182-3.

25. José Ortega y Gasset, 'Vieja y Nueva Política', Lecture in the Teatro de la Comedia, Madrid, 23 Mar. 1914, in Ortega y Gasset, *Discursos políticos* (Madrid, 1974), pp. 69 and 79. Miguel de Unamuno went even further, quoting a poem by Manuel Machado: 'Mi voluntad ha muerto una noche de luna/ en que era muy hermoso no pensar ni querer./ Mi ideal es tenderme sin ilusión alguna...' (My will died one moonlit night/ when it was so beautiful not to think or love./ My ideal is to lie without any dreams at all...) he asserted the nonexistence of national consciousness and will: 'The Spanish as such only seem to want to be left to die in peace. To die, not to live'. Miguel de Unamuno, 'La voluntad nacional', published in *España*, 19 Mar. 1915. See Miguel de Unamuno, *Crónica política española, 1915-1923* (Madrid, 1977), pp. 64-5.

26. C. Seignobos, *Histoire politique de l'Europe contemporaine. Evolution des partis et des formes politiques, 1814-1914* (Paris, 1924), pp. 390-1.

27. On anarchist antipoliticism see José Alvarez Junco, *El emperador del paralelo. Lerroux y la demagogia populista* (Madrid, 1991), pp. 403-30 and 598-9. For

a general view of anarchism in Spain, Pere Gabriel, 'El Anarquismo en España', in G. Woodcock, *El anarquismo. Historia de las ideas y movimientos libertarios* (Barcelona, 1979), pp. 330-88.

28. For a recent example dealing with Cataluña, see Antonio López Estudillo, 'Federalismo, campesinado y métodos de restablecer el control político en la Restauración', in Conxita Mir Curcó (ed.), *Actituds politiques i control social a la Catalunya de la Restauració, 1875-1923* (Lleida, 1989), pp. 191-207.

29. José Rodríguez Labandeira, *El trabajo rural en España, 1876-1936* (Barcelona, 1991), pp. 194-209.

30. Joaquín Romero Maura, 'El caciquismo', in J. A. Gallego (ed.), *Revolución y Restauración, 1868-1931* (Madrid, 1981), p. 77.

31. Richard Herr, 'Spain', in D. Spring (ed.), *European Landed Elites in the Nineteenth-century* (Baltimore, 1977), pp 98-126; Romero Maura, 'El caciquismo'; and Varela Ortega, *Los amigos políticos*, especially, pp. 353-69.

32. 'Caciquismo y Democracia', in Manuel Azaña, *Plumas y palabras* (Barcelona, 1976), pp. 199-203; Gerald Brenan, *El laberinto español* (Barcelona, 1977), pp. 30-2; Antonio Ramos Oliveira, *Historia de España* (Mexico, 1952), vol. II, pp. 316-8 and 417.

33. Herr, 'Spain', pp. 98, 112, 114-5.

34. In support of this interpretation, see also Julian Pitt-Rivers, *The People of the Sierra* (Chicago, 1971). According to this author, *caciquismo*, at least in the early part of the period under study, was true patronage, understood as a relationship between two persons of different standing based on trust and a kind of friendship through which there was an exchange of services. This relationship was also based on certain structural conditions and cultural values. The conditions that Pitt-Rivers stresses are the separation and concentration of power in the hands of the few; and the values highlighted are a strong sense of community, which viewed the village as the natural political unit and was fed by a dominant lively public opinion; acceptance of the economic status quo; and the importance given to personal relations, particularly friendship. A coherent institution with a type of society in which modern rationalist structures coexisted with traditional structures founded on prestige and irrational beliefs.

35. A more detailed analysis of these interpretations is given in Carlos Dardé, 'Vida política y elecciones. Persistencias y cambios', *Espacio, Tiempo y Forma*, Madrid, forthcoming. Variations introduced by universal suffrage in Dardé, 'El sufragio universal en España'.

36. Edward Malefakis, *Agrarian Reform and Peasant Revolution* (New Haven, 1970), p. 98.

37. 'The clientelist network was elevated and became a political system *because* Spaniards were not interested in public debate and this occurred *because*, in much of Spain, the system gave its subjects what these thought reasonable'. Romero Maura, *La rosa de fuego*, pp. 39-40; quoted by Alvarez Junco, *El emperador del paralelo*, p. 444

38. Frank O'Gorman, *Voters, Patrons and Parties. The Unreformed Electoral System of Hanoverian England* (Oxford, 1989) and 'Campaign Rituals and Ceremonies: The Social Meaning of Elections in England, 1780-1860', *Past*

220220 *Elections before Democracy*

and Present, no. 135 (1992), pp. 79-115; and François-Xavier Guerra, 'Les avatars de la représentation au XIXe siècle', in G. Couffignal (ed.), *Réinventer la démocratie. Le défi Latino-Americain* (Paris, 1992), pp. 49-84.

39. Raymond Carr, review of J. Gathorne-Hardy, 'The interior Castle', *Ayer*, no. 10 (1993), pp. 82-3; Brenan, *El laberinto español*, pp. 19-20. Other examples of allusions to ethnic factors in the replies of Ramón y Cajal and Gumersindo de Azcárate to Costa's questionnaire are in Costa, *Oligarquía y caciquismo*, pp. 424-8 and 585-97.

40. Quoted in Costa, *Oligarquía y caciquismo*, p. 380.

41. Andrés Borrego, *Causas del atraso de la educación política de los españoles* (Madrid, 1878). According to this author, the chequered history of the constitutional system in Spain was the cause of 'the mistrust, the scorn, the apathy and the general indifference towards the *res publica* so that there is no party that can summon the help and favour of a true majority in support of its solutions, and this more than anything else explains this apathy and indifference of the nation, and the weakness, the uncertainty, the lack of faith and moral strength of both the government and the opposition parties' (pp. 6-7). The responsibility for this situation, according to Borrego, lay with the upper classes who had not educated the Spanish people who were 'ever ... grateful and docile towards the benevolent patronage of the wealthy' (p. 30).

42. Dardé, 'Significado político e ideológico de la ley de sufragio universal en 1890', in *Anales de la Universidad de Alicante. Historia contemporánea*, forthcoming.

43. Joaquín Sánchez de Toca, *El régimen parlamentario y el sufragio universal* (Madrid, 1889), pp. 287-90; quoted by Francisco Murillo Ferrol, *Estudios de sociología política* (Madrid, 1963), pp. 46-7.

44. Thus, for example, the judgement of the British Ambassador in Madrid, in 1867, contained in an extensive 'Memorandum on Constitutional Government in Spain':

It was thought that the people ... would have shown themselves capable of securing their freedom and the exercise of their legitimate rights ... But one element in their character namely the religious element ... had not been sufficiently taken into account ... The Inquisition ... had done its work among the people more effectually than its authors could ever perhaps have anticipated. It had narrowed intellect, engendered suspicion and distrust in social life, corrupted social ties ...

No sooner therefore was the Constitution system proclaimed than the whole machinery of the Romish Church was set in motion to oppose it and to prevent any intellectual development which might have ensued ...

It was thought that Constitutional Government would curb the vices and remove the prejudices engrafted on the character of the people by this fearful Institution, but its practical application failed to do so, and its first principles even were never recognized or acted on ...

The mass of the people, consequently have never cared for Representative Government as established by the Constitution because care has been taken by the clergy that they should never understand its advantages. They have been taught on the contrary that all their misfortunes have resulted from its introduction ... They know that independent and lawless habits have ever been prevalent but since an unrestricted indulgence in them does not interfere with the Dogmas of the Church they rather encourage them, for real civil liberty is their greatest enemy and they dread its civilising influence. Thus may be explained the apathy and indifference among the lower orders as regards Constitutional Government.

FO 72/1149, no. 16. West to Salisbury, 20 Oct. 1867.

45. See María Luisa Ollero Prieto, 'La tolerancia religiosa en la constitución de 1876. Análisis de la campaña de protesta', *Espacio, Tiempo y Forma*, Serie V (1990), pp. 107-22.

CHAPTER 10

BUILDING ASPECTS OF DEMOCRACY BEFORE DEMOCRACY: ELECTORAL PRACTICES IN NINETEENTH CENTURY CHILE

J. Samuel Valenzuela*

At least once every three years beginning in 1823, unfailingly except for the 1891 presidential contest, Chilean voters were summoned to the polls for presidential, congressional, and/or municipal elections throughout the nineteenth century. Congressional and municipal elections were held every three years, and presidential ones every five. With so many elections there should be a rich historiographic tradition devoted to them, especially since they left a considerable statistical and documentary trail. However, they have only recently become the object of study.[1] Instead of detailed empirical work on the subject, historians since the 1940s have simply enveloped the nineteenth-century's electoral processes in a set of enduring but fundamentally misleading and even inaccurate notions that have been taken as fact, thereby stifling further research. Consequently, the early evolution of Chilean political participation and democratisation has been very poorly understood.

The misleading notions can be stated succinctly in three points. First, the Constitution of 1833 – the first to have more than an ephemeral application – solidified the political domination of the most traditional landed upper class of colonial origin; hence, it established income and property requirements that restricted voting rights, with some exceptions, to relatively wealthy men. Second, the expansion of suffrage to all literate males in 1874 was the product of the rise of financial, commercial, industrial and mining interests that forged an alliance with urban professional and other middle-class groups in an attempt to wrest political power away from the landowners. The electoral reform was championed primarily by the Radical Party, the political expression of the new classes formed by the nation's economic development. And third, despite

* The author gratefully acknowledges the advice and assistance of Erika Maza Valenzuela in preparing this chapter. My appreciation as well to Ivan Jaksic for steering me to some important primary sources, namely the substantial accounts of elections in James M. Gilliss, Ignacio Domeyko and Pedro Félix Vicuna, and to Scott Mainwaring for his comments.

opposition efforts, nineteenth-century elections were nonetheless quite meaningless and unimportant: until 1894 the government-supported candidates always won, and, given the small numbers of voters, the whole electoral process had virtually no impact on the political inclinations of the broad masses. The nation had an 'oligarchic', 'aristocratic', or 'patrician' political and electoral system.[2]

While it is true that the Constitution of 1833 required prospective voters to have certain property, income, or professional qualifications, this did not mean in practice – contrary to the first notion – that only rich property owners were able to vote. In fact, as this chapter will show, a majority of the electorate during the heyday of the 'Conservative Republic' (1830-1871), that was supposedly dominated by landed families of colonial origin, was composed of men of middle-lower- to lower-class background, including public employees. The law specifying the *censitaire* provisions established income levels that could be met by artisans, most if not all adult male salaried workers and miners, and petty merchants. Moreover, all veterans of the wars of independence were exempted from having to show proof of income as well as from the literacy requirement.

As indicated by the second notion, the Radical Party was indeed in favour of most provisions of the 1874 electoral reform. But this is only a half-truth, because the Conservative Party, the one that authors have consistently identified with the wealthy landholding families of aristocratic lineage, was also in favour of the reform. Both parties disagreed sharply over every issue connected somehow to church/state relations, but they forged a short-lived coalition of mutual convenience in congress after 1872 to force the approval of an electoral reform in order to curtail the power of the government, then in the hands of the Liberals, to determine the outcome of elections. And contrary to what might be expected after reading the above quoted literature, the key phrase that expanded the numbers of voters was proposed by Zorobabel Rodríguez, a deputy of the Conservative – not the Radical – Party.[3] It stipulated that 'it is presumed by right that whoever can read and write has the income that the law requires'.[4]

Turning to the third notion, it is true that the governments' official lists of candidates usually won the elections, often by resorting to unfair procedures. However, opposition leaders did run for the presidency, even if unsuccessfully, and opposition candidacies did emerge in many districts or communes in congressional and municipal elections, winning in at least several places in most instances. Thus, as Urzúa Valenzuela notes forcefully, oppositions were an ever-present ingredient in Chile's nineteenth-century politics.[5] And although the numbers of voters was indeed relatively small (a nineteenth century maximum of seven per cent of the total population, about 30 per cent of adult males – or close to 150,000 individuals – were registered to vote in 1878),[6] political divisions and loyalties did extend to a much broader audience in the national society. Elections were not only a concern of those who voted; people who were not registered voters, including many women, participated all the same in the process by attempting to secure its fairness, by protecting the urns, by celebrating the candidates' victories or lamenting their losses, by propagandising in their favour, or by writing in the partisan press for or against specific candidates. As many of the most disputed issues of the day were of concern to the Church – be they control over education, the rights of religious dissidents, or the scope of government versus ecclesiastical authority – the pulpit was a powerful source to crystallise political identities, and it generated an anticlerical reaction. The Liberal, Conservative and Radical Parties emerged from these conflicts. Even if government interference in the elections before the 1890s made them less than democratic, the subsequent development of Chilean democracy cannot be understood without analysing such prior elections in detail. Twentieth-century Chilean electoral and party politics evolved from mid-nineteenth century origins.

This chapter contributes to the analysis of Chilean elections in the nineteenth century by examining the mechanics of voter registration, the voting practices on the day of the elections, the changing occupational composition of the electorate, the creation of candidate lists, electoral campaign strategies and the participation of non-voters in the electoral contests. The chapter refers primarily to the six decades framed between two civil wars, those of 1829-1830 and 1891, that altered the shape of the nation's politics. The first one led to the triumph of the centralist forces that dictated the Constitution of 1833, and the second one set virtually all the nation's parties against the President, José Manuel Balmaceda, who was defeated as his term of office ended. At that point the winning coalition ended official government sponsorship of candidates as well as overt government interference in elections.

Unlike nineteenth-century elections in Argentina, where the polls were open to all males with Argentine citizenship, the compilation of a registry of voters was a key step in Chilean electoral procedures from the very beginning. It is the obvious starting point to analyse them.

Electoral Registrations

After independence, with the exception of a short period in which a system of permanent electoral registries was in force, citizens had to register to vote, or reconfirm their registration, before each electoral year. The registries were opened, with slight variations, in all townships (*comunas*) for four hours a day during the first 15 days of November; congressional and municipal elections were held in March, and those for presidential electors were held in June. The process of re-registering continuously before each electoral year meant that the rolls were largely free of the names of those who had deceased. In 1888, the voter registry was made valid for ten years. There was no legal obligation to register to vote.[7] The short period in which the registries were opened diminished the chances that all those who were eligible to vote would make an effort to register, and it enhanced the proportion of registered voters who were part, somehow, of an organised effort to mobilise voters.

Voter registrations were conducted by a 'Qualifying Junta' (*Junta Calificadora*). Upon registration or re-registration, voters were given a small qualifying certificate, called *calificación*, printed by the national government and bearing its seal. On it, registry officials wrote the voter's name, the date of registration, the book in which the voter's name and occupation was inscribed, and the number assigned to it in the book. The *calificación* was signed by all seven officials on the junta, but it did not contain the voter's own signature.[8] Each citizen had to present the *calificación* at the polls on the day of the election in order to vote; therefore, it had to be kept in a safe place for months before using it. If it was lost, the municipalities were authorised to grant a substitute form on the basis of the voter registry.

The voter registration lists were checked by a 'Revisory Junta' (*Junta Revisora*). In addition to purging the rolls of irregularities such as duplicate registries, the latter was also empowered to review and resolve any complaints by citizens regarding inclusions or exclusions. Its decisions in such cases could be appealed to the courts.[9]

The members of both juntas were appointed by municipal authorities. Despite the fact that all parties were entitled to send observers to oversee the voter registration process,[10] opponents of the national governments argued that the juntas did not have the necessary impartiality to exercise their functions, and that the process itself contained, as a result, many irregularities. Indeed, municipal councillors were generally beholden to the national government because they were usually elected after being included in official lists of candidates prepared by the minister of the interior. The municipal councils were also presided over by the provincial, departmental, or communal representatives of the national executive, namely, either the intendants (*intendentes*), governors (*gobernadores*), or sub-delegates (*subdelegados*), depending on the size and importance of the commune. The representatives of the executive as well as the councillors could also become candidates in the forthcoming elections, and therefore at least some of those who participated in choosing junta members (or in naming themselves to the juntas, as nothing prevented such self-appointments) could even have a personal, and not only political, stake in quickly registering their partisans while questioning the qualifications of those they knew would be opposing them – assuming the latter bothered to make the effort to register during the short period when this could be done.

Moreover, the composition of the juntas was of such significance that national government authorities (and their provincial representatives) took a direct role in selecting the individuals the municipal councils were to place on them. This is illustrated by the following circular sent in 1839 by an *intendente* to all his subordinate *subdelegados*:

> It is extremely important to me to have a list of the individuals that you think you can count on to compose the qualifying tables. The appointments must be made by the Municipalities, but as we do not know the local people I would like to ask you to point them out to me.
>
> Six or seven names will be enough, placing those *you can most count on* at the beginning of the list.[11]

The *intendente* in this case presumably went on to impose the names he accepted on the municipal councils.

After denouncing the lack of fairness in the juntas' voter registration procedures for over two decades, opposition leaders tried in the 1860s to devise a different mechanism to appoint their members. These efforts were finally reflected in an electoral law enacted in 1869. It explicitly excluded the local representatives of executive authority from participating in the *Juntas Calificadoras*, and it changed the character of the *Juntas Revisoras* by drawing its six members by lot from lists of the forty largest taxpayers (*listas de mayores contribuyentes*) of each commune. This latter procedure was introduced by the pro-government congressional majority to counter an indication formulated in 1867 by José Victorino Lastarria, a progressive Liberal intellectual and deputy who was generally a government opponent, that called for the juntas to be drawn by lot from the lists of all voters in the prior election. Subsequently, opposition advocates of electoral reform embraced the idea of drawing junta members from lists of the forty largest taxpayers as the only system that would be acceptable to the government, but would still help ensure the juntas' independence from it. Consequently, this mechanism was instituted in the 1874 electoral law – which was approved when a split in the governing coalition produced an opposition majority in both houses of congress – to compose the *Juntas Calificadoras* as well.[12] Once it was in place, however, government opponents still found reasons to complain that the juntas were biased. They noted that in some communes the lists of the forty largest taxpayers from which the names of junta members were drawn had politically significant omissions. The authorities supplied the lists, and they could indeed be doctored.

Obviously, the political inclinations of those who obtained the qualification certificate to vote in the first 15 days of November prior to each electoral year were of crucial significance for the electoral outcome, and therefore fairness of the juntas which were in charge of the registry was of the essence. In most localities there was a strong if not certain indication of the subsequent electoral results by the time voter registrations were completed. A key aspect of any winning campaign was to make sure that it was well prepared to register its voters, and to denounce fraudulent registries by its opponents. Hence, the electoral campaigns had to begin before the voter registration process took place, especially for opposition candidates who had to make a special effort to mobilise potential voters against the authorities.

The registries were open to all 'citizens' (*ciudadanos*) who met, according to the 1833 Constitution, certain requirements. They had to be 21 years and over if married, 25 and over if single or simply over 21 after 1884; they had to know how to read and write; and they had to have either some real estate, an invested capital, or an income from whatever source, the minimum levels for which were to be set every ten years in an electoral law. These property or income requirements were met simply by being literate. After the enactment of the 1874 decennial electoral law and having been rendered moot by the literacy provision, all mention of them was deleted in the subsequent decennial law of 1884. The word 'citizens' in practice was supposed to mean 'male citizens'. This notion was made explicit in the 1884 electoral law in order to exclude women who had registered to vote in 1876, arguing that the term *ciudadano* was used in the constitution and in the laws in a generic sense, and not in the masculine singular form.[13]

As noted above, the income requirements in the constitution did not mean that the electorate was composed of wealthy voters even before 1874. A key element in the electoral strategy of all the governments during the period discussed here, especially before the 1870s, consisted of generating majorities for official lists of candidates by relying to a significant extent on the votes of two categories of individuals: public employees (including several hundred army officers and policemen), and national guard troops. In an 1869 House of Deputies speech, Lastarria dissected the composition of the 1862 electorate, noting all the voters who were in his opinion subject to the direct influence of the government. His comments are revealing:

> According to the electoral census of 1862, the following were inscribed in the electoral registries: 1) 5,534 farmers (*agricultores*) of whom four fifths are citizens who, given their social and moral condition, are at the mercy of the influences of government agents and do not know the importance of the suffrage...; 2) 3,734 artisans who are, like the farmers, enrolled in the national guard, and are therefore under the direction – and even under the pressure – of the agents of the executive. It is also certain that a majority of these citizens have false ideas regarding the dignity and importance of suffrage...; 3) 1,859 public employees, and 1,110 private employees who work mainly for municipalities, since the latter often extend *calificaciones* to their dependents and servants as private employees. To these employed citizens it is necessary to add 337 army and 55 navy officers.
>
> All of this combines to give the enormous sum of 12,620 voting citizens who formed the basis of the electoral power of the government...[14]

The last figure represented 56.7 per cent of the total number who were registered to vote for the elections of 1864.[15] Most of these individuals lived near or in the nation's cities and towns. Artisans, employees of various kinds, and military officers were mostly urban dwellers, but even the farmers Lastarria mentions had to be in the peripheries of urban areas if they were part of the national guards. As a result the latter's lives were closely connected to urban society. Consequently, the electorate was disproportionately urban at a time when the population was overwhelmingly rural.

The national guard troops were clearly the largest component of the governments' supposedly captive electorate. Reviving a colonial institution that had fallen into disuse with the wars of independence, national guard units were formed in all significant towns of the republic after 1830. Able-bodied men in occupations that were not exempted from service had to enrol in its units, which trained on weekends but could be mobilised on command. The guards were usually led by socially and politically prominent individuals who were appointed at will by the ministers of the interior given their loyalty to the government. This paramilitary force was the principal means for the state to quell serious disturbances of public order, at least until the beginning of the War of the Pacific in 1879, after which the institution declined. The police depended on municipal governments and were undermanned and ineffective (although their numbers and strength increased beginning in the 1870s), and the bulk of the army was stationed permanently in the South to protect against incursions by the Araucanians. Once in full force by the 1840s, there were over 60,000 men in the national guards.[16]

The practice of having national guard troops vote in the elections was so prevalent in the early 1850s that James M. Gilliss, an American naval officer and astronomer living in Chile at the time, noted that 'all who are enrolled as members of the national guard are entitled to the right of suffrage'.[17] This was, strictly speaking, not true, at least in so far as Gilliss presented this practice as an entitlement by right. Gilliss also notes that 'so far as the property and intellectual [literacy] qualifications [to vote] are concerned, the law is dead letter, or at least is openly violated at every election';[18] and while he is correct in observing that men who had little or no property and/or who were illiterate did vote, he was mistaken in implying that such practices, exceptions aside, were illegal. The governments could justify the registration of national guard troops on a legal basis. Illiterates were entitled to vote by a transitory article in the 1833 Constitution as long as they had fought for independence – but who among those who were old enough in the national guard would admit to not having done so?[19] And despite the *censitaire* form of suffrage enshrined in the constitution that has led analysts to believe that only those who were well-off could vote, what really mattered were the minimal property, invested capital, and income levels that were set in the decennial laws to specify the constitutional requirements to vote. The first such law enacted in 1834 set low income levels – 200 pesos in Santiago and 150 in the provinces – and, as demanded by the constitution's article eight, correspondingly low property and capital levels, simply because the authorities needed to have a legal justification to enfranchise the national guard troops. These income levels were never raised before being swept aside by the literacy provision in 1874.

Testimonies of the time contain abundant confirmation that national guard troops were drawn from the lower classes. As Lastarria observed in the above quoted passage, the national guards were composed mainly of artisans and of small property holders in the immediate vicinity of the cities and towns (and who therefore participated, despite their agricultural occupation, in urban social and political life). An Argentine general wrote in his diary while an exile in Chile in the 1840s that the national guardsmen were 'jacks of all trade (*menestrales*), artisans, petty clerks (*mozos de tienda y almacén*), and the proletarian class'.[20] The historian Diego Barros Arana, who was partly a chronicler of the nineteenth-century events he witnessed in his youth, wrote more simply that the guard troops were 'drawn from the working classes'.[21] And regarding their income levels, Gilliss observed in the early 1850s that 'freeholders and artisans ... possess the requisite income [to vote]'.[22] Congressional debates contain confirmations of Gilliss's observation. Thus, while defending in 1874 the presumption that literacy could be taken by right as proof of the requisite income to vote, Senator Manuel José Irarrázabal, the leading figure of the Conservative Party, reminded his colleagues that 'some senators who are now present' had already asserted during the

> previous [i.e. 1864] debate on the decennial law that sets the income citizens must have in order to vote that even the peons [*peones gañanes*], even the lowest of Chileans, could have an income of two hundred pesos, and that is why this figure was set for Santiago and that of one hundred and fifty for the provinces.[23]

A large number of voter registrants obtained their *calificaciones* without having to present any proof-of-income documents. Public employees, including municipal ones, appeared on state payroll lists. Artisans and petty merchants were listed on the municipal treasury books as having paid the requisite local tax (*patente*) for opening their shops. The owners of small plots of land around the towns were included in the national treasury lists as having paid the tithe (the Church's income was drawn from agricultural production), and after 1853 they appeared on the lists of rural property holders that were drawn up to assess the so-called agricultural contribution (*contribución agrícola*) that substituted the tithe. All of these lists were in the hands of the authorities, and anyone on them was presumed to have the requisite income.[24] These were generally the categories of voters who cast ballots in favour of the governments' official lists of candidates. In fact, as many of these individuals were also in the national guards, the commanders usually supervised the process of what turned out to be their virtually automatic registration. The payroll and taxpayer lists could conceivably be adulterated, temporarily omitting certain names from them for political purposes; hence, opposition voters who might appear on them could be screened out from the effortless process of registration. And a reading and writing test beyond the simple ability of signing one's name (ability which was taken to be a sufficient demonstration of literacy), as well as proof-of-income documents could be demanded of any prospective voter, even of those appearing on the voter-qualifying lists.

Consequently, the *censitaire* requirements were simply a tool in the hands of the voter registry authorities who generally acted, as noted above, as electoral agents for the governments. They could simplify the procedures for those they considered secure voters for the official lists of candidates, and they could apply the full extent of the law to those who were not. The literacy test could be done on the spot, and was relatively incontrovertible, but the lack of income documentation, or of what was deemed to be proper proof of income, could be used easily as an excuse to refuse a prospective voter his registration. The Qualifying Juntas could rapidly accept, for instance, the salary certificates given by private employers to known supporters of their preferred candidates while refusing to accept the validity of the same *calificaciones* given to voters favouring, or suspected of favouring, other candidates.[25] This could easily discourage all but the most politicised of voters from making the effort to come back with new documents, or from appealing a negative decision to the Revisory Juntas and, eventually, the courts. As a result, opponents of the government rightly viewed the voter registration requirements, especially the income requirement, as a major obstacle, although the problem was not, as could be assumed at first glance, the income levels that were set but rather the practice of forcing voters to show what was deemed to be its proper documentation. This was a difficulty, in particular, that stood in the way of the qualification as voters of those among the large non-freeholding rural population who could at least sign their names. Even though agricultural labourers apparently had the requisite income, as noted by Irarrázabal in the above quoted passage, they were mostly paid in kind by the large landowners through access to land and pastures. Living generally in a non-monetised economy, they had the greatest difficulty to produce proof-of-income papers. This was the case even for those labourers who marketed part of their production from the plots of land assigned to them.

The difficulty of enfranchising the dependent rural population placed the Conservative Party in a particularly disadvantageous position. The party had strong support among the landowning families of the Central Valley, the most populated area of the country before the rapid growth of the cities towards the end of the nineteenth century. As long as the Conservatives were part of the governing coalitions, they obviously had no need to be particularly concerned with the biases in the voter registration system. However, when the party finally broke its coalition with the government Liberals in 1872, its legislators – who had been elected to the congress on the official candidate lists of the Liberal-Conservative coalition that had governed since 1863 – faced the almost certain prospect of defeat in the next elections. Consequently, they joined forces with the minority opposition of Radicals and 'loose' Liberals in order to reform the electoral law in a manner that would buttress its fairness.

The Conservatives, Radicals and 'loose' Liberals disagreed sharply over substantive issues, but they shared momentarily a strong common interest in minimising the capacity of the executive to place its partisans in elected positions. With the stipulation added to the 1874 decennial electoral law that literacy was to be taken as proof of the constitutionally requisite income, the new temporary congressional majority sought to facilitate opposition voter registrations by eliminating the necessity of consulting payroll or treasury lists, or of having to present proof-of-income certificates and receipts. The opposition legislators could not opt to eliminate the income and literacy requirements altogether because they would have had to reform the constitution, and this they could not do: the Constitution of 1833 could only be changed after a legislature voted in favour of the amendments debated and approved by a previous one. Since the opposition in favour of electoral reform could not count on its own reelection given the electoral practices it was trying to change, whatever constitutional amendments it approved were bound to face certain defeat in the hands of the new pro-government majority that would in all likelihood control the next legislature.

The enactment of the 1874 decennial electoral law eliminating the need for literate citizens to show proof of income when registering to vote led to a threefold expansion – from 49,047 in 1872 to 148,737 in 1878 – of the numbers of registered voters. As could be expected, the registered voters who listed agriculture as their occupation increased most sharply. This can be seen in Table 1, which shows the 1872 and 1878 occupational distribution of registered voters both nationally as well as in Rancagua, a Central Valley district where the Conservative Party was strong.

The registrants listing agriculture as their occupation were the only group to increase significantly not only in absolute terms (from 16,698 to 70,966 nationally between 1872 and 1878), but also as a proportion of the total electorate. Individuals in this category became close to half of the electorate after the change in the voting law. In Rancagua this category increased to about two-thirds of the district's electorate, a fact that reveals the voter mobilisation efforts of the districts' generally Conservative landowners. This effort had already begun by 1872, because only nine years earlier, in 1863, despite the district's overwhelmingly rural and agricultural profile, only 19.2 per cent of its electorate was listed as engaged in agriculture.[26] It should be noted that the 'proprietors and capitalists' group is the only one to have shrunk in absolute terms both nationally (from 6,258 to 4,422) and in Rancagua (from 142 to 11). There must have been a greater tendency in 1878 to list these individuals' occupations either as professionals or as agriculturists.

Table 1

The National and Rancagua District Electorate by Occupational Groups in 1872 and 1878, in percentages

	National Electorate		Rancagua Electorate	
Occupational Groups	*1872*	*1878*	*1872*	*1878*
Proprietors & capitalists	12.8	3.0	9.6	0.1
Professionals, merchants and other middle strata	17.2	13.5	11.3	8.1
Employees, public and private	11.4	7.8	7.5	2.0
Agriculturists	34.0	47.7	52.7	67.6
Artisans and other specialised trades	20.4	21.7	18.0	20.4
Miners	3.9	4.6	0.9	1.5
Workers and fishermen	0.3	1.7	0.0	0.3
TOTAL	100	100	100	100
TOTAL NUMBER	49,047	148,737	1,480	7,722

Source: Chile, *Anuario Estadístico* (Santiago, 1873) vol. 13, pp. 520-21; (Santiago, 1879) vol. 20 , pp. 310-311. A fuller set of figures and a detailed listing of all occupations under these categories appear in Valenzuela, *Democratización vía reforma*, pp. 118-9. Minor errors in the percentages presented there have been corrected for this table.

The Selection of Candidates for Office

During the period discussed here, the outgoing president selected the candidate who would then be presented to the nation as the government's choice to succeed him. Invariably one or more opposition candidates emerged, and yet they never obtained more than a handful of electoral college votes. Citizens voted for slates of electors pledged to the presidential candidates in each province, and with the winner-take-all system in place and the ability of the government to generate majorities for its official lists of candidates, few electors supporting the opposition candidates actually won.

This did not mean that the presidents could choose just anybody to succeed them. They had to select individuals who they knew would be generally acceptable to the parties that supported their governments or, as occurred on one occasion, to their more powerful opponents. This happened with the election of José Joaquín Pérez as successor to Manuel Montt in 1861. As he neared the end, in 1859, of his second term in office, Manuel Montt faced an insurrection which was based in part on the supposition that he was preparing to name his friend and collaborator, Antonio Varas, to succeed him. Montt defeated the insurrection, known as the 1859 Civil War, but decided that he could not press ahead with Varas's name in the face of resistance from Liberals, Conservatives and Radicals, the three parties that had crystallised during his presidency. Hence, he turned to Pérez, a mild man of advanced age who, once in office, made a governing coalition with the Liberals and Conservatives leaving the *Montt-Varista* party, the Nationals, in opposition with the Radicals.

After the parties acquired a clearer configuration during the Montt presidency, they became a more important factor in ratifying presidential succession choices. Their ability to intervene in the process was to a large extent a function of the electoral college system used for the election of the president. Thus, each candidate had to generate a list of names supporting him all over the country, and these individuals, though nominally pledged to support the candidate, could in fact decide to vote as they wished once the electoral college met – although in practice few of them reneged on their pledges. This meant that the sitting president and his chosen successor needed to rely on a nationwide network of political leaders to constitute the electoral college candidacies, and that they could not run the risk of ignoring their sentiments and demands. The institutional design for the selection of presidents therefore made it impossible for the incumbent – unlike the twentieth-century Mexican practice – authoritatively to name a personal choice as his successor. This institutional definition made the next step almost obligatory, namely, the organisation of a party (or a party coalition) convention to proclaim the candidate. Some of the delegates to such conventions could then also become candidates for the electoral college. The first year an official presidential candidate was nominated in a convention with delegates from all over the country was 1876, with the Liberal Aníbal Pinto as the standard bearer. Subsequently such nominating conventions became the norm rather than the exception, and after 1891 presidents were no longer directly involved in the choice of candidates to succeed them.

Opposition presidential candidates also had to rely on party networks to press their candidacies. Again, this was especially true after the 1850s as the parties crystallised into more coherent organisations; opposition figures would either emerge from the parties or, as was more often the case, they would seek the support of the parties that were left out of the incumbent president's coalition whatever their own party position. Thus, in 1871 opposition (or so-called 'independent') parties proclaimed the candidacy of José Tomás Urmeneta, a wealthy mine owner identified mainly with the National Party, in a meeting attended by close to seventy prominent political leaders.[27] In 1876, the same year Pinto was proclaimed in a national convention to head the Liberal-Radical ticket, a separate convention attended primarily by Conservatives proclaimed the candidacy of Benjamín Vicuña Mackenna, who was also a Liberal.

The ministers of the interior, with the collaboration of the intendants (especially when deciding on municipal candidates), drew up the official lists of candidates for congressional and local elections throughout the country. Given this function, the individuals who occupied that ministry towards the end of a presidential term were assumed to be in a strong position to prepare their own campaign for the presidency.

Despite the authorities' capacity to mobilise a significant portion of the electorate, fraudulently or not, for the official lists of candidates, the minister of the interior could not compose the official lists following his own whim. There were certain personalities, like José Victorino Lastarria or Manuel José Irarrázabal, who everyone respected given the force of their intellects and/or the wealth and prominence of their families. Even if they spoke their own minds and were often opposed to the government, it was not possible to ignore them when constituting the official lists for the lower house or the senate. Moreover, there had to be significant signs that the candidates on the official lists would be favourably received by a majority of the most influential local figures in their respective districts ('local' even if the most prominent of them also lived, especially during the winter months, in Santiago). Any attempt to place candidates who were rejected by the local notables on the official lists ran the risk of leading them to set up opposition lists that had significant chances of winning. National opposition leaders would be more than happy to assist in this endeavour. They drafted opposition lists only for the districts where they had a possibility of winning. Hence, the electoral contest between the government and its opponents was only judged on the basis of those districts where the opposition presented a challenge, and any minister of the interior whose official lists were defeated in a sizeable number of those districts by a coordinated opposition effort (rather than various inde-pendent local opposition candidacies) was considered to have 'lost' the election. President Bulnes, for example, fired his minister of the interior, Manuel Camilo Vial, when his opponents won in four of the five districts in which they ran coordinated candidates for the house of deputies in the 1849 elections.[28]

Moreover, even if the minister of the interior decided to pull all the levers of electoral fraud at his command to impose his official list, such a victory was not worth the price of ill feeling it generated among the influential local leaders. Given the paucity of fiscal resources to meet the country's many needs before the great nitrate boom that began in the 1880s, the government had to appeal constantly to the generosity of wealthy individuals, including women, in order to carry out improvement projects.[29] The line between public and private initiative was very nebulous, and the opposition of local notables could lead to a paralysis of construction and repairs to infrastructure, schools, churches and hospitals in the district as the local notables gave a cold shoulder to the representatives of the national government. Consequently, the ministers of the interior usually engaged in a process of consultation or negotiation with influential local notables to establish the official lists of candidates for their districts. These lists (and therefore the congressmen and municipal councilors who were elected) were as a result much more heterogeneous than would appear to be the case. They often included individuals who tended to favour opposition views in the congress and in the municipal councils. For the same reason, the dividing line between majority and minority benches in the congress was not as sharply drawn as could be expected.

In his memoirs, the Conservative congressman Abdón Cifuentes gives an example of negotiations between government authorities and local notables to compose the official list in which the latter took the initiative in presenting the names of the candidates. The case occurred in Rancagua, the already mentioned province with an important number of Conservative landowners, towards the end of the 1860s. At that time Liberals and Conservatives were part of the governing coalition of President Pérez. According to Cifuentes, Rancagua's 'great electors', led by Juan de Dios Correa, met to draw up the list of candidates for the congress, and subsequently took it to the government 'to obtain its customary ratification' (*'la usada venia'*).[30] The minister of the interior objected to Cifuentes's inclusion on the list, but finally accepted it grudgingly when confronted by the insistence of the Rancagua Conservatives. However, he then ordered the local representative of the government to do everything possible to prevent Cifuentes's victory. This did not work out as the minister had planned because the individual who received his order not only did not accept it, but also decided to denounce it publicly, and when confronted with the irate protests of the Rancagua Conservatives, President Pérez personally intervened in Cifuentes's favour. In this case the official list was basically composed by the 'great electors' of the district since a majority of them belonged to the Conservative Party, and it felt entitled to select the candidates in the districts where it had a strong presence given its governing alliance with the Liberals. Moreover, Rancagua's leading figures were individuals who, given their wealth and social rank, were part of the highest circles of Chilean society.

The ministers of the interior had greater room for manoeuvre when dealing with local notables of a lower social standing and living in poorer districts. In these cases the minister could offer some desired position in the local state administration – if not a place on the official list itself, especially for the municipal councils or as presidential or senatorial elector – to an important individual in exchange for his and his family's support for the official lists. Information regarding who should be named to what position was normally provided by the electoral agents of the minister, who were either the government's local representatives or the minister's political and personal friends. For instance, in the following letter an intendant asked Minister of the Interior Antonio Varas to name a certain person to a position in the provincial treasury of Valdivia since that would, he said:

> ...bring us infinite advantages, giving us all the influence of this family, which is the most important in the province. In this municipality alone it has a brother and a son-in-law; the latter's name is Juan Angel Acharán, a person of great value, who belongs to the opposition, but his father-in-law solemnly engages himself to make him work in our favour.

However, the letter also asked the minister to make the appointment on an interim basis 'so that we may', it concluded, 'use this circumstance as a rein in order to guide him in a way that will suit our purposes'.[31]

Using these tactics, the ministers of the interior could even create official lists of candidates in congressional races by naming individuals who had never lived in the region they would represent. This was, again, more common in provinces and districts of little economic importance, whose local notables did not move in the highest circles of national society.

Still, opposition candidacies by either independent local figures or by coordinated national oppositions were a regular feature in elections throughout the nineteenth century. Table 2 presents a comprehensive view of the districts in which there was at least some electoral competition in lower house elections, the number of opposition deputies that were elected, and the number of districts where the difference in vote totals between winning and losing candidates was less than 15 per cent.

Table 2 shows that opposition candidacies appeared in half or more than half of all districts in six of the 20 elections, while there were such candidacies in a quarter to a half of all districts in eight elections. This is a considerable number, given the circumstances. Looking at this dimension from the bottom end, there were only four elections in which there were opposition candidacies in less than 20 per cent of the districts. This latter result is not easy to interpret, because the lack of electoral competition

Table 2
Numbers of Districts with Electoral Competition for Lower House Seats, and Numbers of Opponents Elected to the Chamber, 1831-1888

Year of Election	Districts Electing at least one Deputy*	Districts with Electoral Competition*	Seats Won by opponents	Districts with Close Elections**
1831	32	22 (69)	4	4
1834	37	18 (49)	0	2
1837	36	16 (44)	0	2
1840	38	31 (82)	9	5
1843	38	19 (50)	?	1
1846	38	?	?	?
1849	38	9 (24)	4	0
1852	39	4 (10)	?	2
1855	40	3 (7)	0	?
1858	43	11 (26)	15	5
1861	42	5 (12)	?	1
1864	43	29 (67)	14	11
1867	51	14 (27)	6	3
1870	49	13 (27)	40	3
1873	51	35 (69)	?	6
1876	55	24 (44)	37/28***	12
1879	54	7 (13)	?	1
1882	55	14 (25)	?	1
1885	63	44 (70)	4	2
1888	69	?	14	?

*The figures do not always correspond to the total number of districts because there is no information regarding who, if anybody, was elected in a small number of cases. Some districts chose only one deputy, while most elected two, and a few elected between three and ten (the latter being the case in Santiago).

**Districts with electoral competition are those in which there are more candidates than positions to be filled, even if losing candidates obtain only 1 vote. Close elections are those in which the difference between the winning candidate with the fewest votes and the losing candidate with the most votes is less than 15 % of the total vote. In some districts this result occurred between candidacies competing for the alternate deputy position.

***28 'independents' were also elected that year.

Source: Calculated from figures and reports of electoral outcomes in Urzúa Valenzuela, *Historia política de Chile y su evolución electoral,* chapters 3 and 4.

could be the product of either severe intimidation of opponents by the government (as in 1852 and 1855), of the opening of official candidacy lists to a broad spectrum of candidates (as in 1861), or of the political truce generated by the beginning of the War of the Pacific against Peru and Bolivia (which occurred in 1879). It is noteworthy that competition was quite high in the earlier years, despite the closeness of the 1829-1830 civil war. The elections of 1870 appear as the ones with the most victories by opposition candidates (40 of 99 seats), but this result may be more apparent that real because many liberals were elected as 'opponents' despite having the sympathies of Liberals in the government at a time of tension in the ruling Liberal-Conservative fusion. The elections of of 1876 stand out, therefore, as the ones in which the largest number of opponents were elected, especially since 28 'independents' also won.[32] The 1876 elections also have the greatest number of districts with close results, and they were the first to be held after 1874 reform that expanded the suffrage.[33] It seems to be the most democratic congressional election of the nineteenth century.

The Organisation of Electoral Campaigns

In addition to making provisions to register its voters and to ensure that they actually voted, electoral campaigns also had to present the candidates in public rallies and engage in public discussions of the issues at hand. Already in the 1840s there was a significant arena of public political debate aside from the chambers of Congress, and during electoral campaigns the partisans of one or another presidential candidacy or congressional or municipal list attempted to articulate all the reasons for which voters should support it. The almost nightly custom of evening meetings in private homes (*tertulias*), generally overseen by women and including music and conversation, turned to political discussions especially during electoral campaigns.[34] The major newspapers took positions, and a number of ephemeral ones, often with runs of less than a dozen or so numbers, would emerge to try to argue the case for or against particular candidates. During the 1846 presidential campaign, for instance, Manuel Bulnes, who was up for reelection, was favoured in Santiago and Valparaíso by *El Araucano, El Mercurio, El Progreso, El Orden, El Artesano del Orden, El Rayo, El Industrial, El Cívico de Valparaíso* and *El Mensajero*, while his opponent was championed by *El Artesano Opositor, El Guardia Nacional, El Voto Libre, El Artesano de Valparaíso, El Diario de Santiago, El Duende* and *El Pueblo*.[35]

As these titles indicate, some of the periodicals were specifically directed at an artisanal readership.[36] This is not surprising. Given the governments' early use of the national guards as voters to ensure its electoral victories, the artisanal, working- and lower-middle-class sectors that formed the majority of the civic troops were an important centre of attention during electoral campaigns. Opponents of the government tried to recruit artisans to their cause by sounding populist themes and stressing the need for social equality.[37] This also explains one of the noteworthy characteristics of mid-nineteenth-century Chile, namely, the development of political and cultural circles formed by opposition groups to try to capture the support of urban popular sectors. The first such clubs appear to have been formed in 1845, including one called Democratic Society (*Sociedad Demócrata*) and another one called Caupolicán Society.[38] The purpose, Amunátegui Solar notes, was to 'incorporate distinguished members of the working classes into their ranks, not only to obtain their votes in the elections, but also to take advantage of their influence over the soldiers of the national guard who gave the government great strength in the elections'.[39] The most noteworthy of these clubs became the *Sociedad de la Igualdad* (Society for Equality), which was created in April 1850. Although the majority of the opposition political leaders of the time who were then in the so-called Reform Club kept a certain distance from the Society after it acquired what was for them an excessively radical direction under the inspiration of Santiago Arcos and Francisco Bilbao, they protested energetically against Manuel Montt's government when it forced the Society's dissolution. The governments of the time countered these opposition efforts at organisation by sponsoring the formation of artisanal clubs as well. Such was, for instance, the purpose of *Sociedad de Artesanos de Valparaíso*, created in March 1846 as part of the Bulnes presidential campaign.[40] As a result of these practices, the politicisation of organised popular sectors has deep roots in Chilean republican history.

The increase in the size of the electorate in the mid-1870s was associated with a further development of public campaign styles. As noted earlier, both candidates in the presidential elections of 1876, Aníbal Pinto and Benjamín Vicuña Mackenna, were nominated in political conventions with representatives who came from all sections of the country. The main cities and towns of the central region were already connected by railways, and both candidates took to the trains in order to visit their organised supporters in electoral rallies. The Vicuña Mackenna campaign, opposed by the outgoing Liberal president and supported by the Conservatives, was especially noteworthy for its large gatherings and populist tone. Francisco Encina indicates that Vicuña's campaign stop in the central city of Talca was organised by

> Conservatives and other local notables (*potentados departamentales*) who had also become leaders in the war against the oligarchy... [They] prepared a grandiose reception. Between eight and ten thousand citizens received the candidate at the station and promenaded him triumphantly through the city....

Workers organised a separate rally.... . The 400 place banquet in his honour
that evening was attended by the majority of the high aristocrats of the
area.[41]

Both Pinto and Vicuña Mackenna also campaigned in favour of the
congressional and municipal candidates who belonged to the parties
supporting their presidential bids.[42] These national campaign tours became
an obligatory feature of presidential campaigns from then on.

During the course of the campaign, the ministers of the interior
received regular reports from their electoral agents in order to assess local
opinion and take any corrective measures, if need be, to ensure victory. As
one of Minister Varas's correspondents confidently indicated, 'if there
should arise an opposition we have a thousand means to make it fail'.[43] On
occasion, however, a pessimistic report presaged the victory of an
opposition list:

> It is necessary for me to speak to you in all frankness [began a letter addressed
> to Varas] ...I assured you that you would have many difficulties to overcome
> in order to win [in this district], and anything that may be said to the contrary
> will only come from impassioned men, without any prestige...[44]

In this case the possibilities of the official candidates must have been really
minimal, because the local electoral agents did have a broad arsenal of
tactics at their disposal.

The Mechanics of Voting

Voting took place over a two-day period during six hours each day. The
polls were set up in public places, generally in town squares. The officials
in charge of the proceedings were designated by lot from names proposed
by the municipal councillors, and as a result they normally favoured the
political views of the majority in the councils – which is to say that they
were usually partisans of the national government. However,
representatives of the opposition candidates were normally allowed to
observe the casting of the votes as well as their counting after the polls
closed. The votes were counted at the end of each day of voting. Therefore,
the candidates could assess their chances of winning the election on the
basis of the partial result generated by the first day.

Unlike electoral practices in Argentina, where voters were asked to
voice openly their electoral preferences before polling booth officials, in
Chile voting laws from the very beginning established a 'secret vote'.[45]

The normative expectation was always that each citizen had to be able to cast a vote without revealing its content to others. Violations of this normative standard were frequent, but they were seen as improper and reprehensible, as attested by countless debates in Congress and articles in the press throughout the nineteenth century.

Voters were supposed to present their *calificación* (qualifying certificate) at the voting table, where its number and other information would be checked against the records in the voter registry.[46] They were then allowed to deposit their vote, duly marked and folded to hide its content, in the ballot box. Describing an election he observed in Copiapó during the early 1840s, the Polish scientist Ignacio Domeyko noted that voters gave their ballots to the president of the vote reception table, who would then place it in the box 'rolled up, just as he received it – and in full view of the public'.[47] This practice was probably unusual. Each candidate list or independent candidacy had its own ballot, which had to be printed or written in, on a piece of white paper of a specified size. Voters had to come to the table with their ballots ready to be deposited in the box, i.e., marked, folded and sealed. (It is only with electoral reforms in 1890 that voters were obliged to mark their ballots in a separate area at the polling place before returning to the table to deposit them in the ballot box; this and other measures in the law led Cifuentes to assert that it 'introduced the novelty of the secret vote, to ensure the independence or liberty of the voter'.[48]) After voting, each citizen's *calificación* would be signed on the reverse side by the members of the vote reception board, with a notation indicating that the voter had already cast a ballot (*votó*) in that particular election. This presumably prevented voters from casting ballots more than once.

If these voting procedures had been implemented in good faith, the electoral system could have approximately reflected the distribution of political opinion among the politically active citizens. However, the documentary evidence contains so many references to abuses of the system by the authorities that such good faith was sorely lacking. The result was that many elections contained a significant degree of fraud in favour of the official lists of candidates, and this simply magnified the distortions already contained in the voter registration process.

After the registration of the individuals enrolled in the national guards, most commanders routinely, as Barros Arana indicates, 'collected the *calificaciones* to prevent, so they said, their getting lost'.[49] Many *calificaciones* would then end up on the Minister of the Interior's desk, and he would distribute them to whom he saw fit.[50] The Conservative politician Abdón Cifuentes notes that he even saw 'on the President's table two tall packages of *calificaciones* obtained by policemen' who had dressed in civilian country clothes (as *paisanos*) for that purpose.[51] The *calificaciones* were then given back to the civic guardsmen (or to policemen and petty state employees), who would then be organised by their commanders to vote. The ballots they received were not only appropriately marked to indicate a preference for the government candidate or candidates, but they also had some other external unofficial marking or even a number. In this manner the electoral agents of the government on the vote reception tables could verify that the guardsmen had voted as they were told.[52] Owners of mines, industries and land were also known to collect the *calificaciones* of their employees.[53]

Obviously, the national guard commanders and other officials or political leaders only gave back the *calificaciones* to the troops or other dependents when they were, as indicated by a US observer, Lieutenant MacRae, 'quite sure they will be used only in favour of their own candidates'.[54] Such dependents who tried to vote for the opposition risked brutal treatment on the part of the commanders or the authorities, including lashes and imprisonment.[55] But such events were exceptional. The small size of Chilean communes meant that most voters' political preferences were generally known. Family connections, bonds of friendship, economic dependency to influential individuals with well known political views, participation in political rallies, clubs, and even a close tie to the Church, were all cues that could be taken as signals of political allegiance and voting preference. And even if no effort had been made to mark the folded exterior of the ballots in any particular way, the small variations in the shades of white paper used to print the ballots, in the colour of the ink that was used, or in the size of the ballots made it relatively easy to identify if a voter was casting the appropriate one. Pedro Félix Vicuña even notes that in the 1846 election in Valparaíso 'all employees [public?] voted the first day with marked ballots made with coloured paper'.[56] In sum, given these and many other practices, some crude, some ingenious, the secret vote was not fully guaranteed and the electoral agents could ensure in most instances that their dependants and clientele voted as was expected of them.

But the system for such agents was not fully foolproof. The iconoclastic writer, mine owner and occasional politician, José Joaquín Vallejo, wrote a remarkable account of the tactics his campaign used in order to win a seat in the house of deputies in 1849 as an opposition candidate, and of the reception his victory received in the populace.[57] Vallejo at that point was identified mainly with the Liberal Party, which still retained the early so-called *pipiolo* identity it acquired from the conflicts of the period immediately following independence and of the 1829-1830 civil war.

The governor of Vallenar, one of the two departments in the district where Vallejo was a candidate, organised his electoral forces in the usual way, collecting a sizeable number of *calificaciones*. He then prepared the ballots with a characteristic mark and number, and distributed the *calificaciones* to his friends and family, as well as to Indians from a highland community. He told the latter that their lands would be expropriated if they did not follow his instructions. This procedure meant that the governor did not trust the local national guard troops, and in fact they did not follow his orders when he called on them to help control a crowd that was trying to prevent the Indians from approaching the voting tables. Such insubordination was doubly understandable since the governor was, in essence, pressing non-registered voters to cast ballots by using *calificaciones* that at least in some cases must have belonged originally to the guardsmen themselves. Moreover, the opposition produced ballots that imitated the markings and numbers used by the governor, and managed – given the confusion that occurred as scuffles broke out – to supplant its own ballots for those that the governor had put in a stack to distribute to his electoral contingent. As a result, some of the governor's surrogate voters in fact cast ballots for the opposition list without knowing it.

At the end of the first day the ballots were counted, and the governor was ahead in Vallenar only by a margin of 15 votes. This was not nearly enough to counteract the margin of victory the opposition was expected to receive – and did – in the other department, Freirina, whose governor had not been able to make the necessary arrangements to prevent the opposition majority from being reflected in the ballot box. Vallejo's forces in both departments protected the ballot boxes all night long between the first and the second day of voting. When the polls opened the next day, the same individuals organised to vote by the Vallenar governor showed up at the Vallenar voting tables once again, all in disguise, presenting other *calificaciones*. Liberal protests went unheeded by the vote reception officials, who pretended that all was normal. Many Vallejo voters in the department were unable to go to the polls because the governor had kept their *calificaciones*, and because the municipal authorities refused to give them the legally prescribed surrogate *calificaciones* alleging that they had no access to the voter registry books. Nonetheless, Liberal voters in Freirina once again gave Vallejo a greater margin of victory than the governor was able to secure in Vallenar, leading to celebrations and dancing that lasted well into the night after the ballots were counted. The following afternoon the general election results had to be proclaimed, after re-counting all the ballots from the two departments, in Vallenar. The residents of Freirina – including many women and children – attached a pennant to their ballot box with the words 'Union and Liberty', and marched it in a procession, some on horse back, some on foot, to Vallenar. They stopped at a country house where they were given refreshments, and toasts were raised to the victory expressing the hope that the rest of the Republic will also 'wake up'. Entering Vallenar, the procession was reorganised with 300 men on horseback. They carried the national flag in front, followed by the electoral commissioner with the ballot box. The box was flanked in turn by the new deputy to its right and someone carrying Freirina's pennant to its left. The calvacade made its way into the city through:

> streets full of jubilant and excited people; girls agitated their handkerchiefs and threw flowers as the ballot box made its way in front of their doors. The hurrahs, the rockets, and other exclamations and general happiness gave the festivities an ambience that was reminiscent of the one produced thirty years earlier with the victory of the heroes in the War of Independence.
> 'Thank God!' said a sixty-year-old Liberal (*pipiola*) woman, 'that we have once again witnessed events of our Motherland (*Patria*).'
> After depositing the box in the municipal hall, a banquet attended by citizens of all classes was held.... The dancing lasted until three in the morning.[58]

As this illustration shows, where there was electoral competition the government's agents could not automatically control even the voters in the national guards that were generally most susceptible to their influence. For this reason, in the larger cities there was already in the 1840s a market, in the literal sense of the term, for votes.[59] Some individuals sold their *calificaciones*, their votes, or for a price made themselves available to vote by pretending they were the person whose name appeared on a *calificación* that an electoral agent gave them. Judging from a list of 'new commandments' (*mandamientos nuevos*) that were printed by *El Artesano*, a Santiago newspaper that supported the government and that was directed at an artisanal readership, vote buying was probably a tactic to which oppositions resorted preferentially. Indeed, the very first 'commandment' stated peremptorily 'you will not give your vote for money' (*no darás tu sufragio por dinero*).[60] However, where the market existed, and when the votes of the national guards were not secure or not sufficient, the government also resorted to vote buying.[61]

The prices in this market for votes would increase or decrease depending on which candidate was estimated to be ahead at the time, or after the ballots were counted at the end of the first day, and by what margin. An account of the 1851 presidential elections in Santiago prepared by Lieutenant MacRae notes that under favourable circumstances voters could be paid up to 'half a doublon ($8.62)' for depositing a ballot, or for selling their *calificación*.[62] Electoral agents gave these voters a receipt which they could then exchange, after voting in the expected manner, for a counter-receipt that had to be presented to the campaign 'bank' for payment.[63] Hence, the campaign organisation included a considerable number of operatives to identify voters and others who were willing to engage in these transactions; to agree on a price; to make sure that the voter could reach the voting table through the tight throng of people the contending campaign organisation would also place in front of it to prevent such access; to observe the voting at the table in order to verify that individuals whose votes had been bought actually kept their bargain; to complain to voting-table officials when fraud was committed by the other side; and to deliver the necessary monetary pay-offs after those who had struck a deal had voted as expected. Moreover, the campaigns had to have agents who circulated from one table to the next throughout the city's subdivisions in order to keep tabs on which tables needed reinforcement, i.e., where more money needed to be spent. This information was vital to the central campaign headquarters not only in order to mobilise voters to the deficitary tables, but also to calculate the market price for the votes. Each one of these operators had a special name, as can be seen in MacRae's account:

> Headquarters were established in the house of one of the leading men near the center of the city, and there a bank was formed by subscription of all the wealthy men belonging to the ministerial party. Branch banks, drawing supplies from the central coffer, were instituted near each poll; about which last, three distinct classes of men were employed. The most numerous were the *apretadores* (pressers), whose business it was to jostle or intimidate from the polls as many opposition voters as possible, and facilitate the entrance or exit of their friends. A few intelligent men were stationed inside of the *apretadores*, to answer objections, challenge votes, and exchange checks with those whose votes had been purchased by their friends – a precaution necessary to prevent fraud by the vendor. Outside and circulating among the crowd was the third portion – the purchasers. These, on concluding a bargain, gave the vendor a check, with which and his vote he repaired to the polls, deposited his ballot, and received the counter-check from one of the 'intelligent' gentlemen standing near. This counter-check was an order on the local branch bank for the market value of the vote, regulated by the central institution, through intercourse constantly kept up by men on horseback, whom they called *vapores* (steamboats). Thus, when a steamer arrived from San Lázaro with intelligence that the opposition was very strong, and a majority of the voters were of that party, reinforcements of men and money were despatched there, the former

having orders to hustle their opponents away from the ballot-box, and raise the price for votes one, two, or four dollars, as might be necessary. When another came from La Catedral with news that their friends carried everything before them, the *apretadores* were withdrawn, and a diminution ordered for the sum to be paid for votes. Although there was no actual great necessity for economizing, yet, under this system, no more money was expended than was essential to secure their objects, and uniformity of action was preserved in all the parishes. Their bank seemed inexhaustible.[64]

These illustrations from the provincial north and from Santiago show that even though the procedures were basically fraudulent, the fraud did not consist of stuffing the ballot boxes with a large number of ballots. Voters had to go through the process of registering, and each had to show a *calificación* (whether his own or someone else's) in order to deposit a ballot. The numbers of votes were always fewer than the numbers of registered voters. The irregularities in the procedures centred on mechanisms to control voter access to the ballot box.

Conclusions

Is it appropriate to dismiss the electoral practices of the Chilean nineteenth century as a mere manifestation of an 'oligarchic', 'aristocratic', or 'patrician' system of little relevance to the masses and to the future development of the nation's democracy? This chapter has presented evidence that such characterisations are in need of deep revision.

It is certainly not true that Chile's *suffrage censitaire* meant that only the rich voted. Given the peculiar electoral practices that have been described here, the participation of especially the urban popular sectors was of great significance. Moreover, as elections were observed and celebrated (no doubt on some occasions more than in others) by a much larger number of men, women and even children than the small numbers of actual male voters would seem to indicate, it cannot be said that elections had little impact on national society. The nineteenth-century's electoral practices and political divisions forged enduring partisan loyalties in the electorate. Thus, until the 1920s, the main parties that emerged from the mid-nineteenth century, namely, the Conservative, Liberal and Radical Parties, obtained an average of about 75 per cent of the national vote in congressional elections, and until the late 1940s they received an average of about 56 per cent in the same elections.[65] The parties that emerged in connection with the labour movement, beginning in 1887 with the

Democratic Party, a splinter from the Radical trunk, had difficulty reaching their full electoral potential because the political attachments of many popular sector voters had already been cast by the previous decades. These results were obtained after the 1888 to 1891 electoral law and post-civil-war political changes significantly altered electoral practices: the voting was moved into public buildings instead of being held outdoors, voters were instructed to move to a separate area with a table or desk to choose and mark ballots, the voter registry did not have to be renewed prior to each electoral year, the *calificaciones* that could be used to supplant voters were abolished, the ministry of the interior no longer composed official lists of candidates, and the government no longer intervened directly in determining the outcome of elections. Hence, the parties no longer had to contend with blatant interference by the executive in mobilising voters.

The often noted strength and endurance of the Chilean parties have nineteenth-century origins. They were able to generate loyalties among the populace. Equally important is the fact that they forged strong organisations binding together sizeable numbers of the more militant and politically engaged individuals that exist in any national society. Not only did the parties have to find the necessary individuals to fill all the positions that were available, from local to national government, including membership in the electoral juntas, but they also had to rely on the efforts of a considerable number of individuals to make sure that their voters actually voted, and to control and observe the various phases of the electoral system – from registration to vote counting. The above-noted descriptions of the actual voting show that the process demanded a very exacting and coordinated effort. Paradoxically, it is very likely that the organisational demands on parties would have been much simpler had there been more massive numbers of voters without a voter registry system and much easier access to the voting tables.

The numbers of actual voters for decades after 1891 continued to be relatively small, mostly because a large number of potential voters did not bother to register and/or to vote. Perhaps this was because elections were seen not only as a means to choose political leaders and exercise a right of citizenship, but also as an act of partisanship and militancy – or an opportunity to earn some money by selling one's vote – that many people preferred to shun. If so, this was also a nineteenth-century legacy, given the large numbers of voters who participated in them as part of well-organised groups. The literacy requirement to vote was kept as well; the parties of the centre and the left, in particular, did not favour abolishing it because they relied to a significant extent on the printed word to propagate their views. Moreover, illiteracy was higher in rural areas, where the parties of the right had a stronger presence.

The nineteenth-century's electoral practices, despite their unfairness and irregularities, also had state institution-building effects. The voter registries had to be set up, *calificaciones* had to be printed, records had to be kept of who was and was not a voter, and even tax-payer lists for each municipal ward had to be updated for the registration process. The whole system was also based on the law. Hence, voters who felt they were unfairly treated in the registration process appealed to the courts, which had to hear their cases quickly to settle the matter before the actual election. Moreover, opposition commentators in the newspapers could point to the deviations between the laws and the rights of citizens and the actual practices, and opposition legislators could argue the case in the chambers for legal changes to eradicate fraudulent practices.

By the final decade of the nineteenth century no one openly disputed that electoral practices had to be purified. There had to be a correct registry of voters, there had to be paper ballots, and the vote had to be secret. While complaints of electoral irregularities continued over the next decades – generally centring on vote buying – the electoral results did begin to reflect the relative strength of the Chilean electorate's various political tendencies. In this sense Chile had the essential legal-institutional and party-organisational elements of a democracy in place by the early twentieth century. Yet this was only the case because many of these aspects of Chilean democracy were wrought from nineteenth-century origins as legislators and party leaders sought to free the electoral system from control by the executive in what was, as a result, an authoritarian or pre-democratic polity.

Notes

1. Germán Urzúa Valenzuela, *Historia política de Chile y su evolución electoral (Desde 1810 a 1992)* (Santiago, 1992), is the first book offering a comprehensive view of Chilean elections since the beginning. J. Samuel Valenzuela, *Democratización vía reforma: la expansión del sufragio en Chile* (Buenos Aires, 1985), is the first work that analyses nineteenth-century electoral politics and their contribution to Chilean democratisation.
2. See, for example, Ricardo Donoso, *Desarrollo político y social de Chile desde la Constitución de 1833* (Santiago, 1942), p. 69; Julio César Jobet, *Ensayo crítico del desarrollo económico-social de Chile* (Santiago, 1955), p. 40; Hernán Ramírez Necochea, *Historia del movimiento obrero en Chile. Antecedentes, siglo XIX* (Santiago, 1956), pp. 76-7; Julio Heise González,

150 años de evolución institucional (Santiago, 1960), p. 64; Nobert Lechner, *La Democracia en Chile* (Buenos Aires, 1970), p. 35; Luis Vitale, *Interpretación marxista de la historia de Chile. Ascenso y declinación de la burguesía minera: De Pérez a Balmaceda (1861-1891)* (Frankfurt, 1975), pp. 86-7; François-Xavier Guerra, 'Les Avatars de la représentation au XIXe siècle', in Georges Couffignal (ed.), *Réinventer la democratie: Le défi latino-américain* (Paris, 1992), pp. 52-3. Urzúa Valenzuela, *Historia política de Chile*, pp. 72, 87, 185, 233, firmly reasserts the first two premises, although he also provides evidence that contradicts the first one (see p. 62 for example). There are many differences between these authors on matters of interpretation that go beyond the above noted consensus. One of the main disagreements lies in the assessment of the significance of the 1874 reforms for the landholding groups. The extreme positions are given by Donoso, Lechner and Vitale; a revisionist view is contained in Valenzuela.

3.   See *Boletín de sesiones de la Cámara de Diputados*, Ordinary Session of 16 June 1872, p. 24, for Rodríguez's first suggestion of the key phrase. Although the role of the Conservatives in this crucial aspect of the electoral reform has been documented for the first time in Valenzuela, some prior sources have mentioned in passing that the Conservatives played a part in pressing for the approval of unspecified elements in the electoral law of 1874. For example, Donoso, *Las ideas políticas en Chile* (Santiago, 1967), p. 303, notes the fact that 'Radicals and Conservatives' defended certain aspects of the legislation against the opinion of the government.

However, of the two parties, the Conservatives were the most strongly in favour of reforming the whole electoral system. While the Radicals supported Rodríguez's phrase that expanded the size of the electorate, they broke with the Conservatives when it came to changing the vote counting procedures. The government Liberals were adamantly opposed to the Conservatives' attempt to institute the cumulative vote in all elections. Hence, they offered the Radicals a position in the cabinet if they did not support the Conservatives on this issue. The Radicals accepted the deal, and the cumulative voting system was adopted only for Deputy elections. A majority list system was retained for senators and for the presidential electoral college, while an incomplete list system reserving one third of the seats on municipal councils for the runner-up list was adopted for local government elections. See Valenzuela, *Democratización vía reforma*, pp. 104-5. The new government coalition between Radicals and Liberals was viewed as a sensational development at the time. For details, see Francisco Encina, *Historia de Chile* (Santiago, 1950), vol. XV, pp. 384-7.

4.   The phrase was contained at the end of Article 16 of the 1874 electoral law. The constitution required revisions of the electoral law every ten years in order to set the income and property qualification levels. Article 16 was the key article that fulfilled this requirement. Chile, *Bolétin de leyes y decretos del gobierno*, vol. XLII, no. 11 (Nov. 1874), p. 327.

5.   Urzúa Valenzuela, *Historia política de Chile*, p. 123.

6. See Valenzuela, *Democratización vía reforma*, p. 150, for figures regarding the size of the electorate from 1846 to 1912. The adult male literacy rate in the late 1870s was about 35%. The numbers of voters declined from these levels in the early 1880s because the Conservative party called on its voters to abstain from voting in the presidential elections and in most districts as a form of protest. The number of registrants and of voters declined further in 1885, and did not recover significantly in 1888, probably because there was little interest in participating in elections in which the only opposition force was the Conservatives. Liberals, Nationals and Radicals were all part of the governing alliance during the decade. The 1880s are not, therefore, the best decade to assess the extent of voter participation in the late-nineteenth-century. However, this is what Guerra does in his 'Les avatars de la représentation', p. 52. He is also incorrect in asserting that only five per cent of the 'adult male population' voted in 1885, because that is the percentage of registered voters over the *total* population that year.

7. The legal obligation to vote in Chile was instituted by a 1962 law. It is only then that the numbers of voters increased sharply; the small size of the voting public was first and foremost due to the apathy of potential voters. There is no space to develop this theme further here.

8. For a facsimile of these certificates, see Valenzuela, *Democratización vía reforma*, pp. 148-49.

9. Judicial records show that such appeals were by no means infrequent. For illustrations of such cases when citizens complained of their exclusion from the registry, despite their knowing how to read and write, after 1874, see *Gaceta de los Tribunales*, vol. XXXV, no. 1739 (13 May 1876), case nos. 708 and 709; and vol. XXXVII, no. 1860 (14 Dec. 1878), case no. 4692. The judges ruled in their favour.

10. A reference to such observers appears in the anticlerical newspaper *El Ferrocarril*, 2 Nov. 1875, p. 2. The article stresses that they must know people in the district in order not to be fooled by the practice of registering the same individuals under different names.

11. *El diablo denunciante de los abusos de las calificaciones*, Santiago, no. 1, 5 Dec. 1839, p. 1. *El diablo* was an opposition periodical that printed the circular to denounce this practice.

12. This discussion of the use of municipal taxpayer lists to appoint junta members is based on an anonymous article entitled 'Origen de las funciones electorales de los mayores contribuyentes', *Revista Chilena*, vol. XII (1878), pp. 311-5. Abdón Cifuentes, *Memorias* (Santiago, 1936), p. 105, notes that Manuel José Irarrázabal, the Conservative Party leader and senator, suggested the extension of the largest taxpayer mechanism to the *Juntas Calificadoras*. Though usually reliable, Cifuentes's memoirs, written when he was very elderly, may be incorrect on this point.

13. This matter is discussed in Erika Maza Valenzuela, 'Catolicismo, anticlericalismo, y la extensión del sufragio a la mujer en Chile', *Estudios Públicos*, forthcoming.

14. *Boletín de sesiones de la Cámara de Diputados*, ordinary session of 7 Oct. 1969, p. 462. The speech was part of the minority report of the committee that reviewed the 1869 legislation on electoral registries.
15. Valenzuela, *Democratización vía reforma*, p. 150.
16. Pedro Félix Vicuña, *Cartas sobre la situación de la República y la crisis electoral* (Valparaíso, 1870), p. 21.
17. Lieut. James M. Gilliss, A. M., *The U. S. Naval Astronomical Expedition to the Southern Hemisphere During the Years 1849-'50-'51-'52. Chile. Its Geography, Climate, Earthquakes, Government, Social Condition, Mineral and Agricultural Resources, Commerce, etc., etc.* (Washington, 1855), vol. I, p. 129.
18. *Ibid.*
19. The transitory article stipulated that such illiterates could vote until 1840. In 1842, after a heated congressional debate, the government enacted a law interpreting the transitory constitutional provision as referring only to *new* registrants after 1840.
20. General Tomás de Iriarte, *Panoramas chilenos del siglo XX* (Santiago, 1965), p. 89. The portions referring to Chile in this diary were retrieved from the original manuscript by Gabriel Balbontín Fuenzalida, who wrote its prologue and notes.
21. Diego Barros Arana, *Un decenio en la historia de Chile, 1841-1851* (Santiago, 1906), vol. II, p. 458.
22. Gilliss, *U. S. Naval Expedition*, p. 129. On p. 258, Gilliss notes that *barreteros*, the miners who broke into the ore and hence had higher skills, earned 25 pesos per month, while the *apires*, those who hauled the ore, made 12 pesos per month. The latter (assuming they were of age) would apparently not have the requisite 150 pesos in the provinces to vote, except that miners also received, in addition, food for themselves and their families. Hence, if the value of this food supplement were added to their income, even the *apires* surpassed the required income.
23. *Boletín de sesiones del Senado*, extraordinary session of 28 Sept. 1874, p. 54. Despite Irarrázabal's implication that these income levels were 'set' in 1864, they were simply restated from the earlier decennial electoral laws. As noted above, they were never raised after 1834. By the 1870s, given the expansion of the Chilean economy during those decades, it is very likely that income levels had risen. Inflation only became a persistent feature of the Chilean economy after the mid-1870s.
24. All those with 'public employment' could register automatically, as the president of a Qualifying Junta is alleged to have said in 1839. See *El diablo denunciante de los abusos de las calificaciones*, Santiago, no. 3 (9 Dec. 1839), p. 1. For a typical electoral law stipulating that individuals appearing on these lists were presumed to have the requisite income, see *Boletín de las leyes y decretos del gobierno,* Santiago, vol. XXIX, no. 9 (Sept. 1861), articles 31-7 on pp. 213-5.
25. Gilliss, *U.S. Naval Expedition*, p. 305, mentions a practice he attributes to

landowners, of issuing bogus salary certificates to their dependants to 'qualify' them to vote. He notes that the resulting contracts were later annulled.

26. Valenzuela, *Democratización vía reforma*, p. 119.
27. See Martín Palma, *Los candidatos* (Santiago, 1871), pp. 98-9 for a listing of their names.
28. For a description of these elections, see Barros Arana, *Un decenio en la historia de Chile*, vol. II, pp. 277-85.
29. For an example of an intendant's efforts to solicit the assistance of wealthy individuals to build railways and roads, see *Memoria que el Intendente de Coquimbo presenta al señor ministro del interior dando cuenta de todos los ramos de la administración de la provincia de su mando* (La Serena, 1855), pp. 31-5.
30. Cifuentes, *Memorias*, vol. I, p. 149.
31. Miguel Varas Velásquez, *Correspondencia de don Antonio Varas sobre la candidatura presidencial de don Manuel Montt* (Santiago, 1921), pp. 244-5. In this case the correspondence refers to the presidential campaign of Manuel Montt. The *intendente* later informed Varas that the victory was assured, which meant that he probably thought that the appointment had had the desired effect.
32. Urzúa Valenzuela, *Historia política de Chile*, p. 239. 108 deputies were elected that year, which left the government with a minority of 43 deputies pledged to it.
33 80,346 votes were cast that year, up from 25,981 in the previous lower house election. Valenzuela, *idem*, p. 150.
34. See Gilliss, *The U.S. Naval Astronomical Expedition*, pp. 144-5 for a description of the *tertulias* as social institutions, including the role of women in them; and p. 305 for a reference to their political function during electoral campaigns.
35. This listing is drawn from *El Cívico de Valparaíso. Periódico popular dedicado a los artesanos*, Valparaíso, no. 2 (15 Mar. 1846), p. 1. The first three newspapers were major ones with daily editions and a national circulation.
36. Some, such as *El Cívico de Valparaíso* which was created to support Bulnes's presidential campaign, even circulated free of charge.
37. *El Cívico de Valparaíso*, no. 4 (25 Mar. 1846), p. 1, goes to great lengths in denouncing these opposition appeals, and in condemning a demonstration by artisans in Santiago on 8 Mar. 1846 that led to acts of violence. *El Pueblo*, the periodical published in Santiago, was apparently one of the most radical. It presented 'subversive ideas' according to Amunátegui and Amunátegui, and seems to have had ties to the organisers of the 8 Mar. 1846 demonstration; Miguel Luis Amunátegui and Gregorio Víctor Amunátegui, *D. José Joaquín Vallejo* (Santiago, 1866), p. 126.

Writing from his exile in Perú, where he was sent for attempting to organise opposition to the government in the elections of 1846, Pedro Félix Vicuña, a Liberal leader from Valparaíso, explains that the opposition deliberately tried to capture the support of the militias because it was the most important source of votes for government candidates. Vicuña notes that his party was quite successful in this attempt, and that in the elections the government had to resort to buying votes and to high-handed repression in order to win. See Pedro Félix Vicuña, *Vindicación de los principios e ideas que han servido en Chile de apoyo a la oposición en las elecciones populares de 1846* (Lima, 1846), pp. 40-41, 52.

38. *El Guardia Nacional*, Santiago, no. 1 (6 Feb. 1846), p. 1, mentions the formation in late 1845 of the *Sociedad Demócrata*, for young people, together with 'two or three societies of artisans'. Domingo Amunátegui Solar, *Historia Social de Chile* (Santiago, 1932), p. 93, mentions the *Sociedad Caupolicán*. According to Amunátegui and Amunátegui, *El Pueblo* was also linked to 'various clubs of people of the last class that the opposition had organised', p. 126.

39. Amunátegui Solar, *Historia Social de Chile*, p. 93. *El Guardia Nacional, idem*, also says that the 'societies of artisans ... had the purpose of preparing public sentiments (*espíritu público*) for the elections'. It should be added that the governments and their opponents also saw the guards as a military force that could be a strategic asset if political disputes lead to armed conflict.

40. See *El Cívico de Valparaíso*, Valparaíso, no. 3 (22 Mar. 1846), p. 1. The club appears to have been called first the Society of Order Composed by the Artisans of Valparaíso (*Sociedad del Orden Compuesta de los Artesanos de Valparaíso*). Vicuña, *Vindicación de los principios e ideas*, states parenthetically that the Society of Order only pretended to support the government, and that in fact it 'hoped for its ruin', p. 46. However, he offers no further explanation.

   The conservatives, with their Josephine Worker Societies (*Sociedades Josefinas de Obreros*) and Catholic Worker Circles, also tried years later to establish political support among workers by creating cultural and social circles. Cifuentes, *Memorias*, mentions these groups repeatedly, vol. 2, pp. 149-54; 189-92; 239; 244; 249-51.

41. Francisco Encina, *Historia de Chile* (Santiago, 1955), vol. XV, p. 505.

42. Nonetheless, after the congressional elections had taken place, disagreements developed between Vicuña, who was a Liberal, and the Conservatives. As a result Vicuña finally withdrew his candidacy before the presidential electors were chosen.

43. Varas, *Correspondencia*, p. 264.

44. Varas, *idem*, p. 195.

45. For an analysis of the first electoral laws enacted in Chile, see Juan B. Hernández E., 'Las primeras leyes electorales chilenas', *Revista de Historia y Geografía*, vol. XI, no. 38 (2nd trimester 1921).

46. The qualifying certificates were abolished by electoral reforms in 1888; Urzúa Valenzuela, *Historia política de Chile y su evolución electoral*, p. 234.

47. Ignacio Domeyko, *Mis viajes* (Santiago, 1978), vol. 1, p. 412. Domeyko spent most of his adult life associated with the University of Chile.

48. Cifuentes, *Memorias*, vol. II, p. 288. Cifuentes adds that 'the parties' (not government agents) had invented many tricks to figure out how people voted

despite the changes. And yet, the notion that voting preferences were supposed to be secret was, as noted above, much older than he indicates. The 1890 electoral law also ended the obligation to re-register prior to each election, and introduced a permanent electoral registry. In 1912 the registry was completely renewed. Subsequently, electoral registries were valid for ten years until 1958, when they were made permanent once again.

49. Barros Arana, *Un decenio en la historia de Chile*, vol. 1, p. 99. This practice was so widespread that the pro-government periodical *El Artesano*, Santiago, no. 1 (7 June 1841), p. 3, defended it by saying that national guard officers were not 'robbing us of our property', as claimed by an opposition sheet, but simply acting as 'our depositories' before returning the *calificaciones* the night before the elections.

50. When Antonio Varas took over the Ministry after President Bulnes dismissed Manuel Camilo Vial from the office, he had to figure out who had received the *calificaciones* from Vial and how to recover them. One of his correspondents advised him that 'in this district, with very few exceptions, the only persons who are qualified to vote belong to the civic militia, and to the rural cavalry squadrons. It is known that Vial left the *calificaciones* of these troops with Rafael Cruz.' Varas, *Correspondencia*, p. 82, letter dated 18 June 1850.

51. Cifuentes, *Memorias*, vol. 1, pp. 68-9. The use of the police for this purpose increased in the 1870s as the national guard voters declined as a proportion of the total number of voters.

52. On the markings and even the numbering of ballots see Amunátegui and Amunátegui, *D. José Joaquín Vallejo*, p. 147.

53. See Domeyko, *Mis viajes*, pp. 410-11.

54. Gilliss, *The U.S.Naval Astronomical Expedition*, p. 305. MacRae was a member of Gilliss's scientific team.

55. Gilliss relates that a porter working for his astronomical observatory declined to turn over his *calificación* to a former employer, having since ceasing to work for him 'imbibed in other notions'. After an altercation between the two, 'José was furnished with lodgings at the expense of the municipality', p. 307. For testimonies of beatings of troops who did not follow voting directives see Valenzuela, *Democratización vía reforma*, pp. 65-6.

56. Vicuña, *Vindicación de los principios e ideas*, p. 51.

57. The account was published days after the election in *El Copiapino*, Copiapó, no. 14 (13 Mar. 1849), and is reprinted in Amunátegui and Amunátegui, *D. José Joaquín Vallejo*, pp. 145-56.

58. Amunátegui and Amunátegui, *D. José Joaquín Vallejo*, pp. 155-6.

59. Domeyko also mentions that some voters sold their *calificaciones* in Copiapó, often more than once; *Mis viajes*, pp. 411-12.

60. *El Artesano*, Santiago, no. 2 (20 June 1841), p. 3.

61. This is noted, as indicated previously, by Vicuña, *Cartas*, p. 52.

62. Gilliss, *The U.S. Naval and Astronomical Expedition*, p. 307. These being 1850s dollars, the $8.62 must have represented a tidy sum. The reference

buttresses the notion that where there was electoral competition, and such was always the case in Santiago, it was of great intensity.

63. Gilliss, *idem*, p. 306.
64. *Idem*.
65. These averages include the votes for all splinter groups from the Liberal, Radical and Conservative parties that did not eventually become different parties altogether. The averages are calculated from data in Urzúa Valenzuela, *Historia política de Chile*.

SELECTED BIBLIOGRAPHY

Abel, C. *Política, iglesia y partidos en Colombia* (Bogotá, 1987).

Alamán, L. *Historia de México desde los primeros movimientos que prepararon su Independencia en el año 1808 hasta la época presente*, México, 1850, 5 vols.(ed. facs., Mexico 1985).

Albán Gómez, E. 'Evolución del sistema electoral ecuatoriano' in *Tribunal Supremo Electoral, Elecciones y democracia en el Ecuador*, vol. I. *El Proceso electoral ecuatoriano* (1989).

Almond, G. A. and S. Verba, *The Civic Culture: Political Attitudes and Democracy in Five Nations* (Princeton, 1963).

Alonso, P. 'Politics and elections in Buenos Aires, 1890-1898', *Journal of Latin American Studies*, vol. 25 (1993).

'The Origins of the Radical Party, 1889-1898', unpubl. D.Phil. diss., Oxford University (1992).

Alvarez Junco, J. *El emperador del paralelo. Lerroux y la demagogia populista* (Madrid, 1991).

Amézquita, A. M. *Defensa del clero español y americano y guía geográfico-religiosa del Estado Soberano de Cundinamarca* (Bogotá, 1882).

Amunátegui, M. L. *La Crónica de 1810* (Santiago de Chile, 1911).

Amunátegui, M. L. and Gregorio Víctor Amunátegui, *D. José Joaquín Vallejo* (Santiago, 1866).

An Impartial Statement... of the Late Election (London, 1818).

Anderson, M. L. *Windthorst. A Political Biography* (Oxford, 1981).

'Voter, Junker, Landrat, Priest: The Old Authorities and the New Franchise in Imperial Germany', *American Historical Review*, vol. 98, no. 5 (Dec. 1993).

'The Kulturkampf and the Course of German History', *Central European History*, vol. 19 (Mar. 1986).

'Inter-denominationalism, Clericalism, Pluralism: The *Zentrumsstreit* and the Dilemma of Catholicism in Wilhelmine Germany', *Central European History*, vol. 21, no. 4 (1990).

'Piety and Politics: Recent Work in German Catholicism', *Journal of Modern History*, vol. 63 (Dec. 1991).

Anderson, M. L. and K. Barkin, 'The Myth of the Puttkamer Purge and the Reality of the Kulturkampf', *Journal of Modern History*, vol. 54, no. 4 (Dec. 1982).

Anna, T. *Spain and the Loss of America* (Lincoln, Neb., 1983).

La caída del gobierno español en Ciudad de México (Mexico, 1979).

Anon. *Los partidos políticos en Colombia* (Bogota, 1922).

Anon. *The Franchise and Registration Question* (London, 1841).

Anon. 'Origen de las funciones electorales de los mayores contribuyentes', *Revista Chilena*, vol. XII (1878).

Artola, M. *Los orígenes de la España contemporánea* (Madrid, 1959).

La España de Fernando VII (Madrid, 1968).

Auchmuty, J. J. 'Acton's Election as an Irish Member of Parliament', *English Historical Review*, vol. 61 (1946).

Ayala, E. *Lucha política y origen de los partidos en Ecuador* (1982).

Barón, F. *La reforma electoral* (Bogotá, 1915).

Barros Arana, D. *Un decenio en la historia de Chile, 1841-1851* (Santiago, 1906).

Bayona Posada, E. *Memorias de un ochentón* (Bogotá,1984).

Bellingeri, M. *Conflictos y dispersión de poderes en Yucatán (1780-1831),* in A. Annino and R. Buve (co-ord), *El liberalismo in Mexico* (Hamburg, 1993).

Ben-Ami, S. *Fascism from Above. The Dictatorship of Primo de Rivera in Spain, 1923-1930* (Oxford, 1983).

Berruezo, M.T. *La participación americana en las Cortes de Cádiz (1810-1814)* (Madrid, 1986).

Bew, P. *Land and the National Question in Ireland, 1858-82* (Dublin, 1982).

Blackbourn D. *Class, Religion and Local Politics in Wilhelmine Germany. The Centre Party in Württemberg before 1914* (New Haven, Ct., 1980).

Bodewig, H. *Geistliche Wahlbeeinflussungen in ihrer Theorie und Praxis dar gestellt* (Munich, 1909).

Borja y Borja, R. *Derecho constitucional ecuatoriano* (Madrid, 1950).

Borsay, P. 'All the Town's a Stage: Urban Ritual and Ceremony, 1600-1800', in P. Clark (ed.), *The Transformation of English Provincial Towns* (London, 1974).

Botana, N. R. *El orden conservador. La política argentina entre 1880 y 1916* (Buenos Aires, 1977)

   'La reforma política de 1912', in M. Giménez Zapiola (comp.), *El régimen oligárquico. Materiales para el estudio de la realidad argentina (hasta 1930)* (Buenos Aires, 1975).

Brioschi, P. A. (Archbishop of Cartagena) *El clero y la política* (Cartagena, 1918).

Broderick, J. F. *The Holy See and the Irish Movement for the Repeal of the Union with England 1829-1847* (Rome, 1951).

Brown, R.M. *No Duty to Retreat. Violence and Values in American History and Society* (Oxford, 1991).

Bryce, J. *The American Commonwealth* (London and New York, 1895), vol. II.

Buldaín Jaca, B. E. (ed.), *Las elecciones de 1820. La época y su publicística* (Madrid, 1993).

Bushnell, D. 'El sufragio en la Argentina y en Colombia hasta 1853', *Revista del Instituto de Historia del Derecho*, vol. 19 (Buenos Aires, 1968).

   'La evolución del derecho del sufragio en Venezuela', *Boletín Histórico*, vol. 29 (Caracas, May 1972).

   'Voter participation in the Colombian election of 1856', *Hispanic American Historical Review*, vol. 51 (May 1971).

   'Aspectos de historia electoral colombiana del siglo XIX', *Política y Sociedad* (Tunja, 1975).

'Las elecciones presidenciales,1863-1883', *Revista de la Universidad Nacional de Medellín*, No. 18 (Nov. 1984).

The Making of Modern Colombia (Berkeley, 1993).

'Las Elecciones en Colombia: siglo XIX', *Credencial Historia* (Bogotá, Feb. 1994).

Calibán (E. Santos), *La Danza de las Horas y otros escritos* (Bogotá, 1969).

Callanan, F. *The Parnell Split, 1890-91* (Cork, 1992).

Cantón, D. *Elecciones y partidos políticos en la Argentina. Historia, interpretación y balance, 1910-1966* (Buenos Aires, 1973).

'El Sufragio Universal como agente de movilización', Documento de trabajo, Instituto Torcuato Di Tella, no. 19 (1966).

Carnero Arbat, T. 'Élite gobernante dinástica e igualdad política en España, 1898-1914', *Historia Contemporánea* (1992).

'La modernización del país valenciano durante la Restauración', in J. L. García Delgado (ed.), *España entre dos siglos, 1875-1931.*

Continuidad y cambio (Madrid, 1991).

Carr, R. *Spain, 1808-1975* (Oxford, 1982).

Carter, J. 'The Revolution and the Constitution', in G. Holmes (ed.), *Britain after the Glorious Revolution* (Basingstoke, 1969).

Casas, N. *Enseñanzas de la iglesia sobre el liberalismo por el Ilmo. Sr. Obispo T. de Adrianópolis, Vicario Apostólico de Casanare* (Bogotá, 1901).

Chapman, C. E. 'The Age of the Caudillos: A Chapter in Hispanic American History', *Hispanic American Historical Review*, vol. XII (1932).

Charnay, J. P. 'L'église catholique et les élections françaises', *Politique. Revue Internationale des Doctrines et des Institutions*, nos. 19-20 (July-Dec. 1962).

Chavarri Sidera, P. *Las elecciones de diputados a las Cortes generales y extraordinarias, 1810-1813* (Madrid, 1988).

Cifuentes, A. *Memorias* (Santiago, 1936).

Clark, S. *Social Origins of the Irish Land War* (Princeton, 1979).

Cohen, A. P. *The Symbolic Construction of Community* (Chichester, 1985).

Colombia, Registraduría Nacional de Estado Civil, *Historia electoral colombiana, 1810-1988* (Bogotá, 1988).

Connolly, S. *Religion and Society in Nineteenth-Century Ireland* (Dublin, 1985).

Corish, P. J. 'Irish College Rome: Kirby Papers', *Archivium Hibernicum*, vol. 31 (1973).

'Cardinal Cullen and the National Association of Ireland', *Reportorioum Novum: Dublin Diocesan Historical Record*, vol. 3 (1962).

(ed.), *A History of Irish Catholicism*, vol. 5, fasc. 2 (Dublin, 1967).

Cornblit, O. 'La opción conservadora en la política argentina', *Desarrollo Económico*, vol. 14, no. 56 (1975).

Cosío Villegas, D. *La constitución de 1857 y sus críticos* (Mexico and Buenos Aires, 1957).

Costeloe, M. P. 'Generals versus Politicians: Santa Anna and the 1842 Congressional Elections in Mexico', *Bulletin of Latin American Research*, vol. 8, no. 2 (1989).

Cruz Mina, M. 'Elecciones y partidos en Navarra, 1891-1923', in José Luis García Delgado (ed.), *La España de la Restauración. Política, legislación y cultura* (Madrid, 1985).

Cullen, D. 'Electoral Practices in Argentina, 1898-1904', unpubl. D. Phil. thesis, University of Oxford, 1994.

Cullen, L. M. 'The Hidden Ireland: Re-assessment of a Concept', *Studia Hibernica*, no. 9 (1969).

Dardé, C. 'El sufragio universal en España: causas y efectos', *Historia Contemporánea. Anales de la Universidad de Alicante*, no. 7 (1989-90).

'La larga noche de la Restauración, 1875-1900', in N. Townson (ed.), *El republicanismo en España, 1830-1977* (Madrid, 1994).

'Las elecciones de diputados de 1886', *Anales de la Universidad de Alicante. Historia Contemporánea*, no. 5 (1986).

'El sufragio universal en la práctica: la candidatura de José del Perojo por Santander en 1891 y 1893', in *Estudios de Historia Moderna y Contemporánea. Homenaje a Federico Suárez Verdeguer* (Madrid, 1991).

Deas, M. *Del poder y la gramática* (Bogotá, 1993).

'Algunas notas sobre el caciquismo en Colombia', *Revista de Occidente* (Madrid, Oct. 1973).

'La política', in B. Castro (ed.), *Historia de la vida cotidiana en Colombia*, (Bogotá, 1995).

'San Ezequiel Moreno: "El liberalismo es pecado"',*Credencial Historia*, no. 46 (Oct. 1993).

Deberes de los católicos en las próximas elecciones (Bogotá, 1848).

De Castro, A. *Historia de Cádiz y su provincia* (Cádiz, 1858)

Cortes de Cádiz. Complementos de las sesiones verificadas en la Isla de León y en Cádiz. Extractos de las discusiones, datos y noticias, documentos y discursos publicados en periódicos y folletos de la época (Madrid, 1913).

Deler, J. P. and Y. Saint-Geours, *Estados y naciones en los Andes* (Quito, 1986).

Delgado, J. *La Audiencia de México ante la rebelión de Hidalgo y el estado de Nueva España* (Madrid, 1984).

Demélas, M.-D. *L'invention politique. Bolivie, Equateur, Pérou au XIXe siècle* (Paris, 1992).

De Lara Ródenas, J. C. 'Política y lucha de partidos en la Huelva de la Restauración: las elecciones a Cortes de 1919', *Espacio, Tiempo y Forma*, Serie V, Historia Contemporánea (1990), vol. 3.

De Toreno, C. *Historia del levantamiento, guerra y revolución de España* (Madrid, 1953).

Diario de los trabajos de la Convención Nacional reunida en la capital de la república en el año de 1861 (Quito, 1861).

Di Tella, T., *et al.*, *Argentina, sociedad de masas* (Buenos Aires, 1965).

Ditscheid, Ä. *Matthias Eberhard, Bischof von Trier im Kulturkampf* (Trier, 1900).

Domeyko, I. *Mis viajes* (Santiago, 1978).

Donnelly Jr., J. S. *The Land and the People of Nineteenth-Century Cork: The Rural Economy and the Land Question* (London, 1975).

'The Social Composition of Agrarian Rebellions in early Nineteenth-Century Ireland', in P. J. Corish (ed.), *Radicals, Rebels and Establishments: Historical Studies XV* (Belfast, 1985).

Donoso, R. *Las ideas políticas en Chile* (Mexico, 1946).

Desarrollo político y social de Chile desde la Constitución de 1833 (Santiago, 1942).

Edwards, A. *El gobierno de don Manuel Montt, 1851-1861* (Santiago, 1932).

Elliot, J. H. *National and Comparative History. An Inaugural Lecture Delivered Before the University of Oxford* (Oxford, 1991).

Encina, F. *Historia de Chile* (Santiago, 1950).

Errázuriz, I. *Historia de la administración Errázuriz* (Santiago, 1935).

España, G. (ed.), *Los radicales del siglo XIX. Escritos políticos* (Bogotá, 1984).

Evans, E. J. *The Great Reform Act of 1832* (London and New York, 1994).

Falter, J. 'The Social Bases of Political Cleavages in the Weimar Republic, 1919-1933', in L.E. Jones and J. Retallack (eds.), *Elections, Mass Politics, and Social Change in Modern Germany. New Perspectives* (Washington, D.C., 1992).

Fernández Martín, M. *Derecho parlamentario español. Colección de Constituciones, disposiciones de carácter constitucional, leyes y decretos electorales para diputados y senadores, y reglamentos de las Cortes que han regido en España en el presente siglo* (Madrid, 1885).

Fiaich, T. O. 'Irish Poetry and the Clergy', *Léachtái Cholm Coille*, vol. 4 (1975).

Figueroa, P. P. *Historia de la revolución constituyente (1858-1859) escrita sobre documentos completamente inéditos* (Santiago, 1889).

Font, M. *Coffee, Contention and Change. The Making of Modern Brazil* (Cambridge, Mass., and Oxford, 1990).

Forner Muñoz, S. *Canalejas y el partido liberal democrático* (Madrid, 1993).

Forner, S. and M. García, *Cuneros y caciques* (Alicante, 1990).

Fusi, J. P *Política obrera en el país Vasco, 1880-1923* (Madrid, 1975).

Gabaldón, E. *Las elecciones presidenciales de 1835* (Caracas, 1986).

Gabriel, P. 'El Anarquismo en España', in G. Woodcock, *El anarquismo. Historia de las ideas y movimientos libertarios* (Barcelona, 1979).

García Ceballos, G. *Por un García Moreno de cuerpo entero* (Cuenca, 1978).

Garrido, M. *Reclamos y representaciones. Variaciones sobre la política en el Nuevo Reino de Granada, 1770-1815* (Bogotá, 1993).

Gash, N. *Politics in the Age of Peel. A Study in the Technique of Parliamentary Representation. 1830-1850* (New York, 1953).

Gibson, C. *Los aztecas bajo el dominio español 1519-1810* (Mexico, 1967).

Gilliss, Lieut. James M. *The US Naval Astronomical Expedition to the Southern Hemisphere During the Years 1849-'50-'51-'52. Chile. Its Geography, Climate, Earthquakes, Government, Social Condition, Mineral and Agricultural Resources, Commerce, etc., etc.* (Washington, 1855).

Gilmour, I. *Riot, Rising and Revolution. Governance and Violence in 18th-century England* (London, 1992).

Ginter, D. E. (ed.), *Whig Organization in the General Election of 1790* (Berkeley and Los Angeles, 1967).

González, F. 'Iglesia y estado desde la Convención de Ríonegro hasta el Olimpo Radical, 1863-1878', *Anuario colombiano de historia social y de la cultura*, Bogotá, no. 15 (1987).

González, J. V. *Filiación Histórica del Gobierno representativo argentino* (Buenos Aires, 1937).

González Angulo Aguirre, J. *Artesanado y ciudad a finales del siglo XVIII* (Mexico, 1980).

Götz von Olenhusen, I. 'Die Ultramontanisierung des Klerus. Das Beispiel der Erzdiözese Freiburg', in Wilfried Loth (ed.), *Deutscher Katholizismus im Umbruch zur Moderne* (Stuttgart, 1991).

Graf, W. *Kirchliche Beeinflussungsversuche zu politischen Wahlen und Abstimmungen als Symptome für die Einstellung der katholischen Kirche zur Politik* (Mainz, 1971).

Graf, H. *Die Entwicklung der Wahlen und politischen Parteien in Groß-Dortmund* (Hanover and Frankfurt a.M., 1958).

Graham, R. *Patronage and Politics in Nineteenth-century Brazil* (Stanford, 1990).

Guerra, F.-X. *Modernidad e independencias. Ensayo sobre las revoluciones hispánicas* (Madrid, 1992).

'Les avatars de la représentation au XIXe siècle', in G. Couffignal (ed.), *Réinventer la démocratie. Le défi Latino-Américain* (Paris, 1992).

'The Spanish-American Tradition of Representation, and its European Roots', *Journal of Latin American Studies*, vol. 26, pt. 1 (Feb. 1994).

Guerra, J. J. *Viceversas liberales* (Bogotá, 1923).

Habermas, J. *Strukturwandel der Oeffentlichkeit*, Nuewied, 1962, trad. ital. *Storia e critica dell'opinione pubblica* (Bari, 1971).

Hagen, W. 'The Junkers' Faithless Servants: Peasant Insubordination and the Breakdown of Serfdom in Brandenburg-Prussia, 1763-1811', in R. J. Evans and W.R. Lee (eds.), *The German Peasantry: Conflict and Community in Rural Society from the Eighteenth Century to the Present* (London, 1985).

Hamnett, B. R. *La política española en una época revolucionaria, 1790-1820* (Mexico, 1985).

Hanham, H. J. *Elections and Party Management* (Sussex, 1978).

Head, F. B. *A Fortnight in Ireland* (London, 1852).

Heise González, J. *150 años de evolución institucional* (Santiago, 1960).

Hernández J. B. E. 'Las primeras leyes electorales chilenas', *Revista de Historia y Geografía*, vol. XI, no. 38 (2nd trimester 1921).

Herr, R. 'Spain', in D. Spring (ed.), *European Landed Elites in the Nineteenth Century* (Baltimore, 1977).

Hoppen, K. T. *Ireland since 1800: Conflict and Conformity* (London, 1989).

Elections, Politics, and Society in Ireland, 1832-1885 (Oxford, 1984).
'Politics, the Law, and the Nature of the Irish Electorate, 1832-1850', *English Historical Review*, vol. 92 (1977).
'The Franchise and Electoral Politics in England and Ireland, 1832-1885', *History*, vol. 70 (1985).
'Landownership and Power in Nineteenth-Century Ireland: The Decline of an Elite', in R. Gibson and M. Blinkhorn (eds.), *Landownership and Power in Modern Europe* (London, 1991).
'Landlords, Society and Electoral Politics in Mid-Nineteenth-Century Ireland', *Past and Present*, no. 75 (1977).
'National Politics and Local Realities in Mid-Nineteenth-Century Ireland', in A. Cosgrove and D. McCartney (eds.), *Studies in Irish History presented to R. Dudley Edwards* (Dublin, 1979).
House of Commons, *Appendix to the Minutes of Evidence taken before Her Majesty's Commissioners of Inquiry into the State of the Law and Practice in respect to the Occupation of Land in Ireland* (London, 1845), 672.
Copy of the Shorthand Writer's Notes... and the Minutes of Evidence taken at the Trial of the Longford Election Petition (London, 1870), 178.
Minutes of Evidence taken before the Select Committee on the Mayo County Election Petition (London, 1857), 182 Sess. 2.
Report from Select Committee on Bribery at Elections; together with the Minutes of Evidence (London, 1835), 547.
Return of all Election Petitions alleging Intimidation or Undue Influence (London, 1866), 114.
Return of the Election Petitions alleging Bribery and Corruption (London, 1866), 77.
Return of the Number of Petitions complaining of Undue Returns (London, 1880), 69.
Huard, R. *Le suffrage universel en France, 1848-1946* (Aubier, 1991).
Humboldt, A. v. *Ensayo Político sobre Nueva España* (Mexico, 1965).
Hunley, J. D. 'The Working Classes, Religion and Social Democracy in the Düsseldorf Area, 1867-78', *Societas*, vol. 4, no. 2 (Spring 1974).
Heise González, J. *El período parlamentario, 1861-1925* (Santiago, 1982).
Iriarte, T. de *Panoramas chilenos del siglo XX* (Santiago, 1965).
Jahrbuch für die Amtliche Statistik des Preußischen Staates (Berlin, 1883).
Jensen, R. J. *The Winning of the Midwest. Social and Political Conflict, 1888-1896* (Chicago, 1971).
Jobet, J. C. *Ensayo crítico del desarrollo económico-social de Chile* (Santiago, 1955).
Johnson, T. (ed.), *The Poll for the Election* (Liverpool, 1790).
Jupp, P. J. 'Irish Parliamentary Elections and the Influence of the Catholic Vote, 1801-1820', *Historical Journal*, vol. 10 (1967).
Keenan, D. J. *The Catholic Church in Nineteenth-Century Ireland: A Sociological Study* (Dublin, 1983).
Kerr, D. A. *Peel, Priests and Politics: Sir Robert Peel's Administration and the*

Roman Catholic Church in Ireland, 1841-1846 (Oxford, 1982).

'Under the Union Flag: The Catholic Church in Ireland, 1800-1870', in Lord Blake (ed.), *Ireland after the Union: Proceedings of the Second Joint Meeting of the Royal Irish Academy and the British Academy, London, 1986* (Oxford, 1989).

Kishlansky, M. *Parliamentary Selection: Social and Political Choice in Early Modern England* (Cambridge, 1986).

Knowlton, S. R. *Popular Politics and the Irish Catholic Church: the Rise and Fall of the Independent Irish Party, 1850-1859* (New York, 1991).

Korn, F. *Buenos Aires. Una ciudad moderna* (Buenos Aires, 1981).

Kossok, M. 'Revolución, estado y nación en la Independencia', in I. Buisson *et al.* (eds.), *Problemas de la formación del estado y la nación en Hispanoamérica* (Bonn, 1984).

Larkin, E. *The Roman Catholic Church and the Creation of the Modern Irish State, 1878-1886* (Dublin, 1975).

The Roman Catholic Church and the Plan of Campaign, 1886-1888 (Cork, 1978).

'The Devotional Revolution in Ireland, 1850-75', *American Historical Review*, vol. 77 (1972).

The Making of the Roman Catholic Church in Ireland, 1850-1860 (Chapel Hill, 1980).

Lavrin, A. 'La riqueza de los conventos de monjas en Nueva España; estructura y evolución durante el siglo XVIII', *Cahiers des Amériques Latines*, no. 2 (1973).

Lechner, N. *La Democracia en Chile* (Buenos Aires, 1970).

Lepsius, M. R. 'Parteiensystem und Sozialstruktur: zum Problem der Demokratisierung der deutschen Gesellschaft', in G. A. Ritter (ed.), *Deutschen Parteien vor 1918* (Cologne, 1973)

Lira, A. *Comunidades indígenas frente a la ciudad de México. Tenochtitlán, Tlatelolco, sus pueblos, sus barrios, 1812-1919* (Mexico, 1983).

Lombardo Ruiz, S. *Antología de textos sobre la ciudad de México en el período de la Ilustración (1777-1792)*, INAH, Colección científica, no. 113 (1982).

López Estudillo, A. 'Federalismo, campesinado y métodos de restablecer el control político en la Restauración', in Conxita Mir Curcó (ed.), *Actituds politiques i control social a la Catalunya de la Restauració, 1875-1923* (Lleida, 1989).

Lord, J. *Popery at the Hustings: Foreign and Domestic Legislation* (London, 1852).

Lucas, E. *The Life of Frederick Lucas MP*, 2 vols. (London, 1886).

Luna F. 'Los hábitos políticos después de Caseros', *Todo es Historia*, Año XVII, no. 197, (Oct. 1983).

Lyons, F. S. L. *The Irish Parliamentary Party, 1890-1910* (London, 1951).

MacDonagh, O. 'The Politization of the Irish Catholic Bishops, 1800-1850', *Historical Journal*, vol. 18 (1975).

Macintyre, A. *The Liberator: Daniel O'Connell and the Irish Party, 1830-1847*

(London, 1965).

McCormick, R. *The Party Period and Public Policy. American Politics from the Age of Jackson to the Progressive Era* (New York and Oxford, 1986).

Maiguashca, J. (ed.), *Historia y región en el Ecuador, 1830-1930* (Quito, 1994).

Malo, B. *Escritos y discursos* (Quito, 1940).

Matienzo, J. N. *La práctica del sufragio popular. Breve estudio sobre la ley electoral argentina* (Buenos Aires, 1886).

Martínez de Velasco, A. *La formación de la Junta central* (Pamplona, 1972).

Mecham, J. L. *Church and State in Latin America*, revised edition (Austin, 1966).

Medina Castro, M. 'Proceso evolutivo del electorado nacional', in E. Ayala, (ed.), *La historia del Ecuador, ensayos de interpretación* (1985).

Memorial del señor General don Benjamín Herrera. Respuesta del Excelentísimo señor Presidente de la República (Bogotá, 1924).

Miller, D. W. 'The Roman Catholic Church in Ireland: 1898-1918', *Eire-Ireland*, vol. 3 (1968).

Miller, J. *The Glorious Revolution* (London, 1983).

Mora Reyes, A. *Don Manuel Carrión Pinzano y el gobierno federal de Loja y tres maestros lojanos* (Loja, 1959).

Morales, M. D. 'Estructura urbana y distribución de la propiedad en la ciudad de Mexico in 1813', *Historia Mexicana*, no. 25 (Jan-Mar. 1976).

Moreno Toscano, A. (comp.) *Ciudad de México, ensayo de construcción de una historia* (Mexico, 1978).

Morgan, E. S. *Inventing the People. The Rise of Popular Sovereignty in England and America* (New York, 1988).

Morsey, R. 'Der politische Katholizismus 1890-1933', in Anton Rauscher (ed.), *Der soziale und politische Katholizismus. Entwicklungslinien in Deutschland 1803-1963* (Munich, 1981).

Müller, K. 'Politische Strömungen in der Rechtsrheinischen Kreisen des Regierungsbezirks Köln (Sieg, Mühlheim, Wipperfürth, Gummersbach und Waldbröl) von 1879 bis 1900', unpubl. PhD thesis, Bonn, 1963.

Muñoz, B. N. *Crónicas de Guaca. La ruina de un pueblo* (Cúcuta, 1937).

Muñoz, F. de P. *Escritos y discursos* (Medellín, 1897).

Murillo Ferrol, F. *Estudios de sociología política* (Madrid, 1963).

Murphy, M. 'Repeal, Popular Politics, and the Catholic Clergy of Cork, 1840-50', *Journal of the Cork Historical and Archaelogical Society*, vol. 82 (1977).

Navas Blanco, A. *Las elecciones presidenciales en Venezuela del siglo XIX, 1830-1854* (Caracas, 1993).

Neubach, H. 'Schlesische Geistliche als Reichstagsabgeordnete 1867-1918. Ein Beitrag zur Geschichte der Zentrumspartei und zur Nationalitätenfrage in Oberschlesien', *Archiv für Schlesische Kirchengeschichte*, vol. 26 (1968).

Norman, E. R. *The Catholic Church and Ireland in the Age of Rebellion, 1859-1873* (London, 1965).

Nowlan, K. B. 'The Catholic Clergy and Irish Politics in the Eighteen Thirties and Forties', in J. G. Barry (ed.), *Historical Studies IX* (Belfast, 1974).

Núñez, R. *La reforma política en Colombia* (Bogotá, 1888).

O'Brien, C. C. *Parnell and his Party, 1880-90,* corrected impression (Oxford, 1964).

O'Ferrall, F. *Catholic Emancipation: Daniel O'Connell and the Birth of Irish Democracy, 1820-30* (Dublin, 1985).

'"The Only Lever..."? The Catholic Priest in Irish Politics, 1823-29', *Studies* (Dublin), vol. 70 (1981).

O'Gorman, F. *Voters, Patrons and Parties: The Unreformed Electorate of Hanoverian England, 1734-1832* (Oxford, 1989).

'Campaign Rituals and Ceremonies: the Social Meaning of Elections in England, 1780-1860', *Past and Present,* no. 135 (May 1992).

Ollero Prieto, M. L. 'La tolerancia religiosa en la constitución de 1876. Análisis de la campaña de protesta', in *Espacio, Tiempo y Forma,* Serie V (1990).

O'Shea, J. *Priest and Society in Post-Famine Ireland: A Study of County Tipperary, 1850-1891* (Dublin, 1983).

Ordenanza de la Nobilísima Ciudad de Mexico en cuarteles, creación de las alcaldías de ellos y regia de su gobierno, dada y mandada observar por el Exmo Señor Don Miguel de Mayaga (Mexico, 1782).

Ordoñez Yañez, R. Pbro, *Selección de Escritos* (Cúcuta, 1963).

Ortega y Gasset, J. *Discursos políticos* (Madrid, 1974).

Ozouf, N. *Festivals and the French Revolution* (Harvard University Press, 1988).
La fête révolutionnaire, 1789-1799 (Paris, 1976).

Palma, M. *Los candidatos* (Santiago, 1871).

Parra Pérez, C. (ed.), *La cartera del Coronel Conde de Adlercreutz* (Paris, 1928).

Patee, R. 'La época crítica de la historia ecuatoriana, 1857-1861', *Boletín del Centro de Investigaciones Históricas de Guayaquil* (1941).

Peralta, V. 'Elecciones, constitucionalismo y revolución: el Cusco entre 1809-1815', unpubl. paper presented at the Instituto Ortega y Gasset, Feb. 1994.

Pinzón de Lewin, P. *El ejército y las elecciones* (Bogotá, 1994).

Pitt-Rivers, J. *The People of the Sierra* (Chicago, 1971).

Plumb, J. H. *The Growth of Political Stability in England, 1675-1725* (London, 1967).

Polasky, J. L. 'A Revolution for Socialist Reforms: the Belgian General Strike for Universal Suffrage', *Journal of Contemporary History,* no. 27 (1992).

Posada-Carbó, E. 'Elections and civil wars in nineteenth-century Colombia: The 1875 presidential campaign', *Journal of Latin American Studies,* vol.2 6 , no. 3 (Oct. 1994).

'Elections under the Conservative Hegemony in Colombia, 1886-1930', paper presented at the Latin American Studies Association, XVIII International Congress, Atlanta, 10-12 March 1994.

Potter, A. L. 'The Failure of Democracy in Argentina, 1916-1930', *Journal of Latin American Studies,* vol. 13, pt. 1 (May 1981).

Prest, J. *Politics in the Age of Cobden* (London, 1977).

Prodi, P. *Il sacramento del potere. Il giuramento politico nella storia costituzionale dell'Occidente* (Bologna, 1992).

Quintero, R. 'El carácter de la estructura institucional de representación política en el estado ecuatoriano del siglo XIX', *Revista Ciencias Sociales*, vol. II, nos. 7-8 (1958).

Ramírez Necochea, H. *Historia del movimiento obrero en Chile. Antecedentes, siglo XIX* (Santiago, 1956).

Ramón, G. 'Los indios y la constitución del estado nacional', ponencia al *IX Simposio Internacional de historia económica: las comunidades campesinas de los Andes en el siglo XIX* (Quito, Mar. 1989).

Ranzato, G. 'Natura e funzionamento di un sistema pseudo-rappresentativo: la Spagna "liberal-democratica" 1875-1923', in *Suffragio, rappresentanza, interessi.Instituzioni e societá fra '800 e '900*. Annali della Fondazione Lelio e Lisli Basso-Issoco (Rome, 1989) vol. IX.

Raymond, H. B. 'English Political Parties and Electoral Organization, 1832-67' (Cambridge, Mass., 1952).

Recchini de Lattes, Z. L. *La Población de Buenos Aires. Componentes demográficos del crecimiento entre 1855 y 1960*, Instituto Torcuato Di Tella (Buenos Aires, 1971).

Remmer, K. *Party Competition in Argentina and Chile. Political Recruitment and Public Policy, 1890-1930* (Lincoln and London, 1984).

Repetto, N. *Mi paso por la política* (Buenos Aires, 1956).

Restrepo, J. P. *La Iglesia y El Estado en Colombia* (London, 1885).

Restrepo Posada, Mons. J. *Arquidiócesis de Bogotá. Datos biográficos de sus prelados*, 3 vols. (Bogotá, 1961-66).

La Iglesia en dos Momentos Difíciles de la Historia Patria (Bogotá, 1971).

Reynolds, J. A. *The Catholic Emancipation Crisis in Ireland, 1823-1829* (New Haven, 1954).

Rieu-Millan, M.-L. *Los diputados americanos en las Cortes de Cádiz* (Madrid, 1990).

Ritter, G. A. and M. Niehuss *Wahlgeschichtliches Arbeitsbuch. Materialen zur Statistik des Kaiserreichs 1871-1918* (Munich, 1980).

Roberts, J. (ed.), *Poll Book for the Northern Division* (Chesterfield, 1837).

Rodríguez Ayala, A. 'Elecciones y élites parlamentarias de Cádiz, 1903-1923', *Espacio, Tiempo y Forma*. Serie V, Historia Contemporánea (1990), vol. 3.

Rodríguez Labandeira, J. *El trabajo rural en España, 1876-1936* (Barcelona, 1991).

Rodríguez Piñeres, E. *Por Tierras Hermanas. De Bogotá, por Quito, a la frontera del Sur. Impresiones de un viaje* (Bogotá, 1918).

Robalino Dávila, L. *García Moreno* (Puebla, 1967).

Rohe, K. *Wahlen und Wählertraditionen in Deutschland* (Frankfurt a. M., 1992).

'German Elections and Party Systems in Historical and Regional Perspective:

An Introduction', in Rohe (ed.), *Elections, Parties and Political Traditions. Social Foundations of German Parties and Party Systems, 1867-1987* (New York, 1990).

'Konfession, Klasse und lokale Gesellschaft als Bestimmungsfaktoren des Wahlverhaltens. Überlegungen und Problematisierungen am Beispiel des historischen Ruhrgebiets', in L. Albertin and W. Link (eds.), *Politische Parteien auf dem Weg zur parlamentarischen Demokratie in Deutschland. Entwicklungslinien bis zur Gegenwart* (Düsseldorf, 1981).

Romero Maura, J. *La rosa de fuego. Republicanos y anarquistas: la política de los obreros barceloneses entre el desastre colonial y la semana trágica, 1899-1909* (Barcelona, 1975).

'El caciquismo', in J. A. Gallego (ed.), *Revolución y Restauración, 1868-1931* (Madrid, 1981).

Rosanvallon, P. 'The republic of universal suffrage', in B. Fontana (ed.), *The Invention of the Modern Republic* (Cambridge, 1994).

Ruppel H. G. and B. Groß (comp.), *Hessische Abgeordnete 1820-1933. Biographische Nachweise für die Landstände des Großherzogtums Hessen (2. Kammer) und den Landtag des Volksstaates Hessen* (Darmstadt, 1980).

Rust, H. *Reichskanzler Fürst Chlodwig zu Hohenlohe-Schillingsfürst und seine Brüder* (Düsseldorf, 1897).

Sáenz Peña, R. *Escritos y discursos* (Buenos Aires, 1935).

Sábato, H. 'Citizenship, Political Participation and the Formation of the Public Sphere in Buenos Aires, 1850-1880', *Past and Present*, no. 136 (1992).

Sábato H. and E. Palti, '¿Quién votaba en Buenos Aires?: Práctica y teoría del sufragio, 1850-1880', *Desarrollo Económico*, vol. 30, no. 119 (Oct-Dec. 1990).

Sábato, H. and Ema Cibotti, 'Hacer Política en Buenos Aires: Los Italianos en la escena pública porteña 1860-1880', *Boletín del Instituto de Historia Argentina Dr. E. Ravignani*, Tercera Serie, no. 2 (Sept. 1990). *Sangre y fraude. Testimonio de la tragedia boyacense* (Bogotá, 1949).

Sanucci, L. E. M. *La renovación presidencial de 1880* (La Plata, 1955).

Sargent, C. *The Spatial Evolution of Greater Buenos Aires, Argentina, 1870-1930* (Tucson, 1974).

Schwidetzky, I. *Die polnische Wahlbewegung in Oberschlesien* (Breslau, 1934).

Scobie, J. *Buenos Aires. Plaza to Suburb, 1870-1910* (New York, 1974).

Seignobos, C. *Histoire politique de l'Europe contemporaine. Evolution des partis et des formes politiques, 1814-1914* (Paris, 1924).

Seymour, C. *Electoral Reform in England and Wales. The Development and Operation of the Parliamentary Franchise, 1832-1885* (1915) (Hamden, 1970).

Seymour, C. and D. Paige Frary *How the World Votes. The Story of Democratic Developments in Elections*, 2 vols. (Springfield, Mass., 1918).

Shaw, P. *American Patriots and the Rituals of Revolution* (Cambridge, Mass., 1981).

Silbey, J. H. *The American Political Nation, 1838-1893* (Stanford, 1991).

Smith, H. S. 'Nationalism and Religious Conflict in Germany, 1887-1909', unpubl. PhD diss., Yale University, 1991.

Solís, R. *El Cádiz de las Cortes*, illustrated edn. (Madrid, 1987).

Solow, B. L. *The Land Question and the Irish Economy, 1870-1903* (Cambridge, Mass., 1971).

Sommariva, L. *Historia de las intervenciones federales en las provincias* (Buenos Aires, 1910-31).

Sowell, D. *The Early Colombian Labor Movement* (Philadephia, 1992).

Sperber, J. *Popular Catholicism in Nineteenth-Century Germany* (Princeton, 1984).

Suárez, F. *El proceso de convocatoria de las Cortes, 1808-1810* (Pamplona, 1982).

Stamm, C. *Dr. Conrad Martin Bischof von Paderborn, Ein biographischer Versuch* (Paderborn, 1892).

Steele, E. D. 'Cardinal Cullen and Irish Nationality', *Irish Historical Studies*, vol. 19 (1975).

Steil, H.-W. *Die Politischen Wahlen in der Stadt Trier und in den Eifel-und Moselkreisen des Regierungsbezirkes Trier 1867-1887* (Bonn, 1961).

Stengers, J. 'Histoire de la legislation électorale en Belgique', in S. Noiret (ed.), *Political Strategies and Electoral Reforms: Origins of Voting Systems in Europe in the 19th and 20th Centuries* (Baden Baden, 1990).

Steinbach, P. 'Reichstag Elections in the Kaiserreich: The Prospects for Electoral Research in the Interdisciplinary Context', in L. E. Jones *et al.* (eds.), *Elections, Mass Politics and Social Change in Modern Germany* (Cambridge, 1992).

Suval, S. *Electoral Politics in Wilhelmine Germany* (Chapel Hill, 1985). *The Picture of Parliament or a History of the General Election of 1802* (London, 1802).

Thoma, L. *Jozef Filsers Briefwexel* ([1912] Munich, 1981).

Thomson, G. 'Popular Aspects of Liberalism in Mexico,' *Bulletin of Latin American Research*, vol. 10, no. 3 (1991), pp. 265-92.

Tobar Donoso, J. 'El sufragio en el Ecuador', *Revista de la Asociación de Derecho* (1949).

Tocqueville, A. de *Journeys to England and Ireland*, (ed.), J. P. Mayer (London, 1958).

Torre, J. C. 'La primera victoria electoral socialista', *Todo es Historia*, no. 76 (Sept. 1973).

Torres, C. *Representación del cabildo de Santa Fé de Bogotá a la Suprema Junta Central de España, 1809* (Bogotá, 1960).

Trabucco, F. *Constituciones de la república del Ecuador* (Guayaquil, 1975).

Tusell, J. *Sociología electoral de Madrid* (Madrid, 1969).
Oligarquía y caciquismo en Andalucía, 1890-1923 (Barcelona, 1976).
'Para la sociología política de la España contemporánea: el impacto de la ley de 1907 en el comportamiento electoral', *Hispania*, vol. XXX, no. 116 (1970).

'El comportamiento electoral madrileño revisitado', in A. Bahamonde Magro *et al.* (eds.), *La sociedad madrileña durante la restauración* (Madrid, 1989), vol. II (ed.), *El sufragio universal* (Madrid, 1991).

Tussie D. A. and Andrés M. Federman, 'La larga marcha hacia las urnas', *Todo es Historia*, vol. VI, no. 71 (Mar. 1973).

Unamuno, M. de *Crónica política española, 1915-1923* (Madrid, 1977).

Underwood, D. *Revel, Riot and Rebellion* (Oxford, 1985).

Urzúa Valenzuela, G. *Historia política de Chile y su evolución electoral (desde 1810 a 1992)* (Santiago, 1992).

Valdano, J. *Ecuador: cultura y generaciones* (Quito, 1985).

Valderrama Andrade, C. *Un capítulo de las relaciones entre el estado y la iglesia en Colombia. Miguel Antonio Caro y Ezequiel Moreno* (Bogotá, 1986). (ed.), *Epistolario del Beato Ezequiel Moreno y otros Agustinos Recoletos con Miguel Antonio Caro y su familia* (Bogotá, 1983).

Valencia López, N. 'Periodismo panfletario y excomunión en el suroccidente colombiano (1912-1930)', *Historia y Espacio*, no. 14 (Cali, June 1991).

Valenzuela, J.M. *Democratización vía reforma: La expansión sufragio en Chile* (Buenos Aires, 1985).

Van Aken, M. *King of the Night: Juan José Flores and Ecuador, 1824-1864* (Berkeley, 1989).

Varas Velásquez, M. *Correspondencia de don Antonio Varas sobre la candidatura presidencial de don Manuel Montt* (Santiago, 1921).

Varela Ortega, J. *Los amigos políticos. Partidos, elecciones y caciquismos en la Restauración, 1875-1900* (Madrid, 1977).

Varela Ortega, J. and R. López Blanco, 'Historiography, Sources and Methods for the Study of Electoral Laws in Spain', in S. Noiret (ed.), *Political Strategies and Electoral Reforms: Origins of Voting Systems in Europe in the 19th and 20th Centuries* (Baden Baden, 1990).

Vaughan, W. E. *Landlords and Tenants in Ireland, 1848-1904* (Dublin, 1984).

Vaughan, W. E and A. J. Fitzpatrick (eds.), *Irish Historical Statistics: Population 1821-1971* (Dublin, 1978).

Vernon, J. *Politics and the People: A Study in English Political Culture, c.1815-1867* (Cambridge, 1993).

Vicuña, P. F. *Cartas sobre la situación de la República y la crisis electoral* (Valparaíso, 1870).

Vindicación de los principios e ideas que han servido en Chile de apoyo a la oposición en las elecciones populares de 1846 (Lima, 1846).

Villaseñor y Sánchez, *Theatro americano, descripción general de los reynos y provincias de la Nueva España, y sus jurisdicciones* (Mexico, 1748).

Vintimilla, M. A. 'Luchas campesinas en el siglo XIX y la Revolución Liberal de 1895', *Revista del IDIS*, no.8 (Cuenca, 1980).

Vitale, L. *Interpretación marxista de la historia de Chile. Ascenso y declinación de la burguesía minera: De Pérez a Balmaceda (1861-1891)* (Frankfurt, 1975).

Walter, R. 'Elections in the city of Buenos Aires during the first Yrigoyen administration. Social Class and Political Preferences', *Hispanic-American Historical Review*, vol. 58, no. 4 (Nov. 1978).

Weber, E. *Peasants into Frenchmen* (Stanford, 1976).

Weber, M. 'Beamtenherrschaft und politisches Führertum', in 'Parlament und Regierung in neugeordneten Deutschland', *Gesammelte Politische Schriften* (Tübingen, 1971).

Whyte, J. H. *The Independent Irish Party, 1850-9* (Oxford, 1958).

'The Influence of the Catholic Clergy on Elections in Nineteenth-Century Ireland', *English Historical Review*, vol. 75 (1960).

Williams, E. N. *The Eighteenth-Century Constitution* (Cambridge, 1970).

Wilson, S. *Feuding, Conflict and Banditry in Nineteenth-century Corsica* (Cambridge, 1988).

Wesser, R. F. *A Response to Progressivism: The Democratic Party and New York Politics, 1902-1918* (New York and London, 1986).

Woods, C. J. 'The General Election of 1892: The Catholic Clergy and the Defeat of the Parnellites', in F. S. L. Lyons and R. A. J. Hawkins (eds.), *Ireland under the Union: Varieties of Tension: Essays in Honour of T. W. Moody* (Oxford, 1980).

Wyse, T. *Historical Sketch of the late Catholic Association of Ireland*, 2 vols. (London, 1829).

X.X.X. (pseud), *Por la Iglesia* (Bogotá, 1909).

Zancada, P. *Las elecciones legislativas en España* (Madrid, 1914).

Zangerl, C. H. E. 'Courting the Catholic Vote: The Center Party in Baden, 1903-1913', *Central European History*, vol. 10, no. 3 (1977).

Zapata Restrepo, M. *La Mitra Azul* (Medellín, 1973).

Zeitlin, M. *The civil wars in Chile* (Princeton, 1984).

Zimmermann, E. 'Liberals, Reform and the Social Question: Argentina, 1890-1916, unpubl. PhD thesis, Oxford University, 1990.

INDEX